BEACHCRUISING

AND

COASTAL CAMPING

by
Ida Little and Michael Walsh

Edited by Julius M. Wilensky

All photos by the author unless otherwise indicated

1st Edition—1992

Library of Congress Card No. 92-60226
ISBN No. 0-918752-15-9
SAN No. 210-5810

TABLE OF CONTENTS

3

Photo by Doug Young

Author Ida Little and Michael Walsh. After 5 years of cruising in *Manatee* (17′ canoe) and *Kahoutek* (14′ Hobie Cat), we made the big jump to a 26′x5′x8″ draft beachcruiser. *Dugong* taught us how to look for beachcruisng "anchorages" which we have dubbed "beachorages."

EDITOR'S PREFACE

I learned to sail at an early age. My wife, Dutch, and I bought a sail canoe when we married in 1939, and cruised it in Long Island Sound. We used it for our honeymoon, sailing it in two days to City Island, where we took the bus to the subway and the subway to Times Square. We checked into the old Algonquin Hotel, which is still there, and had a night on the town. Two days later we took the subway to the bus, the bus to the dock, and sailed home to Stamford the same day in a smoky sou'wester. The following year Harry Jobrack and I cruised the canoe for 13 days, circumnavigating Long Island Sound. The 18-foot canoe had sponsons, leeboards, and an outboard rudder, with a lateen rig. We never turned it over though we had to bail frantically at times. In those days there were plenty of beaches to camp on in this heavily populated area. There still are some.

After service in the Air Force (Army Air Corps) in World War II, we bought an Amesbury Pow Wow 17-foot sloop, heavily built lapstrake, flat bottom, centerboard, with an outboard rudder. We cruised Long Island Sound and environs, as far east as Cape Cod. We carried a two-man nylon mountain tent, air mattresses, a sterno stove and a bucket, and we made cruises lasting two and three weeks. Though I learned to sail in the late 20s, and love to cruise, I never owned a boat you could sleep on until 1955.

I was a Boy Scout until age 16 when I discovered girls, but continued to go hiking and camping when I wasn't sailing. I became active as a Scouter for 12 years, and greatly enjoyed taking the boys camping in the woods and sailing on the Sound. At my now advanced age, I still enjoy occasional mild whitewater canoeing, with adult friends or Boy Scouts.

I first met Ida and Michael in 1980 when I was exploring the Florida Keys picking up information to write a cruising guide. I was wandering around Convoy Point, Homestead Bayfront Park, Black Point Park, and environs, like a lost soul when this long-stemmed, tall beautiful young woman came over and asked "Can I help you?" In my head, I was counting the ways, but managed to keep under control and make notes as she guided me around the creeks, parks, and marinas.

I was fascinated with their beautiful 26-foot double ender shallow draft *Dugong*. David Bragdon and I were on a Morgan Out Island 41, and were proud of ourselves for sailing it from Marathon to Miami, inside Florida Bay, without once running aground. *Dugong* was much more practical for Florida Bay, though not nearly as comfortable as our Morgan.

Later that day we had a better look at their boat at a slip in Elliot Key's marina. It was a conversation piece—gathered a crowd wherever they went. We had to anchor out. We invited them aboard for happy hour, and that was the beginning of a long friendship which has resulted in this book.

Though we are kindred spirits in our enjoyment of sailing and camping, I've been a working stiff all my life, and have had responsibilities that

9

prevented my becoming a "beachbum." I could only do it on vacations. Not so with Ida and Michael. They've been at it full time for many years in a great variety of places and boats. No one is better qualified to impart hard-worn wisdom to Beachcruisers and Coastal Campers, than these two "free spirits."

Ida was born in Valdosta, GA, graduated from Chatham Hall, an all-girl boarding school in Virginia, and got her B.A. from Goucher College, outside Baltimore, in 1971. While in college, Ida studied photography at the Art Institute in Baltimore. She spent her junior year at the University of Munich. While there she traveled through Europe, and as far east as Afghanistan.

Michael was born in Argentina. His family moved to Westchester County, NY while he was a teenager, and Michael learned to sail and race the family Herreschoff "S" Class, out of Larchmont, N.Y. Michael graduated 1960 from Clarkson College, where he studied engineering. Until 1970, he worked successively as a sales engineer, teacher, and a portrait photographer.

Ida and Michael met in 1971, and bought *Sheldrake,* a 40-foot wooden ketch. He taught Ida to sail while they sailed it to Bermuda, and then for a year in the West Indies. They lost the boat on a reef off Great Inagua on Valentines Day, 1973.

Starting in December 1973 they went camp-cruising through the Bahamas for five years, cruising Eleuthera, Little San Salvador, Cat Island, Long Island and the Exumas, using a 14-foot Hobie Cat towing a 17-foot Old Town sail canoe. From 1975 to 1985, they managed a fly-in fishing camp in the remote lake wilderness of northwestern Ontario during the short summer season, continuing to beachcruise in southern climes. They beachcruised Martinique in 1978 and 1982 in a 17-foot Old Town sail canoe.

In 1979-80 they built the Phil Bolger designed 26-foot canoe cruiser *Dugong.* They cruised her for four years in the Florida Keys, Florida Bay, and coastal Georgia. They bought *Beachcomber* in 1985, a 36-foot yawl with raked masts, 18-inch draft, flat bottom, and 6-foot headroom! They cruise it in the Abacos every winter and use *Dugong* summers in Cape Cod, where they live in the old Walsh family cottage.

They are not total drop-outs. Both have written dozens of articles for sailing magazines starting in 1974. When we met in 1980, I already knew Ida from her articles. They are acknowledged experts in their field, and Wescott Cove feels proud to publish this massive work, three years in the making.

This is a "how-to" book, packed with information to help you go beachcruising and/or coastal camping, no matter what your level of expertise. While the authors' pertinent anecdotes and lively style keep the book from becoming dry as dust, we wanted to give readers a taste of how beachcruising really is. To this end, we have reprinted four articles written by Ida Little, that give you some of the "flavor" of their adventurous lifestyle. Two of these articles can be found near the end of Chapter 5, and one each following Chapters 7 and 9. These articles are reproduced with the permission of Sail Magazine and Small Boat Journal, where they first appeared.

We have also included some National Ocean Survey chart excerpts, excerpts from other Wescott Cove publications, and Michael's sketch charts showing some of the cruising grounds where they've sailed.

At the end of each chapter there is a bibliography and suggested sources for additional information. This is done by subject within each chapter, and therefore there is a minor degree of duplication. Be careful not to buy anything twice! Reference is made to magazine articles in several chapters. The **addresses** of these magazines are given **at the end of Chapter 2,** and not repeated elsewhere.

If you see anything or have used any gear different than what Ida and Michael describe and recommend, they would be pleased to hear from you. There are bound to be new developments of equipment in the burgeoning fields of Beachcruising and Coastal Camping. Though they're usually off cruising on remote beaches, you can write to them through the publishers, address on the title page. We expect this book to be around for a long time, and your comments will be welcome to Ida and Michael, for inclusion in subsequent editions.

Julius M. Wilensky, February, 1992

Photo by Earle Bragdon

Editor in Greenwich Cove, CT after beaching Earle Bragdon's *Pow Wow* at the end of a beachcamping cruise from Cape Cod, 1952. None the worse for wear except stubby beard. Earle & Julius were the Pow Wow fleet of Long Island Sound

AUTHORS' INTRODUCTION

We aren't purists. The exploration we enjoy with a sailboat others enjoy in power boats and kayaks and inner tubes. We just happen to be attracted to the quiet and the complexity of sailing.

But this is not a sailing book, just as it is not a camping book. It presumes **some** knowledge of boating, sailing and camping, including navigation, fire building, swimming, and map reading; and an interest in the other sub-skills on which explorers rely—first aid, fishing, field cookery, hunting, weather watching, curiosity, and caution.

We write about the unique aspects of boating that apply to camping and on the singular aspects of camping that apply to boating. Some of the equipment is special. The boats certainly are. Few boats are designed to be routinely beached, and rarely would a camper consider the merits of an E.P.I.R.B. (Emergency Position Indicating Radio Beacon) or a VHF radio. Conventional boaters keep their boats moving by staying away from the beach. Conventional campers keep their vehicles (or legs) mobile by staying away from the water. Beachcruisers fall into the gap those others leave free—the shallow fringe between, including the sea and the shore. Only the beachcruiser needs to learn to land her boat through the surf, then slide it up the beach before the next wave comes.

Because much of our sea camping has been in the tropical Caribbean, and because we rely on fresh fish catches to feed us, we've learned to spear fish, and to spin cast on the flats. These skills are esoteric. For this reason a chapter is devoted to them.

The aim of this book is to help you go beachcruising by offering some criteria that will help you select a good cruising area, the right boat to use, the best equipment to bring along, and then how to beachcruise after you've selected the right place, boat and gear for you.

If we hadn't become beachcruisers, we would never have written this book. And so we would like to go back in time here to thank the people and companies who gave us the emotional and material support we needed to get going and stick with it.

Back in 1973, Deane Gray, then President of the Old Town Canoe Co., believed in our wild scheme of cruising the Bahamas in a 17-foot sailing canoe enough to donate a canoe, sail rig, life jackets and paddles. We sometimes think that without the confidence he showed, as a wise, down-to-earth and basically conservative man, we may never have pursued this adventure. Old Town continued to encourage and support our canoe cruises for years.

Our thanks also to Holland America Line for making our dream of canoe cruising in the West Indies come true; to Norwegian Caribbean Line for delivering us and canoe to the Bahamas; and to Royal Caribbean Line for helping us return to Martinique for a second canoe cruise of that island.

We are grateful for the friendship of Corene and Stafford Bain of Little Farmers Cay during our years of living in a tent on a neighboring isle.

Thanks to Mme. Louise de Reynal, we had two wonderful winter cruises in and around Martinique. Without her friendship, help and guidance we might easily have foundered. During the years when we were canoe cruising and tent camping in the Bahamas, we were visited each year by the family who'd made the wonderful tent that was our home. The Stephensons became our friends and in time offered us their home and basement in New Hampshire for building *Dugong*. Jack Stephenson encouraged and supported our project with advice and the very needed place and tools for completing it.

Our beachcruising style may have plateau'd out with *Dugong* if Warren Bailey hadn't come along with his self-designed and built 18-inch draft *Beachcomber*. Thanks to Warren, we now enjoy beachcruising a 36-foot yawl as much as we did our 17-foot canoe.

Many people have supplied information and photos for this book. It has been a real pleasure corresponding with small boat builders and small boat owners. They have made this book more "real" and informative. In particular, we'd like to thank Chris Harkness who provided many of the photographs. He is a talented photographer and a talented writer.

Small Boat Journal Magazine provided past issues, material and information thoughout the three years of research. We are grateful for their help and for their continued publication in the interests of us small boat cruisers.

We are very fortunate to have parents deserving of our enduring gratitude. Michael learned to sail from his father on a Hershoff S-boat. From her parents, Ida received the gift of confidence to go exploring in life. From both sets of parents we learned a love of the outdoors and the camping skills with which to enjoy the wilderness.

For the past four years, we have made the Wilensky home a regular stop on both our northern and our southern migrations. Julius and Dutch Wilensky have made their house feel like our home. We appreciate Dutch's efforts to make us so comfortable and Julius' hard work in putting this book into print.

It is really thanks to Julius that this book has been completed and published at all. When we set out to write a book about beachcruising we had no idea of the amount of work and dogged determination it would require. We're beachcruisers. We want to be outside playing all the time. Julius has kept us on track and given us the professional guidance we needed to get the job done. And best of all, he has been a friend and kindred spirit. Thank you Julius.

Ida Little
October, 1991

CHAPTER 1

BEACHCRUISING: THE EVOLUTION OF A STYLE

"... with the floating clear of the boat, I felt somehow that this escape I had managed myself." Joseph Conrad

WHAT IS BEACHCRUISING?

In this book, beachcruising means cruising a small boat along a shore or a coast with the intention of camping ashore. Though it is possible to use 50-foot schooners to go beachcruising, we are focusing here on small sailboats that are light enough to be lifted or rolled ashore; and sailboats under 30' which are designed to dry out flat on an ebb tide. This book elaborates upon the unique aspects of boating that apply to camping, and upon the singular aspects of camping that apply to boating.

We've been beachcruising almost full-time for 15 years. For us, it is a way of life rather than a temporary break from the real world.

When we started beachcruising in the early 1970s, we had an income of about $100 a month from investment interest. With that $100 and a distinct lack of ambition or interest in indoor plumbing, TV, walls, clothes, and society, we lived the life of royal beach bums. Once we got the hang of things—that is, to make good choices of places to explore, boats to use, and equipment to take—we enjoyed sailing flat seas in a steady trade wind, having miles of white sand beaches all to ourselves, living on a choice of our own tropical islands, swimming in crystal blue seas and diving daily for fresh lobster.

Rather than spend time in an office working for the money to pay for a week's vacation planned by somebody else, or to pay for an eventual retirement at age 60 or 65, we elected to skip the job and plan our own "vacation" now. We just happened to like the beachcruising lifestyle so much that we do it pretty much all the time. But whether you beachcruise for a weekend or for a year, you can enjoy working less and playing more because the expenses are so modest. You can enjoy, as we do, planning your own trip without guides or schedules and go places in ways that **no** amount of money could afford you.

HOW WE GOT STARTED BEACHCRUISING AND THE EVOLUTION OF OUR STYLE

Our beachcruising style evolved from years of car camping, backpacking, canoeing, and yachting. Each had qualities we enjoyed, but each also had drawbacks that were important enough to make us look for another way to go.

Camping

One winter we threw all our camping equipment into a Volkswagon camper and drove down to the west coast of Mexico. The beaches were great and the scenery beautiful in a very stark sense, but everywhere we went, we attracted an audience. If we could get where ever we were, so could other people. Roads make access a little too easy. Therefore, we deviated from the hard-packed dirt roads. Following gravelly, barely discernable tracks, we managed to reach some incredibly remote oases deep in the desert. However, we nearly destroyed our car getting there, could only go as far as our gas supply allowed, and still and all, weren't anywhere near the sea where we really wanted to be.

We went backpacking. We hitched to the New York State Adirondacks, to the California Sierras and to the British Columbia Rockies. With packs on our backs, we hiked into the wilderness. Sometimes we followed trails, sometimes not. Having the choice was a liberating change from car travel. Never did we have a problem finding solitude. There aren't many people willing to exert themselves that much. The occasional few who do don't form audiences, they make good company.

Our problem with backpacking was that it restricted us in terms of supplies. We could carry only so much. In the Sierras we each carried 60 pounds of supplies and camping gear so that we could get far "away from it all" for a couple of weeks or longer. The weight of our packs slowed us

Photo by Michael Walsh

After shipwreck, we hiked the Appalachian Trail, camping for weeks in the Adirondacks where this photo was taken. This 2-person, four-pound tent later became our home for the first three years that we had beachcruised in the Bahamas.

down so much, that by the time we'd climbed into the remote high country, we only had a couple of **days** to stay up there and enjoy it. So there we'd be, surrounded by the most incredible scenery—sheer rock walls, glacial lakes, stunted pines like out of a fairy tale—enjoying so rare a moment in life when vast spaces and beauty are all our own—and we'd have to cut it short. We'd have to pack the tent, disassemble the stove, dive naked into the lake one last time and climb out into the high altitude sun only to pull on rough clothes and start back down into the rest of the world.

Canoeing

We went canoeing. We hitched to Ontario, Canada, rented a canoe, and put the canoe aboard a Canadian National Railway train. Then we hopped aboard to head north into the remote wilderness lakes region. Fourteen hours later, around midnight, we notified the conductor we'd like to disembark at the next river crossing. In the pitch dark, two train employees helped us unload the canoe from the boxcar. Then wishing us good journey, the guys stepped back inside the train and the train moved on.

Pitch dark slowly eased into pale dawn as we carried all our gear to the river's edge. With light came a real appreciation of just **how** far out this

For many years we tried backpacking. Here Michael takes a break from carrying a 60-pound pack—and Ida's guitar!

place was. We might just as well have been dropped out of the sky into the middle of an endless wilderness. This time, we had a vehicle in which to get around and to carry our load. We could choose our own routes. Routes restricted to waterways, yes, but since there was more water than land, that wasn't so bad. Moreover, we could stay "away from it all" for months!

Whole months **did** pass while we canoed, camped, caught pickerel and pike, picked blueberries and raspberries by the bushel, gathered lakeside spearmint by the bunch, and cautiously selected meaty mushrooms by the bucket.

Perfect as so many things were about our canoe trip in the Canadian wilderness, there were still a couple of problems. One, we got tired of paddling. Unlike the enormous bodies of water like Lake Superior, Lake Michigan and others, the smaller inland lakes don't have the fetch for a steady wind. The flukey wind made sailing just no good. We're both experienced sailors and even we had a hard time sailing anywhere without swamping, much less just staying dry. For us, the other problem with Canadian lake canoeing was that we missed the sea. We missed the vast horizons and the extended waterways. We yearned for wide beaches, snorkeling, diving, and warm sun for nudity year 'round.

Cruising In a Deep Draft Sailboat

So we went ocean cruising. We got a 40-foot ketch with a 6-foot draft and took off for the Caribbean. Bermuda, Puerto Rico, the Windward and Leeward Isles, Venezuela, Los Roques and Los Aves—spectacular! We saw more vast horizons, sea, diving, deserted islands, wide beaches and endless hot sun than we'd dreamed of.

However, after a year of cruising the Caribbean, we were **more** frustrated about what we were missing than when we'd started. Aboard our 6-foot draft, 12-ton ketch *Sheldrake*, it seemed like every time we found a secluded cove, the anchorage was either too shallow, too deep, or poor holding. Every time the anchorage was good, the place was not secluded. Along the uninhabited coast of Dominica, we disregarded the poor anchoring conditions and tied *Sheldrake* betweeen a tree and a boulder. The place was perfect: secluded, tropical, and lush. Ashore, wild avocado trees were dropping so much fruit that they littered the forest floor in layers. It was paradise complete with a clean, fresh, waterfall and pool. But it was not for us. We no sooner stepped ashore to get a taste of the fruit than on onshore wind piped up and we had to go. The place was absolutely right but the anchorage was all wrong.

In the Virgin Islands, we found a small, deserted island protected by a half-circle of reef. We conned our way in. At sunset we were happily lounged on the sandy beach watching the flames of a driftwood fire. It was so lovely we decided to spend the night there on the warm sand. Ah, to spend one night **off** the boat. Forget it. Dawn found us back on board struggling against onshore winds to retrace our route out through the reef.

Again and again we glimpsed paradise, a thin, one-dimensional profile, from a fathom depth away. In popular Fort de France, Martinique, the harbor offers good, deep secure anchoring. From here we did explore the jungled mountains of land extending beyond the coastal facade. However, having left *Sheldrake* in a crowded foreign harbor, we felt compelled, as always, to return that same day to secure our interests for the night.

Sheldrake was our one and only home, chock full of the few precious possessions we owned. To the islanders she was a YACHT: a vessel for rich, idle Americans to travel around in, loaded with exotic electronic goodies and no doubt **wads** of American greenbacks. Between our own interests and the lust of others, we felt we should keep a guarded watch most of the time. Sometimes we weren't careful and we let our guard fall. We came back to the boat once and saw she'd torn her anchor free and was drifting over the horizon. Another time, we invited some South American Indians aboard and were subsequently robbed of our disappointingly small bundle of *plata* (money). It took **some** persuading to convince them that all Americans are not *ricos*.

When we hauled out in Puerto Rico, we wished we **were** *ricos*. Big boat (40 feet); big maintenance (500 linear feet of seams to caulk). Big fees; in 1972 these were $300 for the haul-out, another $200 for the bottom paint. Supply costs were also denominated in hundreds. All this time, consumption took place in less than pleasant surroundings.

Sheldrake was big enough to require three of us to handle her initially. When our friend "saw the light" and retreated to his farm in Minnesota, the two of us novices carried on. The School of "Learning by Experiencing" was a demanding taskmaster and we sure learned fast. Still, it was six months before each of us could take the helm with confidence. Six **months**, and **never** did either of us feel confident about single-handing. In fact, it was a major dread.

The frustrations mounted. Time and again we were denied the Gardens of Eden we were in fact on this journey to enjoy. In 10 months we visited the Chesapeake, Bermuda, Puerto Rico, the West Indies, the north shore of South America, Haiti, and the Bahamas. What we knew best and remembered most after all those months, were our impressions of *Sheldrake*. It was the boat, sailing and anchoring that consumed our energies, our money and our devotion.

We were on our way to the States to sell the boat when we wrecked in the Bahamas. Perhaps if we hadn't wrecked, we'd have given up boating as a lost romantic cause. Instead, the wreck helped us realize what we really wanted. The reef-fringed bay that claimed our boat claimed our hearts. This was what we'd been looking for. It's just that we could never get in here and stay here to enjoy it with a big boat.

Realization!
The concept of beachcruising that we talk about in this book was actually conceived the morning we wrecked *Sheldrake*. I suppose it was all

that had gone before—the camping and canoeing and backpacking and ocean voyaging—suddenly came together in this place where we found ourselves shipwrecked. There we were, stranded on a remote Bahamian beach, looking out at our broken ship, and what did we see? A crystal clear blue lagoon protected by a rim of rose-colored reef, wavelets lapping across a long, white sand beach that lifted inland to gentle dunes shaded by long needled pines. We saw beauty, solitude, vast horizons, sea, and sun. We saw the ideal place to camp for a long, long time.

I can't pretend we were thrilled to be there. For two people who have just come out of a wreck and stumbled ashore in a strange place, having just lost their home, all of their belongings and almost their lives, it's incredible that this tropical beach **could** make as remarkable an impression on us as it did.

With our makeshift backpacks, a can of potato soup, and the clothes on our backs, we started walking in the direction of the only small settlement on the whole island. Towards evening of the following day, we reached Matthew Town where we relinquished rights to salvage.

In the weeks following our shipwreck, we did a lot of backpacking while we licked our wounds. We rehashed what had gone right and what had gone wrong with our trip aboard *Sheldrake*. We'd been dissatisfied enough with our lifestyle on *Sheldrake* that we'd been planning to sell her long before the shipwreck. Again and again our discussions led to the irony of our shipwrecking right where we really wanted to be all along. It was exactly the sort of isolated, spectacular, wild place we wanted to go to and live for weeks or months at a time. A boat like *Sheldrake* couldn't take us there (obviously). And we couldn't carry enough equipment to hike there for any length of time.

And so we conceived of beachcruising in a boat small enough that we could sail right up to any shore, then lift or roll the boat out of the sea. We could carry enough gear and supplies to last us months, yet be free of roads, deep waterways, and public anchorages.

WE START BEACHCRUISING

In December of 1973, a little less than a year after our shipwreck, we started beachcruising. We got a 17-foot Old Town sailing canoe in which to carry all our gear while cruising, and a 14-foot Hobie catamaran to carry us and to tow the canoe. We packed camping gear, fishing gear, some food staples, and hardware into the canoe, then trailered the boats and gear to south Florida. There we practiced sailing both boats, singly and in combination, for a couple of months in preparation for cruising the Bahamas.

We, both boats, and all our gear crossed the Gulf Stream aboard the *Starward*, a Norwegian Caribbean cruise ship. In Nassau, we disembarked from the lap of luxury into what we term Terror Incognita. Loosely translated, it means terror associated with doing something new, or going somewhere new without knowing what to expect. In this case, the terror was heightened by our awareness that nobody else had ever done anything quite the same as what we intended to do. We didn't have any precedents to give us an idea of how it all might turn out.

We had a lot to learn our first few months in the Bahamas, but essentially the whole rig did work as we'd hoped. We cruised down Eleuthera, out to Little San Salvador and Cat Island, to the Exumas, and on down to Long Island. We could see or not see people for as long as we wished. Our gear and rig supported us for months at a time without need for supplies.

The cruise-camping life style worked so well that we continued beachcruising the Bahamas for six years.

When we'd had our fill of the flat, desert dry isles of the Bahamas, we loaded a 17-foot sailing canoe onto the Holland America cruise ship *Rotterdam* and journeyed down to the West Indies. For two winter seasons we beachcruised the lush jungle coast of French Martinique.

Dugong

By 1980, we'd been more or less permanent beachcruisers for seven years. Our small canoes and catamaran had carried us and our camping gear through wilderness Canadian lakes, Lake Superior's Apostle Islands, Block Island and Cuttyhunk Island off Rhode Island and Massachusetts, the Bahama Out Islands, and Martinique. There was never a night that we had to worry about our boats, and rarely a time when we lacked for spectacular, secluded campsites.

So, why mess with a good thing? "If it's working, don't fix it," goes the saying. However, we thought we **might** enjoy a little more mobility and space aboard a larger boat. It was a big maybe. My own fear was that we'd end up back where we'd left off with *Sheldrake*. That is, back with anchor watches, public harbors, too much focus on the boat, and not enough focus on coastal explorations. To guard against the Big Boat Syndrome, we went to Phil Bolger, N.A., for a deviant hull design. We were looking for a design that would allow the boat to float in depths of less than a foot and to dry out upright on an ebb tide. Phil designed for us a 1 ton, 26' x 5'x8" draft, flat-bottomed canoe cruiser. We learned to loft lines, scarf stringers and cold mold veneers to build our *Dugong* over a period of about a year and a half.

Our intentions with *Dugong* were to continue beachcruising as before, albeit with a more limited choice of campsites due to our not being able to haul out, yet with a greater open-sea cruising range and wider choice of cruising areas. With *Dugong*, we expected to be able to sail across somewhat greater distances of open water to reach remote isles and shores than we'd been able to do with our smaller, open boats. Also, we could cruise areas where camping ashore is not possible or not allowed. We'd have a comfortable boat in which to sleep and cook when necessary, yet still have the choice of sailing right up to the shore and camping there.

With 26' *Dugong*, we learned how beachcruising is possible with a larger boat. For several hundred feet there is *no* water at low tide—a perfect "beachorage."

We launched *Dugong* in south Florida on Halloween. We expected to practice sailing around Biscayne Bay for a while, then hop on across to the Bahamas. ***Editor's note:*** *That's where we met them. Ida was ashore when I landed our dink at Homestead Bay Front Park, and she offered to help when she saw me wandering around like a lost soul. Later we rendezvou'd at Elliot Key where Dugong could get into the shallow marina, and our very comfortable Morgan Out Island 41 had to anchor offshore. We enjoyed their company, observing how they coped, and we've been together many times since. Ida didn't have to look for a publisher when she wanted to put this book together. We became friends.* After sailing around south Florida for a month, though, we realized that, given the winter storms, *Dugong's* poor performance in hard seas, and her lack of auxiliary power, we did not want to attempt a 50-mile crossing of the Gulf Stream. So, in fact, *Dugong* did not allow us the greater offshore cruising range that we'd expected. She did, however, allow us more flexibility in choice of shores and islets to cruise, right there in Florida (which is fortunate since that's where we were when we needed Plan B). Because we had a small cabin, comfortable for sleeping, and a 6-foot cockpit in which to cook and eat, we could cruise areas where either no campsites were possible (most of the Everglades) or not legal (most of the islands in Florida Bay and the islands west of Key West). Being able to sleep aboard *Dugong* allowed us to satisfy the legal restrictions on camping that disallow sleeping ashore, while still being able to enjoy a daytime shore camp for cooking, eating and lounging. With *Dugong* secure in a "beachorage," dried out nice and level right next to shore, our sea and shore life became completely integrated.

In this respect, we were very pleased with *Dugong's* design. We'd never used a sailboat of her size and weight to beachcruise. As you know by now, we hate **having** to anchor out. We turned our backs on deep draft vessels for that reason. We like exploring and camping ashore as much as we like sailing.

When we started cruising *Dugong* we made the same presumptions most sailors make: When you've got a big boat you're **supposed** to anchor off a ways so as to be out of danger of being swept ashore. Naturally we grumbled and complained every time we threw over the anchor, blew up the inflatable, and rowed ashore like everybody else.

Finally our instincts saved us from the straight and narrow. With *Dugong* we could attempt the unconventional and get away with it. All it took was too much frustration with cruising in a way that we thoroughly disliked, and finding a place that lured us into saying to hell with worrying about shallow water and running aground. The beaches fringing the low-lying mangrove bird sanctuary islets west of Key West stood back behind 50 to 100 yards of inches-deep mud/sand flats. Where we wanted to be, naturally, was 'way over there.

Screwing up our courage for a trip into Terror Incognita once again, we sailed *Dugong* across the flats, bumped bottom, slid across underwater sand hills, and skidded to a stop against the slope of the beach. We lowered the sail, stepped out, and walked the anchor a few feet up the beach.

I remember thinking, sure, it's great to be right here, but we sure better keep an eye on the tide. Mere inches' drop in depth could mean the difference between getting out of here and being stuck for the next 12 hours. It did. We were gone for over an hour walking the beach, hiking inland, watching the frigate birds, and climbing through the mangroves. We were like kids at recess. When we got back to *Dugong*, the tide had fallen 5 inches. *Dugong* was resting comfortably high, dry and level on the firm sand flat. Far out on the horizon, the sea still retreated. I could not conceive of staying here with not a bit of visible protection. Yet there was no sea that could reach us for 12 hours, and even then, only 8 inches of it at most.

From that moment on, beachcruising took on a whole new dimension. We enjoyed beachcruising and camping with *Dugong* through Florida Bay, the Everglades, the scattered islands west of Key West, the Intracoastal Waterway from south Florida to north Georgia, and the creeks and islands off the Georgia coast.

Beachcomber

Our years of beachcruising *Dugong* proved to us that this way of cruising is possible with big boats, given the right hull design. Today, we beachcruise *Beachcomber* in the same style as we enjoyed in our 17-foot sailing canoe and with our 26-foot *Dugong*. *Beachcomber*, a 36' x 8' x 18" draft canoe cruiser, dries out flat on the ebb and serves as bedroom/kitchen as well as mobile camp. We still make a daytime camp ashore and "anchor" our boat, high and dry on tidal flats, right where land meets sea. So, while we have gone bigger, we still enjoy the aspects of beachcruising that attracted us to it in the first place; the pleasure of sailing in moderate seas right next to shore, freedom to choose our own route off the beaten track, mobility, land and sea explorations with secure sleeping and living on or next to shore, with our boat firmly aground, level, and safe from storms and seas.

Photo by Michael Walsh

We cruised on *Sheldrake*, a 40′ x 11′ x6′ draft ketch for a year before we could identify which parts of cruising we really enjoyed. Ocean passages were not among them.

Author's *Beachcomber* resting securely on the tidal flats at Allans-Pensacola Cay in the Abacos. Look in the distance where the deep draft boats have to anchor

CHAPTER 2

THE GOOD NEWS AND THE BAD NEWS ABOUT BEACHCRUISING

FIRST, THE BAD NEWS. . .

Loneliness

One of the disadvantages of being so free to sail, anchor, dry out or haul out almost anywhere, is loneliness. There are still many more big-boat cruisers than beachcruisers. These big boats are way out there, sailing outside the one fathom line all day. At night, when most boaters socialize, they're all anchored out in the deeper, more exposed, part of the bay. We find ourselves sometimes abandoning our perfectly safe "beachorage" for the exposed, but more social, anchorage.

Lack of Prestige

Tagging along as a corollary to the loneliness factor comes a lack of prestige. Putzing around in small sailboats is definitely no way to increase your status in the neighborhood. The only small boaters who manage a response of admiration from regular society are the daredevils and extremists. Don't expect a lot of interest or curiosity from others about the short forays you make into the fascinating mazes of your nearby river. The people you impress will be few and far between.

Limited Cruising Range

Compared to big boats, the small size and light weight of a beachcruiser are limiting in terms of range over the open sea. We wouldn't dare sail our canoe to Bermuda, for instance, as we'd been able to do on 40-foot *Sheldrake*.

Limited Capacity

A small boat is limited to, at best, a month's supply of food and water. By comparison to big boats, this means less time between stores. Big boats carry more gear and a greater variety of foods and so feel less dependency on stores. They are also more likely to have capacity for carrying coolers, ice boxes, or refrigerators, so can carry some of the foods and drinks that beachcruisers miss.

Discomfort (or Character Development)

The Boats Themselves

Small open boats are not comfortable. There's no place to sit comfortably for long; there's seldom a way to get out of the sun or rain underway; there's rarely relief from the helm, and often no motor to take over when the wind dies. When you're finished sailing for the day, there's no cushy settee on which to rest your tired body, nor spacious place to stretch out below, out of the wind, rain, or sun. The larger cuddy boats provide some shelter underway, but not without cost. Their additional size and weight make it difficult—to impossible—to haul them out and above the high tide line.

Exposure to the Elements

Since comforts are not built into small boats, beachcruising demands a lot of attentive energy in living with the elements. This means providing, day to day, a shelter from the elements. On our first cruise in the Bahamas, it took us about two weeks before we figured out that the sun was burning us alive. We cut the sailing time down from 8 hours to a max of 4 hours a day. We learned to avoid exposure to storms by getting ashore before they hit. We bought the highest quality foul weather gear. And, we'd always make an adequate shelter for sleeping each night, even when we were very tired.

Ashore, though we are more secure and more entertained than when anchored out, we have to contend with Nature in the raw. We're either seeking shade or seeking sun; looking for a soft place to sit or looking for a tree to block the wind. Other times, we want a breeze and there's none to be had. It's then that we suffer the worst problem of all—BUGS. First and foremost, Biting Bugs: deerflies, horseflies, houseflies, blackflies, greenhead flies, mosquitoes, sand gnats and no-seeums. Then there's the non-biting varieties such as gnats that swarm 'round your mouth when you're trying to eat. Fine mesh screening and insecticides will screen out the bugs. However, sometimes we've been cooped up in the tent or down below longer than we like.

Animals

Besides bugs, there are land pests like crabs that will steal your toothbrush; rats that will try to eat through your plastic containers; raccoons that will filch food from your locked ice chest; and snakes that will try to sleep next to your warm body.

Need for skills

Going cruising in small sailboats requires **some** skills that must be learned. None of us are born knowing how to swim well or to sail a boat.

Backpacking is accessible to anyone who's mobile. Learning to run a small boat motor doesn't take long. But sailing, **well** now. Sailing is at first mysterious and totally frustrating. So, those into the "gimme now" mode will have trouble dealing with the initial skill-learning stages.

NOW FOR THE GOOD NEWS

Simple and Easy to Use

Though learning to sail takes time and practice, learning to sail and maintain a **small** boat is relatively easy. It's easy to get to know the boat in its entirety. In little time anyone can master a small boat confidently enough to go off cruising by themselves. It's not intimidating by its weight, bulk, or size. You can accidently jibe it, run it aground, flip it over, and laugh about it. It forgives easily and rarely holds a grudge (scar). Lack of experience and training in manipulating big objects, using hand tools, understanding electricity or plumbing or celestial navigation, make no difference in beachcruising. Mastery and control of a small boat comes quickly, and so does the confidence for enjoying the whole trip.

Low Cost

For what would be many big boats' cost of insurance for just one year, we can buy and equip a beachcruiser. For a few dollars more, we can build up an inventory of spare cleats, some stainless rigging, and some fiberglass and epoxy for future maintenance and repair.

We do our own maintenance and repairs either in the field or at home. Our boat doesn't have to sit in a dusty, noisy shipyard waiting for work to be done at the yard's convenience, and cost. Since our boats are small, lightweight, and flat bottomed, they can be car-topped or trailered easily. We can launch and retrieve without assistance. And when we're finished cruising, we can take the boat home and store it there. This independence saves us costs that steadily erode the budgets of most big boat cruisers. Compared to many adventurous styles of voyaging, beachcruising is downright inexpensive. We don't pay for guides or outside transport. Since we can get up and go so easily, we're never obliged to forfeit deposits on arrangements for a trip we were forced to make weeks in advance.

On the whole, since beachcruisers **are** so easily used, they're used more often than big boats or even recreational vehicles. On a per use cost, their expense is negligible.

Great Freedom in Choosing Routes

Beachcruising a small boat is like this: we sail our canoe into Georgetown, Great Exuma, through the back door. We skid over mangrove flats, pull through river channels, sail among the maze of unmarked Brigantine Cays, poke into innumerable cul de sacs, portage over a rusted drawbridge and reach the main harbor with some regret. We are having such exhilarating fun exploring unmarked waters and uninhabited shores that it is hard to stop.

By contrast, our deep draft boating was like this: we steer our 6-foot draft *Sheldrake* into reef-rimmed St. Georges, Bermuda, on a moonless night. In the narrow channel, we nearly collide with an unlit sailboat anchored by one of the channel markers waiting for dawn's light. Next day there are varying reactions to our carefully negotiated night landing. "Brilliant!" is one. "Idiots!" another. What do **we** feel? Whew. Glad to be in, anxious to drop anchor, dinghy ashore and stand on solid land. Relief. This relief in successfully negotiating rigidly limited channels is usually our experience. It's like taking an exam, giving the right answers, and receiving a good mark. Briefly rewarding, and mostly a relief.

Unlike traveling by road, by trail, **or** by marked channel, beachcruisers are free to **create** routes as they will. This precious opportunity is one we cherish dearly.

Photo by Michael Walsh

Beachable boats cavorting in Biscayne Bay, Florida. Left to right: Drascombe Dabber, Sea Pearl with leeboards, Bolger's *Brick*, Sea Pearl with centerboard, Bolger's *Micro*

Security

We experience a great thrill from **not** having to survive The Big Storm. Thanks to the kind of boats we use, the slightest threat of storm merely sends us scurrying for the best ringside seat to enjoy the drama. We cruise close to shore and can quickly get our boat hauled out to safety or tucked into the tiniest of bays.

Though we were never enamoured with the Romance of Ocean Cruising, we had opportunity to enjoy some of the many romanticized aspects. Encountering The Big Storm was one. Our ocean passage to Bermuda included a nearly direct hit with Hurricane Agnes. Ever been so tired you don't even feel scared any more? So tired you don't mind contemplating death because at least you'll get some rest? And nowhere to run; nowhere to escape. The quick security our beachcruiser affords us is more acutely appreciated. We now **enjoy** the opportunity of watching some of the most spectacular shows that nature puts on.

Small, simply-built boats are easy to maintain. We can check vital parts ourselves and be sure that they are in good shape.

The Many Varied Pleasures of Beachcruising

Though we have always imagined ourselves exploring near water of some sort, we never fantasized about being out in the ocean, out of sight of land, for days on end. We aren't obsessed with dreams of sailing to foreign ports, or dreams of anchoring in popular harbors. We rarely revel in the successful negotiation of a trail or marked channel.

It's no wonder we weren't satisfied with backpacking or trailer camping, and that we fought big boat cruising all the way. And no wonder we fell in love with beachcruising.

What we **do** fantasize about, and actually enjoy, is gliding over shallow waters near shore, paying much less attention to a trail or a course than to what's around and under us. Among the small islands west of Key West, Florida, where the water is muddy and opaque, we sail in shallow enough depths that we're able to see rays, nurse sharks, barracuda and conch. It's like flying, suspended over another world. In the Bahamas, where the water is crystal clear to 40 feet, our attention focuses on purple sea fans, orange corals, and gaudy parrot fish. That is, when we aren't absorbed in the osprey nest, driftwood or ghost crabs on the nearby shore.

Beachcruising exposes us to an enormous variety of sensual entertainments. Water and sky are a part of our visual world, but they don't dominate it. We find we appreciate sky and sea much more with the relief of landscapes and underwater scenes.

Intimacy with Nature and Wild Creatures

Creatures reward us for spending time ashore. We have had a mockingbird eat out of our hand, a banana twit drink from our cups and hummingbirds collect our hair for their nest. We've watched newborn herons and nesting nighthawks. The rare Bahamian iguana has tracked across our camp with an arrogance that only lack of human contact allows.

A wild, remote, secluded shore attracts us. Our dozens of shore camps with small boats along domestic and foreign coasts are far more fun and entertaining than public campgrounds and commercial anchorages.

Freedom from Intrusion

Though beachcruising seems to imply greater vulnerability to human intrusion, we've found it to be in fact not so. With our small boats, we can tuck into isolated places to which there is no path or water route for the average boat. Of course, there are some crowded shores where the **only** landings are inhabited. We avoid these places or learn ahead of time if the natives there make good neighbors. In Martinique, where much of the coast is populated, we weren't bothered at all. The Martiniquais behaved like Orientals accustomed to living in paper houses. They respected pri-

These two black skimmers slept on our Florida Keys beach during mid-day, then awakened to forage the flats at sunset. The Florida Keys are a haven for sea birds!

vacy. In Mexico, the natives were intrusive. They gawked and swarmed 'round us constantly.

As for threats from the locals, in 14 years of beachcruising, leaving our boats and gear sometimes for days at a time completely unattended, we've only once been robbed. That time was by the Bahamian police who were making a search of our belongings. Our Bahamian neighbors were as incensed as we. But **never** have our lives been threatened.

As beachcruisers we have little to offer. In fact, we're a laughable anomalie to most robbers who seek to "upgrade" while we have obviously chosen to "downgrade." We aren't worth bothering with.

Intimacy with Local Culture

Before cruising, Michael and I had traveled, both independently and together, through South America, Yugoslavia, Turkey, Afghanistan, Canada, Hawaii, Mexico and almost all of Europe. We'd walked, ridden public buses and trains, hitchhiked and occasionally driven our own Volkswagen camper. After cruising 40-foot *Sheldrake* for a year through the West Indies and South America, we decided that this mode of travel actually compared **unfavorably** to our former modes of travel. We seemed to become slaves to, and completely oriented toward, the boat. With this focus, we naturally adopted the Ulysses Factor creed—have boat, will travel—and travel—and travel—ever onward to new horizons!

Beachcruising compares favorably to all the other modes of travel we've tried. We find we stay put for longer periods and really get to know where we are. Cruising Martinique with a 17-foot sailing canoe, *Crapaud*, we got to know and make friends with Martiniquais because we necessarily made ourselves available to them. We pulled our boat ashore regularly, without regard for tourist amenities or safe anchorages where most tourists would go. We entered into local life as part of that life. We shopped in their rural shops, bought local foods, ate exactly what they ate, hurried to the *boulangerie* for bread early every morning. We washed our laundry in the same streams. Our boat looked like their boats. We became part of the culture. We didn't just pass through or anchor off, dinghy in, spectate awhile, then move on. We hadn't come to notch another port into our sailing log or travel diary. We'd come to live, learn, and enjoy familiarity with their culture.

Pleasant Associations

Throughout our years of beachcruising, we've tended to roam in remote and isolated places. On the few occasions we meet others traveling in similar fashion, though, there is without exception an immediate sense of camaraderie. For the four years we've been working on this book, we've enjoyed an association with beachcruisers all over the world.

The kind of people who are attracted to beachcruising are as unpretentious and playful as their boats. They enjoy the doing more than the show. The Dovekie newsletter, Wayfarer logs, and Lightning bulletins represent the unassuming attitudes representative of beachcruisers in general. It's a real pleasure having an activity that attracts the kind of people you'd be looking for as friends.

Variety of Cruising Grounds

Oddly enough, a small boat gives us the greater variety of cruising and exploring within a given area than does any other mode of travel. We use waterways to sneak into shallow bays, run up tidal creeks, and cruise shoal areas with abandon. Where sandbars and reef protect a shore from intrusion, we can explore every inch of coast in solitude. Land travelers need roads or trails or open terrain. Deep draft boats cruise so far off shore, beyond underwater hazards, that they don't intrude. Unless they roam in dinks, they can't get close enough to appreciate what we're enjoying.

We don't have to go far to enjoy the solitude of the wilderness. It's as close to the nearest lake, coast, river, lagoon or creek.

SOURCES FOR ADDITIONAL INFORMATION

Magazines That Have Articles About Small Boats and Cruising in Small Boats

Boat Journal, 21 Powers Ferry Rd., Atlanta, GA 30339

Ask for the eight-page index to back issues which includes a two-page section of boat reviews and enclose a #10 SASE. Boat Journal is devoted to small boats of all sorts. Every issue offers information about small boats and their gear, modifications, and cruises.

Photo by Chris Harkness

Early each May, beachable boats gather at Cedar Key, Florida, for a weekend of fun and fellowship.

Messing About in Boats, 21 Burley St., Wenham, MA 01984

This is the least commercial small boat magazine on the market. The style and content truly reflect an attitude of using boats for fun rather than prestige.

Cruising World, 5 John Clarke Rd., Newport, RI 02840

This magazine is not devoted to beachcruising small boats but does run articles about cruising in them from time to time. The information is both interesting and well told.

Sail Magazine, Charlestown Naval Yard, 100 First Ave., Charlestown, MA 02129-2097

Although most of this magazine favors ever more—bigger boats and fancier equipment—you will from time to time come across beautifully presented pieces devoted to the beachcruising rogue. Note especially pieces by James Beck and Norris Hoyt.

Nautical Quarterly, 373 Park Ave. So., New York, NY 10016

This hardback high quality quarterly occasionally runs pieces about beachcruisers. In issue #46 (1989), they ran a piece entitled "A Big Day For Small Craft," which will reassure those of you who think tiny boat cruising is nowhere. This piece assures us that it's the coming thing and that any of us into it now are in the forefront of fashion.

Sailing Magazine, 125 E. Main St., Port Washington, WI 53074

This large format magazine publishes occasional stories about small boat cruising. Note especially pieces by Chris Harkness, such as "The Simpler Cruising Life: Open Boat Shore Cruising or Beachcombing under Sail," and "Happiness is a Small Boat" (Oct. 1988).

WoodenBoat Magazine, P.O. Box 78, Brooklin, ME 04616

This classy and well written magazine is devoted to wooden boats of all sizes.

More publications that are helpful on beachcruising are listed at the ends of Chapters 4, 5, 6 and later chapters.

Book

Castaway by Lucy Irvine, 1985, $4.50, Dell Publishing Co., New York A how-not-to book. A very well written and entertaining account of two people who think they can get away from it all by escaping to a deserted tropical isle.

Magazine Articles

"In Praise of the Beachable Boat" by Michael Walsh, 8-'84, Cruising World, 5 John Clarke Rd., Newport, RI 02840

"Cruising's a Beach: In Praise of Running Aground" by Ida Little, Florida Waterways Magazine, Peter Smyth, Stuart, FL 34995

"Jim Melcher: Portrait of a Shoalie" by Ida Little, 8-'86, Sailors Gazette. Back issues available through libraries. Magazine ceased publication

Associations

Trailer/Sailors Association, Pete Bowman, Montgomery Manor, Beecher Rd., Hudson, MI 49247

Directory; and newsletter "Clipper Snips" with information about all aspects of trailering, launching, and sailing small boats. President: Jerry Belanger, 2604 Freeman Dr., Lake Orion, MI 48035

Seven Seas Cruising Association, 521 S. Andrews Ave., Suite 10, Ft. Lauderdale, FL 33301. Monthly newsletter full of current information from cruisers all over the globe.

Michael and a tired pelican hold a staring contest. The pelican won! When it's so easy to pull up to a beach, you land frequently

CHAPTER 3

PLACES TO BEACHCRUISE

How to Choose Good Areas to Beachcruise

There are ideal places to beachcruise—places where the seascape geography is small, shallow and intricate; where a warmed, gentle wind blows steady; where we land, picnic, walk about, camp, gather firewood, without intruding on the privacy of others; where there are few stinging, biting creatures or insects; where we can find abundant fresh water and restock our larder conveniently along the way; where the shore is visually entertaining as we coast along. We've found some in the Caribbean, in the Gulf of Mexico, in the Great Lakes, in desert lakes and along Pacific and North Atlantic shores. There are so many reported by others, we'll never enjoy half of them.

While the coasts along which we cruise are more varied and interesting, less of their area qualifies for beachcruising than for stay-aboard ocean passage cruising. Our coastlines are not as expansive as the oceans. Yet a major thrill of coasting is discovering small, secret places and secret people. Places and people that are exceptional yet without status. Places to which we return with appreciation; people to whom we return with friendship.

Because we don't carry the elaborate shelter of a big boat, beachcruisers need a friendlier climate and gentler weather. Because it's not fun to sail a little boat on a big ocean, we want smaller waters. Because it's not fun to paddle a heavy load, and few of us carry an engine and fuel, we want a steady breeze. If we've chosen to rely on power, then our area is even more restricted to those places where fuel is available. Finally, because we need and enjoy the shore, we must cruise in places where our landings, our shore camps, our explorations, our very presence, won't attract or provoke the attention of land dwellers—like insects, rude natives, or bears.

One late night we pitched our tent on a dark and deserted beach on the southern shore of Cap Cod. Because it was a warm, still night and we had no tent, the mosquitoes didn't let us sleep well. We slept late. We awoke to the yelling of an angry mob. I peeked from under the sheet to see what was going on. It was we who were the center of interest! We were surrounded by an angry mob of children, mothers, and fathers working each other up to a pitched indignancy at our sleepy intrusion upon their suburban shores. As we put on clothes and stuffed the bedding into the canoe, they were pitching sand at us. Those on power boats escorted our departure with threatening insults and wakes. Nobody helped us leave. Few shore populations are as mean as that. However, many are just as intrusive.

On the beaches of Pacific Mexico, the locals encircled our camp. And watched. And watched. All day it was up to us to entertain them. In the

34

Bahamas and in Martinique, it was quite the contrary. We were uncertain we were even visible to those who passed by. On one small, isolated, uninhabited islet, we happened to be camped on the very day the lighthouse crew made an annual inspection. They acknowledged our presence with tentative reluctance—as if they found beachcruisers camped on all the lighthouse rocks.

However, that rare treat is unlikely to occur in North America. Fortunately, in North America, there remain many lake and sea coasts without defensive inhabitants. It is these more remote shores that are inviting and entertaining for the variety and discoveries they offer. Sometimes the shores are difficult or dangerous to the unprepared. Usually they are seasonal.

We learn of places we might like to explore in many ways: from magazines like National Geographic, Small Boat Journal, Islands, Cruising World, or Canoe; from cruising narrative books like "Alone in the Caribbean" and "Enchanted Vagabonds"; from cruising guides like "Cruising Guide to the Abacos and Northern Bahamas", "Yachtsman's Guide to the Windward Islands", or "Baja Sea Guide"; from small and large scale maps and nautical charts; from the verbal reports of sailors we meet; and from the listings of "adventure travel" companies.

If written guides are available, these are usually the most comprehensive and detailed resource. Sometimes a guide will cover an area nearby the one of interest, so it at least describes the seasonal wind and weather patterns to be expected. The geography and topgraphy we learn from nautical charts and topo maps and flight maps. We deduce the intensity of population and commerce from a common road map. We seek out places without roads—places accessible only by boat. This would have prevented our unpleasant Cape Cod experience. Small islands attract us. Undeveloped peninsulas are a second best. Large areas of flat, low, lake-flooded lands, like the Canadian Shield, are certain to be wild and become our temporary home for decades.

For cruising on rivers, across small lakes, or seas near mountains, we know we'll have to rely on oar or paddle power. Massive lands make for unreliable winds. For a short distance, a short time and a light load, we have relied on paddle power. On long voyages without reliable winds, where fuel is available, we have relied on motor power.

There are places we avoid. We keep away from places where the local population is aggressively unfriendly or hungry. Long, unbroken coastlines are dangerous—even if the shore is a gently sloping beach. Not without reason is the coast of southwestern Africa named the Skeleton Coast. Coasts of uninterrupted mangrove are even deadlier than those beaches. Coasts of steep-to cliffs are obviously scary. Except within each bay, the Gulf of Alaska might be named "The Other Skeleton Coast." Most of Pacific North America is equally formidable, but there are small and large areas along even those steep-to shores that invite beachcruising.

PLACES

The Pacific Northwest

The Pacific Northwest, from Seattle northward, includes two seas connected to the Pacific and one another by stormy straits—Juan de Fuca leading to Puget Sound, and Queen Charlotte leading into the Strait of Georgia. Between these two basins lie the **San Juan Islands.** Within these two basins are hundreds of channels and islands and fjords forming such a confused maze as to challenge the skills of the best coastal navigator. The choices are infinite. Indeed, Captain Juan de Fuca experienced the area so immense as to describe it as "a broad inland sea." **Puget Sound** alone encompasses more than 2,000 square miles. The Strait of Georgia, to the north, is much larger, reaching widely between the lofty Cascades and the mile-high peaks of Vancouver Island.

The Pacific Northwest is one of the rainiest places in the world! On Olympic Peninsula, abutting Puget Sound, grows the only tropical rain forest in North America. In fact, most of the rain does fall on the Olympic Mountains—250 inches a year; and that, between October and May. In the lee of the mountains, some summers are almost dry.

The fog on the water persists longer than the rains—even into summer nights and mornings. As long as it's foggy, it's usually calm, good for paddling and motoring quietly. These seas are popular among kayakers and power boaters. By early afternoon they've made a destination and are appreciating the sunshine as they make camp, gather firewood and shellfish, and bathe in a nearby hot spring.

Wind direction and strength are variable. Combined with the 15-foot tidal range, tidal currents of up to 6 knots, the heaviest concentration of commercial traffic in the world, and log floats a half-mile long, relying on sail can be frustrating even after the fog burns off. Unless you plan to skim along the shore like the kayakers, a radar reflector is necessary, and a radar transceiver is desirable.

On some beaches and rocky landings, open fires are prohibited. Logging companies make the rules. Better bring along a good cooking stove.

Farther inland the climate is a little dryer. There is excellent boating on many large and small lakes and rivers. The **Hood River Gorge** on the **Columbia River** attracts champion sailboarders with reliable afternoon breezes of 30 knots.

In 1980, Mary Pederson and Steve Gropp circumnavigated **Vancouver Island** during July, August, and part of September in a 16-foot open, Gloucester-type, wooden rowing dory. The sail was a helpful and hopeful relief to their steady rowing between evening camps ashore. John Burleson and his family enjoy less arduous beachcruising inside their 15-foot outboard powered lapstrake skiff.

Baja California

For a friendlier year-round climate, western sailors look to Baja California as their cruising ground. Steady, gentle, winds and sunny skies make its 2000 miles of coastline a year-round attraction. Much of the coast is parched and arid, and supports no life or boating facilities. Southward of Ensenada to Cabo San Lucas, sailors are on their own. Moreover, the endless Pacific surf makes landings uncertain and risky. In the winter of 1933, Dana Lamb and his bride, Ginger, began their two-year beach cruise along this coast in a 16-foot, decked, sailing canoe. (Their cruise ended in Panama.) Since them, others have sailed and camped along sections of this coast. **Scammon's Lagoon** and **Magdalena Bay** are especially popular. These two huge sea-lakes offer protection and security not found along the open Pacific coast. To get to these, boaters trailer overland along a dirt road that is no better provisioned and only slightly less bumpy than the ocean they avoid. However, at 15 miles an hour, the road makes for a safer and faster passage.

Sea of Cortez

Baja California is a peninsular "territory" of Mexico. Most sailors, and especially power-boaters, limit their cruising to the inside of this peninsula—to the Sea of Cortez.

While these shores are no less forbidding than the Pacific coast, they don't suffer the constant and huge Pacific rollers, and the Sea of Cortez offers a string of small harbors, bays and islets, behind which a small craft might shelter; and villages at which to provision and make human contact.

What makes this territory so forbidding is that it is a desert. The lack of water limits all life forms, especially human development and its attendant mutual support systems. A boater must be totally self reliant outside of the few, small, almost frontier outposts—Ensenada, San Lucas, La Paz, Loreto, Mulege, Santa Rosalia, and San Felipe.

In cruising and camping along this coast, we have had to hike well inland up the arroyos in search of fresh water. Sometimes we've been lucky to find an oasis pond, complete with flitting song birds, croaking frogs, colorful flowers, and the tracks of mountain lions. Because the air is so dry and the land so barren, visibility is good. Be watchful for snakes. There are venomous species. Like all life in Baja, they are scarce, but the antivenin is scarcer still, and far away.

In summer, the climate becomes very hot, particularly when the wind's calm. It blows between 5 and 15 knots from the northwest in the mornings and from the southwest in the afternoons. Winters keep it northwest longer, and summers keep it southwest longer. It's gentler and more frequently calm during summer, except during the rare tropical storms. These depressions are easily identified. Be sure to shelter well inland. Don't shelter in a dry stream bed. Don't shelter in the bottom of a canyon. **Never** shelter on those tempting sand banks piled up where a stream flows into the sea. A rainstorm, one far inland, of which you can't be aware, can send a wave of mud and sand and water that has washed campers out to sea.

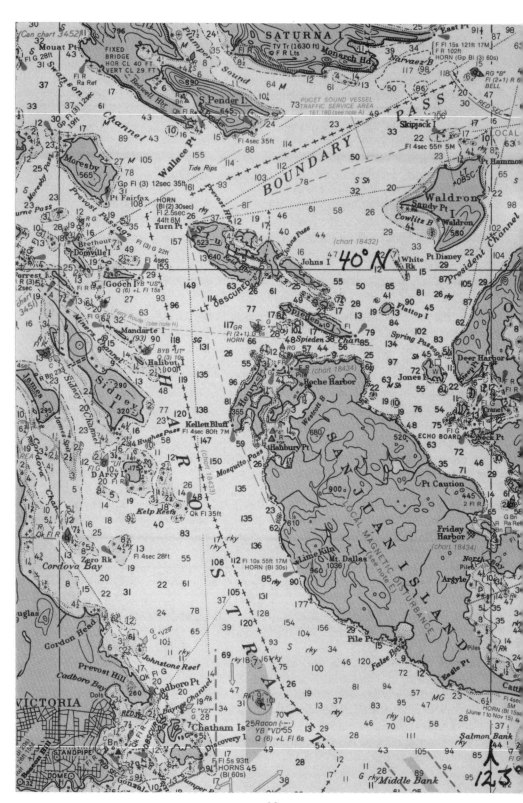

San Juan Islands, NW USA, and portion of Canadian Gulf Islands upper left, and portion of Vancouver Island, British Columbia lower left.

18400 SCALE 1:200,000

39

Except at the northern bight of the Sea of Cortez where the range is 20 feet, the tides around Baja are moderate with a mean range of 3 to 5 feet. Around the entrance to bays and between islands, the wind sometimes drives the currents to 5 knots. In breezy conditions, we approach these and headlands with caution. If possible, we land the boat and make an exploration on foot before risking the unseen by sea.

Because Baja is a territory of Mexico, paperwork and documentation is necessary for each foreigner and foreign vessel upon entry. While it is easier than for those entering the U.S., plan to spend a half-day on this. Also recognize that the officers rely on tips for part of their income.

Many small boaters, including beach camping sailors and kayakers, cruise the Sea of Cortez and the large estuaries of Pacific Baja. They are attracted by the sea life, including whales; and by the wild solitude of the shores. It is not unusual to see schools of fish 5 to 10 miles long. There are spiney lobster under the rocks and shellfish under the sand. There are choice beaches, bays, and islands that afford sheltered landings and private camping. The local population, centered at the few settlements and seasonal fish camps, are friendly and helpful. If you speak a little Spanish, you'll find it much easier to purchase your needs. The words *agua fresca* are especially useful in Baja.

The sanitary standards of mainland Mexico do affect the quality of fresh water. In Baja it is scarcer and no purer. Plan to boil it. Alternatively, take along iodine crystals. These have an infinite shelf life. If the water is warm, iodine will kill all the bacteria in 20 minutes. If you can't plan your thirst that long in advance, you can purchase an effective filter through which you can pump a quart through in 90 seconds. Remember to wash fresh fruit and to brush your teeth with purified water. Mexican beer is safe, excellent, and inexpensive.

Across the Sea of Cortez, on the Mexican mainland, the coast is almost as wild and unspoiled. Between bold headlands, small beaches provide landings within easy reach of each other. On some you'll see fishermens' shacks. Only 300 miles due southward of Tucson, **Guaymas-San Carlos** is the launching and provisioning center for this coast.

Inland Lakes and Rivers of the U.S.

Between the seacoasts, North America is dotted with navigable lakes and rivers. Except on the largest of these, the **Great Lakes**, the winds are so influenced by the surrounding lands, so variable in strength and direction, that we don't recommend reliance on sail. For short or downhill (downwind or downstream) cruises, kayaks and canoes work well. We've made longer, extended, inland cruises in aluminum skiffs powered by an outboard. Other people use houseboats. A friend built a platform on pontoons. On the platform she had space for a big standing-room tent and a front porch galley.

The Delta is an inland extension of San Francisco Bay. In order to explore and enjoy overnighting on these waters, we had to have self-contained sleeping accomodations. A boom tent or a small cuddy is a minimal must. Houseboats and trawlers are a more common sight. On our aluminum skiff we didn't have the room to stretch out. We found enough motels accessible from the shores.

On the shores of **Lake Mead** and **Lake Powell** on the **Colorado River**, it was easy to make camps ashore. The scenery is dramatic—even astounding. The spring and autumn weather, along with the stark privacy of the surrounding desert and canyons, invites nudity. Watch out for squalls. One caught us on the water as we raced it toward our camp. We didn't make it. The rain filled the boat and the hail cut our bare flesh as the wind swept the boat across a surface we could no longer see. Where we crashed ashore, we sheltered under the overturned boat, shivering until the squall passed. Without our compass and chart, we couldn't have figured out where we were. We never did find our camp. It had blown away. We returned to the parking lot under cover of night. Cold.

Like most rivers and man-made lakes, the **Sacramento California Delta, Lake Mead** and **Lake Powell** in Arizona and Utah, the **Mississippi River, Lake Barkley** and **Kentucky Lake** near the junction of the Tennessee and Ohio Rivers, have muddy, dark, obscure waters. Neither the water nor the winds on these lakes make for steady, relaxed or reliable sailing. However, for those who live inland, these are the largest available bodies of water on which they can lose themselves. We have tried sailing, paddling, and motoring on each of these. Sailing is frustrating. But as shoreside camps are easily found, and because we planned on only short trips, we enjoyed the quietness of a canoe. It let us hug the pretty shores close enough to appreciate the flowers and surprise the wildlife.

During our exploration of inland lakes, we carried our canoe on a car rack and towed a Jayco "pop up" camping trailer. With such a comfortable wilderness camp to return to, most of our paddling was limited to day trips. The Jayco camper was so easy to set up and put in tow, we explored more of each lake than if we'd been carrying our camp in the canoe. Often we would hitch a ride back to the Jayco and car and drive it to where we'd left the canoe.

Between Lake Barkley and Kentucky Lake lies a long expanse of park and campgrounds administered by T.V.A. Although it is possible to make an inconspicuous camp anywhere, we preferred to climb the short hill to the administered sites where we filled our Jerry cans with clear water and washed under a hot shower.

Only in the upper **Mississippi River** in Minnesota, have we enjoyed exploring and camping on this river. Downstream, we've been offended and crowded by the smell of commerce and development. Here again we've limited our cruises to paddling a few days along the nicest sections.

We've enjoyed short sections of other rivers in the same way—the **Saint Croix** in Minnesota, the upper **Hudson River** into **Lake Champlain,** the **Saint Johns River** in Florida, and Florida's **Suwanee River** have given us

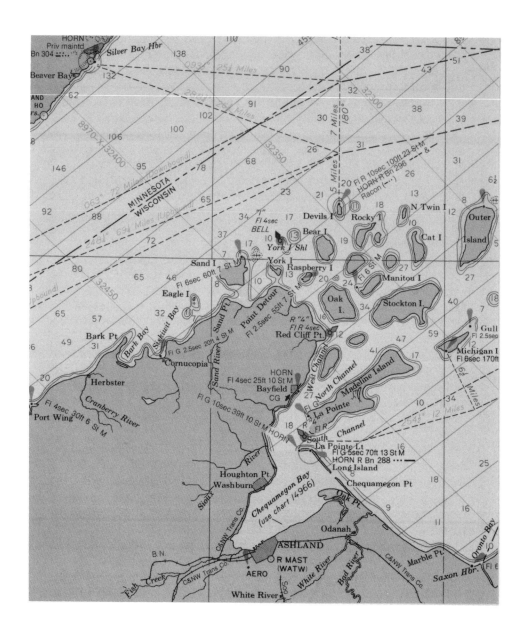

The Apostle Islands in Lake Superior off the north shore of Wisconsin are a National Seashore Park. Only Madeline Island is permanently inhabited. We were never bored on these beautiful islands, but few shores are sloped enough to land on. Kayaks and canoes can be hauled up these steep banks. The water is frigid—too cold to swim.

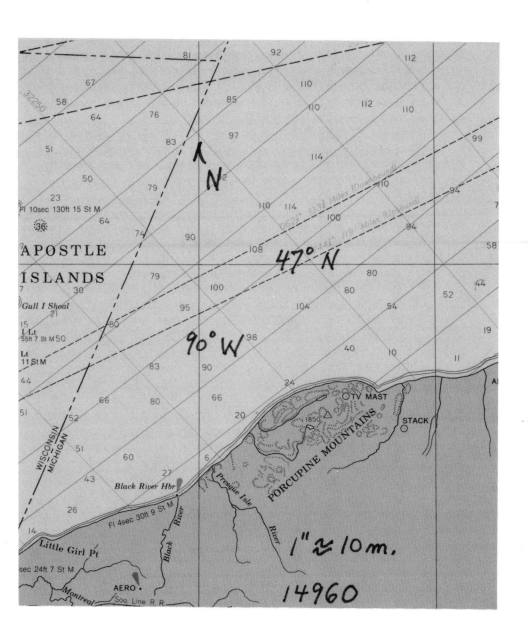

days of paddle-powered pleasure. Less muscled enthusiasts can enjoy these and other larger lakes and rivers with a small outboard on a canoe or small aluminum skiff that is easily trailered, launched, and retrieved. Just around the bend from the roadside ramp, you'll have the river to yourself. For aluminum skiffs to 14 feet, and canoes to 18 feet, weighing under 140 pounds, we don't need to find a ramp.

Along all these watery inland places, come prepared to defend yourself from insects. Seasonally (at hatching time), they become so numerous as to make breathing unlikely. The air is foggy with the little wings. Humans don't adventure during these times. Other times are enjoyable only with effective defences.

The Great Lakes

The enjoyably remote sections of even the expansive inland seas, the Great Lakes, are equally forbidding for the stinging and biting insects that hatch along the shores. No-see-ums, gnats, sand flies, mosquitoes, black flies, and deer flies take hungry turns while we're ashore. In the calm evenings and mornings, while we make supper and breakfast, the insects strike hardest. It's a boater's schizophrenia: to hope for gentle winds so we can put to sea, yet hope for strong winds so we can get ashore without being eaten alive.

It's on these lakes that we've most enjoyed inland, fresh water sailing. Seasonally. From October through May, it's too cold and storms are violent. We did once winter camp on an island in **Lake Superior.** We got out there in an enclosed cabin on a 40-foot passenger toboggan ferry, banging over hills of shore ice, across the thick snow drifts that covered the surface ice, then dropping 3 feet into holes to float across water, then bash into the edge of surface ice on the other side of these holes and sled for miles on a bumpy snow surface. The huge, enclosed, snow toboggan was built of steel plate and did 20 knots powered by an airplane engine and prop. It was home-made by our pilot. We were its only passengers and the only campers during that week that we stayed on the island.

Not that there are ever many beachcruisers on these lakes even during the gentler summers. From late June into September, the winds generally blow out of the southwest at 15 to 30 knots. Around Lake Superior, warm afternoons will cause onshore winds to clock around the lake. In our other favorite, the **North Channel** and **Georgian Bay** of **Lake Huron,** the winds are more westerly, then sometimes easterly.

Cold fronts and thunderstorms are fast moving, violent, and call for seeking immediate shelter. We listen to weather conditions from stations to the northwest (where from come the storms) and watch for any thunderstorm anvil tops coming our way. The Canadian Wayfarer Association, 980 Concession Street, Hamilton, Ontario, Canada 18T 1A1, publishes detailed log-books describing their many fleet cruises of the Great Lakes.

Around the **Apostle Islands,** and among the islands scattered along the

Canadian shores of **Lake Superior**, we can always hide in a lee. We keep close to a shore and mindful of the nearest place we can force a landing. The water never gets warm enough for immersed survival. Hypothermia is a likely consequence of a capsize or falling overboard. Along a gentle shore, in a calm, sunny bay at mid-day, we'll plunge in for a bath. In the evening, we warm a bucket over the coals. We do appreciate this abundance of clear, fresh water. If dipped up from deep water, some yards offshore, we've found it safe to drink. Water dipped from shoreside is sometimes safe to drink. However, the larvae and algae make it appear less, uh, fresh. Other times, I know that shore water is likely to be contaminated with wildlife fecal protozoa which may cause giardiasis and other nasty intestinal disorders.

On cold lakes where hypothermia is a risk, small boating is safe only **very** close to shore. This is one reason why buddy boats and fleet cruises are attractive. If you are compelled to keep close to shore, where the winds are least favorable, then consider a canoe or a powered skiff. A canoe can be easily kept close to shore; and a powered skiff can make open crossings faster, hence safer. Our sailing experiences on cold-water lakes has been a little risky, cautious, limited, and sometimes disappointing. We've usually enjoyed short passages—out to an island on which we'd set up a base camp and from which we made day trips to surrounding islands. For extended trips, paddle power and outboards have served us better. When the lake got lumpy, we've made a fast retreat, sometimes up a stream. On those calm, warm evenings, when the insects might have carried us away, the canoe was easy to conceal while we retreated to a road and hitched to a motel. If you plan extended cruises under sail on cold water, then you must take special precautions to not capsize, to not fall overboard, to recover from a capsize (self-rescue) and defend yourself from hypothermia. A dry suit would help. A quickly inflated inner-tube might make a personal, good life raft.

The warmer lakes and rivers allow safer beach cruising and playful sailing. We've even enjoyed day sailing a Sunfish in the high Rockies, but those playful inland winds make for uncertain cruising. For cruising inland waters, we rely on the canoe, sometimes with a small outboard on the stern bracket. Even along the **sea** coasts in the lee of the West Indies, we've found it more certain to rely on the paddle than on the wind. Larger boats can risk finding those certain winds that blow 1 or 2 miles off shore. On little boats, we're apprehensive of being blown away. It's happened to others.

East Coast of Canada

It is the eastern and Gulf coasts of North America that are seasonally blessed with just the combination of conditions appropriate to small boat sailing and coastal camping—warm protected waters and moderate, reliable winds. Some of the shoreline is heavily populated, but enough marginal land is still open to provide a landing, a walk, and an overnight

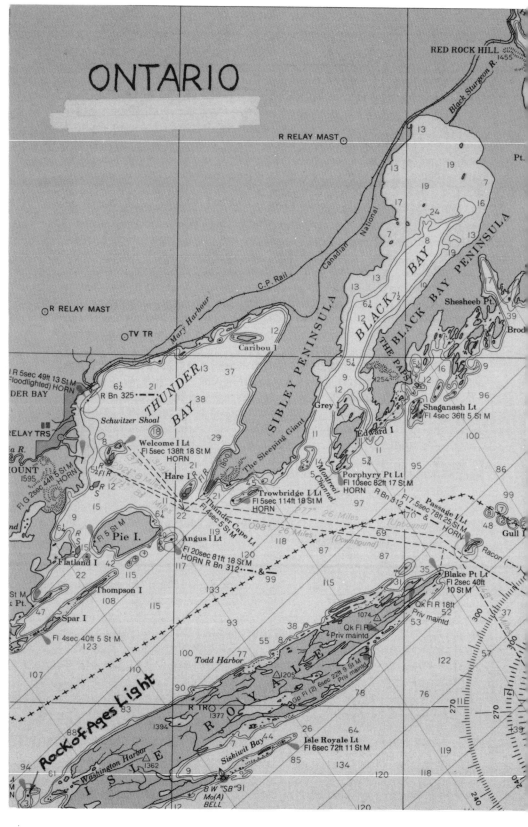

ONTARIO

RED ROCK HILL 1455

Black Sturgeon R.

R RELAY MAST

R RELAY MAST

TV TR

BLACK BAY

Shesheeb Pt.

THE BLACK BAY PENINSULA

Brod

SIBLEY PENINSULA

THUNDER BAY

Caribou I

Mary Harbour

C.P. Rail

Canadian National

Schwitzer Shoal

Welcome I Lt
Fl 5sec 138ft 18 St M
HORN

Hare I

Pie I.

Angus I Lt
Fl 20sec 81ft 18 St M
HORN R Bn 312

Flatland I

Thompson I

Spar I
Fl 4sec 40ft 5 St M

Todd Harbor

Rock of Ages Light

Washington Harbor

Siskiwit Bay

The Sleeping Giant

The Montreal Channel

Trowbridge I Lt
Fl 5sec 114ft 18 St M
HORN

Grey I

Edward I

Porphyry Pt Lt
Fl 10sec 82ft 17 St M
HORN

Shaganash Lt
Fl 4sec 36ft 5 St M

Passage I Lt
Fl 7.5sec 78ft 25 St M
HORN

Gull I

Racon

Blake Pt Lt
Fl 2sec 40ft
10 St M

Qk Fl R 18ft
Priv maintd

Qk Fl R
Priv maintd

ISLE ROYALE

Isle Royale Lt
Fl 6sec 72ft 11 St M

B W "SB"91
Mo(A)
BELL

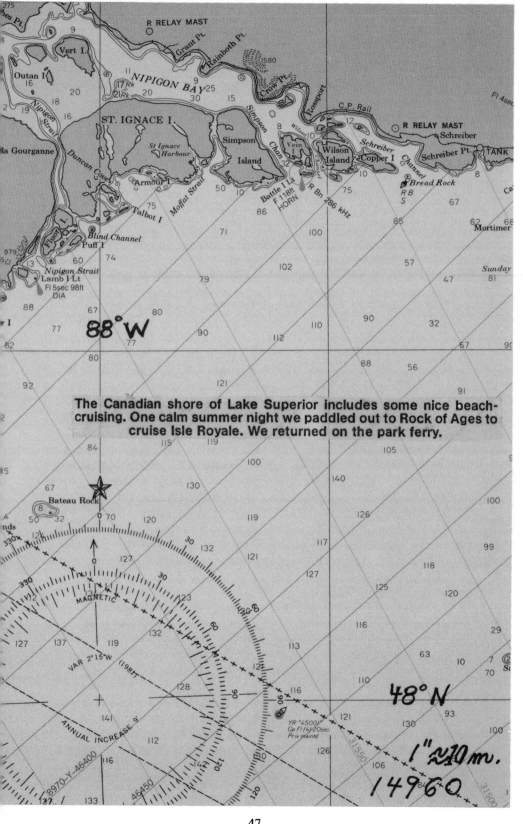

The Canadian shore of Lake Superior includes some nice beach-cruising. One calm summer night we paddled out to Rock of Ages to cruise Isle Royale. We returned on the park ferry.

camp. What has been lost by way of Nature's accomodations can be overcome by exploiting some of the varieties of High Culture. When we can't find a comfortable and secure camp, then we can go to a restaurant, a movie, and spend the night in a hotel. Not all shore folk are like those of Cape Cod. A few have welcomed us to a shower, a meal, friendship and a bed.

Northward of Cape Cod, the seas never warm. Northward of Portland, Maine, the shore population becomes less dense and more friendly. But the weather, even in summer, becomes less friendly and less reliable. Fog and rain are as common as in the Pacific Northwest. The tidal range becomes even more exaggerated. Day trips, even two-day trips, can be light fun in fair weather. On longer cruises, it's realistic to count on some foul weather. Fortunately, as far northward as Halifax, Nova Scotia, there's enough shore development to easily retreat into the comforts of a village. From Halifax through Labrador the summer weather gets no worse, though summers are shorter. In these latitudes we've cruised prepared to be fully on our own, as settlements are fewer and farther between.

The **Labrador** coast is frontier country accessible by ferry boat from Lewisporte, northern Newfoundland, to Goose Bay, thence by coastal steamer to Nain, northern Labrador—The Last Stop. Goose Bay (it's a very wide, long, big bay), might be a good place to make a shakedown cruise. Geoffrey Heath has made two extended cruises of northern Labrador. First with Dave Getchell, Sr., in an 18-foot aluminum outboard skiff; and the next year, alone, in his Wayfarer sailing dinghy, reported in issue #44 of Small Boat Journal. He did carry a two-horsepower outboard and 5 gallons of fuel. He didn't admit to carrying an E.P.I.R.B. or polar bear repellent. I would recommend carrying both when cruising Labrador.

In Labrador, the solitude is overwhelming. The giantness, the starkness, the geography and remoteness are persistent reminders of the frailty and brevity of human life. Geoffrey Heath observed that he didn't talk with anyone for 22 days. Robert Perkins made a longer cruise of this coast in a small canoe. Then he portaged the Torngat Mountains into Ugava Bay. He, too, became attracted by the intensity of the solitude. Along eastern North America, Labrador is singular in offering coastal campers such a grand seclusion.

The **Bras d'Or Lake in Cape Breton Island,** Nova Scotia, is a more accessible, less forbidding, cruising area. Here we haven't been able to cruise for 22 days without speaking with another. But in parts of West Bay, we might have been the only souls on earth. There is something to being in a place so remote that you know there are not others even within reach. Particularly when it's quiet and still and peaceful, the experience of seclusion is rare and uncanny. To some it's unsettling. We recommend it as a singular human experience to be enjoyed by boat cruisers. In "Against Straight Lines—Alone in Labrador" by Robert F. Perkins, 1983, Little Brown, Robert Perkins describes well his encounters with himself in the Torngat Mountains of Labrador.

Northeast U.S.

From Labrador southward, the experience of seclusion becomes less likely as the weather becomes seasonally gentler, and human enterprise more abundant. Yet there are hundreds of uninhabited islets, coves, marshes, bays, beaches and pockets where the only other sounds you're likely to hear are the wind and the waves. East of **Bar Harbor, Maine,** there are few other boaters. All over Maine, the shore folk are as friendly as the summer weather.

Along the **Northeast coast** of the USA, summer winds are predominently from the southwest at 10 to 15 knots. About once a week, a cold front sweeps through, preceded by rain and followed with a day or two of clear, dry winds out of the northwest. The predominent southwest wind eases during the evening to be replaced by an offshore breeze that may last until mid-morning. By mid-day, the southwest wind is at its strongest and will have blown the fog off.

Along this part of the coast the tides are at their fullest. A fall of 15 feet is common and makes the tidal currents severe. The daily plan must reckon with both. If you plan to sail, you must plan to row, or motor, or anchor, to stay in place. The depth of water, right up to the shore, is in places over 30 feet. Anchoring calls for a long rode. Sometimes tying to the shore is more effective.

Even in hot mid-summer, the seas eastward of Cape Cod don't warm for comfortable swimming. A fast plunge is all we've ever dared. A prolonged capsize would certainly lead to hypothermia. Don't cleat the main sheet.

On shore, insects are numerous. Black flies are a bloody nuisance until the first hot spell in June. Mosquitoes continue right through September. We've used head nets while setting up the tent.

Photo by Ron Johnson

Cruise camping at its finest. A *Sea Pearl* and a cat boat enjoy a sandy isle all to themselves, Cedar Key, FL

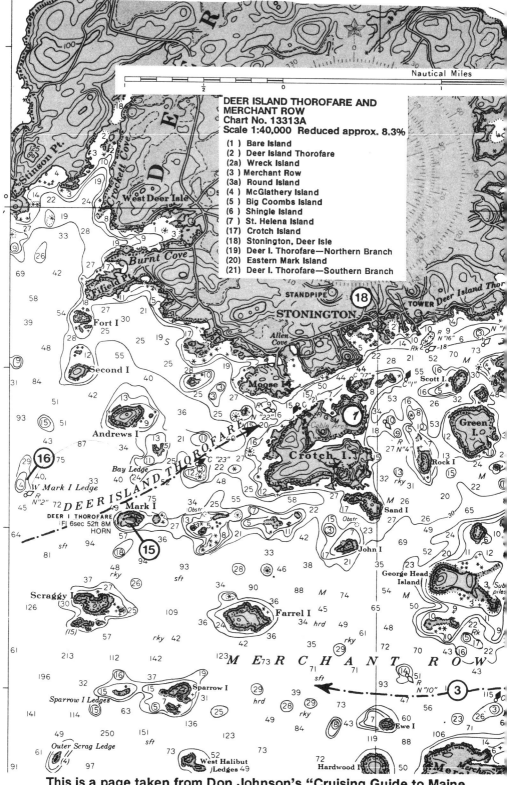

DEER ISLAND THOROFARE AND MERCHANT ROW
Chart No. 13313A
Scale 1:40,000 Reduced approx. 8.3%

(1) Bare Island
(2) Deer Island Thorofare
(2a) Wreck Island
(3) Merchant Row
(3a) Round Island
(4) McGlathery Island
(5) Big Coombs Island
(6) Shingle Island
(7) St. Helena Island
(17) Crotch Island
(18) Stonington, Deer Isle
(19) Deer I. Thorofare—Northern Branch
(20) Eastern Mark Island
(21) Deer I. Thorofare—Southern Branch

This is a page taken from Don Johnson's "Cruising Guide to Maine, Volume II," published by Wescott Cove Publishing Co., Box 130, Stamford, CT 06904. This shows a very small part of Maine's 3000-

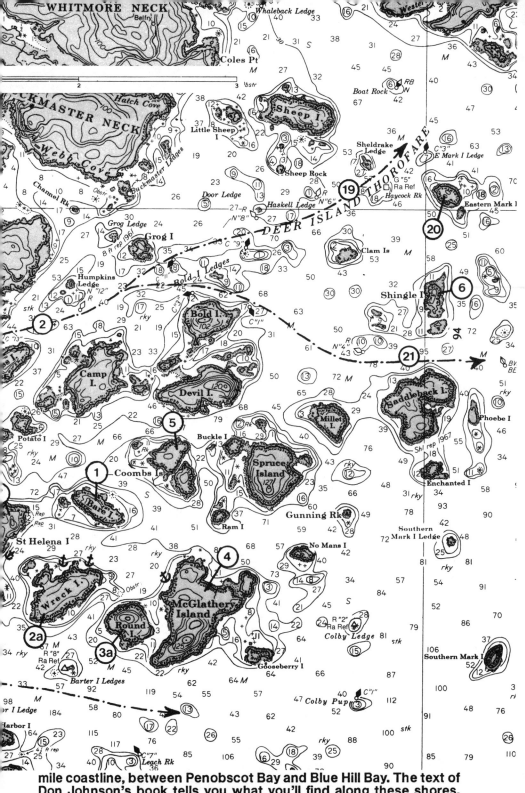

mile coastline, between Penobscot Bay and Blue Hill Bay. The text of
Don Johnson's book tells you what you'll find along these shores.
Though these waters are cold, we've found inland ponds swimmable
at the end of a sunny August day.

51

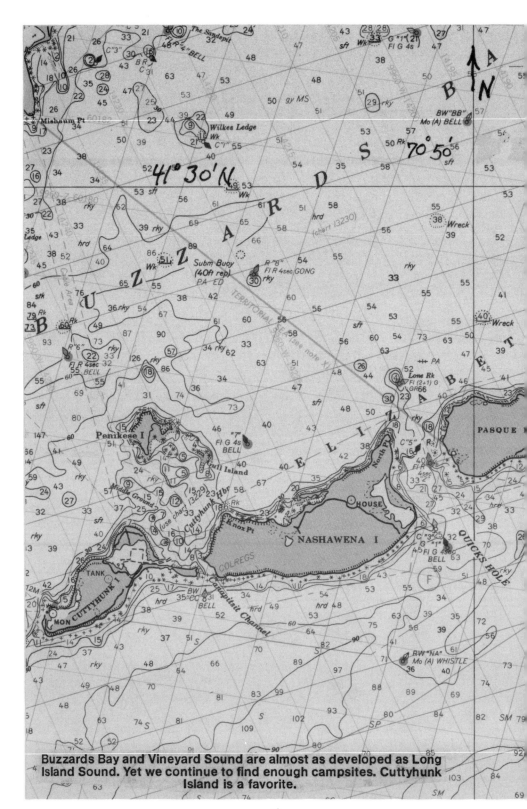

Buzzards Bay and Vineyard Sound are almost as developed as Long Island Sound. Yet we continue to find enough campsites. Cuttyhunk Island is a favorite.

Along the southern shores of **Cape Cod**, the water warms up, summer seas are swimmable. Because of it, much of the shoreline is thickly populated with year-round homes. Also, because of the warmer seas, we do much of our sailing around here. A shore camper must keep a low profile and be ready to move on. A boom tent or sleeping cuddy adds manifold choices to a cruise in any such populated area. We may not be welcomed, but as sleep-aboards, we will be tolerated for the few days we plan to enjoy a locale.

Thanks to the **Cape Cod National Seashore** and other more local parks, we've been able to enjoy shore camps in a few remote sites even along thickly settled shores. **Great Island** and **Sandy Neck** on **Cape Cod Bay** are remote and undisturbed by even the park rangers. Inside **Nauset** and **Monomoy**, we've been able to enjoy days of beach camping and warm swimming.

Across Nantucket Sound, on **Martha's Vineyard, Nantucket Island,** and on the **Elizabeth Islands**, we've found beautiful shore camps sufficiently remote that our presence has disturbed no one. Neither have we advertised our presence by erecting our tent conspicuously during the day on a beach, or by lighting bonfires at night.

The places where you're likely to shore camp undisturbed are obvious on any detailed road map. If no roads approach a shore, then there's **probably** no private interests your presence will upset. Getting detailed, good quality maps of the area that interest us, we've usually been able to find some shores to which roads don't approach. A few times we've left the boat at anchor or concealed the canoe in the bush, put our camp and stores in the backpacks, walked through town, inland, to set up camp by a pond or stream. We've become very aware of poison ivy. It's a serious hazard—even along the shores.

Because the eastern seaboard is such a developed coast, we've found it expedient to be prepared to sleep aboard or in a motel. (Cooking ashore, even in Manhattan Island, is not a problem!) Thus we enjoy many more places; we're relieved of the uncertainty of finding a shore camp; and we can more frequently appreciate the High Culture—local architecture and food, museums, shops and entertainment opportunities. Along suburban shores, we usually anchor. Sometimes we can get into a dock that no other boat can use and enjoy a hot shower at the marina. We've found that if we're going to keep sailing each day, it's more convenient to keep the housekeeping aboard rather than make and break a shore camp daily. Along much of this seaboard, sleeping aboard has frequently been more enjoyable than camping ashore. We particularly appreciate the privilege when we find an inviting shore, as we did on Washburn Island in Waquoit Harbor on Cape Cod; on Duck Island Roads in Long Island Sound; and around Block Island, Rhode Island.

If getting permission to camp on private land looks likely, then we're not shy to ask. The owner of a beach estate in Martinique invited us to stay for months! It's nice to meet local residents on favorable terms. More often it's a whole lot easier to ask forgiveness than to get permission.

From **Buzzards Bay**, Massachusetts through **Long Island Sound**, and the connected bays that fringe Long Island's south shore, there is a lifetime of cruising. No wonder this area has such a concentration of boats. Weekends are crowded with wall-to-wall boats. But during the week, even here, there's few enough that we find ourselves waving to one another. **Barnegat Bay** and **Chesapeake Bay** are like this too. Busy weekends, dominated by power boats in a hurry, quiet during the week.

Mid Atlantic Coasts of U.S.

Southwestward from Long Island, the prevailing summer southwest winds become gentler and tentative. And hot. The best sailing is in the spring and fall. **Barnegat Bay** and **Delaware Bay** are the least likely places to enjoy shore camping or high culture from the hull of a small boat, but on **Chesapeake Bay** we've enjoyed both. Again, poison ivy is common; and dense foliage on those rare, undeveloped shores requires some zeal to get through. The waters are swimmable during spring and fall. In the summer, when it might be most enjoyed, it becomes infested with nettles, and jellyfish that inflicts severe and immediate contact stings. As the waters are frequently opaque from river runoffs, don't dive in before first making a gentle exploration of what lies obscured under the surface. You might dive into a submerged log.

On the Atlantic side of the **Delmarva Peninsula**, there are more remote, more interesting, smaller bays to explore in a small boat—**Chincoteague Bay** and **Hog Islands Bays** to the southward. Again, dense foliage, including poison ivy is to be expected. Mosquitoes and ticks are not unknown. These bays and associated streams are small enough for canoeing.

Southeast U.S.

Moving southward in the fall, we've lingered in the Albermarle and Pamlico Sounds of North Carolina. As in the bays to the northward, these river-fed bays are muddy and the shores are even lower and are marshy—even swampy in places. Where there are towns, the elevation is at least 2 feet above high tide. Other high shores are usually cut off from the mainland by marshes.

We've sailed across to camp on the barrier beaches of **Hatteras** and **Ocracoke Islands**. Out there on the **sounds**, we've always felt exposed, vulnerable, and apprehensive. The area is expansive. **Pamlico Sound** is 70 miles long and averages 20 miles wide. That's 1500 square miles. Hard winds blowing across these fairly shallow sounds develop a real nasty chop. There may be a prevailing wind force and direction, but we've never gotten an assured grip on it. Of course, we've been there only in the spring and fall, the seasons of change, when winds are least prevailing. During these uncertain seasons, we've felt more confident sailing farther

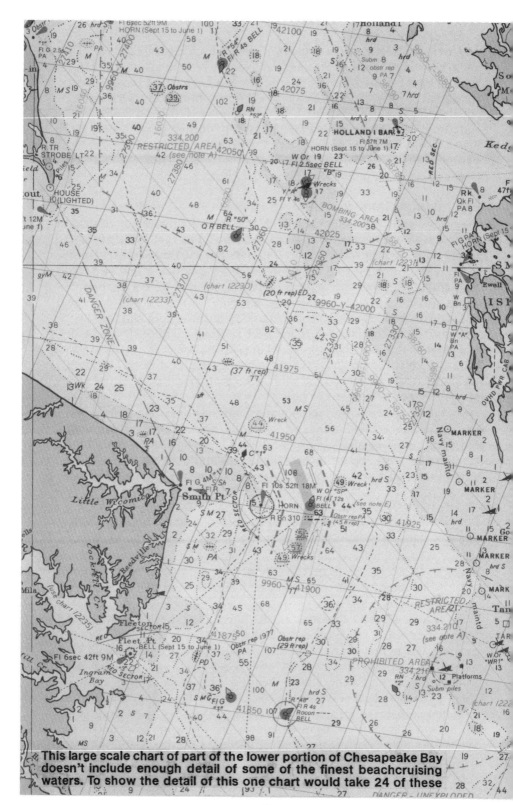

This large scale chart of part of the lower portion of Chesapeake Bay doesn't include enough detail of some of the finest beachcruising waters. To show the detail of this one chart would take 24 of these

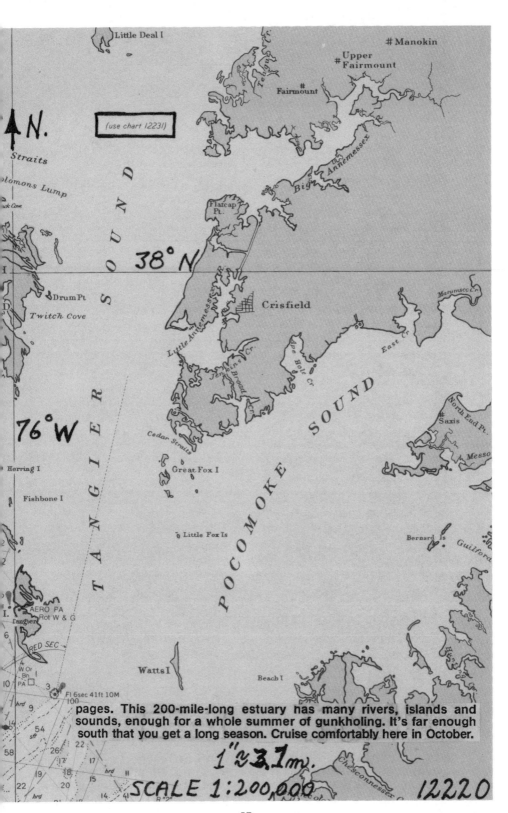

pages. This 200-mile-long estuary has many rivers, islands and sounds, enough for a whole summer of gunkholing. It's far enough south that you get a long season. Cruise comfortably here in October.

SCALE 1:200,000

1" ≈ 3.1mi.

12220

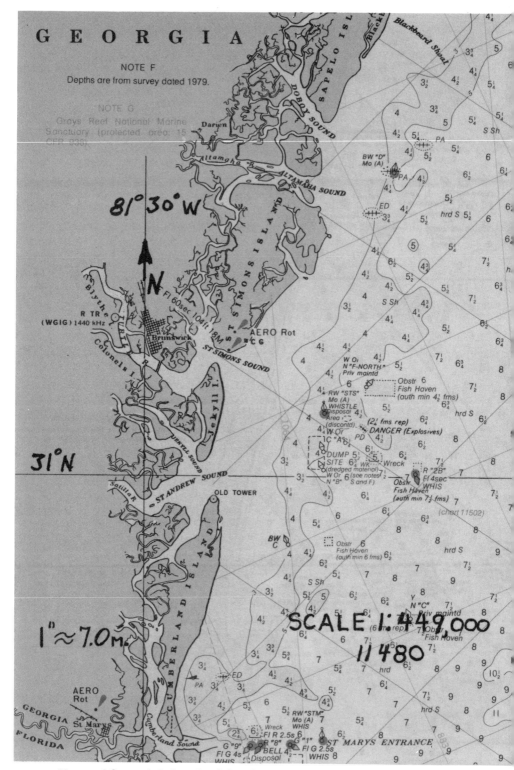

Many of Georgia's barrier islands can only be reached by boat. Tidal currents and tidal range must be considered. Cumberland Island is our favorite. There are dunes, deer, ruins, great beaches, and hot showers.

southward, along coastal **Georgia.** Here, behind the barrier islands that extend southward to Miami, we've felt more protected from the unpredictable elements of spring and fall. Among the **Florida Keys** it's been warm enough even in winter.

Most of the coastal islands of Georgia are still islands. They don't have bridges connecting them to excessive exploitation. Most are separated from the mainland by expansive tidal marshes through which meander pathways of tidal rivers. Some of these are wide and deep. The smallest dry out on the ebb.

The tidal currents flow strongly, often 3 knots. Because these rivers wind and meander so that in places the wind is sure to come against your direction, reliable power is highly recommended. Matt Layden travels this waterway annually in each direction. He frequently has to wait for the tide to turn. Even with a motor, passage along coastal Georgia is slow. In the wide sea inlets, between islands, a hard blow can build up a mean chop, especially when the wind and tide are opposed.

When we've cruised the Georgia isles, we've been there to explore them rather than passing through on our way to another destination. Slow passage hasn't frustrated us. We were there to appreciate the wildness and the beauty at a slow pace. We were where we wanted to be. Even the mainland side has places of remote solitude accessible to camping. We prefer the islands. **Blackbeard** and **Cumberland** are our favorites. These are replete with forests of gargantuan oak and hickory trees, high sand dunes, wild horses and feral pigs, deer, man-eating crocodiles, fresh inland ponds, many miles of wide open beaches, and very few people.

While the weather is uncertain, the passages are narrow, hence offer real security even during a wild squall. On these islands we've left canoes and *Dugong* overnight, with certainty they'd be there when we returned, and we've met nice people with whom we've made friends.

Southward of Cumberland Island lies **coastal Florida.** While the waterway behind the barrier islands is narrow and developed, it is a playful passage that includes sufficient small side pockets at which to set up an overnight shore camp. Better yet, sleep aboard anywhere along the waterway and enjoy daytime landings.

Along this **Intracoastal Waterway,** we've enjoyed a few of the occasional, scattered, overnight campsites along the shore—up a side creek or canal, on a spoil islet, up a bay, in state and local parks. We've always been on our way, and not lingered even in those few undeveloped places. Otherwise we might have resented the insects, and the constant hum of traffic—boats, cars and trucks.

A few miles inland, Florida's **Saint Johns River** provides a wider and wilder waterway, but the insects, particularly during late spring and summer, are a Major Distraction. Once, our timing was so imperfect, it was impossible to breathe without a dust mask. The stingless mosquitoes were that thick. Eating wasn't easy either. Everything was coated with their bodies. At least they don't sting. And we did enjoy swimming with the

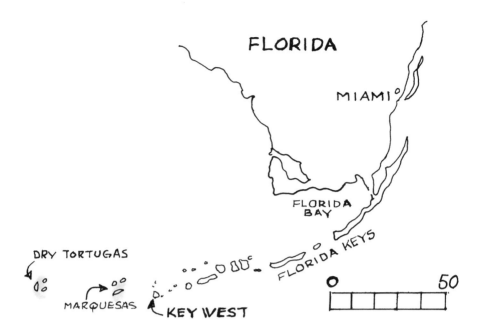

manatees in clear, sweet, spring waters erupting from deep, underground caverns. These are comfortable swimming year-round, a constant 70°. We've been back there in the fall and been only slightly bothered by stinging mosquitoes during the calm evenings and mornings. We found it enjoyable by canoe.

By canoe, we continued on to explore and camp along **Lake Okeechobee** and the **Kissimmee River** in southern Florida. This lake is open enough for steady sailing, and at times too windy for paddling. Much of its shoreline is a 30-foot high, sloped earth dam. State and local parks along the shore provide facilities for camping. Only 100 miles farther southward, in the **Everglades** and **Florida Bay** and the **Keys,** we've found wilder cruising and better beach camping.

Biscayne Bay is a good place to start a cruise. We've made a number of prolonged shakedown cruises here. The marina and grounds of **Elliot Key National Park** afford a convenient and comfortable base. This bay, the **Everglades, Blackwater Sound, Largo Sound** and the **Florida Keys** are all connected by sea and offer sufficient camping with convenient access to remote wilderness and shopping malls. Between them, you can find groomed and popular campgrounds whose facilities and society have refreshed and entertained us.

Our first winter in the Florida Keys, we were surprised, no, shocked and shaken at how cold and windy these tropical seas can become. A hard norther, a cold front, blew the water out of **Florida Bay.** We couldn't sail to a phone to call home for blankets until the winds clocked to the east.

Typically, summer winds are hot and gentle out of the southeast, interrupted by occasional hurricanes as autumn approaches. Don't get caught

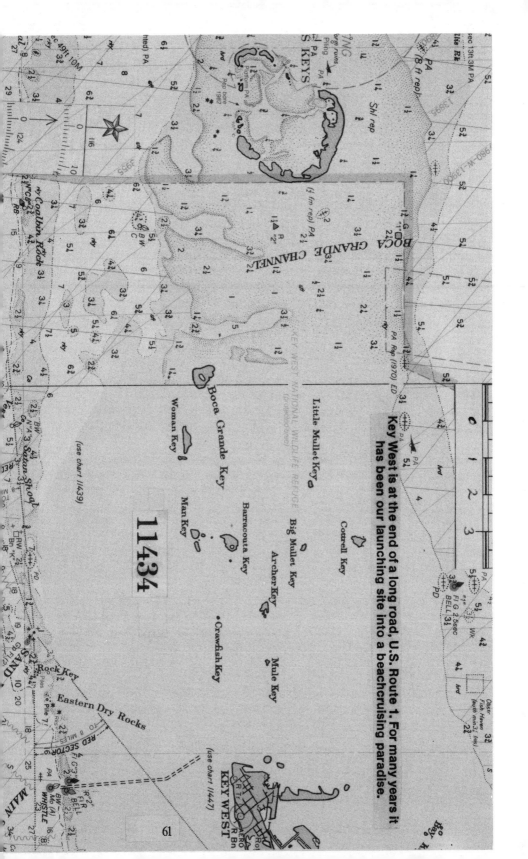

Key West is at the end of a long road, U.S. Route 1. For many years it has been our launching site into a beachcruising paradise.

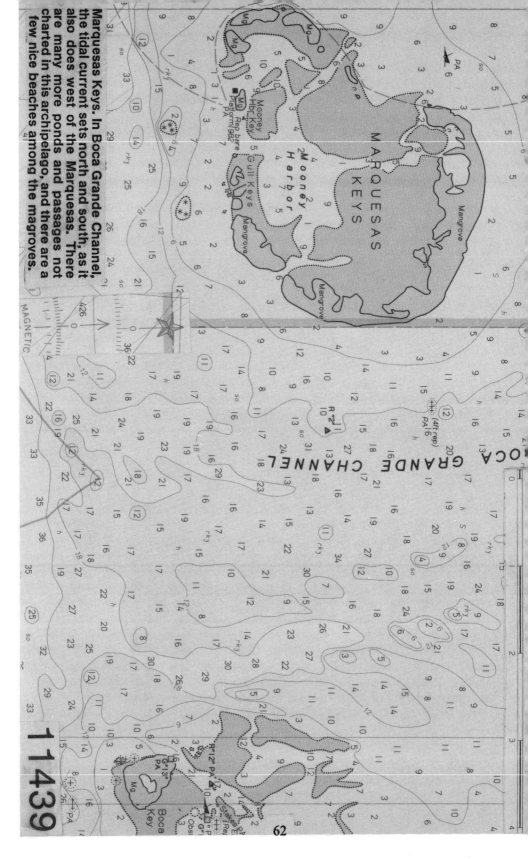

Marquesas Keys. In Boca Grande Channel, the tidal current sets north and south, as it also does west of the Marquesas. There are many more ponds and passages not charted in this archipelago, and there are a few nice beaches among the magroves.

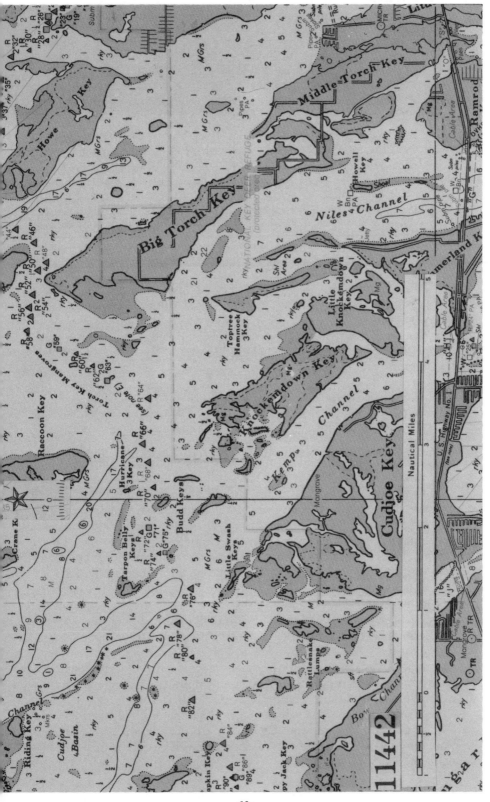

North of Route 1 and east of Key West are vast shallows and many islands where our shallow draft lets us sail, camp, snorkel, and dive.

63

anywhere near the sea if one of these approaches. None of the shore is very elevated, and it is known that thousands have perished in a single storm. As winter comes, cold fronts become more frequent and intense. Between these, winds prevail from the east and northeast. As each front approaches, winds clock to the southeast then south, then may blow hard out of the southwest and west, to be followed by a Black Horizon rolling down from the northwest. Avoid exposing yourself to these Black Horizons. During the mid-winter, these fronts arrive weekly, and often enough the cold, hard blow out of the north and northeast will last six days. It takes some experience to select landings and beach camps secure to winds that clock weekly. Particularly hard to find are ones that combine that security with sufficient breeze to minimize mosquitoes and no-see-ums.

Warmed by the Gulf Stream, and being the most southerly part of the U.S., these clear seas and islands are our favorite beach cruising grounds of North America. We've made a permanent base camp for several years on one or another of the many uninhabited islands off the Florida Keys. Once a month we'd day sail, occasionally with an overnight at anchor, to **Key West** or **Marathon** for supplies, water, the library, a movie and mail. Before it became intervally (time sharing) owned, Key West was an entertaining and real community.

Gulf Coast of U.S.

From the Everglades National Park northward, it is the **western coast of Florida,** on the Gulf of Mexico, that is least developed. Along this coast, beach camps are easy to find. Much of the coast is so remote that your presence won't be noticed. From **Fort Myers** to **Tarpon Springs,** you'd want to keep moving or stay at regulated campsites in order to minimize your intrusion. Beyond this concentration of human industry, the Gulf Coast of Florida offers opportunity for relaxed coastal camping and unrestrained exploration. If unexpected, hurricanes, insects, snakes, and even small mammals like raccoons, can be more than a nuisance. Once, our camp was attacked by so many raccoons, even clubs and rocks didn't discourage them. They'd already crippled one another so badly that they were immune to physical pain. In the Canadian Shield, we've been attacked by hundreds of chipmunks! Less prepared, more innocent campers have lost much of their food and all their drinking water during the raccoons' nocturnal forays. They easily puncture plastic, open latches, tear apart tents and carry away cans. They're good swimmers too. Only rats are as bad. One winter we killed 54 rats in our camp traps. One even got around the rat stops on the lines and boarded the boat. Before we caught it, it caused quite a bit of damage.

The Gulf Coast gets shallow even miles from shore. Winds stir the silty bottom and muddy the water. Tides are a moderate 4 feet or less. The winds and barometric pressure will sometimes affect the depth more than the moon.

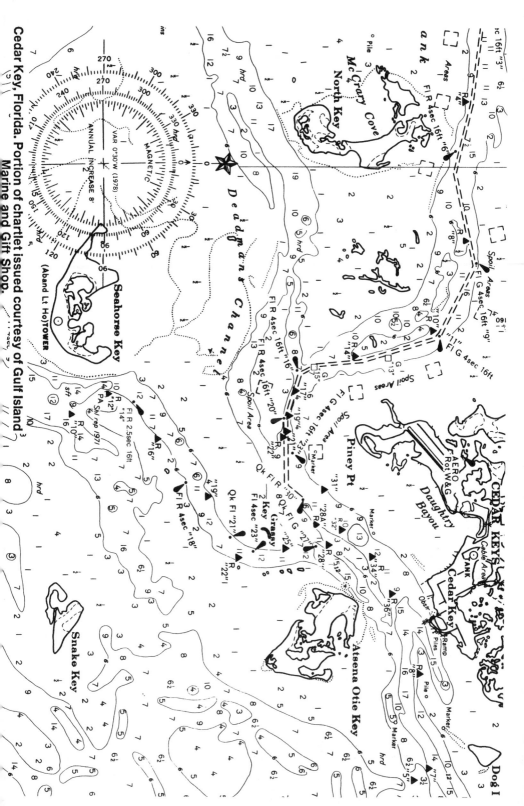

Cedar Key, Florida. Portion of chartlet issued courtesy of Gulf Island Marine and Gift Shop.

65

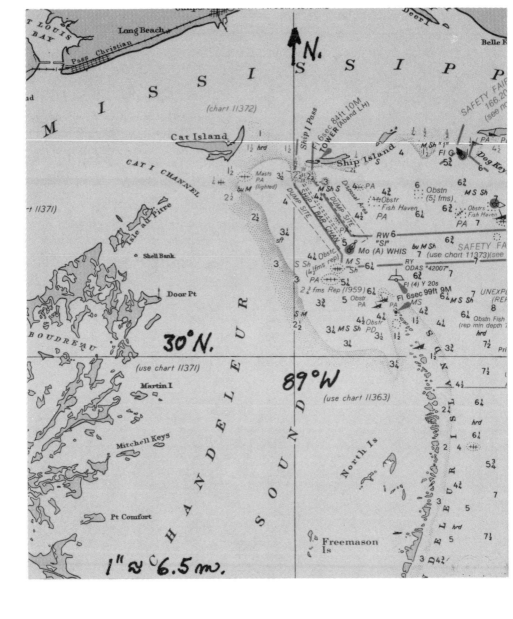

If your boat is lightly laden and reliably powered, the streams and rivers offer secure shelter and inland exploration. Of these, the **Suwanee** is deservedly famous as it leads through forested high banks to fresh springs and into the trackless Okefenokee Swamp. Yet it is neither wide nor fast flowing. The **Waccasassa,** the **Steinhatchee,** and the **Aucilla** are smaller and as interesting. The **Apalachicola** is bigger, yet not so developed that shore camps are hard to find.

Except in a few places, cruising along this Gulf shore offers little protection. While the waters are too shallow for large waves to build, a hard

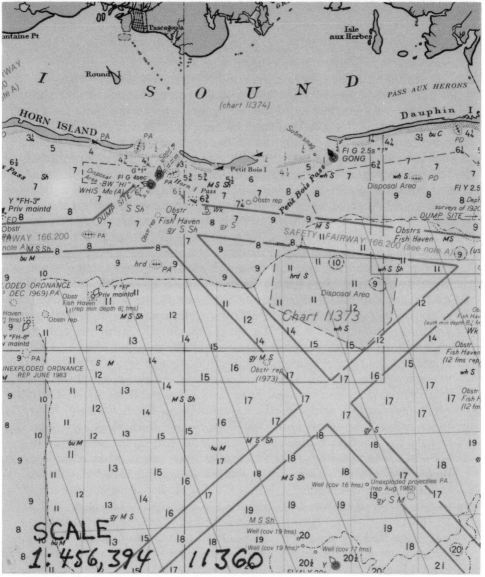

The Gulf Islands of Mississippi Sound. The islands are 5 to 10 miles from shore. The sound is 65 miles long and will develop a sea in a blow. Our editor had Army Air Corps basic training in Biloxi, and was fascinated by these offshore isles.

onshore blow can cause such a nasty chop as to make boating dangerous. In iffy weather, always have a planned destination and a retreat to sheltered waters. While outside it raged for days, we sailed peacefully throughout **Whitewater Bay** in the **Everglades**.

Alternatively, limit your cruise to the bays within which you'll always find protection from the worst of the rages. Along the Gulf, westward from the Florida panhandle, there are many such little seas formed inside the barrier islands. On these islands and in sections of the mainland shore, there are countless good landings, hundreds of beaches, and campsites within easy sailing range of one another.

We've found **Saint George Sound** and **Apalachicola Bay** especially appealing. Around the corner, **Saint Joseph Bay** can be reached in a day. Between Saint Joseph Bay and **Mobile Bay**, we've found the shore too exposed for relaxed shore cruising, and the beaches too developed for camping. In certain weather, day sailing is commonly enjoyed. Mobile Bay is a very industrial waterway. West of Mobile Bay and around the Mississippi River Delta, we've found safe waters and accessible shore camps. Of these, **Mississippi Sound** and the **Gulf Islands** have got to be a high point. As these lie about 10 miles offshore, we waited for settled weather to make the crossing. Once out there, the crossings between the islands are no less intimidating. Be prepared with plenty of insect repellent while cruising this tropical delta.

Only during spring and fall does this area offer a tolerable climate. Winters are too cold for exposed boating. Summers are calm and hot. Of the two good seasons, fall is likely to be dryer and less buggy. In the fall, be watchful of changes in weather. Thunderstorm squalls are severe and lightning is attracted to masts. If a hurricane enters the Gulf, be ready to make a hasty retreat to high inland ground. Most of this low coast becomes awash in the 10-foot or more rise of hurricane seas. The big waves are on top of that rise. For reasons of haste, insects, and uncertain winds, locals of the Delta use enclosed power boats and small cabin cruisers in which they explore and enjoy the bays and ways. The Mississippi River Delta is 100 miles across and goes 50 miles inland—5,000 square miles equally and randomly divided between land and water, and a mix of both. Many outlying bays are at least 25 miles across. **Chandeleur** and **Breton Sounds** are 50 miles across, fringed with uninhabited islands.

The most westward cruising on the Gulf of Mexico is inside the barrier islands that fringe Texas from **Galveston** to **Brownsville.** This waterway is 5 to 10 miles wide and 150 miles long. It is narrow enough for secure open sailing, yet long enough to accommodate a wide and continuing choice of routes, movement, and exploration. The best part of it is **Laguna Madre**, behind **Padre Island**, now a national seashore. Away from Corpus Christi, shores on either side of this long lagoon are undeveloped and easily approached for landing and camping. There are no settlements to obtain provisions and water. Winds are a steady 10 to 15 knots out of the east and blow well into the night. The wind and the arid, barren landscape, ease the insect problem. There is little shade to moderate the sun, and no features break the wind or provide a landmark. It takes a strong, well-anchored tent to stand up to these conditions, particularly when the squalls of the thunderstorm blow across. Once, during a day sail, we neglected to lower the tent. When we returned to camp, quite shaken and in need of shelter, there remained nothing but shreds of fabric on pieces of broken poles. That the tent was old made us feel little better. Since then, we've not forgotten to lower it to the ground, and to cover it with an old sheet to protect it from the disintegration of the sun. If we plan to linger, we set up a wind break, more for ourselves than for the tent.

Beachcruisers' ability to snuggle into small spaces lets them find room in the most crowded harbors, like this scene in Camden, ME. The largest boat on the left side of the dock is a *Lightning* with a homemade cabin conversion

Photo by David Buckman

The Bahamas

We have and continue to do most of our winter cruising in the **Bahama Islands**. Few of us are able, willing, and interested in devoting as much time, distance, energy and resources, to beachcruising. Yet these islands do offer the most perfect setting in which to beachcruise—short distances across shallow, clear, azure seas; gently sloped beaches defended from the seas by offlying reefs and islets; constant, warm, trade winds; a benign climate; a sparse and concentrated, friendly local population; good seafood; shade, hills, and fresh water; scattered settlements at which to provision; political stability; and proximity to the U.S. It's no wonder we continue to beachcruise.

We are not alone in our choice. Small boats handled by experienced seamen frequently make the **Gulf Stream** crossing from south Florida to the **Bahamas**. Large vessels, even handled by experienced sailors, sometimes don't get across. The cause of losses is usually some failure of some part of the boat, sometimes aggravated by the violence of the weather.

If such a long crossing is planned, check every fastening and linkage of the boat. Try to cross in company with other boats of the same speed. Carry safety devices—minimally, a hand-held VHF transceiver, an E.P.I.R.B. and a personal life raft. The weather in Florida and the Bahamas is more settled, reliable, and gentle during summer. The southeast trade winds blow at 5 to 10 knots. Boats have rowed and paddled across in summer! The major interruption to the trade winds are depressions that develop into an easterly wave and occasionally into a hurricane. So even in summer it is necessary to heed weather forecasts.

Winter winds are more commonly violent and unreliable. Cold fronts reach into the Bahamas with weekly regularity. These masses of cold, heavy air, blowing against the 2-knot flow of the Gulf Stream, create very mean seas. Fifty-knot squall winds are not uncommon, and sustained winds of 30 knots are frequent. These gross winter conditions can be avoided by heeding weather forecasts. Plan to make your crossing and landfall well before the passage of a cold front or easterly wave, or just after them.

Many, including us, have sometimes shipped their boats to the Bahamas in a crib on the deck of one of the many weekly freight runs that originate from West Palm Beach, Fort Lauderdale and Miami. Shipping and handling charges for a 16-foot boat, carried as deck cargo, are about $500 each way. In addition, a bond equal to 10 percent of the price of the boat must be posted, and the boat must be out of the Bahamas within 6 months if the bond is to be recovered. Anyone contemplating this alternative should carefully question commercial shippers for details and costs as well as to make specific arrangements.

•

This chapter is not an exhaustive and complete, nor fully detailed guide of places to cruise. It is, like the selected charts, intended to help you choose a place to cruise through the descriptions of the places we've enjoyed.

The charts serve as instruction and example of places where beachcruising has been enjoyed. At the end of this chapter is an annotated bibliography of resources from which additional information regarding specific areas may be learned.

Before investing much of your resources in beachcruising or in exposing yourself to unknown geography, you can charter local craft in some locations. Some outfitters offer guided beachcruising and coastal camping tours. Doug Knapp guides a few boats at a time on weekly tours of the Sea of Cortez. Bill and Fran Blatter charter shoal draft sailboats at **Key Largo** to those interested in exploring Florida Bay. Other outfitters listed in the bibliography offer more exotic tours from Maine to China. This is the best way to determine if you might enjoy beachcruising, and to gain first-hand experience of an area at minimal cost and risk.

Our mockingbird pal in the Bahamas. He lived in our camp and ate out of our hands. Beachcruising allows us to live with wild creatures, not just observe them.

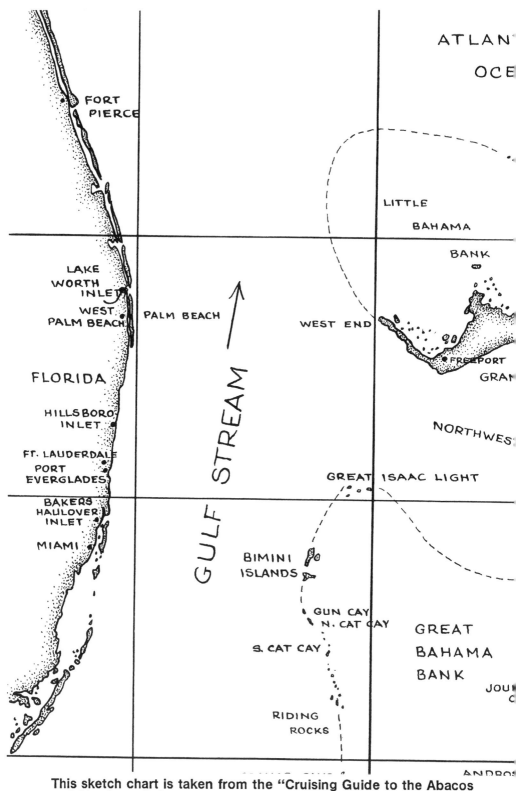

This sketch chart is taken from the "Cruising Guide to the Abacos and Northern Bahamas," published by Wescott Cove Publishing Co., Box 130, Stamford, CT 06904. We have been cruising this area

Northern Bahamas

SCALE

0   10   20   30   40   50   60

NAUTICAL MILES

C N

WALKER CAY

GRAND CAY

CARTERS CAY

GREAT SALE CAY

ALLANS-PENSACOLA CAY

ABACO ISLANDS

27°

∞

SPANISH CAY
POWELL CAY

LITTLE ABACO

GREEN TURTLE CAY

GREAT GUANA CAY

TREASURE CAY

MARSH HARBOUR

MAN-O-WAR CAY

HOPE TOWN

DEEP WATER

TILLOO CAY

BAHAMA CAY

MORES ISLAND

LITTLE HARBOUR

CHEROKEE SOUND

GREAT ABACO ISLAND

PROVIDENCE

GORDA CAY

SANDY POINT

26°

CHANNEL

NORTHEAST PROVIDENCE CHANNEL

GREAT STIRRUP CAY

HOLE IN THE WALL

GREAT HARBOUR CAY

SPANISH WELLS

BERRY ISLANDS

HOLMS CAY

HARBOUR ISLAND

BONDS CAY

CURRENT ISLAND

WHALE CAY

CHUB CAYS

ELEUTHERA ISLAND

ER YS

NICHOLL'S TOWN

ROSE ISLAND

NASSAU

25°

NEW PROVIDENCE ISLAND

for five winters. Most of the land area is remote and uninhabited. There are vast shallows perfect for beachcruising, settlements enough for supplies, great beaches, marvelous reefs for snorkeling and diving.

73

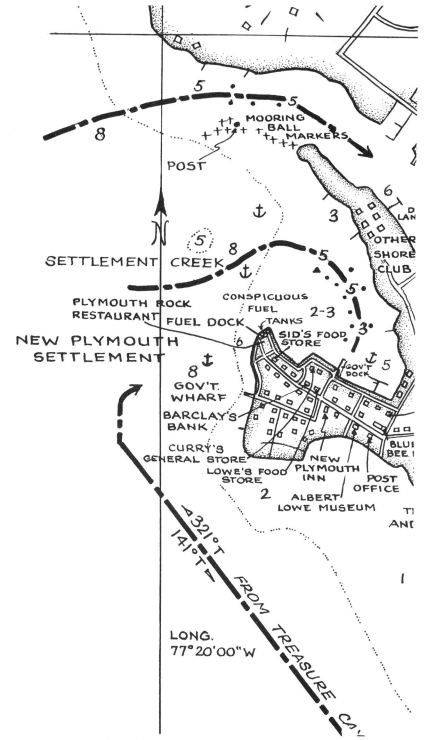

This sketch chart is taken from the "Cruising Guide to the Abacos and Northern Bahamas," published by Wescott Cove Publishing Co., Box 130, Stamford, CT 06904. New Plymouth is the main settlement on Green Turtle Cay. It's one of the most charming villages in the Bahamas, and is an excellent supply port. The mail boat restocks the island once a week.

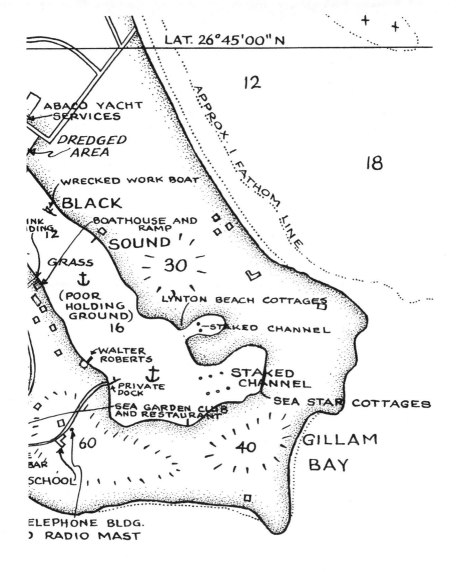

LAT. 26°45'00" N

12

APPROX. 1 FATHOM LINE

18

ABACO YACHT SERVICES

DREDGED AREA

WRECKED WORK BOAT

BLACK

BOATHOUSE AND RAMP

SOUND

30

INK IDING 12

GRASS

(POOR HOLDING GROUND)

16

LYNTON BEACH COTTAGES

STAKED CHANNEL

WALTER ROBERTS

PRIVATE DOCK

STAKED CHANNEL

SEA GARDEN CLUB AND RESTAURANT

SEA STAR COTTAGES

60

BAR

SCHOOL

40

GILLAM BAY

ELEPHONE BLDG.
RADIO MAST

DETAIL OF

New Plymouth

SETTLEMENT

AND BLACK SOUND

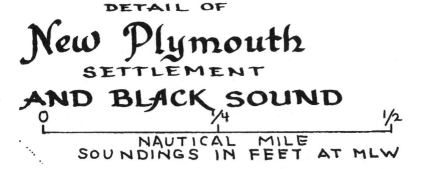

| 0 | 1/4 | 1/2 |

NAUTICAL MILE
SOUNDINGS IN FEET AT MLW

An "armchair" way of learning about beachcruising places is by reading appropriate magazines and newsletters. We've found Small Boat Journal, Messing About in Boats, Canoe, and Sea Kayaking to be especially helpful. Other, conventional boating magazines devote themselves to Big Boats.

For many of the areas we've cruised, we've found that privately published cruising guides and privately published charts include more useful nautical detail in a handier size, than the charts published by government agencies. The descriptive texts in these guides are a bonus.

In considering specific places, we've found cruising guides to be the most helpful resource. These guides are written by people with intimate, extensive, concentrated, and exhaustive knowledge of a specific area. Although these guides are written for the Big Boater, there's enough appropriate detail to be valuable to a beachcruiser. We've been surprised of what odd places to which cruising guides have been published. I wouldn't be surprised if there were a cruising guide to the Falkland Islands! *Editor's note: There is.*

Charts (See also Chapter 9 "Government Charts")

"Chart" is a name given to maps of interest to mariners. Like land maps, charts come in a variety of scales. Sailors crossing oceans need a large scale that covers a big expanse with little detail—1:3,000,000 plus. Beachcruisers need a lot of detail, don't usually cross a big expanse, and seek a small scale chart—1:40,000 or lower. Most sailors are neither ocean crossers nor beachcruisers and use the medium scale charts.

For this book, we've selected assorted scales of charts of interesting cruising areas to which we've been. Nautical charts come in big sheets, usually at least 3 feet square. For this reason, the charts printed in this book are only small portions of a large sheet. If we condensed the whole chart to fit on these pages, it would not be legible.

Nautical charts have a latitude scale along the left and right edges that can be used to measure distances on the same chart. Each latitude minute mark (1/60th of a degree) is a nautical mile (6,076 feet). Do not use the longitude scale on the top and bottom edges to measure distances.

Learn to look at the scale noted on most charts. Learn that 1:63,360 is the same as 1 inch per statute mile; 1:72,993 is the same as 1 inch per nautical mile. Whatever scale be the chart you're using, say 1:639,400, just divide by 63,360 to get miles per inch; 639,400 is about 10 miles per inch. The symbol $\approx$ means almost equal or about. We usually move the decimal four places to the left and divide by six. That's close enough for eyeball beachcruising.

Depths are the little numbers scattered in the water areas of a nautical chart. These are either in fathoms (6-foot units), meters, or feet. One meter is 3.28 feet. Check each chart to learn what unit it's using for depths.

SOURCES FOR CHARTS AND PUBLICATIONS

Charts

Bluewater Books & Charts, 1481 SE 17th St., Fort Lauderdale, FL 33316; 800-942-2583

Armchair Sailor, Lee's Wharf, Newport, RI 02840; 401-847-4252 or 800-29CHART

Sailorman, Inc., 350 E. State Rd. 84, Ft. Lauderdale, FL 33316; 800-331-5359

Landfall Navigation, 354 W. Putnam Ave., Greenwich, CT 06830; 203-661-3176

All of the above stock a wide selection of books and charts devoted to coastal cruising. They provide good mail order service. Catalogs available.

A good **Road Atlas** is a useful start for preliminary survey of potential cruising grounds. **State Road Maps** can usually provide additional detail. **Topographic** and **Hydrographic** charts provide the most detail. Use a **State Atlas and Gazetter** when one is available.

Another good source of inspiration and detail are the past issues of **National Geographic Magazine** on file at local libraries.

Distribution of topo maps and the index therefore is handled by the **U.S. Geological Survey,** Reston, VA 22092.

Hydrographic charts of U.S. waters are published by the **National Ocean Service,** Distribution Division, 6501 Lafayette Ave., Riverdale, MD 20840. Their chart catalogs all contain lists of chart agencies where you can buy charts over the counter.

Additional detail and convenience is available in privately published **Chart Kits, Chartbooks,** and **Cruising Guides.** Contact Bluewater, Armchair, or Landfall, distributors for any of these. They also carry charts of international waters which are published by **Defense Mapping Agency.**

Charts of Canadian waters are published by the **Canadian Hydrographic Service,** P.O. Box 5050, Burlington Ontario, L7R 4A6, Canada. Small craft guide charts are available from the **Canadian Hydrographic Distribution Office,** P.O. Box 8080, 1675 Russell Rd., Ottawa, Ontario K1G 3H6, Canada.

Tours

For beginners and novices, group tours led by experienced boaters with local knowledge are a safe introduction to beachcruising. Check tours listed in Boat Journal, Sea Kayaker, and Canoe magazines. Also check "adventure travel" listings published for travel agencies. There are many guides offering raft and dory runs down many U.S., African, Asian and South American rivers.

General Books

If you are interested in exploring TROPICAL coasts, then *Exploring Tropical Isles & Seas: An Introduction for the Traveler and Amateur Naturalist,* by Frederic Martini, 1984, $27.95, paperback edition $15.95, now

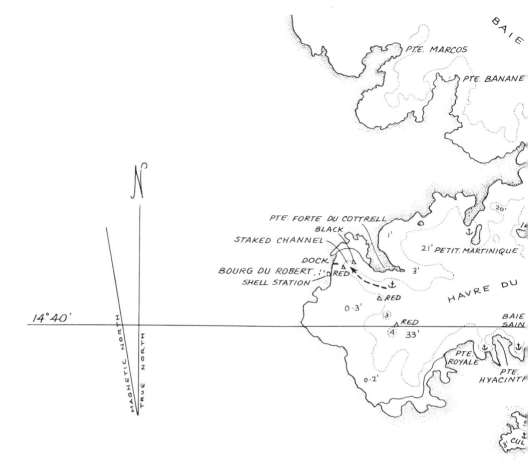

François and Havre du Robert
Eastern Coast, Martinique

BG. DU FRAN

0   1   2   3

NAUTICAL MILES

This sketch chart is taken from the "Yachtsman's Guide to the Wind-ward Islands," published by Wescott Cove Publishing Co., Box 130, Stamford, CT 06904. We bought our French bread, brie, and paté at the Bourgs du Robert and du Francois. These are big coastal towns, originally fishing villages, but now also small resorts and populated by some commuters to jobs at Lamentin or Fort de France.

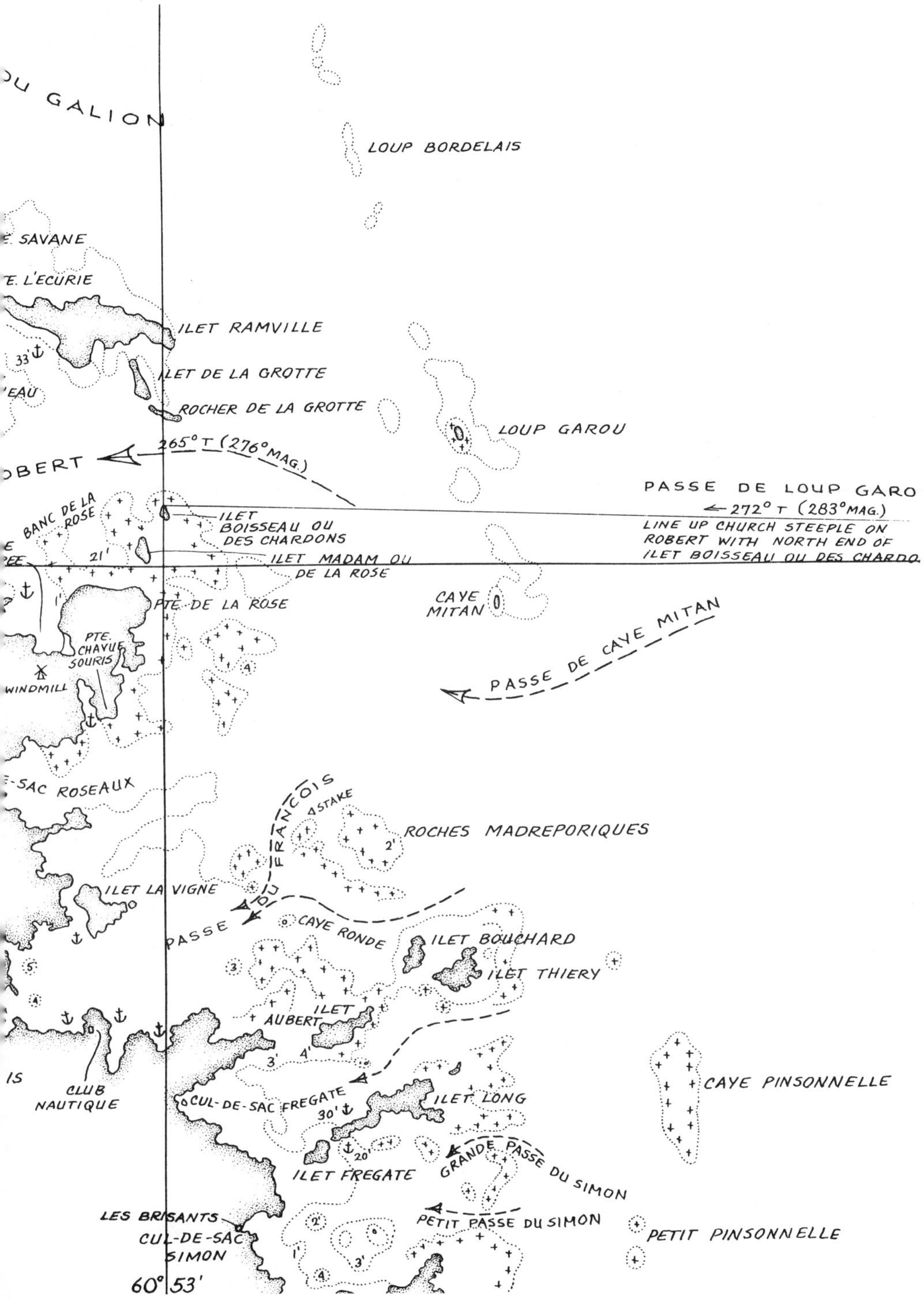

OU GALION

LOUP BORDELAIS

E. SAVANE

E. L'ECURIE

33' ⚓

ILET RAMVILLE

ILET DE LA GROTTE

'EAU

ROCHER DE LA GROTTE

LOUP GAROU

OBERT ← 265° T (276° MAG.)

PASSE DE LOUP GARO

← 272° T (283° MAG.)

BANC DE LA ROSE

ILET
BOISSEAU OU
DES CHARDONS

LINE UP CHURCH STEEPLE ON
ROBERT WITH NORTH END OF
ILET BOISSEAU OU DES CHARDO.

E

21'

ILET MADAM OU
DE LA ROSE

⚓

1'

PTE. DE LA ROSE

CAYE
MITAN

PTE.
CHAYU
SOURIS

4

WINDMILL

PASSE DE CAYE MITAN

E-SAC ROSEAUX

PASSE DU FRANÇOIS

STAKE

ROCHES MADREPORIQUES

2

ILET LA VIGNE

0

⚓

PASSE DU

CAYE RONDE

ILET BOUCHARD

3

ILET THIERY

5

4 ⚓

⚓

ILET
AUBERT

CAYE PINSONNELLE

3 4

IS

CLUB
NAUTIQUE

CUL-DE-SAC FREGATE

30' ⚓

ILET LONG

⚓ 20'

GRANDE PASSE DU SIMON

ILET FREGATE

LES BRISANTS
CUL-DE-SAC
SIMON

2

PETIT PASSE DU SIMON

PETIT PINSONNELLE

3

60° 53'

4

79

out of print, but is in many libraries. This is a helpful introduction to life above and below sea level. May be available from Bluewater Books & Charts, 1481 S.E. 17th St., Fort Lauderdale, FL 33316, or The Armchair Sailor, Lee's Wharf, Newport, RI 02840.

Every kind of map and chart on earth and even some of off the earth are listed and described in *The Map Catalog*, by Joel Makower, 1986, published by Vintage Books.

Sailing America, by Larry Brown, is an account of his personal inland trailer sailor adventures.

Your Right to Anchor, by Phillip Hodes, 3137 Capri Rd., Lake Park, FL 33410 reviews legal tactics devised to intimidate anchoring and recommends courses of action when confronted by these tactics.

•

Editor's note: I try not to go where I'm not wanted, and if I'm challenged, I don't argue, I up my anchor and leave. Recent trends limit anchorages. Many popular anchorages have become restricted to local boats, boats that have bought expensive permits, or have been declared no discharge, no overnight, no liveaboard, and what won't they think of next! Some organizations that try to make sense out of this snowballing trend are:

Gulf Coast: Boating Trade Association, 2600 South West Freeway, Suite 1000, Houston, TX 77098; 713-526-6361.

East Coast: Sailors Total Anchoring Rights Society (STARS), c/o Annalemma House Publishers, 3137 Capri Rd., Lake Park, FL 33410; 407-622-6129. Open Harbors Association, 56 Harrison St., Suite 301, New Rochelle, NY 10801.

•

Out of Print Books

Some books recommended in this appendix may be out of print. You can probably obtain them from University Microfilms International, P.O. Box 1346, Ann Arbor, MI 48106.

Baja California

The Forgotten Peninsula, by Joseph Wood Krutch, 277 pages, 1986, U. of Arizona Press, 1230 N. Park, No. 102, Tuscon, AZ 85719. An excellent naturalist introduction to the Baja landscape.

Baja Adventure Book, by Walt Peterson, $16.95, 264 pages, 1987, Wilderness Press, 2440 Bancroft Way, Berkeley, CA 97044-1676. An experienced account of camping in Baja.

Camping and Climbing in Baja, 4th Edition, by John Robinson, $4.50, 1983, La Siesta. Emphasizes inland and mountain exploration.

Hidden Mexico—Adventurer's Guide to the Beaches and Coasts, by Rebecca Bruns, $12.95, 456 pages, Ulysses Press, Box 4000H, Berkeley, CA 94704. Has excellent descriptive coverage of camping along all of coastal Mexico, including Baja.

Baja California Diver's Guide, by Michael and Lauren Farley, $12.95, 224 pages, 1984, Marcor Pub., Box 1072, Port Hueheme, CA 93041. An invaluable guide to specific spots along the Baja coast that offer unique diving experiences.

Sea of Cortez Guide, second printing, by Dix Brow, $19.95, Western Marine Enterprises, 4051 Glencoe Ave., Suite 14, Marina Del Rey, CA 90292-5607. One of the earliest guides to the Sea of Cortez by an author who knows the area best.

Cruising Guides and detailed strip Nautical Charts of selected areas of the Baja coast are available from Box 976, Patagonia, AZ 85624.

Charlie's Charts to Mexico, by the late Charles Wood are useful. Sections of the Baja coast are available from Box 1244, Station A, Surrey, B.C. V3S 4Y5, Canada. These and others listed are also available from Bluewater Books & Charts, 1481 SE 17th St., Fort Lauderdale, FL 33316; The Armchair Sailor, Lee's Wharf, Newport, RI 02840; and Landfall Navigation, 354 W. Putnam Ave., Greenwich, CT 06830.

Baja Cruising Notes, by Vern Jones, Sea Breeze Enterprises, P.O. Box 75, Julian, CA 92036. Reveals the less frequented nooks along the coast.

Baja Boater's Guide, Volume II, by Jack Williams, $26.95, 1988. Features hundreds of aerial photos of the Sea of Cortez. Volume I, $24.95, 1989, covers the Pacific Coast. Both published by H. J. Williams, 191 Santa Rosa Ave., Sausalito, CA 94965.

The Log from the Sea of Cortez, by John Steinbeck, $4.95, 416 pages, 1977, Penguin, New York. An excellent and personal account of a cruise he made along the Sea of Cortez in the company of a good friend and naturalist interested in collecting specimens and adventures.

Enchanted Vagabonds, by Dana and Ginger Lamb, 1938. Harper & Brothers, New York. Must reading in preparing for any beachcruise of Baja. Epic account of coastal cruising and seashore camping. This book is out of print, but many libraries have it.

When cruising Baja, other Central American or some African coastlines, remember that local people are not likely to observe the tidy and sanitary practices of more prosperous western countries.

U.S. West Coast

Pacific Boating Almanac, Northern California and Nevada Edition; Southern California, Arizona, Baja Edition, both by Peter L. Griffiths, each $12.95, Western Marine Enterprises, 4051 Glencoe Ave., Suite 14, Marina Del Rey, CA 90292-5607. Written by and for blue water cruises. It does include coastal data that is valuable to a coastal sailor.

Sea Marine Atlas, Southern California, by William P. Crawford, Sea Publications.

Cruising the Pacific Coast, Acapulco to Skagway, by Carolyn and Jack West, $10.95, 345 pages, 1984, Pacific Search, 222 Dexter Ave. N., Seattle, WA 98109.

California Coastal Passages, San Francisco to Ensenada, by Brian M. Fagan, $16.95, 159 pages, 1981, Chart Guide Ltd., 300 N. Wilshire Ave., Suite 5, Anaheim, CA 92801.

Bob Smith's Complete Guide to Harbors, Anchorages and Marinas, Southern and Northern California, two separate editions, $19.95 each, 1985, "C" Books, Box 548, Del Mar, CA 92014.

Beachcombing the Pacific, by Amos L. Wood, $9.95, 225 pages, 1987, Schiffer Publishing Ltd., 1469 Morstein Rd., West Chester, PA 19380.

The Big Tomato: A Guide to the Sacramento Region, by Dorothy K. Leland, 112 pages, Tomato Enterprises, Box 162455, Sacramento, CA 95816.

Cruising the California Delta, by Bob Walther, $15, 192 pages, Aztex Publishing, Box 50046, Tucson, AZ 85703. The only detailed picture guide that includes boating facilities of the delta. (ISBN 0-87799-058-1)

Pacific Northwest

Exploring the Coast by Boat, by Frieda Van der Ree, $14.95, 1979, Gordon Soules BK., 1916 Pike Pl., Suite 620, Seattle, WA 98101. Navigational advice and sketch charts for cruising Puget Sound, the San Juan Islands, Gulf Islands, Vancouver area, Strait of Georgia, Desolation Sound and Discovery Islands.

Gunkholing in the San Juans, by Al Cummings and Jo Bailey, $11.95, 1984, Nor'westing, Inc., Box 1027, Edmonds, WA 98020. Navigational advice and small reproductions of government charts. Used by many Puget Sound sailors.

The San Juan Islands, Afoot & Afloat, by Marge Mueller, $10.95, The Mountaineers, 306 Second Ave. W., Seattle, WA 98119.

The Gulf Islands Explorer, The Complete Guide, by Bruce Obee.

Guide to the Queen Charlotte Islands, by Neil G. Carey, $9.95, 100 pages, 1989, Alaska Northwest, Box 3007, Bothell, WA 98041-3007.

An Explorer's Guide to the Marine Parks of B.C., by P. Chettleburgh. Guide to anchorages and campsites of 30 parks.

Glacier Bay National Park: A Backcountry Guide to the Glaciers & Beyond, by Jim DuFresne, $8.95, 144 pages, 1987, The Mountaineers, 306 Second Ave. W., Seattle, WA 98119.

Sea Kayaking Canada's West Coast, by John Ince & Hedi Kottner, $14.95, 240 pages, 1989, Gordon Soules BK., 1916 Pike Pl., Suite 620, Seattle, WA 98101. An excellent and personal account with friendly photos of what a camp cruiser may expect.

Many of the above are available from Ecomarine, 1668 Duranleau St., Granville Island, Vancouver, B.C. V6H 3S4, Canada.

Great Lakes

A Gunkholer's Guide to the North Channel, by Pat & Judy Nerbonne, $7, 1984, P.O. Box 748, Amherst, MA 01004.

Summer Sail—Cruising Green Bay's Historic Waters and *Summer Sail II of Northern Lake Michigan*, both by John B. Torinus.

Well-Favored Passage: A Guide to Lake Huron's North Channel, 3rd edition, by Marjorie C. Brazer, $18.95, 184 pages, Heron Books, 536 Ann Arbor Hill, Manchester, MI 48158-9701.

Cruising Guide to the Great Lakes and Their Connecting Waterways, by Marjorie C. Brazer, $22.95, 496 pages, 1985, Contemporary Books, 180 N. Michigan Ave., Chicago, IL 60601.

Sweet Water Sea: A Guide to Lake Huron's Georgian Bay, by Marjorie C. Brazer, $18.95, 200 pages, 1987, Heron Books, 536 Ann Arbor Hill, Manchester, MI 48158-9701.

Cruising Guide to Lake Superior, by Bonnie Dahl, $16.95, Eastern National Park & Monument Association, Apostle Islands National Lakeshore, Route 1, Box 4, Bayfield, WI 54814.

Camping in the Apostle Islands National Lakeshore, free brochure available from Apostle Islands National Lakeshore, Route 1, Box 4, Bayfield, WI 54814. Tells which islands you can camp on, describes facilities, regulations, etc.

List of Publications and Charts for the Apostle Islands, and Lake Superior, free from Eastern National Park & Monument Association, Apostle Islands National Lakeshore, Route 1, Box 4, Bayfield, WI 54814. Contains prices and ordering information.

Charts of Great Lakes Canadian Waters may be ordered from Chart Distribution Office, 1675 Russell Rd., P.O. Box 8080, Ontario K1G 3H6, Canada.

U.S. Inland Lakes & Rivers

The U.S. Army Corps of Engineers publishes a variety of chartbooks of inland rivers and waterways. Each Corps district takes a different approach to chart type, style and format. No two are alike and no two have the same price. None are very good, but often these are all there is. Call Bluewater Books & Charts, 1481 SE 17th St., Fort Lauderdale, FL 33316; The Armchair Sailor, Lee's Wharf, Newport, RI 02840; or Landfall Navigation, 354 W. Putnam Ave., Greenwich, CT 06830, for what is available.

For the **Colorado River and its lakes,** contact: U.S. Geological Survey, Box 25286, Federal Center, Denver, CO 80225.

For the **Sacramento, San Joaquin and tributaries,** and for the **Hudson River** and **Lake Champlain,** contact: National Ocean Survey, C 41, 6501 Lafayette Ave., Riverdale, MD 20840. They also handle charts of the **St. Johns River of Florida.**

Lake Winnipesaukee Cruising Guide, by David Buckman, $7.95, 102 pages, 1984, Eastern Publications, 18 Ridgwood Ave., Gilford, NH 03246. Very helpful guide to this summer cottaged lake.

Quimby's Boating Guide, $10, 188 pages, Mildred Quimby, Box 85, Prairie du Chien, WI 53821. A handy reference for boaters on the Kentucky,

Mississippi, Illinois, Arkansas, Tennessee, Ohio, Allegheny, Cumberland, Monongahela, and Tennessee-Tombigee waterways. Includes harbors and marina indexes and black & white maps.

On The River: A Variety of Canoe & Small Boat Voyages, by Walter M. Teller, $13.95, 1988. Available from Bluewater Books & Charts, 1481 SE 17th St., Fort Lauderdale, FL 33316; The Armchair Sailor, Lee's Wharf, Newport, RI 02840; and Landfall Navigation, 354 W. Putnam Ave., Greenwich, CT 06830.

Cruising Guide to Lake Champlain, by A. & S. McKibben, $19.95. Available from Landfall Navigation, 354 W. Putnam Ave., Greenwich, CT 06830.

Cruising Guide to Lake Champlain, by Pierre Biron, $25, 108 pages, 1984, bilingual (English/French). Available from The Armchair Sailor, Lee's Wharf, Newport, RI 02840.

Chicago to New Orleans: A Cruising Guide, by Don Haig, 1985, 18386 North Shore Estates, Spring Lake, MI 49456.

Sailor's Guide to the Tenn-Tom, by Doug Adams. Navigational advice on cruising this newest of the Big Ditches made by The Engineers.

Small Boat Journal magazine, 2100 Powers Ferry Rd., Atlanta, GA 30339, has back issues for sale. Among these are articles describing many inland cruising areas.

Lakeland Boating, 106 Perry St., Port Clinton, OH 43452, is a magazine that specializes in fresh water sailing, and is useful for discovering inland cruises and products.

Northeast U.S. and Canada

Cruising Guide to the Nova Scotia Coast, by John McKelvy, $20, 1988, available from International Marine, TAB Books, Blue Ridge Summit, PA 17294-0840. Includes Prince Edward Island and the Magdelans. Originally published by the Cruising Club of America and updated by the author. For each harbor, entries include position, chart number, directions, anchorage, remarks and facilities. Introduction includes comments on weather, winds, and customs.

Cruising Guides to Newfoundland and Labrador may soon be available. Check with Bluewater Books & Charts, 1481 SE 17th St., Fort Lauderdale, FL 33316; The Armchair Sailor, Lee's Wharf, Newport, RI 02840; or Landfall Navigation, 354 W. Putnam Ave., Greenwich, CT 06830, for availability and cost.

Cruise Cape Breton, by the Cape Breton Development Corp., $14.50, 245 pages, 1982. An excellent guide to the Bras d'Or Lakes, Strait of Canscok Lennox Passage, Isle Madame, and Inhabitants Basin. Detail includes approaches, sketch charts with anchorage and facility information, government chart numbers, tides, lights and customs.

Cruising Guide to Maine, by Don Johnson, edited by Julius M. Wilensky, Volume I, $24.95; Volume II, $29.95, Wescott Cove Publishing Co., Box 130, Stamford, CT 06904. An exhaustive guide to the coast and the islands in two volumes. It includes complete charts, facilities and photos.

Your Islands on the Coast, by Dave Getchell, Bureau of Public Lands, Dept. of Conservation, Station 22, Augusta ME 04333. Describes what islands along coastal Maine may be accessible for landing.

Cruising Guide to the New England Coast, by Roger F. Duncan and John P. Ware, $29.95, 732 pages, 1987, Putnam, New York. The classic guide for the well-heeled yachtsman. Covers the whole coast, so it cannot go into detail, nor provide enough charts.

Embassy's Complete Boating Guide to Long Island Sound, $29.95, 1988 and *Complete Boating Guide to Rhode Island and Massachusetts*, Embassy Marine Publishing, 37 Pratt St., Box 338, Essex, CT 06426. More detailed guides to smaller portions of the N.E. coast. Contains advertising.

Chart Kits and **Chartbooks** are large format colored charts and photos of selected cruising grounds.

Chart Kits from Better Boating Assoc., Box 407, Needham, MA 02192: Region 2, Canadian Border to Block Island, $89.95; Region 3, New York to Nantucket and Cape May, $89.95; Region 4, Chesapeake and Delaware Bays, $89.95; Region 6, Norfolk to Jacksonville, $74.95; Region 7, Florida's East Coast and the Keys, $89.95; Region 8, Florida's West Coast and the Keys, $89.95; Region 9, Bahamas, $99.95.

Waterway Guide Chartbooks from Waterway Guide, 6255 Barfield Rd., Atlanta, GA 30328: Newport to Canada, $49.50; New York Waters, Block I. to Cape May incl. Hudson R., $49.50; Chesapeake and Delaware Bays, New York to Norfolk, $49.50; Norfolk to Jacksonville, $49.50; Jacksonville to Miami, $45.50; Florida's West Coast, $49.50; Lower Florida and the Keys, Lake Okeechobee to the Keys, $49.50.

U.S. East Coast

Cruising Guide to the Chesapeake, by William T. Stone and Fessenden S. Blanchard, $29.95, 446 pages, 1989, Putnam, New York.

Guide to Cruising the Chesapeake Bay, $24.95, 400 pages, published annually by Chesapeake Magazine, 1819 Bay Ave., Annapolis, MD 21403.

A Gunkholer's Cruising Guide to Florida's West Coast, by Tom Lenfestey, $9.95, 1983, Great Outdoors, 4747 28th St. N., St. Petersburg, FL 33714. This coast is accessible only to gunkholers!

A good **road map** or **road atlas** would be a big help to cruising this coast. DeLorme Publishing Co., Box 298, Freeport, ME 04032 publishes an excellent atlas.

Cruising Guide to Coastal North Carolina, 3rd edition, by Claiborne S. Young, $17.95, 1989, John E. Blair Publishing, 1406 Plaza Dr., Winston-Salem, NC 27103. Includes guiding advice and charts. Another volume covers South Carolina. In fact, a third volume covers the eastern coast of Florida and the Saint John's River.

Cruising Guide to Coastal South Carolina, by Claiborne S. Young, $17.95, 1985, John E. Blair Publishing, 1406 Plaza Dr., Winston-Salem, NC 27103.

Cruising Guide to Eastern Florida, by Claiborne S. Young, $21.95, 1987, Pelican Publishing Co., 1101 Monroe St., Gretna, LA 70053.

Cruising Guide to the Florida Keys, 6th edition, by Frank Papy, $14.95, 198 pages, 1988. It's all there is, in a handy size.

Boating, Anchoring & Liveaboard Laws in Florida, by Patricia B. Link. May be helpful in dealing with authorities. I prefer the more aggressive posture recommended in *Your Right to Anchor*, published by Analemma House.

Boater's Photographic Chartbook to the Florida Keys, by Air Nav Publications. Compares aerial photos and nautical charts of popular anchorages and cuts.

Boater's Photographic Chartbook to the Bahamas, by Air Nav Publications. A more superficial parallel coverage of a much bigger area.

Boater's Photographic Chartbook of Florida's West Coast, by Air Nav Publications.

Yachtsman's Guide to the Bahamas, now edited by Meredith Fields, $18.95, Tropic Isle Publishers, Box 610935, N. Miami, FL 33261-0935. An excellent resource for any cruiser in these islands.

Cruising Guide to the Abacos and Northern Bahamas, by Julius M. Wilensky, $24.95, Wescott Cove Publishing Co., Box 130, Stamford, CT 06904. A very detailed guide to this popular section of the Bahamas.

Cruising Guide to Northwest Florida, by Doug Adams, 1987. Navigational advice for the Big Bend and Panhandle regions of Florida.

Gulf Coast

There are not many cruising guides to this coast.

The Waterway Guide, Southern Edition, $16.95, 6255 Barfield Rd., Atlanta, GA 30328. A moderately useful compendium of commercial facilities along this coast.

A good **road map** combined with corresponding nautical charts would serve small boat campers well.

For extensive cruising along this coast, the **Chart Kits, Region 16, Panama City to New Orleans, $84.95; Region 17, New Orleans to Texas Border, $84.95;** and **Region 18 for Texas Coast and Offshore, $18.95,** are the most useful marine guides.

For information on the **Gulf Islands** write: Assistant Superintendent, Gulf Islands National Seashore, 350 Park Rd., Ocean Springs, MS 39564. Also, *The Horn Island Logs of Walter Inglis Anderson*, by W. I. Anderson, $37.50, 180 pages, 1985, University Press of Mississippi, 3825 Ridgewood Rd., Jackson, MS 39211. Very useful reading to anyone contemplating a cruise along this coast.

Texas Cruising Guide, by Lettalou and Lawrence Sexton, 4th edition, $18.95, 239 pages, P.O. Box 561414, Houston, TX 77256. The Bible to cruising the Texas coast.

Texas Gulf Coast Mariner's Atlas, by A. P. Balder, $40, Lone Star Books, P.O. Box 2608, Houston, TX 77252. Provides more coverage for the money than any other privately printed charts. These are small (10 x 14) and edges don't always include the lat/lon scale.

Consider that South Padre Island borders Mexico and the standards may be considered trashy by some people.

Beachcruisers using *Sea Pearls* enjoy Robbit Key in Florida Bay. Only shoal-draft cruisers can land here

CHAPTER 4

SELECTING A BEACHABLE SAILBOAT

As in selecting an area that offers good beachcruising, so is choosing a beachable boat more restricted than if we were going deep water cruising. The boats, like the places, are more interesting and varied.

Although this chapter is specifically devoted to sailboats, many of the factors considered apply equally to paddle boats and power boats because the underlying requirement is that the boat is to be routinely beached.

DESIGN CONSIDERATIONS

Material
Routine beaching limits the hull material and hull shapes to those that will not be compromised when they are aground or dried out. Wood is compromised by repeated wetting and drying. For this reason we recommend boat hulls made of fiberglass, metal (usually aluminum), or epoxy saturated wood, which is really plastic reenforced wood. We also recommend hull shapes that will remain upright on firm, level sand or shingle.

Keels, Centerboards, Leeboards, and Bilgeboards
Most sailboat hulls are shaped so as to cause the boat to lean or fall substantially to one side or the other when allowed to dry out. Even most shoal draft sailboats designed to sail in very shallow water include a permanently affixed keel on the underside of the hull. This keel is usually big enough to tip the boat at an uncomfortable angle when the boat dries out on firm, level ground. Most centerboards don't fully retract into the well and cause the same problem. On many boats the weight of the loaded hull concentrated on the keel or centerboard will cause catastrophic damage to the hull. It's pretty easy to tell what boats will dry out level by looking at their bottoms, or by letting them dry on firm ground, not soft mud.

Beachable boats, omitting the keel with which conventional craft are handicapped, introduce different complications. A major bugaboo is the question of stability. If a heavy mass of lead keel is omitted from the underbody, what is to keep the boat upright under a press of sail? In fact, boats that are fitted with deep and heavy keels, do rely on the keel for stability and stiffness. Boats without keels are designed to gain their stability from the shape of the hull; and, because they are lighter, are moved with a more conservative sail plan.

A second function of a keel is to produce lateral resistance, without which a sailboat could not make headway against the wind, or abeam the wind, as it would be blown sideways over the surface of the water. Canoes and power boats have modest keels to help them "track." On sailboats, it is this lateral resistance of the keel against the water, and the movement of the keel through the water, that allows a keeled sailboat to go against and across the very wind that drives it.

Beachable craft rely on hull shape and on centerboards, bilgeboards, leeboards, and the rudder to produce the lateral resistance. These are not as effective as a deep keel. The difference is only apparent when beating to windward, and then only if the keel-less boat can't gain an advantage by cutting over shoals or by sailing on calmer waters closer to shore.

A few custom designed and made sailboats have hull shapes so designed that they need no boards. Most commercially available beachcruisers are fitted with centerboards. A few come with leeboards or bilgeboards.

Leeboards have the advantage of not intruding into the limited interior area of a small boat. Because they are fitted outside the hull, on each side, rather than into the bottom, leeboards don't compromise the integrity of a hull. Their disadvantage is that they must be handled each time you change tack—the board to windward raised and the board to lee, the lee board, lowered. On our leeboard boats we overcame this disadvantage by building leeboard retainers, running-boards, above the waterline, outboard of each leeboard. This kept both boards in a slot, between the hull and the running-board. Thus we could keep both boards down without tearing off the one to windward. On *Dugong* the boards were heavy. Keeping the windward board down (out), reduced the heeling, and the running-boards made a convenient boarding and hiking step.

This catboat has a retractable daggerboard that will not pivot up if the boat grounds or strikes an underwater hazard. We recommend selection of a boat with a centerboard that will pivot up by itself when struck.

Dovekie off Cedar Key, Florida. Note the use of leeboards instead of a centerboard or daggerboard. *Dovekie* also has an awning over the cockpit, nice on a hot day.

Another disadvantage to leeboards is that as they are outside, rather than within the hull, they are a cosmetic intrusion to those of pure vision. The corresponding advantage is that they are more easily observed and maintained than centerboards or bilgeboards which are concealed within enclosures (called box, trunk or well) inside the hull.

Despite their intrusiveness into the limited space on a small boat, centerboards are easier to sell. So most beachcruisers, most small boats, come fitted with centerboards. Inspect the design and construction carefully. Will the board get jammed by mud or stones? How will you free it when it does get jammed in the trunk? Will the board rattle noisily as you're trying to get to sleep on the gently rocking boat? Is the trunk solidly and stiffly built? It must be immovable! Is the trunk sealed? If it's open on top, will it take on water while underway or when the boat becomes partially submerged?

When Webb Chiles crossed the Pacific Ocean in a 16-foot centerboard Drascombe Lugger, he was distressed to find himself unable to bail out the water once it filled above the centerboard well. The water came in through the top of the well faster than he could bail it out! Indeed, almost all centerboard wells do have at least a hole through which the line that raises and lowers the board is led into the cockpit.

Consider, can the centerboard be removed for inspection and repair? Is the pin on which the board pivots, inside the hull? If so, may it leak? Will the centerboard pennant or pennant knot break if the board falls abruptly? Is this line, wire, or rod easy to inspect and replace? Is there a pin or other mechanism by which the centerboard may be locked up and/or locked down? It is preferable to have that choice. On *Beachcomber* we have a breakaway pin that may be used to lock the board down. This is in addition to the regular swivel pin. If we hit bottom, the breakaway pin will shear off and the board will come up. In practice, we seldom engage the breakaway pin. It is useful only to hold the board in place during a capsize.

Many boats can be fitted with any of these types of boards and pennants. Regardless of what board choice you make, consider what the board(s) will do if when in the down position, unpinned, the boat turns over. **Heavy** boards have been known to fall through, tearing out the trunk and fittings on their way. If you contrive a pin to lock the board down, consider what will happen when you strike a shoal with the pin in place.

Any beachable boat should have a kick-up rudder, shown here on *Sea Pearl*. If the boat you like doesn't have one, *make* one.

While we have not personally experienced conditions that approached rolling us over, those who have contend that by raising the board the boat rides more securely than a keel boat. Captain Voss and Warren Bailey have written that with the board raised, their boats slid down the waves much more easily; no longer tripping the boat into a broach and/or capsize as a keel would.

Beachcruisers without boards rely solely on the rudder and the hull shape for lateral resistance. The 14-foot Hobie catamaran uses asymmetrical hulls. Monohulls use a hard chine, reenforced with a chine "log" or runner. In sliding sideways down a sea, these boats easily "trip" into a capsize. But then, with no board to foul, a capsize is less traumatic. These boats are easily righted.

Matt Layden's Experience

Matt Layden, returning to the Connecticut River from a 5-month cruise of the Bahamas in his 13-foot boardless beachcruiser, wrote:

"From Allans-Pensacola it took me the better part of a week to get 'down' to West End against persistent westerlies. Then, due to an incredible concatenation of oopses, beginning with a busted radio a couple of days before and ending with a non-functioning port running light on an

In choosing a boat, test stability by standing on the gunwale or sitting to leeward under sail. Push the boat's performance to get a feel for its limitations.

92

Some people prefer sculling to rowing. This catboat owner mounted an oarlock astern to make sculling easy for him.

approaching tanker on a PITCH black night, I found myself swimming at the end of my harness line behind my poor overturned swamp buggy, among the Gulf Stream sharks, about 15 miles eastward of West Palm Beach.

"Blame me, not the boat (well, blame the damn tanker captain too), as she's been through plenty worse and never been knocked down more'n 60 degree, AS LONG AS I REMAINED SEATED. In this case, I was standing up, with the cockpit cover wide open, trying to see over the wave tops whether my evasive tactics re said tanker were going to work. (They did. Just as well she never got close.) Well, not being able to see anything, and beyond sight of the compass, I let my course get a wee bit ragged. So that suddenly a good sized breaker hit us right abeam and in my face. Instead of rolling with it, ole' quick wits grabbed the weather rail and pulled the boat over on top of himself.

"Well, after rolling her back up and clearing the worst of the floodwaters before the sea snakes could locate me and attack, I decided, with the wind veering southerly and blowing along pretty well, that I had no intention of close reaching up for West Palm, and that the U.S. Customs could cry in their coffee. If they can spot my 13-foot plywood boat in mast-high seas and heavy rain, let them do their worst. Up helm and ran off for Saint Lucie inlet—which is not the greatest place in an onshore sea. But I knew the entrance and would have flood tide.

"The rest of the return cruise was much better. After a couple of days 'desalinating' above the first lock of the Okeechobee Waterway (Oh,

Blessed Fresh Water!), I started northward at a leisurely rate, slowing down and exploring a bit through the Georgia Isles then Pamlico Sound and associated waters (beautiful!), and spending a month in the Chesapeake. Delaware Bay, despite its reputation, is great for a shallow, maneuverable boat, with all its little unspoiled marsh creeks and a few isolated (well, not really) fishing towns. It's not as polluted as they say. And the shoals keep the heavy traffic miles away, out in the middle, as well as mitigating the infamous wind/tide chop, which is bad only in the main channel.

"Don't know that I'll make it out to the Bahamas next winter as I want to get back up here in the early spring. I have a pretty definite offer from a friend to use his yard and equipment to build a steel boat, and my ideas are starting to gel."

Effect of Chines

Boat designer Warren Bailey comments on Matt's design:

"Your chine protrusions are an excellent idea for gaining lateral resistance in shoal waters.

"Back in '35, Key West sponging dingies had about a 4-inch radius on their chine protrusions, called a 'knuckle-V.' I made a cruising sailboat of one of these, and was amazed at the way she'd surf sideways in a breaker—wouldn't trip over as ordinary hard chine boats did. Nowadays this relieved chine is called a non-trip chine; which you may want to consider in the light of your capsize while surfing sideways."

A couple of years later, Matt sailed out to the Bahamas in his next boat. It is 16 feet long by 4.5-foot beam on deck. It is fitted with a centerboard and the chines are gently radiused. The balanced lug rig gives ample power for carrying two months of food and water. Instead of oars, the auxiliary is a sculling sweep. Note photos on page 93.

If you're planning on beachcruising, then avoid hulls that won't dry out level or that have any big fixed things (like bilge keels, rudders, shafts, or propellers) sticking out from below the hull. Centerboards and leeboards, rudders and propellers, that can be pulled up completely above the bottom, allow a boat to dry out without damage. Beware of "dagger" type centerboards. These don't "kick up" on their own with the forward movement of the boat, but must be raised by hand vertically through a slot. When dagger boards strike the bottom or an immovable object, they either break off, or they tear out the dagger board well and the bottom of the boat.

Need for Rugged and/or Reenforced Hull Construction

A boat that is to be routinely beached should have a stronger and thicker hull than one that's to be kept afloat. In getting in and out of a "beachorage," we sometimes bump and scrape hard things with the bottom of the boat. We sometimes overlook a rock, a conch shell, or a partially buried spike, and let the boat dry out on them. Conch have been

HULL SHAPES

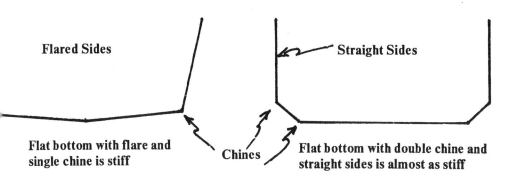

Flared Sides

Straight Sides

Flat bottom with flare and
single chine is stiff

Chines

Flat bottom with double chine and
straight sides is almost as stiff

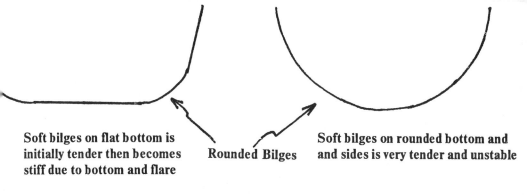

Soft bilges on flat bottom is
initially tender then becomes
stiff due to bottom and flare

Rounded Bilges

Soft bilges on rounded bottom and
and sides is very tender and unstable

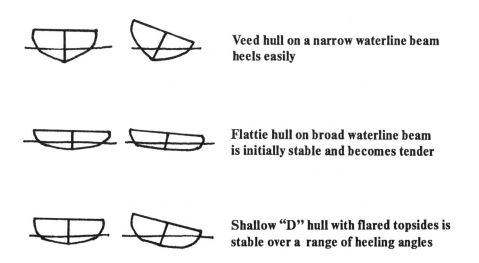

Veed hull on a narrow waterline beam
heels easily

Flattie hull on broad waterline beam
is initially stable and becomes tender

Shallow "D" hull with flared topsides is
stable over a range of heeling angles

known to walk under our hull while it was afloat just to test the bottom when we dried out on them at ebb tide. A thick, strong hull keeps such incidents from become a repair stop. We sheathed the bottom corners of *Kohoutek's* hulls with stainless steel. *Dugong's* 2-inch thick flat bottom is sheathed with 1/16-inch thick ultra high molecular weight polyethylene (Durasurf ™). This is the stuff that's used on the bottoms of skis and river dories. Our current live-aboard beachcruiser, *Beachcomber*, is defended by a 2″ x 14″ greenheart (Ocotea Rodiaei) that runs the centerline of her bottom. The bottom is 1-inch thick plywood sheathed with ¼-inch thick fiberglass.

Weight Considerations

Strengthening a hull necessarily adds weight. However, unless the boat is to be lifted or hauled onto beaches, adding weight to the bottom while strengthening is a good thing. Once the boat weight exceeds what we can lift, our landings become restricted to beaches where we float in on the flood tide, or where we might slide or roll the boat out of the surf.

With our lightweight catamaran and canoe cruising boats (*Kahoutek* and *Manatee*), we frequently landed along shores that had **no** beaches; and on steep beaches pounded by surf. We'd anchor off while we swam and waded ashore with our camping needs. Once emptied of cargo weight, the two of us could lift each boat and carry it above the tide line. This allowed us to enjoy places that others could not reach.

The most devoted example of the advantages of a small and light vessel is Ms. Ann Southerland who used an inner tube. Her accounts of coastal cruising, landings, and camping along the most forbidding shores of Hawaii are published in her book titled, "Paddling My Own Canoe." River cruises are often made in inner tubes. Though they don't sail well or paddle easily, they are easily carried by the rivers' current.

Once we exceed our ability to lift, slide, or roll our boat ashore, it doesn't really matter how much the boat gets to weigh. As we elaborated our beachcruising, we wanted more range, more comforts, and more security. It's quite practical to cruise locally for two or three weeks. For that long, we can do with only a weekly bath and we can forfeit a comfortable chair in which to rest and read. For short cruises, our needs can fit into a boat that's light enough to lift or slide. It's only when we want to beachcruise for hundreds of miles over several months that some want a daily bath, a gentler mattress, more books, a comfortable chair, and a larger and quieter, more secure shelter. Because we beachcruise for five months of each year, and because we've been doing this since 1974, we now have a boat that's too heavy to even roll. *Beachcomber* weighs about 9,000 pounds. We let the tide float us onto firm sand flats. Sometimes the tide doesn't refloat us for a month. Even the prop and shaft retract into the hull.

Size Considerations

In considering your choice of beachcruiser, first determine how much capacity you need to enjoy the length of your cruise. On boats, VOLUME capacity is usually the limit reached before WEIGHT capacity. If you can possibly fit your needs into a boat that you can lift, you'll have a much wider choice of landings. This is one major reason why most Pacific beachcruisers use kayaks. Kayakers can land their boats through the surf and lift them onto rock ledges. Some have learned to use the waves to land on the rock ledges!

A major determinant on the size of craft you'll want is the number of persons the boat will have to accommodate. We met a charming family of four doing very well in their third full year living aboard and beach-cruising an 18-foot sloop, about the size of a Flying Scot. They were happy and without a worry when we met them on their way to coastal Carolina from the Florida Everglades. Few of us are as compatible or as humble, but most of us can do half as well for a couple of weeks. If you can't find one boat to suit your needs, consider two boats. This is how we initially cruised the Bahamas—with a Hobie cat and a canoe.

Photo courtesy Phillip Miller

Sea Hike **is fast and light. Between the daggerboard and sheet arrangement, she's too cramped for more than a solo sailor. Be sure that the boat you choose has room for the people you plan to sail with.**

The kayak cruisers keep only one person in each boat, yet they keep their little boats close to one another to feel they are together (there are two-person kayaks).

We solved this choice with two different boats. We put all our camp gear and supplies in a 17-foot Old Town covered canoe which we towed behind a 14-foot Hobie catamaran on which we sat. We sailed together; had boats light enough to lift; had generous cargo capacity in the canoe; and, once camp was set up ashore, we each had a boat to sail separately or together. The catamaran was our choice for speed, sport, visiting nearby islands (now we use sailboards), and diving on the reefs. The canoe was used for fetching water, or for sailing to a nearby settlement for flour, sugar, rum, mail and visitors.

Rigging Considerations

In contriving such a bastardized combination, we introduced some severe complications. Most manufacturers of small boats have designed them to perform adequately as day sailers. The designers and builders don't make the boats for such exotic, severe service as that of beach-cruising. It's a bit like using a sports car to pull a house trailer. You've got to expect to do some modifying even after you've selected an acceptable craft.

With the strengthened bottom, that weight, added to the weight of your camp, and food and water and clothing and diving equipment and entertainment needs, is likely to add up to more than the boat was designed to carry. While all that weight is likely to add stability to an already stable design, unless the sail plan is enlarged, the boat may bog down to an unmaneuverable speed. Even if you don't need to enlarge the sail plan, the added weight will stress the rigging beyond its design load. Unless the boat is already heavily rigged, you must plan on adding heavier wire, lines, and fittings.

We learned these lessons on the Hobie cat and the canoe. Our intention had been to follow the inspiration of Fred Fenger who had beach-cruised the West Indies in a small, decked, sailing canoe. But once we loaded our needs into our larger canoe, there was no room for us. The Hobie cat is known for its lack of stability. Indeed, it sails at its best while balanced on only one of the narrow hulls, from which position it frequently capsizes or dives under and catapults. But it is almost as easily righted.

We changed all the wire rigging on the catamaran to the next larger size. In five years of heavy service, we had no rigging failures. The first few times it nosedived, we were so confused that it took us too long to get *Kohoutek* righted. The wind and surf, pushing as it they do the underside of the trampoline, caused the mast to impale on the shallow bottom. The rigging and fittings survived even that test. Don't let the mast impale the bottom in seas of over a foot as the mast and mast step of any boat is sure to be broken. In a capsize, first keep the mast tip afloat, maybe by tying a

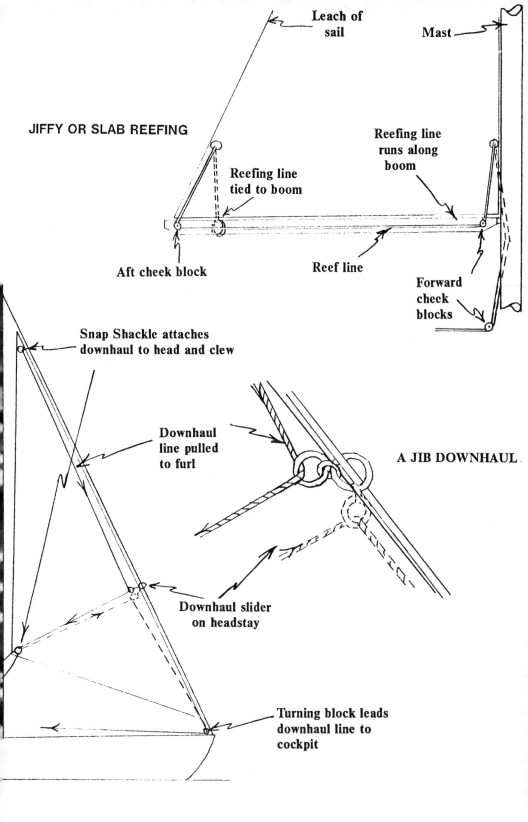

JIFFY OR SLAB REEFING

Leach of sail

Mast

Reefing line runs along boom

Reefing line tied to boom

Reef line

Aft cheek block

Forward check blocks

Snap Shackle attaches downhaul to head and clew

Downhaul line pulled to furl

A JIB DOWNHAUL

Downhaul slider on headstay

Turning block leads downhaul line to cockpit

life jacket on it, then swim it around to windward, then try righting the boat by standing on the board and hanging out as far as you can with a line on the gunwale.

In those days, the 14-foot Hobie was not rigged to carry a jib. Like all multihulls, it is slow and sometimes impossible to bring about. This was the more so with a heavy load on the trampoline and a heavily laden canoe in tow. We carried two paddles on the trampoline. More than once we used them to paddle hot, becalmed miles, as a black, cold, squall line rolled from the north.

A rigging failure is the single most likely cause of boat losses while underway. Inspect the rigging and the fittings at both ends before each major cruise or passage. The second most likely cause is failure of the steering linkages and loss of rudder. Take a good look at the quality of the steering mechanism. Simplicity and ease of inspection and repair while underway is necessary. If rudder loss is remotely possible, then install an oarlock at the stern so that you can use an oar to steer the boat to a safe landing.

Rarely are small boats (or big ones) fitted with adequately sized and mounted cleats to which to fasten the anchor rode. For each 1,000 pounds of boat weight, the anchor cleat must hold 300 pounds. As a precaution, most boaters carry their rode around the mast after cleating.

Editor's note: For about 10 years, we beachcruised in an 18-foot sail canoe, and a 17-foot flat bottom wood lapstrake centerboard sloop, an Amesbury (Mass) Pow Wow, marconi rigged. The canoe was lateen rigged, and had leeboards and sponsons. We always beached the canoe, and nearly always anchored heavily constructed Pow Wow offshore. I built a sea chest for the sloop which we installed aft of the centerboard trunk. The camping gear stowed under the foredeck, with the anchor and rode, and everything else went into the sea chest.

Both craft served us well. We never once capsized either boat. The canoe had only auxiliary paddle power, but we had an outboard for auxiliary power on the sloop, and we carried extra fuel for it.

We always sailed the canoe with both leeboards down. She didn't heel much because of the sponsons. Though both boards down caused more strain on the rig, we found that we made less leeway. We only broke the crosspiece once in 5 years.

We never did any extra rigging on Pow Wow. Though she was weighed down, her large main and small jib let her move well and gave her stability. We used rollers only once when the tide stranded us at Horse Island in Joshua Cove, west of Sachem Head, CT. The stays pulled loose at the mast tangs when we sailed in a thunderstorm, trying to make shore at Plum Island east of Long Island's (NY) north fork. The spruce mast bent, but held until we got canvas off. Though we heavily loaded both boats, that was the sum total of damage to either boat over long periods of use.

Our centerboard was heavy wood with a bronze rod pennant. To lower the board, we raised the handle and pushed down the rod. It was not locked. When we grounded, the board would come up, raising the rod.

The handle locked the board up. I don't believe in locking it down. Groundings never caused damage to us because the centerboard was free to come up into its trunk.

We never cruised more than three weeks at a time in these boats and our cruising range was Long Island Sound and environs to Cape Cod. We sailed overnight weekends and 3-day weekends whenever we could. This was beachcruising as defined by Ida Little, but we didn't do it five months at a time, and therefore didn't have to carry much paraphenalia. We carried only a tool kit, food, storm gear, clothing, cushions, life preservers, a two-man nylon mountain tent left over from World War II, a bucket with a home-made wooden seat, and a two-burner Sterno stove. If this will be your cruising mode, there are many stock day sailers that will fill your bill. We have friends who go beachcruising in Lightnings, in Rhodes 19's, and in every conceivable beachable sailboat and motor skiff. They haven't had to soup up the boats or the rigging because they only go on short trips.

Photo by Chris Harkness

When selecting a boat, go sailing on several different designs. Don't forget to drop your rudder to its down position! This is *Black Pearl*.

Necessity for a Reefing System (See Page 99)

We neglected to have the Hobie sail modified so we might reef it. When it got over 18 knots, we had to make a landing and stay ashore until the wind moderated. If a beachcruiser is to be safe, it **must** be provided with a way to quickly and easily reduce sail. Reducing sail is called "reefing."

Sailors agree that the best reefing system is either slab reefing or "roller" reefing. Loose-footed sails (like the jib) are usually rolled. Boomed sails are usually slab reefed, though there also are roller reefing systems for main sails. If your sailboat is not already fitted with an effective way to reduce sail area, preferably from within the cockpit, then have a sailmaker and rigger modify the sails and rig the boat. Practice reefing and shaking out the reef before you begin any cruise, and always reef as a precaution—before you need to. While underway, if you consider reefing, then do it immediately. If you have a good system, it will be easy to shake out once the threat is past.

A sail that can't be easily reefed should not be considered for cruising. The lateen rig on most canoes and sailfish-type boats provides no way to reduce sail. The conventional "marconi" rig is easily reefed and is the sail with which most boats are fitted. It is a tall rig that may overpower some tender, unballasted, small boats. A lower rig that is easily reefed is the one Matt Layden uses. It's called a "balanced lug." Because it's cheap to build, easy to maintain, powerful yet of low aspect, fast to raise and strike, easy to control and to reef, the balanced lug is probably the best sail rig for small boats.

Without any reefing provisions on our Hobie rig, our only choices were to put ashore or go full speed ahead. The canoe, *Manatee,* fully loaded and in tow, was not designed to move over seas in a full speed ahead mode. The narrow bow would slice into each wave and throw a bow wave that would slide up the hull, slide under the edge of the cover, slowly fill the canoe, and eventually unsnap the cover. As the canoe filled, it created such a load on the catamaran, that *Kahoutek* would nosedive, even with both of us on the stern of the windward hull. By the time we learned all this, we were in the Bahamas and without the resources to modify the sail for reefing. Instead, we found some PVC tubing on a beach. We cut the 8-foot long tube in half, lengthwise, so as to make two 8-foot long C-sections. Each of these was screwed and glued onto each side of the canoe, from the bow to amidships. These acted like a deflector and broke the bow wave. We still went dangerously fast, but the canoe no longer filled, the cover stayed on, and our camp and stocks stayed dry and salt-free.

Comfort Considerations

On *Kahoutek*, sitting as we were without backrests, on a hard, high-speed trampoline only inches above the water, often inches under the wave tops, we had no expectation of dryness or comfort. The time limit to our sailing day was our fatigue and our endurance to heat and cold (usually four to five hours a day). In considering a choice of beachcruiser, comfort in sailing is often compromised because we plan to find comfort ashore. Nonetheless, ease of motion, a comfortable, wide seat with backrest, and modest dryness and shade while underway should be at least sought. Some beachcruisers do offer some of these.

We recommend sleeping on the seats rather than on the floor of the cockpit. Thus you can have wider seats than if the width was left for sleeping on the floor, and wider seats accommodate more stowage under them.

Don't be tempted to widen the seats by eliminating the side decks. Side decks add significantly to seaworthiness and explain how a kayak can turn turtle without taking on but a few drops of water. Under the side decks is the most effective place to add flotation. They also make an effective place to sit in a hard blow.

On *Dugong* we got to appreciate a comfortable cockpit—wide, cushioned seating with a backrest and leg room; space enough to move around and vary our positions. Eventually we installed an awning that kept us shaded and dry. But *Dugong* is a 26-foot decked canoe. Few beachcruisers are big enough to include that much comfort aboard. Yet oddly enough, it is the smallest ones, the kayaks, that have the most comfortable seats!

Safety Considerations

Rather than comfort, our overwhelming concern in choosing a small boat is safety. And so it should be. Our need to be assured of survival

One person can raise the *Dovekie* mast which pivots on deck. It helps to be tall!
Select or modify a boat so that raising and lowering the mast is easy.

103

must be the primary consideration. Any small boat used for cruising should be unsinkable and be able to support the crew and stores when filled with water. This is assured by including air-tight, foam-filled compartments of sufficient volume. These flotation sections should be placed above the waterline along each side, not on the bottom. It is usually easy to add flotation to a boat that lacks it. It is usually difficult to remove flotation that has been misplaced and become waterlogged.

If your boat doesn't have side decks, consider adding a fabric "skirt" along each side within the cockpit. By supporting the inside edge of the skirt with elastic shock cord, it will stretch out of your way when you lean against it. Even such a temporary side deck will significantly reduce the amount of water taken into the cockpit in a capsize and make recovery from a swamping much more likely.

We beachcruisers are most likely to fill our boats with water by holing the boat, than by taking on a heavy sea. But we are as vulnerable to a capsize as are the ocean cruisers. Most small boats don't have small cockpits that are quickly self-draining or that can be quickly sealed. A capsize is quite certain to fill our boats. In conditions that cause a capsize, we aren't likely to be able to bail our boat faster than the seas refill it. If you plan to recover from a capsize, be sure to have side decks and add a skirt to additionally enclose the lee side of the cockpit.

On our canoe, *Crapaud*, in which we cruised the coast of Martinique, the snap-on cover kept the seas and heavy rains out. The cover had two holes at each end through which we sat in the canoe. These holes were fitted with sewn-in skirts with elastic waist-band ties. Inside, under the cover, our legs were dry and shaded while our upper torsos were necessarily exposed. However, when the seas threatened to capsize us, as they did every time we landed through the surf, we crawled out of the cocoon and sealed each cockpit skirt tightly with the waist band. Now we'd sit on, rather than in, the canoe. Our legs dangled over the sides, feet in the water. *Crapaud* did get broached, washed over, and rolled as we approached a beach through 6-foot breaking surf, and we were washed off. As we and the paddles were tethered to the canoe, and bow and stern painters were trailing, we pulled her ashore without loss. Inside it usually got a little wet, but everything was in watertight bags, dry and undamaged. Choose or devise a cockpit that won't cause a catastrophe in the event of a capsize.

On *Kohoutek*, the Hobie catamaran, we had no cockpit. That was a safe, uncomfortable way to solve the problem. Frequently, a cockpit can be temporarily reduced or covered in threatening conditions. If you can't or won't defend your cockpit, then do take along a couple of inner tubes and provide for quick inflation of them. They'll displace water and add to the buoyancy.

Survival can be assured only if the boat carries a reserve of buoyancy sufficient to float the hull a few inches above the water with the crew standing dry on the deck or gunwales. This buoyancy must be distributed so as to keep the vessel in an upright position when fully swamped; and the crew must have practiced getting the boat sailing after a capsize or swamping. It is little known that most laden kayaks and canoes can not be reentered or recovered from a swamping or capsize at sea.

Stiffness

Another solution would be to find a boat that can't be capsized. While this is not currently possible, some boats are more resistant than others. These are safer and more comfortable to sail. This characteristic, to stay upright under the press of sail or crew movement, is called "stiffness." A boat that rolls easily is called "tender." Canoes and tree logs are very tender. Barges and sand boxes are very stiff. Some hull shapes are initially

Such a big sail on such a small boat requires vigilance at the helm. Note oars placed handily along the gunwales.

tender, say to an angle of 15 degrees, then become impossible to heel further. Others are intially stiff and fall over once a threshold is reached. Most boats become stiffer as weight is put aboard. The best, and maybe the only, way to tell if the boat you're considering is stiff enough for comfort and security, is to put aboard a representative load and take it out for a sail in a stronger than normal wind.

On small boats the main determinant of stiffness is hull shape. Rounded hulls are tender. Flat-bottomed hulls are stiff. Wide bottoms are stiff. Narrow hulls are tender. We advocate wide, flat bottoms; with hard chines; and topsides with moderate flare.

Freeboard and Load Carrying Factors (See Page 95)

The hull shape will also determine the load you carry. A hull that floats deeply in the water as you add the weight of stores and people has less to recommend it than a boat that floats at the same level regardless of the load. The more weight you can put aboard to make the waterline only 1 inch higher, the better the boat will sail, and the greater will be its load-carrying capacity. We also favor "freeboard"—the distance from the water to the gunnel.

Little touring kayaks include sufficient volume under their decks to provide the paddler with a week of clothing, food and water, and reading. If you plan to cruise with more than one person for longer than a week, then you must carefully evaluate your choice of boat for available stowage volume. Put all the things you want to carry into a pile and measure how much volume you need to contain the pile. When you look at boats, use a tape measure to determine how much stowage volume each boat provides. Consider the backpacking experience. Excluding water, a backpack carries all a climber's needs for 10 days within two cubic feet. The full pack usually weighs under 65 pounds. Fresh water for 10 days would equal those numbers—per person.

A safe rule of thumb is that a small cruising sailboat should be able to accommodate at least 18 pounds of crew (weight) for every foot of waterline length. Thus a boat of 16 feet at the waterline should be built to accommodate **at least** two people. Specialized craft, such as canoes and kayaks, rely on special design or special handling for safety.

Another safe rule of thumb is that the entire crew must be able to sit on the same gunwale (gunnel), amidships and at the cockpit, without causing the boat to take on water or capsize. Our sailing canoe, *Crapaud*, fails this test. Hence the full cover. A boat whose beam is **at least** the cube root of the waterline length squared is usually safe. Thus a boat whose waterline is 16 feet long must be at least 6.4 feet wide.

Sail Before You Buy

Even if you choose one of the classes of beachcruisers discussed in the next chapter, going out for a sail is the only way to check the condition of a particular boat. While hull stiffness is a consequence of the design of a boat, it is strength, integrity, and the condition of the components that are more likely to affect your safety. These you will have to inspect on each particular boat you consider.

Try to not be influenced by the quality of the finish or by the repairs and modifications you can yourself accomplish. If the mast step is weak, as many are, it is fairly easily strengthened. On small boats, the cost of additional rigging and refitting is minor—and usually necessary.

However, if the sailing rig won't fit inside the hull when not in service (such as while stored or trailering), it may be costly to make acceptable provisions for it. When you go out for a sail, observe whether you have good visibility from the steering position. Are you protected from the weather? Can you rig a dodger? An awning? A tent? Do you stay dry as you sail or does the boat throw each wave back at you? Can you handle the sails from the cockpit—raising, furling, and reefing as well as sheeting? Can you handle the anchor from the cockpit, or must you crawl forward inside or on deck? Anchor? Well, with good planning it shouldn't happen too frequently.

Once you've inspected the basic design and construction and determined the boat seaworthy, the next step is to go for a sail in genteel conditions. In getting off, consider the ease of difficulty in setting sail. Once underway, does the boat respond to the helm at various points of sail? Is it maneuverable? Does it track or does the tiller require constant adjustment? If you let go the tiller will the boat ease into the wind and assume a hove-to position? A slight weather helm in the puffs is desirable. Try varying the setting of the centerboard or leeboard. Pretend an unexpected

Photo by Ron Johnson

Choose a boat popular in your area. You can join a class association, providing a network of people and information, and the opportunity to cruise in company. These are *Sea Pearls* rendezvousing on Sea Horse Key off Florida's west coast. These owners have such an association.

squall and go through a reefing drill. Throw a floating cushion over the side and try to recover it. Try taking down all sails. Will they come down in a blow? Or can you easily add a downhaul and brail to get them down? Are the sails in the way when dropped? Can you add lazy jacks?

As you move along, determine if you have total visibility from your steering station. Will you have to cut windows in the sails? Or through the foredeck? Or sit in a high chair?

Critique the layout of the standing and running rigging for ease of handling, simplicity, and maintenance. Make a beach landing and pull the boat ashore. Have a picnic. Go to a place and drop anchor. Does it stay in place at anchor, or will it take a second anchor to keep it from sailing around the rode?

On your return, consider the speed. Does the boat move easily in response to the wind? Or not at all? Try pointing as high as she will and note within how many degrees (on the compass) she points on the other tack. The Cup contenders can tack inside 60 degrees. We're happy if we can go about inside 100 degrees. If there are waves or wakes to sail into, consider the sedateness of the boat's motion, or does it shake and jar and toss you around? And does she throw a spray of sea into your face as well? Or does she help you stay dry?

After it takes you back, note how easily and quickly you can stow the sails and get off her leaving the boat secured. If all these considerations satisfy you, then look over her accommodations and stowage volume to determine suitability to your beachcruising plans.

Trailering

A beachcruiser is likely to be trailered more frequently than it's anchored. Unless you own your own choice of shore, pick a boat that is easily trailered. The bottom must be strong enough to not flex, even when the boat is on the trailer, loaded with all your camping comforts, and bouncing along a back road at 50 knots. The sailing rig must not take much time or muscle to raise or lower.

With other kayakers, including his wife, John Dowd had cruised from Trinidad through the West Indies and the Bahamas to Florida. In 1980, Jeremy Barnard and James Meadows sailed from Friendship, Maine to New Orleans—3,200 miles in 149 days—each in a 14-foot *Phantom* Sunfish-type boat. In 1985, Christopher Cunningham came 2,600 miles down the Mississippi from Pittsburgh, Pennsylvania to Cedar Cay, Florida, in 75 days on a self-built, 13.5-foot "sneak-box."

Instead of cruising such long distances, we've preferred to trailer our boats to the areas we want to explore. In choosing a boat that we plan to trailer, the ease of launching and retrieving, including the time it takes to rig and strike, determine how frequently we'll go out sailing. Before you invest in a boat and trailer, be sure to go through the launching drill yourself. and don't forget to keep a line to the boat for when it floats off the trailer. We've seen a few smooth launchings marred by the boat drifting away unmanned and untethered. Be watchful of overhead power lines within range of your raised mast!

Auxiliary Power

The time may come when you've got to row, paddle, or outboard power your boat. Is it possible? Is it easy? Can it be done with the sailing rig down and stowed? We enjoyed taking our 26-foot *Dugong* through the inland waterway. Loaded as she was, she was a pig to row. Yet, because the small Seagull was attached to the rudder, the outboard was frequently drowned by the wakes of the big power boats. We'd row to a side canal to get the motor running again. Once beyond these rude canals, we moved along at 5 knots and used a quart of fuel per hour—20 miles per gallon. Almost as good as a car!

•

All boats are compromises. Don't expect any boat to be totally satisfactory, particularly if your own interests are uncertain, ill-defined, or variable. Over the years of practicing beachcruising, our needs have changed. Our choice of boat has evolved from a 17-foot canoe to a 36-foot beachcruiser.

Our current home, *Beachcomber* is 36 feet on deck. Nonetheless, her flat bottom and 18-inch draft allow us to dry out, aground and level on firm sand most of our cruising year. To toss the Aerobie and fetch water from the well, and to beachcomb, we step off and walk to dry shore inland and across the island. When friends come for tea, they've a long walk to *Beachcomber*, across sand flats, from where their **dinghy** has gone aground!

Michael Walsh inspecting a *Capri 14.2* on a trailer at Kentucky Lake. She's shoal draft, centerboard, with a flat bottom.

ADDITIONAL SOURCES OF INFORMATION
ON SELECTING A BOAT

Local Newspapers from around watery areas nearest where you live or plan to sail are the most likely economical resource for gaining both sailing experience and a good buy on an appropriate boat. Meet the boats and the owners through the classified "marine" listings.

Local Classified Monthly "rag" publications such as Boat Trader and Pennysaver are usually found near the magazine racks at convenience stores. These, like the newspaper classifieds, list boats for sale and sometimes include photos.

Local monthly boating news journals, such as Latitude 38, Box 1678, Sausalito, CA 04066; Soundings, 35 Pratt St., Essex, CT 06426; and Messing About in Boats, 29 Burley St., Wenham, MA 01984, list boats for sale by local owners.

Monthly national boating magazines such as Wooden Boat, Boat Journal, Canoe, Sea, Kayaker, Soundings, Yachting, or Cruising World may have a listing within range of your pocket and geography.

Books We've Found Helpful to Define Our Needs

Ocean-Crossing Wayfarer' by Frank and Margaret Dye, $12.95, 144 pages, 1977, David & Charles, Box 257, North Pomfret, VT 05053.

Sailing on a Micro Budget, by Larry Brown, $15.60, 163 pages, 1985, Seven Seas Press, TAB Books, Inc., Blue Ridge Summit, PA 17294-0840.

Dinghies for All Waters, by Eric Coleman, Hollis & Carter, 9 Bow St., London, England WC2E 7AL.

Dinghy Book, 2nd edition, by Stan Grayson, $14.60, 160 pages, 1989, International Marine, TAB Books, Inc., Blue Ridge Summit, PA 17294-0840.

Dinghy Cruising with Phillips, A Manual on Camping and Sailing in Small Open Boats, by Alan Phillips, available from Ken Elliott, 56 The Esplanade #403, Toronto, Ontario M5E 1A7, Canada. Includes a list of the Wayfarer log anthologies.

Any of the books by naval architect **Philip C. Bolger** usually published by International Marine, TAB Books, Inc. Blue Ridge Summit, PA 17294-0840, will have the effect of releasing the reader from the narrow conventions of boat design. His words and designs instruct and inspire and sometimes entertain.

Sailboat Buyers Guide, by Alan Chappell, $12.95, 374 pages, 1983, Seashore Publications, Long Beach, MS 39560. Includes photos and line drawings of over 1,000 sailboats.

Enchanted Vagabonds, by Dana and Ginger Lamb, 1938, Harper & Brothers, New York. While no longer in print, this book is worth searching out along with Fred Fenger's *Alone in the Caribbean*. These are the only epic accounts of coastal cruising and seashore camping. Many libraries have these books.

CHAPTER 5

USING CANOES FOR BEACHCRUISING

HOW YOU CAN USE CANOES

Small boat beachcruisers tend to enjoy a variety of water activities. We like windsurfing, river paddling, white water running, daysailing, racing, power boating and overnight camp-cruising. We can afford to be democratic in our interest for two good reasons.

First, our vessels, our toys, are not expensive investments. We can have two or three different sorts of small boats. Or, if we just have one, we don't feel compelled to use it every free moment because it's there and it's costing us. We can rent a different water toy or go off on someone else's boat without feeling guilty.

Secondly, our small boats can be metamorphosed to match mood, conditions and/or geography. A sailing canoe converts into a white water runner, a lake paddler, a dinghy, a fishing boat, a grocery boat with power, and a "cruise ship." For this reason, we include canoes (and kayaks) as beachcruisers. Many of us already have a canoe, and if not, you may choose to get one because it's got so many uses.

On the down side, canoes and kayaks do not qualify as stable, or stiff, vessels. Far from it. They're tippy and will go right on over easily.

Photo by Chris Harkness

Man and best friend canoeing along Cedar Keys on Florida's west coast during the annual small craft meet.

Swamped, they're difficult to re-enter, and in the case of a canoe, impossible to bail once swamped at sea. Both require quite a bit of practice and experience for skillful handling.

Although these small, light craft are about the least expensive mode of beachcruising, a **new** canoe with cover, sail rig, rudder and leeboards, will run you about $2,000. On the other hand, they're less expensive than other daysailer craft, and they're extremely versatile and light enough to carry on top of your car or on board a train or light plane. For their size, canoes are capable of carrying a heavy, bulky load of cruising gear.

We have used open canoes for paddling, river running, sailing and cruising for many years. Our first sailing canoe, *Manatee*, was a 17-foot Old Town canoe. For five years in the Bahamas she served as both our beachcruiser and our covered supply wagon. Our next 17-foot Chipewyan canoe, *Ahmic*, we used for cruise-camping through the lakes of northwestern Ontario, Canada. Our canoe *Crapaud* carried us on two winters' cruises along the coast of Martinique, French West Indies. In each case, we had wonderful cruises with lots of fun sailing and camping for as long as four months at a stretch.

Editor's note: In 1940, we circumnavigated Long Island Sound in 13 days in our 18-foot, canvas-covered, wood sail canoe, camping on beaches, with no auxiliary power except paddles. Although there are fewer places to camp now, we still see small boats carrying campers to beaches all over New England. More recently, I've taken Boy Scouts on canoe camping trips in New Jersey's Pine Barrens and on rivers in New England, and have done some mild whitewater rapids running, and have enjoyed camping-fishing trips in canoes in northern Ontario. You can have a lot of fun in canoes. At Boy Scout camp in Wingdale, NY, at a very early age we jousted in 12-man canoes, and here I am still canoeing at an advanced age!

Our 17' Old Town canoe *Manatee* was our taxi, dive boat, grocery boat, fun boat, and storage container. Triangular leeboards are Michael Walsh's design to increase strength over daggerboard type

Author enjoying kayaking off Cedar Key, Florida

Kayaks

Kayaks, although they have minimal carrying capacity, have the unique advantage of being foldable. Kayakers enjoy cruising in as far-away places as the Amazon or Tierra del Fuego. They simply fold the kayak into a suitcase-like bundle and carry it on the plane with them.

Because we have little personal experience with kayaks, we leave that subject to people who do. The appendix at the end of this chapter lists kayak reference books and periodicals which are both entertaining and educational.

SELECTING A CANOE
A COMPARISON OF MATERIALS

ABS Plastic (Acrylonitrile-Butadiene-Styrene)

This material is tough, will snap back into shape if dented or bent, is easy to repair if holed, feels ever so comfortable to your body, requires no rivets, screws, or ribs, is as light as aluminum, and is as quiet as wood. Our canoe *Manatee* slipped anchor in the Bahamas once and washed up on a shore of razor sharp coral. She spent the whole night lifting and falling with the waves—fully loaded with about 500 pounds of gear. Yet when we found her the next morning, abandoned by the tide, and balanced on two sharp coral spikes, she showed only minor dents and scratches! Our canoe *Crapaud* was picked up by her ends, fully loaded with 600 pounds of gear, yet she did not buckle and fold.

On the other hand, ABS deteriorates over time no matter what you do. *Manatee* took quite a beating from the sun and heat over five years of cruising in the Bahamas. To protect her from destructive UV rays from the sun the last three years, we covered her with palm fronds or tarps when she was ashore. On her seventh birthday, when a violent wind tossed her into the air and abruptly dropped her on a steel stake, we weren't too surprised that she cracked. In her youth, she'd have come through **completely** unscathed. However, we **were** surprised to find that she'd gone stiff and brittle all over, especially the plastic gunwales and the bow and stern where the flexing of her belly really showed.

In fact, we had to spread patching compound over the fatigued areas in order to keep her afloat. At that point, we no longer considered her a safe vessel. *Ahmic*, the same model canoe we used in Canada, lasted almost twice as long as *Manatee*. She wasn't used as vigorously, and was carefully stored in cool, shady places. Also, she was never exposed to tropical sun and heat. Nonetheless, *Ahmic* too turned brittle after 10 years. *Crapaud*, in tropical Martinique, aged on the same schedule as *Manatee*.

Because ABS plastic is molded with such inherent strength in itself, it requires no ribs or hull reinforcers. This is nice when you're sitting in it and when you're stowing gear in it, but it causes fatigue problems over time. The hull flexes as it travels through the water. It's a nice feeling, actually, as you sit with it waving underneath you. Eventually, this "oil canning" fatigues the material. At bow and stern, the plastic becomes brittle and cracks easily. The flexibility of the hull also slows down the boat. Under the same conditions, an ABS plastic molded sailing canoe will move slightly slower than a stiff hull.

Aluminum

Aluminum lasts much longer than ABS and is almost as lightweight. Aluminum canoes are less flexible than ABS canoes, and marginally faster.

Aluminum boats need frames and a keelson to provide stiffness and strength. However, the rivets that hold the frames to the hull wear and tear over time. They slowly work loose and begin to weep. While this weeping won't usually sink you (you can easily bail faster than the rivets ooze), it'll keep the inside of the canoe continually wet. Some rivets are easy to get at and can be patched or re-hammered or replaced. Others may be hidden so that you cannot get at them. Guess which rivets will leak first!

You can field repair aluminum with tape or aluminum patching compound. Permanent repairs must be welded. ABS takes a lot more beating before needing patching or repair. Coral would rip aluminum like a tin can.

The bumps and ridges of ribs inside an aluminum canoe are uncomfortable to sit on. The aluminum itself is cold to the touch, and very noisy.

Wood

Wood looks pretty, feels good, and moves quietly, but it's fragile and needs a lot of maintenance. It's repairable in the field, enough to get you by, but more difficult to repair more permanently. *Editor's note: we repaired the canvas with canvas patches held by Ambroid glue.* Wood canoes are pricey. Cruising in a lightweight canoe compares to running jeep trails with a Rolls Royce. Because of its expense and relative fragility, you would be less likely to risk damaging it by "playing around." To us, that's one of the joys of small boats—being able to use them more casually and with greater abandon.

MODIFYING A CANOE FOR CRUISING

Hardware for Sheets and Halyards

We added cleats and blocks to make handling the sail easier and quicker. Our 55-square-foot lateen sail was hoisted with a line halyard which we led through a small block on the gunwale, back to a clam cleat within reach of the helm. Thus we could quickly drop sail without moving from the helm. To make sheet handling a lot easier, we added a block with clam cleat mounted on the stern. It's impossibly tiresome to hold the sheet with no mechanical relief. We just have to be very careful to ease the sheet when the winds are strong and puffy. If the sheet is not released immediately, a canoe is easily thrown over in a hard puff. On the cold Canadian lakes of northwestern Ontario, we never cleated the sheet. As on all small lakes, the winds are flukey, fluctuating quickly in intensity and direction. In Florida and the Bahamas, winds blow with constant force and direction. It's usually only when we sail close to shore, where the land deflects the breeze, that we have to watch for flukey winds.

Tiller and Rudder

We never had a problem with the very lightweight aluminum rudder or tiller. Our mistake, though, was not disassembling the parts often enough. Over time, the pin holding the rudder to the gudgeons corroded, so that we could no longer remove the rudder from the back of the canoe. Aluminum parts have a habit of corroding if they sit together too long in salt water. Our tiller came with an extension arm. If it hadn't, we'd have added one. Often we are hiked out on the windward gunwale from where it's impossible to reach a short tiller.

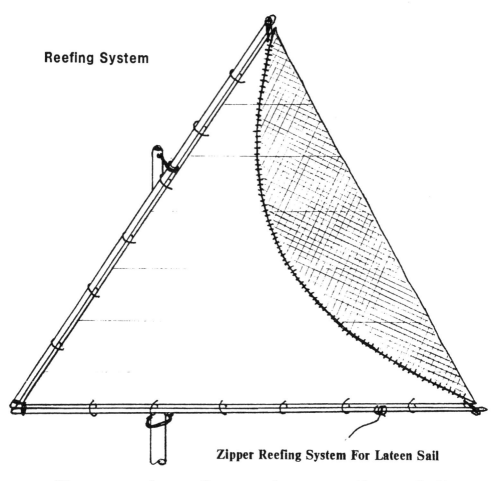

Reefing System

Zipper Reefing System For Lateen Sail

We never created any reefing system for our canoes' lateen sails. Since 55 square feet is a small area to begin with, we just never bothered. Today we definitely would make part of the sail removable with a zipper system, as we do on our windsurfers. Even though we rarely sail more than a few hundred yards offshore, all it takes is getting caught out once. We had zippers sewn in our windsurfing sails so we could just unzip a section out of the leech. I thought I'd never have to use it but it's amazing how fast the wind can come up and how impossibly far a hundred yards to shore can become.

Leeboards

We were tacking across a large lagoon, in the middle of a very remote and uninhabited Bahama island, when our leeboard broke off. We heard a loud snap and suddenly skidded off to leeward. For a frozen moment, neither of us understood. Then Michael leaned outboard and picked up a piece of wood and I wondered why, at a time like this, he'd bother to pick up a piece of driftwood. Soon we were aground and jumping out to assess the damage. That driftwood was our leeboard. The aluminum angle iron that supports the 3-foot long dagger-shaped board had broken. It was im-

116

possible for us to repair in the field, and we hadn't even considered bringing along a spare. It had looked very strong and beefy. However, over the four months of constant and sometimes demanding stress, the aluminum had fatigued at the angle. In bad blows, we had left the windward board down, allowing it to unduly stress the bracket outward. We could now see the other bracket was cracked and ready to snap as well.

We were lucky. We were cruising in two boats and didn't **have** to sail the canoe. When we got back to an inhabited island, we made improvements on the leeboard rig so that we wouldn't be disabled again.

First, we ordered a strong leeboard bracket made with steel instead of aluminum. Then we installed outboard slots to keep the windward board snug against the hull. With this added support, we are able to leave the windward board down without worrying about fatiguing the bracket as we had done. The leeboard slot, or brace, was so successful on *Manatee* that we added hefty ironbark braces when we built *Dugong*, our 26-foot leeboard canoe cruiser (described under Cuddy Boats in Chapter 7).

To further reduce the strain on the leeboards and fittings, Michael redesigned the leeboards. He made shorter, triangular boards to replace the traditional dagger boards. These reduce our draft from 3 feet to 1 foot, with no appreciable change in sailing performance. Our new leeboard arrangement will support about 80 pounds of weight at the ends of the boards, enough so that the two of us can hike out on the gunwales without causing leeboard or bracket damage. Anyone contemplating sailing, and particularly cruising, a canoe, should test the boards. Hang at least 70 pounds at the end of each board with the force **away** from the hull. This is easily done by turning the canoe on its side, on blocks, and hanging 9 gallons of water in a bucket from the end of the board.

Rubberized Canoe Cover

The Old Town canoe cover comes with two wood slats sewn in to athwartship pockets. When the cover is snapped on, these slats hook against the gunwales, forming two arches. This shapes the cover to shed water. We found that by piling our gear under the saggy places we could totally prevent the formation of puddles. The cover and canoe snaps must be greased regularly.

CANOE CRUISES

Ed Gillet, age 26, only a few years ago, crossed 2,200 miles from Monterey, California to Maui, Hawaii in 63 days, in a 21-foot kayak. The only discomfort he admitted was the lack of a sense of gravity. He said, at the end of his journey, that it felt good to stand up. On the more positive side, he said he felt pleased to have survived and actually enjoyed much of the very unique experience.

The kind of cruising we like includes shores, beaches, as much walking (plenty of gravity) as sailing, and as much land as sea. There are plenty of kayakers and canoeists who enjoy and recommend the writings of certain experienced kayakers. Much of the cruising experience related to kayak cruising applies equally to canoe cruising. John Dowd's "Sea Kayaking: A Manual for Long-Distance Touring" makes wonderful, informative reading. Like us, he believes in relaying information based primarily on his personal experience. For example, when you read his method for handling a rescue, you know he's writing from experience, not from library research and hearsay. Other kayak cruising sources are listed at the end of this chapter.

Our Cruise of the Sail Canoe *Manatee* in the Bahamas

Our inspiration for choosing a sailing canoe for cruising was reading of Frederic Fenger's cruise through the West Indies in 1911, in his 147-pound, 17-foot, partially-decked canoe named *Yakaboo*. His book, "Alone in the Caribbean," was the only descriptive account we could find of seacoast cruising that fit our vague ideas of what we wanted. Interestingly, Fenger's inspiration came from the mid-1900s when Capt. John MacGregor wrote about canoe cruising in England.

Since discovering Fenger, we have uncovered other adventurer canoe cruisers for inspiration. Dana and Ginger Lamb built a partially decked canoe and cruised for years along the coast from San Diego to the Pana-

Photo by Michael Walsh

Our 14' Hobie Cat *Kohoutek* towing our 17' Old Town canoe *Manatee* through shallows in the Exumas Cays in the Bahamas. We cruised the Bahamas for four years with this rig. Note full splash cover on the canoe, described on page 117.

ma Canal. Their book, "Enchanted Vagabonds," published in 1938, tells of their adventures in *Vagabunda*. While their cruise thrills the soul and inspires primitive and heroic fantasies of self-reliant living, it doesn't quite fit the bill for inspiring an average person to get out and have fun in a canoe! What it does do is reassure any reader that her scheme to putz along a secluded shore is well within the realm of possibility. After all, if the Lambs can brave such wild shores under such terribly difficult conditions, without anywhere near the amount of security features we have today, then surely we can safely hop in a sailing canoe and cruise for a week or two or even months in—in the Bahamas?

Anyway, that was what we thought. The only problem was, there were no sailing canoes big enough for the two of us and all the stuff we wanted to carry for the unlimited amount of time we wanted to carry it. *Manatee*, a 17-foot Chipewyan Old Town canoe **looked** big enough, but when we loaded her up with all our gear, there was no room left for us. Because we planned to be cruising the Bahamas indefinitely, we had a lot more gear than that required for a two-week cruise. Here's an idea of the gear we actually did end up carrying with us:

• Two 24-quart beer cooler chests stuffed with: typewriter; cameras; film; typing paper; batteries; three flashlights; a tiny AM/FM radio; stationery; notebook paper; notebooks; reference books on trees, sea fish, and shells; an assortment of adhesive tapes like scotch, duct, and electrical; tubes of superglue; five-minute epoxy; silicone rubber; cassette player and tapes; underwater camera; film; the games of chess and Go; cards; candles; matches; spare hand compass; charts; guide books; binoculars; address books; wallets; and money.

• Two 5-gallon collapsible water jugs (usually filled).

• A large canvas bag holding kitchen/galley gear, aluminum nesting billies, frying pan, grill, kerosene stove, fuel, and cutlery.

• A supply of two to four bottles of rum.

• One large backpack stuffed with tent, 5-foot foam sleeping pads, two sheets, a thin blanket, a space blanket, two ripstop nylon tarps, two rain ponchos, and clothing. Backpack pockets held three flashlights, toilet articles like razor, soap, comb, toothpaste and toothbrushes, spare whistles and medical kit.

• A duffel bag of spare boat parts, tools, machete, hatchet, folding shovel and waist satchels.

• One large net bag of dive gear: flippers, masks, snorkels, gloves, and wet suits.

• Two large waterproof Voyageur™ packs full of food staples like rice, flour, pasta, sprout seeds, powdered milk, coffee, potatoes, etc.

Individually packed were: hammock, guitar, paddles, canoe mast and sail, and spears for the Hawaiian slings.

It was too much. Too much for a little 17-foot canoe. So for the most part, we cruised with *Manatee* loaded as a floating supply wagon towed behind our 14-foot Hobie Cat, *Kohoutek*. When we established a secure base camp, however, we enjoyed cruising in *Manatee* for day- or week-long side trips. When we did this, the two of us sat aft of the center thwart, leaving the forward section free for a week's supply of camping gear and food. The sail rig handles fine with the spray cover in place over the front half, so we never shipped much water.

Two particularly attractive features of the canoe are its simplicity and its light weight. One or two can cruise comfortably in a canoe carrying a tent, food supplies, water, spare parts and tools for about two weeks. Once Michael stayed at our base camp while I cruised *Manatee* through the shallow Pipe Creek area of the Exumas for two weeks. It was my first solo cruise and I can't think of a nicer boat for it. She was easy to handle, easy to fix and easy to check for potential problems. By using a simple boat fender, I could roll her up a beach each night and roll her in each morning.

Our Cruise in the Sail Canoe *Crapaud* in Martinique

"I don't invest much time in planning a long journey on the water," writes Christopher Cunningham in the sidebar to his article about cruising in a sneakbox (Small Boat Journal, Feb./Mar. 1987). He then goes on to explain: "Travel in a small boat is necessarily determined by water and weather conditions, not by the rower's itinerary. Instead, I prepare and equip myself to make the best of whatever situations I might find myself in. The distinction between planning and preparation is important."

Never was this distinction felt so poignantly as when we were dropped off on the island of French Martinique instead of the former British island of

"At home" in our Bahamas base camp. Hobie Cat *Kohoutek* is covered with palm fronds. Michael constructed table and chair from driftwood.

Crapaud, our 17′ Old Town sail canoe fit right in among the heavy Martinique *gommiers.* We set up camp right on the beach. In foreground is fishing net on the sand.

Dominica where we had planned to canoe cruise. The planning (charts, landing, language) went by the boards. But the preparations—the fruit cakes, equipment, spares—served just as well. So well that we ended up cruising Martinique for the whole six months, rather than going on to Dominica. What we lacked in the way of French vocabulary we made up for in friendliness. And thanks to the style of our cruise, so simple and non-threatening, native Martiniquans smoothed our way.

Because we were cruising in a 17-foot canoe (exactly the same Old Town ABS model as we'd used in the Bahamas), our supplies were limited to the two weeks' worth we could carry. Since drinkable, fresh water abounded in the rivers and streams, our limited capacity wasn't taken up with water jugs. Unfortunately we could not supplement our grocery stocks with freshly caught or speared fish. The water is too murky and the fish are almost all gone. We really depended on local grocery stores.

The charm of Martinique lies in its culture and its geography. So it didn't matter that we couldn't enjoy the same amount of isolation and solitude as we'd savored in the Bahamas. We enjoyed the daily stops in small villages and the occasional forays away from people into the jungles. The canoe, being light and sturdy, was easy to leave while we explored inland.

As in our canoe cruise through the Bahamas, we got to know the natives by living among them more like neighbors than as tourists or yachtsmen. The Martinique people, delighted and intrigued by the style of our journey, took us in as one of them, and treated us with what now comes across as "old fashioned" hospitality. This is probably one of the greatest attractions of cruising in very small boats.

Our Cruises In the Sail Canoe *Ahmic* In Canada

You can't beat a canoe for versatility in the lakes of northern Canada. They paddle, portage, motor, and sail better than any other kind of boat. You have to count on most of these qualities even if your plan is to sail-cruise. First, you have to get the boat to where you want to cruise (by train, car, or "bush plane"). Then you have to be able to travel in the boat from lake to lake which usually entails some portaging, so you've got to be able to carry the thing. A motor is optional. A paddle is necessary. Sails are mostly a handicap.

We planned our first cruise in the northwestern Ontario lake system with the idea of sailing most of the time and paddling the rest. We ended up paddling almost all of the time and just stowing the sails. The winds blow so haphazardly that even we, who had been sailing canoes in the Bahamas for years, couldn't stand up to the wind. We spent our time leaping onto the gunwale then back down into the canoe and up again. It was more work than fun. Since downwind sailing is the only sensible direction for sailing on these lakes, a heavy plastic garbage bag supported by a couple of sticks would work just as well, and take up less room!

The cruising is delightful even if we do have to propel the boat ourselves. All the fresh water, good fishing, solitude, and silence we could want.

We've returned to the northern Canadian lakes many summers, always with a canoe without the sail rig. Sometimes we hire a float plane to fly us and canoe to a lake beyond the northern reaches of roads and tracks. Sometimes we rent a canoe and put it on a train. We ride the train into the "bush country" where we are deposited at whatever river or lake we choose. Once in a while we take our canoe on one of the old logging roads and put in at a lake.

Unlike the populated shores of Martinique, the lake shores of the north country have little or no habitations. For this reason, we always carry in the supplies we need for the whole cruise, including fishing poles and lures.

SOURCES FOR ADDITIONAL INFORMATION

Magazines

Canoe Magazine, Box 3146, Kirkland, WA 98083

Sea Kayaker Quarterly, 1670 Duranleau St., Vancouver, B.C. V6H 3S4, Canada

Books

Canoes and Kayaks: A Complete Buyer Guide, by Jack Bronsius and Dave Le Roy, $5.95, 1979, Contemporary Books, 180 N. Michigan Ave., Chicago, IL 60601

Sea Kayaking: A Manual for Long Distance Touring, by John Dowd, $14.95, 298 pages, 1988, University of Washington Press, Box 50096, Seattle, WA 98145-5096

Derek C. Hutchinson's Guide to Sea Kayaking, by Derek C. Hutchinson, $13.95, 122 pages, 1985, Globe Pequot Press, 138 W. Main St., Chester, CT 06412

The Coastal Kayaker: Kayak Camping on the Alaska and B.C. Coasts, by Randel Washburne, $11.95, 224 pages, 1983, Globe Pequot Press, 138 W. Main St., Chester, CT 06412

Coastal Kayaker's Manual: A Complete Guide to Skills, Gear, & Open Water Safety, 2nd edition, by Randel Washburne, $12.95, 288 pages, 1989, Globe Pequot Press, 138 W. Main St., Chester, CT 06412

The Voyage Alone in the Yawl Rob Roy, by John MacGregor, $13.95, 224 pages, 1987, published by Collins in England, distributed in USA by Sheridan House, 145 Palisade St., Dobbs Ferry, NY 10522

Alone in the Caribbean: Being the Yarn of a Cruise in the Sailing Canoe Yakaboo, by Fred Fenger, 1917

Enchanted Vagabonds, by Dana and Ginger Lamb, 1938, Harper & Brothers, New York

Both of the last two books are the only epic accounts of coastal cruising and seashore camping. Both are out of print, but many libraries have these books.

Magazine Articles

"Lake Powell in a Sailing Canoe," by Ron Swartley, Small Boat Journal #65, Feb./Mar. 1989

Equipment

Ecomarine Ocean Kayak Center Catalog, 1668 Duranleau St., Vancouver, B.C. V6H 3S4 Canada, 604-689-5926

Wildwater Designs Catalog, 230 Penllyn Pike, Penllyn, PA 19422

Easy Rider (spinnakers for single and tandem kayaks), Box 88108, Seattle, WA 98188

Expeditions

Check current periodicals and canoe/kayak centers for current information. Trips are available thoughout the USA and as far away as New Zealand.

Following is an article from Small Boat Journal #35 February/March, 1984. It is reprinted here with their kind permission. It describes one of their cruises through the Bahamas in a Hobie Cat, towing a canoe!

BAHAMA SOJOURN

An open-boat idyll
by Ida Little

Just 50 miles off Palm Beach, Florida, lies the upper extremity of the Bahama Islands, an insular commonwealth that extends some 800 miles in a south-easterly direction to the north coast of Haiti. Most of the 700-island archipelago is undersea reef and sand, but 5,000 square miles break the surface and give each 40 inhabitants one square mile to share. Because the topsoil is so thinly infertile and fresh water is so rare, Bahamians have been forced to abandon the lands and cluster into the tourist societies of Nassau and Freeport, or into 60 scattered settlements that serve the cities with fish and sea salt.

This status quo could have left about 4,500 square miles on 650 islands completely uninhabited. However, smuggling fines and import duties are insufficient to support the expense of democracy. So, at the cost of $1,000 an acre, 100 islands have been purchased from the governors by development speculators, wealthy hermits, and yacht clubs searching for their place in the sun. This happily leaves 550 rocky and barren islands for adventurers to share with a few hardy birds and lizards. And, more importantly, provides a varied base and access to a coral sea.

For two years our home has been a lightweight nylon tent set in the shade of casuarina pines on one or another of these islands. It's taken that long for my husband and I to make ourselves at home. Here, along the cays on the Bahamian littoral, we have come to feel increasingly at ease—have found a challenging privacy and isolation in which we are privileged to search for our own destiny.

Certainly, such privacy exists elsewhere. But rare, and nonexistent within our ken, is the combination with such a favorable year-round climate, easy accessibility to the resources and friendships of North America, and availability of edible wild game and fish.

In March, I wrote home from Eleuthera: "By now, we had expected to be approaching the lower Bahama Cays. But we're having too fine a time, and we'll probably not reach them until *next* summer. Between Nassau and here, we've made thirty camps on seven islands, sailing over two hundred miles." I wrote from a campsite that we'd found while cruising our Hobie Cat along Eleuthera's one-hundred-mile lee shore. And what a find!

A spectacular beach and reef at the south tip of Eleuthera Island posed exclusively for the eye of an overlooking lighthouse. Before we sailed around to the windward shore, we beached in the lee and climbed the high weather-whitened coral cliffs to the lighthouse to see what was on the other side. We looked down over a wide unending reef, lining an unvisited beach that stretched beyond sight. Breeze ruffled palms, and pines patched the dunes behind the shoreline. Picture-postcard clouds drifted toward us from infinity, and we had to sit and catch our breath. We had never seen the underwater world so clearly from so high. Ranges of reef, ranges of water, ranges of cloud, all way out there in full color and stereophonic sound, and we were IN it.

In another hour, we'd brought *Manatee* and *Kohoutek* (canoe and catamaran respectively) around the point and were sailing just inches above the scene. We surfed onto the windward beach and lifted *Kohoutek* above the tide. We rolled *Manatee* up the beach on fenders, unloaded, and set up camp behind the dunes, amongst a mixed stand of casuarina and coconut palms.

From the canoe, we brought our four-person nylon tent, which weighs five pounds and packs into a six-inch by twelve-inch roll. The small Svea stove we left stashed. We've learned that wood fires work better, are easier, and don't need messy store-bought fuel. The rest followed: waterproof canoe packs that keep clothing and sheets dry ashore and in *case* the canoe swamps (it has); folding chairs, a hammock and lots of books for relaxing; duffle bags for holding the food organized into Nalgene lab containers; five-gallon collapsible jugs full of fresh water; large beer cooler to protect typewriter, paper, books, tape player and cassettes, the Nikonos and Minolta underwater cameras; candles for night reading; snorkeling and spear-hunting equipment for two.

Tired of the daily pack-up-and-move-on, and delighted with this camp, we decided to linger. It's warm enough here for nudity. And private enough, too. Thanks to the scarcity of fresh water and fertile soil, most natives choose to live in one of the few other towns or settlements. This place is one of hundreds that offer solitude. There are more than five whole islands we could "have" to ourselves. A week evolved into months at our camp on Eleuthera, and a routine emerged from a sense, now, of home.

In the morning, we awoke as the sun gave the tent's inner sanctum a soft green glow. We switched on the tape deck and "Carmina Burana" set a mood. A mockingbird is inspired. He joins the monks. Slowly, we sat, then crawled out to meet another warm, delicious day. Over hot coffee, we talked about what propitious activities we should plan. At noon the tide'll be low. Perfect conditions for a dive hunt. But we need water, too. So this morning we carry our jugs to the public faucet at Bannerman. Wash the sheets. Shampoo hair.

This walk was a long enjoyment. Barefoot we strolled three miles down the pink sand beach. At the lighthouse we put on tennis shoes for the inland miles, and sandspurs quickly covered them. From the lighthouse, a path leads through coarse bracken to Bannerman Town. Here, the McPhees are the only residents among a score of abandoned and dilapidated cottages. Yet there is sweet water at the street faucet.

While we bathed and laundered, the children played ball around us. Older ones watched bashfully from dark windows. They rarely see white people bathe and launder in public, just like them! Tom McPhee and Michael traded grapefruit and tomatoes for fish, then chatted while I gave his wife, May, another driving lesson. She wants to drive a car, so she can sell hot lunches to the construction workers at Cape Eleuthera. Salt of the earth, the McPhees. So are all these Out Island natives. We understand one another.

Back at camp, first we swam, then ate salty sausage-and-cabbage sandwiches. No time to relax. Noon already. We packed the diving gear into our wet-suit tunics and tied the bundle to straps on *Kohoutek's* trampoline. *Kohoutek* weighs over two hundred pounds with gear and anchor and is a hefty load to lift and carry to the water's edge. A hundred yards out, at the main line of reef, we lowered sail. The paddles came out, and we maneuvered around, looking for coral formations that are likely to provide shadowed cave homes for grouper or spiney lobster.

The water was so clear and flat that we would see five-inch grunts, yellow and blue streaks flashing twenty feet below. A long, dark-silver shadow observed them with us, jaws working. We dropped anchor and watched it flutter and sink, coming to rest under the edge of a convoluted brain coral. Taking masks, slings, and gloves out of our flippers, we put everything on and slipped gently off the trampoline with spears poised in the slings. A quick paranoid scan below and around assured us that we weren't being stalked. Both of us dived twenty feet to the base of the head, looming upward from the sandy ocean floor. We conserved oxygen by moving slowly, gracefully, bodies loose and flexible. Michael drew his spear, turned upside down, and aimed beneath a mushrooming coral. He shot. The water reverberated with grunts; the spear thrashed against sand. We surfaced. While Michael recovered his breath, I dived down to retrieve the catch, a Nassau grouper twitching on the point. As I turned to surface, I saw feelers waving in a nearby head. Soon *Kohoutek's* trampoline held all the seafood we could eat. We put away the spears and just played, shooting each other and the scene with the Nikonos.

At camp, we fried the fish in a fritter batter, which makes it keep longer. It is especially tasty and nutritious on a long exploration or passage, when preparing food on board is impossible. It was for just such a passage that we prepared, having decided to cross from Eleuthera to the Exumas, thirty miles westward.

We had to wait two days for the weather, but on the third morning gentle, southeasterly winds promised pleasant sailing. By noon, we were well on our way, *Manatee* towing easily behind. Besides the compass, we had a navigator's dream—color-coded clouds that reflected water depths, which in turn key to the chart. Though we sighted Highborne Cay after an easy four hours, we ended up *paddling* into Ships Channel Bay just an hour before dark. That night a storm hit and ferocious northerly winds lashed seas under the floor of the tent.

One late afternoon in midsummer, we were somewhere along the west coast of Great Exuma. The Bahama Guide, worn and wrinkled from daily handling, rested beside the jerry bottle of tepid water. I suggested that it didn't really matter where we were, as long as Great Exuma was to port. And this was true, except that we needed to find the small channel between Great and Little Exuma to make the shortest route to Georgetown. In spite of wet teeshirts and French Legionnaire-style hats, we were getting tired and literally burnt-out. The rudders scraped bottom and made steering hard. So we headed away from Exuma toward a string of islands on which we might be able to make camp. As typical on the westward banks, these islands are low, scrubby, and skirted with mangroves; it was too late to look for anything better.

After tying the boats to a couple of mangrove roots, we unloaded gear for just the night. Half an hour later, the hammock was strung between a couple of peely red gumbo-limbo trees, and the food was stashed on it. In the one flat area that got enough breeze to discourage the awesome cloud of insects, we pitched the tent. Nearby, Michael scooped out a shallow pit for the fire, over which we heated leftover fritters. Before dinner, we bathed, then rinsed the salt off with fresh water. Somewhat refreshed, we sipped rum-punch cocktails and watched the distant shore of Great Exuma slide into darkness. We hadn't seen a boat all day. Too

Photo by Michael Walsh

Author takes Old Town canoe *Manatee* for a sail to Little Farmers Cay in the Exumas chain of the Bahamas to pick up groceries and mail.

shallow. We were cozily alone now and at peace, grateful for the beauty of such a far-out space. And exhausted! Ten hours in an open boat is too much. We crawled into the tent and passed out.

Around midnight, I felt a jab in my ribs and awakened in a panic. Michael urged, "You better get up!" For a minute, I flashed on the old days, when Michael's tone of voice meant 'we're dragging anchor.' Same edge. I couldn't see anything. But I felt . . . water? The tent was afloat and nearly adrift. That night was the once-a-year highest tide, and we, of course, were in the once-a-year lowest campsite. We sloshed out, gathered up soggy sheets, climed into the mangroves and waited for the tide to recede.

More to our liking were the campsites that encompassed miles of beach and offered inland explorations. And that's what we found at Little San Salvador, a verdant, uninhabited island between Eleuthera and Cat Island. It's big—some miles long and less than a mile wide. Long sand beaches face northward and drop quickly into depths of twenty to thirty feet that nourish coral so abundant that even we, jaded by constant hunting, were impressed. Low dunes back the beach and provide a footing for the long-needle casuarina pine. By all rights, we should not have been there, gliding along a windward shore, but a northerly weather system caused the winds to veer southwest. We surfed ashore on gentle ocean rollers, then walked down the beach and climbed to the rim of dunes. The chart showed an inner lagoon and a thicket of palmetto somewhere on the other side of us. We thrusted down the back side of the dunes to reach the edge of a shallow, brownish lake. Frigates circled overhead, making no sound. Like discovering The Lost Lagoon, we thought. We'll return in the morning. But now we have to set up camp. It's getting late.

No problem, we thought, plenty of high ground and tree shelter for the tent. My sister has a saying that goes, "If it's not one thing, it's five." One of those "things" there was the bugs—so many, so hungry, so active in the calm air, that we had to spend the night walking up and down the beach pursued by stinging swarms.

The second "thing" on our karmic agenda happened the following day when we portaged *Manatee* across the lagoon for a little exploration. A twenty-five-knot wind wailed across the lagoon when we set sail. We tacked across the deepening shoals. With such wind, it took all our concentration to keep the sail working but not overloaded, balanced with the right amount of hiking to windward and the sheet free to fly. The movements were a delicate dance. Suddenly, a loud snap and *Manatee* skidded to leeward; we reeled off balance. I heard a shout and Michael lurched overboard. Very soon we were in ankle-deep water and jumped out to see what happened. The aluminum angle iron that supports the three-foot dagger-leeboard wasn't strong enough. It had fatigued and fractured.

That afternoon, Michael designed shorter, triangular boards and external slots into which the boards fit to brace against the topsides. The new boards cause less strain on the bracket. Because they are such an improvement over traditional dagger-leeboards, our triangular boards deserve a little description. They are cut from 3/4-inch marine plywood, appropriately flared, glassed, and painted. The equilateral triangle is designed to be mounted to the angle bracket by one corner so that an edge and the other two corners are in the water, board down. The design is to have about 180 square inches per board in the water. Braced against the hull as ours are, these boards cause so little stress that they have not fractured even the commercial cast aluminum angle bracket which pivots them on the thwart. As a plus, the boards cut our draft from three feet to one foot, with no appreciable change in sailing performance.

127

Manatee served us well. She sails easily and fast. Her stowage capacity allowed us to use her as a shopping basket in the small villages. She even served as a taxi, relaying our guests to and from local airports. She won't sink even if we break her into little pieces. And we've tried (though unwittingly). One night she slipped anchor, washed up on a razor-sharp coral, and spent the whole night lifting and falling with the waves—fully loaded with about five hundred pounds of gear! Yet she showed only minor dents and scratches when we found her next morning, abandoned by the tide and balanced on two sharp coral spikes. If she *is* ever holed (she never has been), the ABS plastic is easily repaired with an inexpensive field kit. One more test we put to her. When we had the canoe shipped to Martinique, a crane picked her up by the ends, fully loaded with a thousand pounds of gear. Horrified, we waited to see her buckle. She didn't.

The catamaran is a fast sailer, a great dive platform, and an efficient tug. We cruised effortlessly along at five knots, found those far-out uncharted and uninhabited shores, sailed our boats over reef and sandbars with only four inches of water, carried and rolled them onto the beach, made camp and lived off the sea and land. We had a few maintenance labors or expenses. It took just minutes to set sail and be off. We sailed to get water, to get food from a reef or a settlement, to check out an exposed sandbar for shells, to have fun.

•

Getting There

Boats can be shipped to the Bahamas from the Miami/Ft. Lauderdale area. For a current list of ships that serve the port to which you wish your boat shipped, check the Yellow Pages, write to the companies, and write to the port officials in the Bahamas. Palm Beach Steamship Agency, 4 East Port Road, Suite 404, Riviera Beach, FL 33404, will ship a boat to the Abacos.

In the Bahamas, you will have to post a bond for your boat. To find out the cost of this, you can write to the customs office of the port in the Bahamas. This bond is refunded when you leave Bahamian waters if you stay no longer than six months.

Outfitting

The object in fitting out is to make yourself as independent of stores as possible. Take spare parts and a few tools; diving equipment; Hawaiian slings, spring-steel spears, flippers, and mask with snorkel; containers in which to store water and food; a comfortable tent if you aren't sleeping aboard; books; travelers checks. (Out-island natives are very friendly and generous. Too often I've seen them taken advantage of by travelers who come ill equipped to take care of themselves.) Food and water are available from nearly every settlement. "The Yachtsman's Guide to the Bahamas," has the charts and information you need. DO NOT leave it behind.

A Word to the Wise

Some islands and some pieces of islands are private. If you wish to land, immediately ask for permission from the owner or caretaker. Most of the land is Crown Land, and it is officially against the law to camp on these lands. It would be unwise to stay on them longer than a few days. Most of the good camping spots are not far from the small settlements. The people are friendly, and you are less likely to be asked to move on than you would be if in a more isolated area. Today, there is a greater problem with drug smugglers and the police. It's better to stay out of the way of both. Your small boat is your greatest asset.

•

Our friend, Judy, visited our camp in the Bahamas, bringing the current year's magazines. During the heat of mid-day, we sat in shade under tarps.

Following is another article by Ida Little that was printed in Small Boat Journal #52, December/January 1987. Their editor, Richard Lebovitz, gave us permission to reprint it here. Their address is 2100 Powers Ferry Road, Atlanta, GA 30339.

As mentioned in the Editor's Preface, we are including reprints of four magazine articles by Ida Little, that give you some of the flavor of their adventurous life. Besides the two articles found here, others are at the ends of Chapters 7 and 9.

CANOE CRUISING IN THE CARIBBEAN: IN SEARCH OF ANSE DUFOUR

A lightweight canoe opens up new vistas for explorers of the Caribbean.
by Ida Little

Though we wear wide hats with neck flaps, and keep our shirts wetted with sea water, we are still roasting alive. Sweat drips down my forehead, stings my eyes, and fogs my glasses. To starboard, the dry, rocky coast of Martinique floats in and out of focus. My mind reels from the sun.

Michael squirms in the sweat slippery canoe. Two gommiers, native fishing canoes, row by and distract us from the heat. One man begins casting a net over the side, much like a planter scattering seed across a field. The rowers move the gommiers in a wide circle, while the crew hurl stones, bang sticks, and slap the water, scaring the fish into the seine as we sail farther and farther away. Lordy, it's hot!

Faith, I tell myself, Louise assured us that if we keep sailing up the coast about 10 miles past St. Pierre, we will come to the bay named Anse Dufour. There, *sûrement,* we will find the cool, secluded, jungle paradise we seek.

In this heat, it's easy to forget that's why we came here three weeks ago. Actually we didn't plan to come to Martinique at all. We meant to go to Dominica, a West Indian island 20 miles north of here. An island of such savage, uncontrollable jungle that few people can survive it. At least, that's how we imagined it from the comfort of an air-conditioned library while looking over a colorful National Geographic map. We hoped these extreme conditions could assure us isolated, jungle-bound beaches to explore and enjoy.

The selection of Dominica four months ago was the culminating decision of a vague longing started one hot day in the desert dry Bahamas. We'd just finished replenishing our stock of precious fresh water from a neighbor's cistern. I turned to Michael, sweating from the exertion, and said wistfully, "You know what I'd really like? I'd like to go to some cool, lush, wet jungle dripping with fresh water and vines."

That vision floats across my mind as I pull off my shirt and dip it in the sea. Even the shore looks sun-burned. Dry, rocky, and bare. Brown grasses wave from the crests of tall cliffs; the cactus gesture obscenely. Lush jungle, indeed.

The Best Laid Plans

My mind retreats to the cool library. Big soft chairs. Gentle lights. So easy to imagine taking a 17-foot sailing canoe and cruising the coast of tropical

Dominica. We'd cruise close to shore, just as we'd done for years in the Bahamas (see "Bahama Sojourn," *SBJ#35*), and we'd enjoy all the fine details of isolated coast. Rugged, no doubt, but more than compensated for in wild grandeur and solitude, the stuff we thrive on.

Getting there with all our gear was a problem, though. Airlines couldn't handle the canoe. But the *Rotterdam*, a luxurious cruise ship, agreed to carry us and all our gear the 1,500 miles.

After all our planning and equipping for the six-month cruise, it was a great relief to actually be under way. The crew of the huge ship slung our canoe *Crapaud* on board like a child's toy and tucked her into a corner of the foredeck. We could finally relax. We lounged by the pool. Feasted on seven-course meals. Danced. Slept in a plush stateroom. Forgot about tomorrow, except for that one unresolved problem: The *Rotterdam* did not stop in Dominica. We'd have to disembark at nearby Martinique . . . and what then?

The most crowded, hassled place on Martinique is Fort de France. And that's where the *Rotterdam* pushed us out of our nest. Right into a rain squall. Steep seas swamped the canoe, soaked the gear, and made a hell out of our landfall. We wallowed to the nearest dock and tried to figure out what to do.

I walked into town with a sinking sensation, hoping to find a hotel. Not only did I not speak French, but I looked like a freak. Straggly wet hair. Pink shorts and bright orange life vest. A look of panic and desperation. A cross between tourist and refugee. Cars jammed the streets, people crowded the sidewalks. Horns blasted, people yelled and pushed. I tried, but nobody understood; they were all in a hurry.

"It's no use," I reported to Michael. "We might as well get on with it."

The relief to finally be off and on our own came as a surprise to both of us. We had everything we needed. A tent, sleeping pads, small stove, kerosene and kerosene lantern, 5-gallon water jug, a box of books, a 10-pound fruit cake, and a classical guitar. Too much! There was barely enough room for us.

Since the wind was blowing hard out of the north, we elected to head south. After careening across the Fort de France bay, we crash landed on the first available beach—a pretty beach, but like most lovely accessible beaches, cluttered with people, umbrellas, and lounge chairs. So here we were, a thousand miles from home, in a country with a strange tongue, sailing in search of wild, secluded jungle beaches and we end up on a French Riviera.

Que será será. We stripped to our suits and joined the people in the pool.

Michael was making a dive off the board when he noticed a small islet a mile or so offshore. We'd hardly noticed it on the chart, but considering the lack of privacy here, a speck of island looked like just the thing.

We crossed the choppy water and landed in the lee. No people, but a picnic table made us suspicious. We scouted around for signs of use. Nothing recent. We explored farther and found a trail, steep and overgrown, leading up the side of the islet to the ruins of an abandoned 17th-century fort. Nobody around. Perfect.

We hid the canoe and carried all our gear up the trail. We pitched the tent on a concrete roof and set up a kitchen on an old stone bench. Below us lay the bowels of the fort. Around us, fortress walls and cannon slots. Perched on the edge of the wall, feet dangling into space, we munched sardine sandwiches and watched boats sail across the bay.

We were still there long after the sun set. By dark, Fort de France twinkled in strands of light . . . a fallen piece of starry sky. We didn't say much. Just sat there, feeling a little odd and very private.

The old fort was just the first of a series of unusual encampments during our first weeks in Martinique. There just weren't many good campsites along the southwest coast. When the winds became favorable for heading north, we sailed past Fort de France and found only one tiny beach on which to pitch a pitiful camp. And it was right in front of a lovely villa.

"No privacy. No shade. No jungle. No beautiful streams. We have got to get to Dominica somehow . . . *soon,*" I wrote in my logbook.

Michael suggested we get the people in the villa to mail our letters. Fat chance, I thought, but I was wrong. Louise de Reynal offered us her beach-side lean-to as a *base camp!* This whirlwind of a 65-year-old was enthusiastically sympathetic to our voyage and to our company. If not for her, we would never have heard of Anse Dufour.

She'd been there as a child some 60 years ago. Her father had hired a gommier to ferry the family the 3 miles from Grand Rivière. There was no other way to get to the small bay lying in the shadow of a volcano. No road. Not even a trail. Still isn't. The jungle is too thick and the mountains too crumpled and steep to penetrate. Any time anybody has tried, a cyclone lashes out and washes the effort away, or earthquakes collapse it.

Minimal Cruising

"Better head out a little," Michael warns. Ahead of us a lone gommier rides at the beginning of a long seine. Two men in ragged shirts and conical straw hats haul on opposite ends of the net. Hot, frustrating work. We've seen gommiers labor over an hour, locating the fish, throwing out the nets, hauling it in, only to harvest one kilo of 6-inch ballyhoo. In Florida, fishermen use ballyhoo for bait. Here, the villagers prize them as one of the few fresh fish available.

Everybody's in luck today. The gommiers have filled the boat with flapping needle-nosed silver. They row towards shore, and we sail for the dock in the middle of St. Pierre. Since this is the last sizable village between here and Anse Dufour, we want to buy our fresh food here.

We weave our way through to the central, open marketplace. Vendors sit, stand, lean, talk idly behind their tables. We stroll down one row, then another, stopping to purchase red ripe tomatoes, shriveled purple and yellow eggplant, prickly pale yellow *christophene,* dirty brown *ignam,* foot-long sweet peppers.

The sellers are all sturdy, black women who've grown or collected the produce for the market. And they are fair to a fault. No skimping on weights or coins. If anything, they are too generous. With armloads of veggies, we move down the street to a *supermarché* where we collect powdered milk, coffee, sardines in tins, local sugar, local rum, camembert cheese, and smoked ham. From there, we go to a nearby *boulangerie* and purchase a dozen flaky fresh pastries.

By the time we finish our shopping, the streets are clogged with noonday shoppers. It is a relief to climb into *Crapaud* and be off. Too many people. Too close. Time to find a place where we can be alone.

It's not that we hate people. It's just that when cruising in a small, open daysailer we depend on the shore for private space. Five years ago, we were here in our 40-foot *Sheldrake,* and when we got tired of hassles and crowds ashore, we just retreated to our flaoting island. It was shelter, security, stowage, a means of maintaining our distance. It was our space, and our spaceship.

But these blessings of a big cruiser were also its curse. Instead of cruising *in* different places, we cruised *to* and *from,* *around* and *between.* The Virgin Islands, Puerto Rico, Venezuela, the West Indies. In my mind, they're all a blur of anchorages.

I remember more about *Sheldrake* than of the places we visited. I was too busy and distracted worrying about her. Every time I went ashore, part of me stayed behind to "protect our home." She and the goodies inside represented "big investment." I wasn't about to go traipsing off with *Sheldrake* at anchor in a strange harbor. No, sir! With *Crapaud,* though, we surrender ourselves to the place, its people, and its culture. It's what gives our cruise character.

And so we choose our cruising ground carefully. We study its geography, climate, and culture. We prepare ourselves with equipment and information to be self-supporting and self-sustaining. We plan ahead (see sidebar "Planning Ahead". *Editor's note: It's at the end of this chapter.*)

Some don't. The two Antioch students who came to the Bahamas while we were there had decided to go to a deserted Bahama island to experience "solitude and independence," a sort of survival test trip. Well, they didn't have a boat. So old man Kirky gave them a lift in his dory to a barren, buggy island. His island. A tin shack and a wood fire had been his "comforts of home" for 10 years or more. The students set up their pup-tent a few hundred yards away. Soon they were begging water from Kirky.

And when Kirky cooked coffee over his fire, they horned in on that too. A week later, smelly, hungry, burned, and fatigued, they hailed us for a ride to the mailboat. They hadn't researched or equipped themselves with the neccessities of sustaining an independent survival trip. And they left as dumb as they came.

Paradise

A rancid stench reminds me that we are still abreast of the St. Pierre garbage dump. Martinique must be adrift and moving northward with us.

"What's the deal?"

"Wind slacked off," Michael tells me, "quite a while ago, space cadet."

We fold the sail rig, stash it along the gunwales, and take up the paddles. The burning garbage dump falls behind. I paddle mechanically. The shore shakes off the signs of enterprise.

The heat of the day is passing, thank God. I no longer have to wet my shirt. I suggest we land, if only for a moment, at Anse Ceron. Four people, near shore, cavort in the waves. One brave girl tries body-surfing and for several moments disappears in the froth. Michael says he'd rather keep on going so that we're sure to reach Anse Dufour before dark. I hastily agree. The seas increase as we approach the north end of the island. Atlantic rollers surge. On the top of one we catch sight of the village Grande Rivière and far beyond—Dominica!

The sun slants an orange glow onto the massive cliffs towering overhead. Cape St. Martin. I get a crick in my neck looking up. Michael says he sees why nobody's tried to put a road across this part of the coast. "C'est formidable!" said most of the Martiniquais who'd been here. Overwhelming green broken by brown slashes of avalanching earth. House-sized boulders threatening to fall.

I'm thrown off balance as a roller surges under and beyond us. It races full speed at the shoulder of the cliff to heave thousands of Atlantic miles of momentum into a smash of white.

We are nearly beyond the next bay when Michael says, "Hey, Ida, that's it, I think . . . Anse Dufour." Unfortunately, it all fits. There's the river just like Louise described. But *no beach.* Bare rocks washed by surf. I know Michael is thinking about cosmic rhythms bringing forth sand and washing sand away. The universe is a mighty tiny place right now. To my right, solid cliff. To the left, a tall jagged rock. A wave lifts under us and speeds on. Twenty-five yards from shore it crests, hovers, then crashes. Froth surges through the rocks then falls back in a great sigh. Stones tumble and rumble in the backwash. I can sense what is going to happen to my body. Mind and body are in full accord. Run! But it's too late in the day to turn back now.

I laugh, nervously. Michael continues staring ahead. Without a word, we each begin to prepare for a landing. I feel as if every motion is against my will. Michael lifts his legs and straddles the bow; I lift mine over the gunwales, and snap the canoe cover closed.

We wait, poised like anxious riders at the gate, pulsing with each heaving sea. The moment comes. There's no time for hesitation or doubt. We paddle in a mad dash for the shore. Harder! The waves roar up from behind, shoving me so high that Michael looks as if he's far below. The bow digs under as the stern whips around. *Crapaud* trips, throwing us both into the sea. A line lashed my face and I grab on to it just before *Crapaud* careens into the cliff. Frantically, we half-swim to where we can get our footing and wrestle *Crapaud* out of the sea. Each wave washes and pounds her higher. And suddenly it's over. We've made it. The canoe is safe. Energy spent, we collapse in a gasping heap. But not for long. We've got to clear a site for the tent before dark.

We awaken warm, listening to frogs chirpings in a background of pounding surf. Step from the tent into the hot glare of sun. Plunge into the cool virgin river and awaken our flesh, our minds, to admire and explore. For days. Alone.

We build a dam in the river to form a deep pool. In the pool, we float sweet smelling jungle blossoms. Tiring of body surfing in the sea, we lie on a bit of warm black sand, and watch Dominica fade in and out of sight. Then cool in the pool. Come out fresh for a lunch of French bread, smoked ham, camembert, a glass of wine.

We climb up the mountain. Learn to know our way by the clump of bamboo here, the tall fern tree there, the slope of the hill as it rises to the ridge. Discover the ruins of an elaborate plantation effort. Roof tiles. Broken dishes. A bottle. The traces of an aqueduct. Heavy stone walls. Farther up, through bamboo thickets, a herd of wild goats grazes.

Evening rum punch. Playing "count the eels swim up the river" by kerosene light. Another bath in the moonlight. A crayfish tries to feed on me. It's cold. To-night we use a light blanket. Rain. The tree frogs peep all night. Exploring up the river, we discover coco trees with yellow fruit on one bank. Farther up, the jungle darkens into a solid canopy a hundred feet above, supported by buttressed tree trunks 8 feet across. Water cascades into deep pools. Crayfish hide under rocks. Too fast to catch. Higher upstream, hot water streams from a cliff crevice. Return to camp to swim. And when tired, to bathe and be refreshed.

This solitude, this feast for the senses, this paradise—this is Anse Dufour.

•

Planning Ahead

Equipment
• 17-foot ABS Old Town Canoe with sail rig and complete, snap-down cover: The canoe is rugged, comfortable, and light. The sail rig was minimally useful as we usually stayed too close to the west shore to catch the never-ending easterly wind.

• 4-man, 6-pound Stephenson tent: It's home. Large but lightweight and not bulky, and insect proof. ("Warmlite," Gilford, NH)

• Voyageur Waterproof canoe bags (Voyageur's, Ltd., PO Box 409, Gardner, KS 66030). They kept our cameras, bedding, papers, books, and other necessities dry

• Optimus stove and small kerosene lantern

• Collapsible water jugs

• Sling chairs. Sitting on the ground with no backrest is no fun.

Food for Thought
We researched general conditions of West Indian islands that would affect us as campers; especially climate, specific dangers, and social conditions. We learned, for example, to avoid bathing in streams that might carry schistosomiasis and

to keep an eye out for the deadly fer-de-lance snake on Martinique.

Words to Those Who Would Follow

Times change. Places change. Today the old fort island is blocked; and one beach campsite is taken by an enormous electrical plant. Anse Dufour, happily, remains as elusive and isolated as before.

•

Preparing to launch *Crapaud* on the SW coast of Martinique. We first carry her to the edge of the sea, then load our gear aboard.

CHAPTER 6

SOME OPEN BOATS RECOMMENDED FOR BEACHCRUISING

People who like to go exploring by water will go in just about anything. One lady cruised with an inner tube. Plenty of people cruise with open board boats, windsurfers, and undecked catamarans. We list a few board multihull boats that are designed for sailing in shallow water and beaching. All these boats have been used at some time for beachcruising.

ADVANTAGES OF OPEN BOATS

So, why go with an open boat and not a boat with a sleeping cuddy? We cruise in open boats because they are small and light enough to lift or drag ashore. But there are many good reasons for wanting an open boat instead of a cuddy boat. Being small and lightweight makes them easy to lift, haul on a trailer, put on top of a car, carry up a beach, and stash away. They don't cost as much to buy or to maintain. They're easier to sail, more easily sailed alone, and may sail better than their bigger cuddy cousins.

Open boats are almost all cockpit. You go out in them to be outdoors. If there is no cuddy, you cannot "go below." You either sleep out under the stars, or erect a tent. With a cuddy, you are more likely to sleep "indoors" and a lot less likely to bother setting up a tent ashore. When you need shelter aboard an open boat, you can erect a fabric cockpit tent. You have a choice of whether to have a "cabin" or not, and the material for making one doesn't have the burdensome weight that a solid cuddy cabin has.

For you project-oriented types, open boats are easier to modify and change than cuddy boats. When you start out with less, there's less to change, and more room to create. There's an article about modifying some open boat or other in most issues of Boat Journal.

More people own, sail, race and cruise small open boats than small cuddy boats. So open boaters have more opportunity to enjoy cruising and racing camaraderie through class associations.

DISADVANTAGES OF OPEN BOATS

As a general rule, open boats are more uncomfortable than cuddy boats. Not "less comfortable," because small cuddy boats are not what you'd call comfortable. Just, more uncomfortable. In an open boat you get wet from rain, burnt from sun and wind, and splashed with spray. Small seats can't provide much leg room, good back or fanny support. You cannot stand up to stretch your legs easily or for long. If you sleep aboard, open boats are more difficult to protect against mosquitoes and no-see-ums than cuddy boats.

Open boats are less stable than the heavier cuddy boats, so you not only stand up less, but you move around less and with more caution.

Weight and bulk matter a great deal to an open boat. You've got to pack more frugally and with more attention to space-saving equipment. There's not much room, much less protected room, for stowage in small open boats.

SOME OPEN BOATS RECOMMENDED FOR BEACHCRUISING

Editor's note: In their vast beachcruising travels, Ida and Michael have seen a variety of small open boats used for beachcruising. These are their picks for the best of the lot. As described in Chapters 5 and 7, canoes, cuddy boats, and even larger boats are suitable. So are other designs of open boats that can be converted for beachcruising. So if you do not have or can't afford one of these beauties, don't let this deter you from beachcruising in whatever boat is available to you. We had a great five years cruising a 17-foot flat-bottom, centerboard, lapstrake and heavily constructed open boat, camping on beaches. We see other people doing this for short periods in just about any kind of boat, including outboard-powered skiffs of all sizes and kinds.

Following this list are more detailed descriptions of each recommended boat.

Holder 14 MKII

L.O.A. 13′ 8″
L.W.L. 12′
Beam 6′ 2″
Draft board up: 5″; board down: 3′ 2″
Weight: 275 pounds
Capacity: four adults, gear, and outboard
Sail Area: main: 70 sq. ft.; jib: 37 sq. ft.; spinnaker optional
Sail Rig: Marconi sloop
Reefing System: roller furling jib optional; none for main
Hull: fiberglass and foam. Hard chine
Cockpit Length: about 8′, self bailing
Mast Length: 18′ 7″
Centerboard and Rudder: spring loaded for kick-up
Stowage: under decks fore and aft
Builder: Hobie Cat, P.O. Box 1008, Oceanside, CA 92054

Holder 14 Mark II under sail

Courtesy of Hobie Cat

Pacific Pelican (Kit Boat)

L.O.A 14' 7"
Length on the Floor: 13' 1"
Beam: 6' 1"
Draft board up: 5"; board down: 3' 8"
Weight: if ⅜" glassed: 600 pounds; if ¼" glassed: 540 pounds
Sail Area main: 105 sq. ft.; jib: 40 sq. ft.
Sail Rig: standing lug sloop (with boom and yard)
Reefing System: handled from the cockpit; not jiffy
Hull: Banks dory/pram with Oriental sampan bow
Cockpit Length: about 8'
Flotation: self-rescuing
Centerboard and Rudder: kick-up
Designer: Jim and Edward Barlow

Builder/Source of Plans: Bay Boat Co., 350 Demeter St., E. Palo Alto, CA 94303

Built since 1984

Good Points: instruction book gives step-by-step instructions that help the builder deal with both materials and tools

Cost: flyer $6; book, plans and paper patterns: $85

Courtesy of Edward Barlow

Pacific Pelican **under sail with her lug rig**

Drascombe Dabber

L.O.A. 15' 6"
L.W.L. 13' 7"
Beam: 5' 10"
Draft board up: 8"; board down: 3'
Weight: 550 pounds
Capacity: two people and gear for a week's cruise
Sail Area main: 83 sq. ft.; jib: 21 sq. ft.; mizzen: 14 sq. ft.
Sail Rig: standing lug; loose-footed
Reefing System main: reef points provided, and cringle; jib: none
Hull: lapstrake, double hard chine, rounded sides. Fiberglass with replaceable hardwood keel and bilge "rubbers"
Decks: none
Cockpit Length: about 8½'; self bailing: no; side decks: no; floorboards: yes
Flotation: built-in expanded polystyrene foam; will float and support crew
Self-rescuing: no
Mast Length: about 15'; 9 kg. weight (about 20 #). How stepped: through thwart onto the keel. Stays: fore and side stays
Sheeting Arrangement main: on the tiller; jib: amidship cleats; mizzen: cleated at stern
Rudder: kick-up: no. Mounts: gudgeons (hardware to receive pins on the rudder) on stern
Centerboard Tackle: blocks and line. Case: open. Weight: about 55 pounds
Rowing Ability: oarlocks provided
Motoring Provision: outboard well for up to 4 H.P. motor
Racing: no
Stowage: aft locker with padlock. Not watertight. Under seats and forward beside centerboard
Covers: cockpit cover for mooring/trailering. Flat overall cover for storing. Folding pram hood canopy
Good Points: replaceable bilge and keel hardwood rubbers. Bilge pump for bailing under floor boards. Aft covered compartment makes comfortably wide seat
Bad Points: rudder doesn't kick up. Bow sprit makes jib harder to get at; forestay interferes with jib sheet. Lug rig slightly unwieldy; jiffy reefing system would have to be installed. Three stays to rig and maintain. Three sets of sheets to handle besides centerboard and rudder
Modifications/Additions: jiffy reefing. Kick-up rudder

Ida and Michael take a *Drascombe Dabber* out for a sail

Chris Harkness launching his *Drascombe Dabber.* He can go sailing on the spur of
the moment because the launch only took 10 minutes

Drascombe Lugger

L.O.A. 18' 9"

L.W.L. 15'

Beam: 6' 3"

Draft board up: 10"; board down: 4'

Weight: 748 pounds

Capacity: five adults plus gear for one week, including 40 gallons of water

Sail Area main:74 sq. ft. ; jib: 36 sq ft.; mizzen: 22 sq. ft.

Sail Rig: gunter lug, yawl; loose-footed (no booms)

Reefing Arrangement main: reef points provided and cringles; jib: roller furling

Hull: lapstrake; double hard chine

Decks: none

Cockpit Length: 6'

Flotation: built-in polystyrene foam

Self-rescuing: no

Mast: wood, about 18' long; about 24 pounds. Pivoted into notch in thwart

Sheeting Arrangement main: traveler across back of cockpit with block; jib: cleats amidships; mizzen: cleated far aft just ahead of transom

Rudder: kick-up rudder optional (but must be removed when beached). Mount: through a rudder trunk

Centerboard: about 24 pounds

Drascombe Lugger   *Courtesy Honor Marine*

142

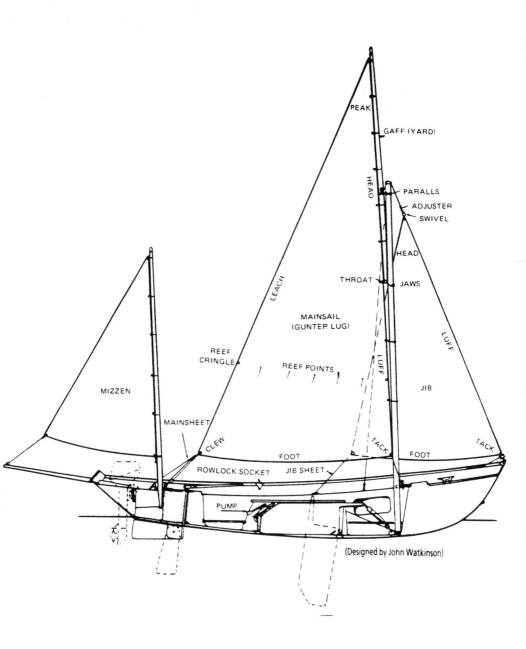

PEAK

GAFF (YARD)

HEAD

PARALLS

ADJUSTER

SWIVEL

HEAD

THROAT

JAWS

LEACH

MAINSAIL
(GUNTER LUG)

LUFF

REEF
CRINGLE

REEF POINTS

MIZZEN

LUFF

JIB

MAINSHEET

CLEW

TACK

FOOT

TACK

ROWLOCK SOCKET

JIB SHEET

FOOT

PUMP

(Designed by John Watkinson)

Line drawing of *Drascombe Lugger*

Courtesy Honor Marine

Drascombe Longboat

L.O.A. 21' 9"

L.W.L. 18'

Beam: 6' 7"

Draft board up: 1'; board down: 4' 2"

Weight: 880 pounds

Capacity: six adults and gear

Sail Area main: 94 sq. ft.; jib: 56 sq. ft.; mizzen: 22 sq. ft.

Sail Rig: sliding gunter, yawl

Reefing Arrangement main: reef points and cringles provided; jib: roller reefing

Hull, Decks, Flotation: same as Dabber

Cockpit Length: about 10'; about 24 pounds; floorboards

Mast Length: about 21'. Stepped by pivoting on foot into slot in thwart

Sheeting Arrangement main: traveler on stern with block; jib: cleated amidships; mizzen: aft of cockpit

Rudder: kick-up but must be removed to beach. Mounted through a rudder trunk

Centerboard: about 88 pounds

Rowing Ability: three pairs of oarlocks; 8½' oars

Motor Provision: outboard well for 6-8 H.P. motor

Racing: no

Stowage: locker under aft compartment. Four cave lockers under side benches. Side bench locker

Covers: cockpit cover. Flat overall cover. Pramhood canopy. Cockpit tent complete with hoops

Good Points: roller furling jib. Bilge pump. Main choice boat of the members of the Dinghy Cruising Associations of England and America. Proven to perform well in 15–20 knots with wind with a steep chop (off Baja). Carries a maximum load for its length. A lot has been written about cruising this boat. Choice boat of cruise camp outfitters. Used with success in charter business in Baja California. Carries a lot of weight for its size. Moves well in chop

Bad Points: three sets of sheets, halyards, rudder, and centerboard line to handle. Rudder can jam inside the trunk if bent

Modifications/Additions: cuddy cabin, smaller jib and add genoa

Drascombe Dabber, Lugger, and Longboat

Designer: John Watkinson

Builder: Honnor Marine (U.K.) Ltd., Bridge Mills, Staverton; Totnes, Devon TQ9 6AP, U.K.

Cost: delivered to nearest container port in U.S.: Dabber, $6,500, 800 built; Lugger, $7,795, 1,600 built; Longboat, $9,000, 950 built

Books/Articles/Cruises

Dabber: *The Drascombe Dabber* and *The Elbow of the Neuse* by Chris Harkness in Small Boat Journal Feb./Mar. 1982

Lugger: *Lugger in the Keys* by Betty Willauer in Small Boat Journal Nov. 1980/Jan. 1981

Books by Ken Duxbury: *Lugworm On The Loose; Lugworm Homeward Bound; Lugworm Island Hopping*

Books by Webb Chiles: *Open Boat-Across the Pacific; The Ocean Waits*

The Seagoing Drascombe by Hans Vandermissen, available from Honnor Marine

Dinghy Cruising Association Bulletins—see additional information at end of this chapter

Baja Expeditions: crewed trips in the Sea of Cortez in Drascombe Luggers and Longboats: Douglas Knapp, Small Boat Cruising Center, P.O. Box 881-833, San Francisco, CA 94188-1833

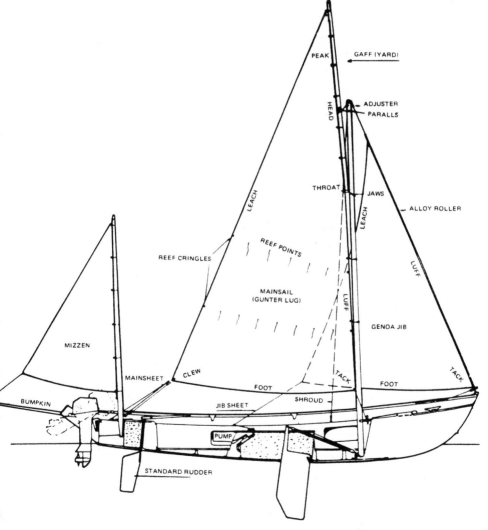

Line drawing of *Drascombe Longboat*   *Courtesy Honor Marine*

Wayfarer

L.O.A. 15' 10"

L.W.L. about 14' 10"

Beam: 6' 1"

Draft board up: 8"; board down: 3' 10"

Hull Weight: 372 pounds

Capacity: about 600 pounds (the company says there's capacity for a family of six)

Sail Area main: 95 sq. ft.; jib: 30 sq. ft.; genoa: 46 sq. ft.; spinnaker: 145 or 195 sq. ft.

Sail Rig: Marconi sloop

Reefing System main: none; jib: none

Hull Shape: double hard chine with slightly rounded bottom. Material: wood or fiberglass

Decks: at bow and stern

Cockpit Length: about 9'. Width: wide enough for a medium to slim build adult to lie down alongside each side of the centerboard. 6" side decks. Removable floor boards

Flotation: watertight compartments fore and aft. Self-rescuing (Ensolite buoyancy pocket at mast head helps)

Mast Length: about 25'. Stepped: by pivoting into tabernacle in deck. Material: wood or aluminum. Stays: side and fore stays

Sheeting Arrangement main: traveler on stern then forward to mid-cockpit; jib: jam cleats amidships

Rudder: kick-up. Mounted on stern gudgeons

Rowing Ability: no provision

Motor Provision: outboard motor mount on stern; or outboard may be clamped to transom. 2½ H.P. motor moves fully loaded boat at 3½ knots

Racing: numerous racing fleets

Stowage: watertight compartments fore and aft; below seats

Covers: boom tent available from manufacturer

Good Points: strong class membership, association, and cruising groups. Long history of being cruised and many accounts of cruises. Proven seaworthy by extreme tests made at sea by Frank and Margaret Dye

Bad Points: side and forestays to rig and maintain. Main sheet interrupts cockpit

Modifications/Additions: storm jib; spray dodger for those "marvelous wet thrashes"; jiffy reefing system for mainsail; jib downhaul; lanyard to rudder pin for quick release; cam cleats for sheets; fasten copper strips on keel with adhesive instead of screws which "work" then begin to leak

Designer: Ian Proctor in 1957 for cruising off the South Devon coast of England

Builder: fiberglass version: Abbott Boats Ltd., 1458 London Rd., Sarnia, Ontario N7S 1P7, Canada. Builder for over 35 years. Over 9,000 built. Cost: $4,500. Wood kit version: Wayland Marine Ltd., Ron Mueller, 8686 West 68th Ave., Arvada, CO 80004. Approximate number of man hours to build: 432. Cost: $3,300

Associations and Newsletters: U.S. Wayfarer Association, 688 Glenhurst, Birmingham, MI 48009. 150 members, quarterly publication called the Skimmer. Canadian Wayfarer Association, 980 Concession St., Hamilton, Ontario L8T 1A1, Canada. Alan Phillips, Honorary Librarian. Ask for Cruising Library Catalog: 15 years of cruising stories from members' logs. A deposit of $10 per anthology is refunded if the anthology is returned within three weeks. The anthologies are grouped geographically. Membership Secretary: 16 Pottery Crescent, Bramlea, Ontario L6S 3S3, Canada

Books: Books by Frank and Margaret Dye: *Open Boat Cruising,* and *Ocean Crossing Wayfarer.* Published by David and Charles, Brunel House, Newton Abbott, Devon, U.K. *Dinghy Cruising with Phillips* by Alan Phillips. Available from Ken Elliott, 56 The Esplanada #403, Toronto, Ontario M5E 1A7, Canada. The Wayfarer Cruising Anthologies available from the Canadian Wayfarer Association

Articles: Wooden Boat Mar./Apr. 1983. Article by David Brooks about building a Wayfarer kit and cruising in Maine. Small Boat Journal #36, May 1984, "The Wayfarer Logs" by Frank and Margaret Dye. Small Boat Journal #44, Aug./Sept., 1986 Wayfarer to Labrador by Geoff Heath

Courtesy U.S. Wayfarer Association

Wayfarer dinghies getting ready for a race. Hand grips on gunwales are for lifting

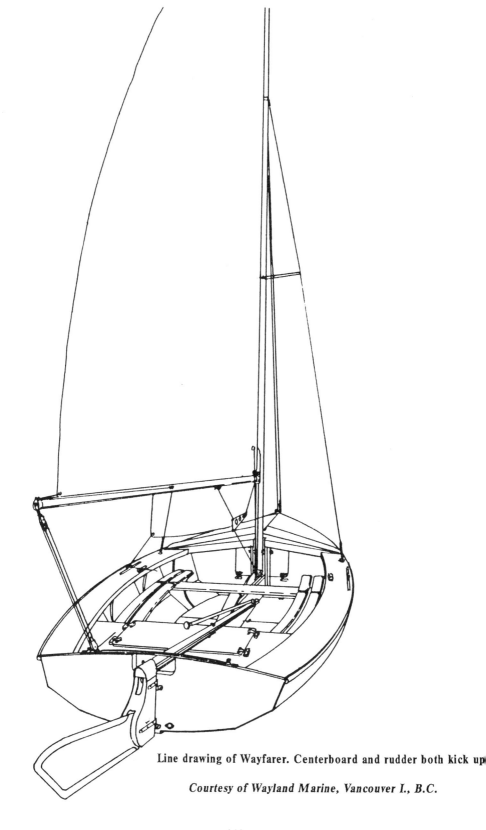

Line drawing of Wayfarer. Centerboard and rudder both kick up

Courtesy of Wayland Marine, Vancouver I., B.C.

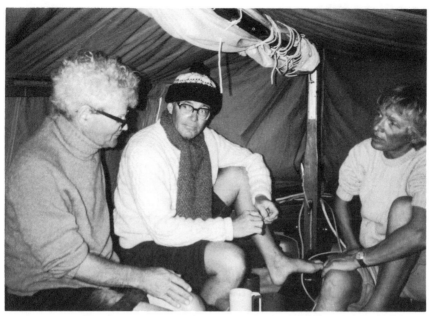

Michael Walsh (center) visiting Frank and Margaret Dye aboard their Wayfarer. The Dyes have rigged a boom tent over the 9-foot cockpit

Courtesy of Ken Elliott

Stowage inside a *Wayfarer*. Aft side-benches removed. Nets under side decks. cockpit area is clear. That's an anchor, chain, and 100 feet of rode, plus the braided line

Town Class Townie

L.O.A. 16' 6"

Beam 5' 9½"

Draft board up: 7"; board down: 2' 4"

Weight wood version: 650 pounds; fiberglass version: 800 pounds

Sail Area: main and jib total 152 sq. ft.

Sail Rig: Marconi sloop

Hull: rounded lapstrake sides, dory-like flat bottom

Mast Length: about 24'

Rudder: kick-up rudder optional

Centerboard: 52 pounds made of brass

Motor Provision: transom reinforced for an outboard

Racing: designed as town class racing boat

Designer: Marcus and Percival Lowell in 1932 as a safe, yet racey, daysailer for summer camp programs. The town of Marblehead, MA, adopted the simple boat as a town class boat that would attract townspeople

Modifications: on the wooden model, the wood below the waterline needs fiberglassing so that it will not dry out when out of the water; reefing system adapted

Builder: Pert Lowell, Co. Lane's End, Newbury, MA 01950. Builder since 1936. 1700 built, with fleets from Maine to Florida

Cost: wood version: (sails are $550 extra from the company) $6,000; fiberglass version: (Ditto on sails) $7,500

Town Class "Townie" Articles: "The Townie's Back in Town" by Bob Hicks. Small Boat Journal #50 Aug./Sept. 1986

Photo by Ron Johnson

The National Park Service allows camping on only a few of the many isles in Florida Bay. Here's a group of *Sea Pearl* cruisers enjoying Rabbit Key.

Line drawing of *Town Class Townie*

Courtesy of Pert Lowell Co.

O'Day Daysailer 3

L.O.A. 16' 9"

L.W.L. 16'

Beam: 6' 3"

Draft board up: 7"; board down: 3' 9"

Weight: 575 pounds (hull alone); 628 pounds (with rigging)

Capacity: 640 pounds (approximately four adults)

Sail Area main and jib total: 145 sq. ft.

Sail Rig: Marconi sloop

Reefing Arrangement main: roller reefing gooseneck available to be used with a claw which the buyer must install; jib: roller furling optional

Hull: wide, flat bottom with flaring sides. Fiberglass

Cockpit Length: about 8'. Floorboards: none. Side decks: 6". Self-bailing: yes

Flotation: high foam buoyancy for possible self rescue

Mast Length: 24' 3". Material: Aluminum with foam filler. Stays: fore and side stays. How stepped: on tabernacle on deck. Weight: 27 pounds

Sheeting Arrangement main: center cockpit with quick release mainsheet cam cleats; jib: cleats amidships

Rudder: kick-up; mounted on stern gudgeons

Centerboard: fiberglass, about 28 pounds. Single line for raising and lowering

Rowing Ability: no provision

Motor Provision: up to 8 H.P. long shaft motor mounted on reinforced transom or optional outboard bracket

Racing: locally; as a class. 89 active daysailer fleets

Stowage: decked forward with lockable wood closure. Built-in ice box and provision for outboard fuel tank in cockpit

Covers: none standard

Good Points: non-skid surfaces. Self-bailing cockpit. Large area of lockable stowage forward

Bad Points: centerboard reputed to stick in its case. Reefing system only partially complete

Modifications: downhaul for jib. Jiffy reefing or roller reefing for main. Make forward stowage watertight. Hinge the mast step

Designer: Uffa Fox, about 1959

Builder: built by the O'Day Corporation for over 30 years. In continuous production until 1988, with over 16,000 built. Now available from your local O'Day dealer.

Warranty: 1 year limited warranty

Cost: $4,600

Associations and Newsletters: Daysailer Association, P.O. Box 1918, Gulf Shores, AL 36542. The Daysailer Quarterly. 650 members

O'Day Day Sailer 3, one of the most popular day sailers ever built. More than 13,000 are still sailing, many in New England. The *3* has a roller furling jib, easily-reefed main, kick-up rudder, centerboard and a flat bottom for beaching

Line drawing of *O'Day Day Sailer 3*

Courtesy of O'Day Corp.

Lowell's 18' Sailing Surf Dory

L.O.A. 18'

Length on Bottom: 14'

Beam: 5' 4"

Draft board up: less than a foot; board down: about 2'

Weight: 340 pounds

Capacity: four adults and gear for a week (this design is particularly capable of carrying a heavy load)

Sail Area for Loose-footed Gunter Sloop main: 97 sq. ft.; jib: 25 sq. ft.

Sail Area for Loose-footed Gunter Yawl main: 97 sq. ft.; jib: 22.5 sq. ft.; mizzen: 21 sq. ft.

Reefing System main: reef points and cringle; jib: none

Hull Shape: Swampscott Dory: lapstrake, round sided, flat bottom, rounded bilges; high end and tombstone transom. Shape gives extra stability in following seas and when beaching through surf. Material: oak and pine with epoxy finish below the waterline which reduces leaks by keeping the wood from drying out and shrinking when stored on a trailer

Cockpit Length: about 9' divided almost in half by center thwart. Floorboards: optional

Flotation: wood, not self-rescuing

Mast Height: about 15'. How stepped: through thwart in bow. Material: Sitka spruce, about 18 pounds rigged. Stays: none on surf boats under 20' in length. Gaff sprit: about 10 pounds

Sheeting Arrangement main: block on transom sheer; jib: cleats amidships

Rudder: kick-up, mounted on gudgeons on stern

Centerboard: lead-weighted wood or aluminum. Block and line for lifting

Rowing Ability: oar locks provided; the dory rows very well

Motor Provision: outboard well, forward of stern seat, with notch in the transom to permit beaching; 4.5 H.P. recommended

Racing: no racing fleets

Stowage: lockers fore and aft

Covers: none provided

Good Points: beautiful looking. Each boat unique. Stable: used by U.S. Life Saving Service (the nearly forgotten past of the Coast Guard) for over 100 years; used by fishermen because it is so stable in a sea with a heavy load. Custom work available: for lockers, seats, etc. No stays. Rows, motors, sails very well. No boom on sail. "Wearfoots" under forefoot and twin skegs for beaching

Bad Points: wood to maintain. Frames infringe on inside floor of cockpit (floorboards are a help in this regard). No bailing arrangement. Floor too short for sleeping

Modifications and Additions: make tent cover and dodger. Create sleeping space using seats and plywood boards. Cam cleats for jib sheets. Block and cam for main sheet. Add styrofoam for higher flotation if swamped

Designer: Simeon Lowell, in 1793 built the first true "dory"

Builder: Jim Odell, Lowell's Boat Shop, 459 Main St., Amesbury, MA 01913. Builder since 1793. Lowell's is the oldest continuously operated boatshop in the USA. Sailing Surf Dories available up to 24' long. Over 160 dories built. Pattern plans available. Jim Odell will tell you cruising stories that he hears all the time from dory owners who stop by the shop

Cost: $8,000

Cruises/Articles: Thor Thorson sailed his 14' Surf Dory from Massachusetts to Nova Scotia three times; he sailed twice to Penobscot Bay, Maine once with another couple aboard. "The Sailing Surf Dory," by Mason Smith. Small Boat Journal #45, Oct./Nov. 1985. A rowing adventure in a dory boat: "Around Vancouver Island in 80 Days", by Steve Gropp, Small Boat Journal, Dec./Jan. 1982

Photo by Mark Halevi

Lowell's *Sailing Surf Dory* underway. The unstayed mast and loose-footed main make her easy to rig and cruise

Lightning

L.O.A. 19'

L.W.L. 15' 3"

Beam: 6' 6"

Draft board up: 6"; board down: 4' 11"

Weight: 700 pounds

Capacity: 900 pounds (or six adults)

Sail Area main: 125 sq. ft.; jib: 52 sq. ft.; spinnaker: 300 sq. ft.

Sail Rig: Marconi sloop

Reefing System main: none; jib: downhaul

Hull Shape: hard chine, slight V bottom. Material: foam cored fiberglass or wood

Decks: foredeck, small stern deck

Cockpit Length: about 9'. Self-bailing (Mueller Boat's Lightning). Side decks: 8"

Flotation: foam core with 7" in the bottom; buoyancy tanks mounted high inside to help keep the boat from turning turtle after a capsize. Self-rescuing

Mast Length: about 25'. How stepped: through the deck. Material: aluminum. Stays: fore, side and back stays

Sheeting Arrangement main: aft then to center of cockpit; jib: cam cleats amidships; spinnaker: continuous sheet through the transom

Rudder: does not kick up. Mounted on gudgeons on stern

Centerboard: 125 pounds; stainless steel. Uses large drum with 10:1 differential

Rowing Ability: needs 8' oars and does not row comfortably

Motor Provision: uses a standard outboard bracket on the transom for a 3 H.P. motor. Older versions have an outboard well

Racing: this boat was designed for racing, with more than 500 racing fleets across the USA

Stowage: no watertight stowage. Decked space forward, up to within 3' of the bow; decked space aft

Covers: cockpit and full covers available: Service Canvas Co., Inc., 131 Swan St., Buffalo, NY 14203. Most local sailmakers will make covers for your Lightning

Good Points: hard chine stability in hull. Heavy, stainless steel centerboard. Old and proven successful design. Self-rescuing. Many racing fleets

Bad Points: no watertight stowage. Rudder does not kick up. Has no reefing system

Modifications/Additions: install kick-up rudder. Use a plywood sleeping board to span the opening between seats and centerboard to create a 30'-36" sleeping area. Sculling arrangement on the stern. Genoa: approximately 100 sq. ft. for light airs. Jiffy reefing. Hard cabin à la David Buckman (see Books and Articles below)

Designer: Olin Stephens (of Sparkman and Stephens), in 1938

Builders: Allen Boat Co., Tom Allen, 655 Fuhrman Blvd., Buffalo, NY 14203; McLaughlin Boat Works, Mike McLaughlin, 4737 Adams Rd., Hixson, TN 37343; Mueller Boat Co., Jack Mueller, 1809 Root Rd., Lorain, OH 44052. More builder's names and addresses available from the International Lightning Class Association. 14,300 Lightnings built continuously since 1938. Over 500 active racing fleets

Cost: $6,500 (without sails)

Associations and Newsletters: International Lightning Class Association, 808 High St., Worthington, OH 43085. Monthly bulletin: Lightning Flashes. Yearbook: includes cruises, and list of current boat owners and their addresses. Over 4,000 members

Books/Articles: *Lightning Manual—Tuning, Tactics, Technique, Sailing*, edited by Tom Bierman and Tryg Jacobsen; available from the I.L.C.A. Yearbook (includes such remarkable cruises as the one in the 1980 Yearbook titled, "Cruising Hawaii in a Lightning," by Morrie and Barb Craig; available from I.L.C.A. Yachting Magazine Dec. 1938. Small Boat Journal 1979 #4 and #5 (parts 1 and 2 about modifying a Lightning for cruising). Cruising World May 1979, "Barebones Cruising: The Simplest Way to Go" by David Buckman. Small Boat Journal, June 1980, "Down East Cruise" and "Domesticating A Lightning" (designing and building a cuddy cabin), by David Buckman. WoodenBoat Magazine #53 July/Aug. 1983, "Building the First Lightning" by Susan Kennedy. Sail Magazine, Dec. 1985, "Barebones Cruising: A Decade of Lightning Adventure" by David Buckman. Small Boat Journal #40, Dec./Jan. 1985, "Long Live the Lightning!" by Susan Peterson

Courtesy International Lightning Class Ass'n

Looking down on a *Lightning*

Line drawing of *Lightning*

Courtesy Patrick M. Royce

An International Racing Class.

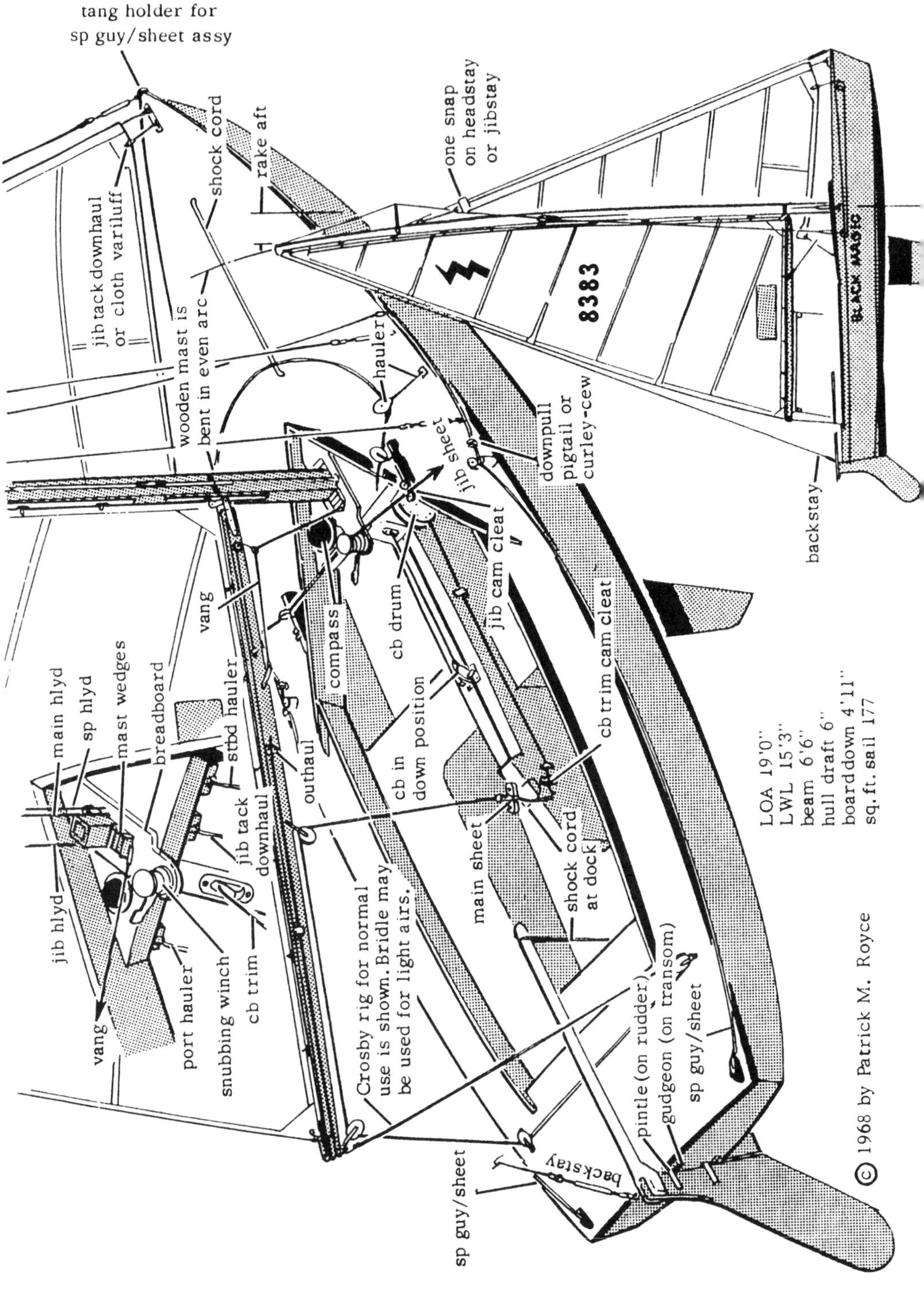

tang holder for
sp guy/sheet assy

one snap
on headstay
or jibstay

shock cord

rake aft

jib tack downhaul
or cloth variluff

wooden mast is
bent in even arc

hauler

hauler

jib sheet

downpull
pigtail or
curley-cew

8383

BLACK MAGIC

backstay

vang

compass

cb drum

jib cam cleat

cb trim cam cleat

main hlyd

sp hlyd

mast wedges

breadboard

stbd hauler

outhaul

cb in
down position

jib hlyd

jib tack
downhaul

cb trim

main sheet

shock cord
at dock

vang

port hauler

snubbing winch

Crosby rig for normal
use is shown. Bridle may
be used for light airs.

pintle (on rudder)

gudgeon (on transom)

sp guy/sheet

LOA 19'0"
LWL 15'3"
beam 6'6"
hull draft 6"
board down 4'11"
sq.ft. sail 177

sp guy/sheet

backstay

© 1968 by Patrick M. Royce

158

Here's a *Lightning* with a home-made cabin. Many people beachcruise *Lightnings* as an open boat, but this conversion adds little weight, has sitting headroom aft, and there are two 7' berths either side of the centerboard trunk. Cabin or no, look at her go! She was designed to race, but is fun to beachcruise

Flying Scot

L.O.A. 19'

L.W.L. 18'

Beam: 7' 6"

Beam at Waterline: 6' 9"

Draft board up: 8"; board down: 4'

Weight: 675 pounds stripped; 850 pounds with sail rig

Capacity: designed for a crew of three. Cruised long distances by two adults with camping gear. Approximately 500 pounds

Sail Area main: 138 sq. ft.; jib: 53 sq. ft.; spinnaker: 200 sq. ft.

Sail Rig: Marconi sloop

Reefing System main: jiffy reefing system available; jib: none

Hull Shape: wide, flat bottom (planing hull) skiff. Material: fiberglass with balsa core

Deck: large decks fore and aft

Cockpit length: about 7'. Self-bailing. Side decks: about 12"

Flotation: styrofoam under side decks; balsa core sandwich deck and hull

Mast length: about 26'. How stepped: on deck. Material: aluminum. Weight: 40 pounds. Stays: side and fore stays

Sheeting Arrangement main: through a block on the tiller to center of cockpit; jib: cam cleats port and starboard

Rudder: kick-up. Mounted with gudgeons on stern

Centerboard weight: 105 pounds (80 pounds lead in tip). Fiberglass. Lifted with 5:1, or 16:1 differential drum winch. Case is completely closed. No pivot pin used

Rowing ability: paddle only

Motor Provision: standard outboard bracket may be mounted on stern

Racing: designed for racing. 162 active racing fleets

Stowage: beneath bow and stern decks

Covers: tent type, over boom, closed forward, open aft. Cockpit cover that drains onto seats and thence overboard for mooring, trailering

Good Points: centerboard falls easily and lifts easily. Class design demands strict building codes so Hull #1 remains competitive today. Hull very stiff initially. Builder very supportive with spare parts, etc.

Bad Points: tall mast. Poor sleeping space in cockpit (needs board across seats). Can turn turtle when capsized. Won't go to weather as well as the finer entry bow designs

Modifications/Additions: use sleeping board across seats

Designer: Gordon "Sandy" Douglass in 1957

Builder: Gordon Douglass Boat Co., Inc. , Eric Ammann, Rt. 4, Box 9K, Deer Park, MD 21550. 4,500 built (about 125 per year) since inception over 30 years ago

Warranty: five years on hull; two years on rigging

Cost: $8,000

Associations and Newsletters: Flying Scot Sailing Association, c/o builder. Bi-monthly publication called Scots N' Water. 1,872 members

Books/Articles: Sailing World, Nov. 1987, "The Secret of the Scot's Success," by Susie Evans. Small Boat Journal #62, Aug./Sept. 1988, "The Flying Scot: An Enduring Family Daysailer Enters its Fourth Decade," by Fred Miller

Cruises: Related in editions of Scots 'N Water. Cruises include the Chesapeake Bay, North Carolina's Outer Banks, the Mississippi River, etc. In the March, May, June, July 1983 issues, "An Epic Scot Journey" Don Stuart describes his cruise from Moosonee, Ontario on James Bay, into Hudson Bay and up the coast of Quebec. A fascinating account. John Harrod of Boston cruises his Scot in the Bahamas for a few weeks every winter.

Photo courtesy Gordon Douglass Boat Company

Flying Scot flies downwind. This popular racer and beachcruiser has 150 active fleets, 4500 built. She comes with boom tent and trailer, and has full flotation

Wilce's Sharpie "Heron"

L.O.A. 19' 3"

L.W.L. 18'

Beam: 5' 7"

Draft board up: 4" (empty), 9" @ 2,000 pound displacement; board down: 2' 8"

Weight: 450 pounds

Capacity: 1,600 pounds

Sail Area fore main: 72 sq. ft.; aft main: 72 sq. ft.

Sail Rig: Bermuda spritsail, cat schooner

Reefing System: roller; the schooner rig also has the option of taking one mast down and re-stepping remaining mast amidships

Hull Shape: Sharpie: flat bottom, appreciable rocker (the bottom of the boat has a curve in it like the legs of a rocker), hard chine with flaring sides. Material: thermoplastic sheet with plastic foam core 3" thick

Cockpit length: about 4'. Width: 22" between seats. Partially self-bailing

Flotation: foam core. Self-rescuing

Masts length: 20'. How stepped: through the deck into PVC tubes. Material: wood (fir). Weight: 30 pounds maximum with sails attached. No stays

Sheeting Arrangement: foresail sheet: cleated near aft mast, handy to helmsperson. Aft sail sheet, cleated at transom

Rudder: kick-up. Mounted on gudgeons on stern

Centerboard: high density polyethylene; open case

Rowing Ability: oar locks provided for moderately easy rowing

Motor Provision: transom designed to handle 3-6 H.P. motor

Stowage: two forward lockers next to centerboard case with 34-cubic foot hold. One aft locking locker. Covered outboard tank bay or lazarette

Covers: boat covers and cockpit tent available through Hogin Sails of Alameda, CA.

(Refer to general information regarding Wilce boats folowing Sea Venture 22)

The *Heron* Sharpie and the 20' *Navigator* Cruising Dinghy are boats with similar dimensions, rigs and functions, but emphasizing different qualities. The ultralight *Navigator* is built to maximize beaching, rough water handling and a general excellence of performance with sail, oar or power. She's narrow, and her initial stability is low. The *Heron*, a foot shorter, has nearly twice her capacity and is much roomier and more stable. *Navigator* has good storage and ergometrics for boats in her class; *Heron's* are lavish.

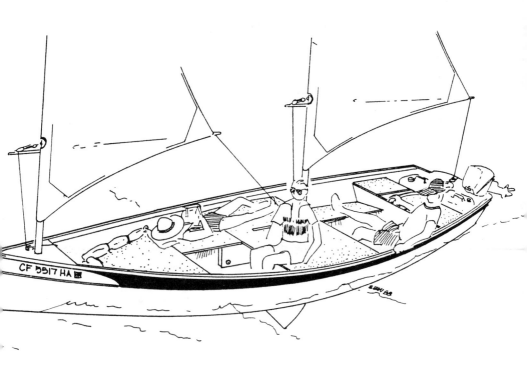

Heron 19' Sharpie Schooner

Line drawings courtesy of Stephen Wilce Boats

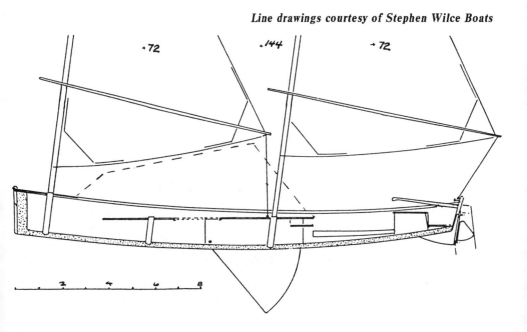

Wilce's "Navigator"

L.O.A. 20' 2"
L.W.L. 18' 6"
Beam: 5'
Draft board up: 8"; board down 2' 4"
Weight: 280 pounds empty; 335 pounds rigged; 445 pounds with trailer
Capacity: 900 pounds
Sail Area main: 72 sq. ft.; mizzen: 50 sq. ft.
Sail Rig: Bermuda spritsail, cat ketch
Reefing System: roller (around mast); slab
Hull: hard chine; thermoplastic sheet
Cockpit: about 5' long. Entire boat self-bailing
Flotation: foam core. Self-rescuing
Mast length (main): 18–20' (in two sections). How stepped: into PVC tube through mast partner. Material: tapered aluminum. Weight: 16 pounds **with** sail. No stays. Booms: tapered fir; 2½ pounds each
Sheeting Arrangement main: through central deadeye to cam cleat at mizzen mast; mizzen: through central deadeye and cam cleat on transom
Rudder: kick-up. Mounted on gudgeons on transom
Centerboard: ½" high density polyethylene: 18 pounds. Lifting tackle: single part, halyard to cam cleat
Rowing Ability: bronze oarlocks and 8½' oars provided for moderately easy rowing
Motor Provision: motor mounted on transom for 2–4 H.P. outboard
Stowage: 23 cu. ft. cargo hold 12" deep under central "deck." Lazarette locker with padlock
Covers: optional tent and dodger. Optional boat cover

Photo by Steve Wilce

Steve and Lee Wilce aboard *Navigator* under tow off Pt. Reyes, CA. She throws a small wake for a 7-knot speed. Her foam core provides flotation

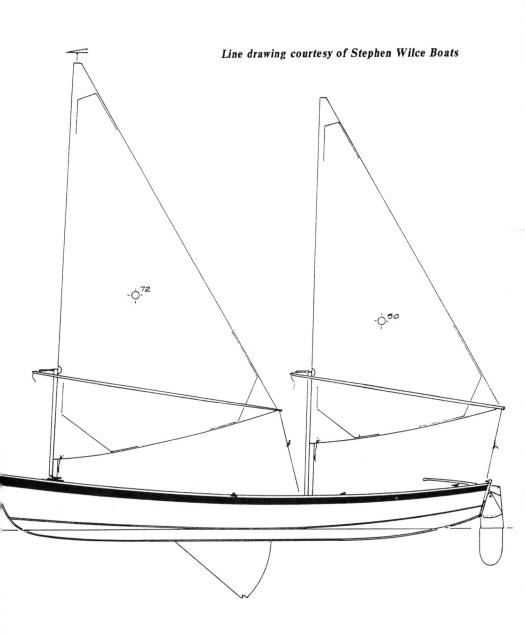

Line drawing courtesy of Stephen Wilce Boats

Navigator 20' Cruising Dinghy comes with optional tent and dodger

165

Wilce's Sharpie "Sea Venture 22"

L.O.A. 22' 6"
L.W.L. 19' 3"
Beam: about 6' 6"
Beam on bottom: about 3' 6"
Draft: 7½" @ 2,000 pounds displacement
Weight: 500/600 pounds
Capacity: approximately 1,600 pounds
Sail Area main: 90 sq. ft.; mizzen: 63 sq. ft.
Sail Rig: Bermudan spritsail ketch
Reefing System: slab
Hull: Sharpie (like Heron); thermoplastic sheet with foam core
Flotation: integral from foam core construction. Self-rescuing
Centerboard: 34 pounds
Masts length: forward mast: 21'; aft mast: 19'. How stepped: through thwart onto step. Material: wood. No stays
Sheeting Arrangement main: cam cleat at mizzen mast; mizzen: cam cleat on transom
Rudder: kick-up. Mounted on gudgeons on transom
Motor Provision: up to 10 H.P. Long shaft on transom
Stowage: covered hold amidships. Locker aft

The Good Points of Wilce's Boats

Hull Material: the Kydex PVC-Acrylic Alloy (thermoplastic) is engineering quality thermoplastic, superior to consumer grade plastics such as ABS. Developed as a durable fire-resistant material for the aircraft industry. All of Wilce's boats are semi-custom in that they are somewhat responsive to each buyer. None of the boats use stays. Thick foam core provides good temperature and sound insulation

Heron: has twice the capacity of Navigator; roomier, more stable. Will almost entirely self-bail

Navigator: good storage; cheaper and lighter than Heron. This model can be rolled ashore by one person alone. All sail controls lead aft to helmsperson. Will bail herself completely dry with a load of 250 pounds. Proven by Wilce family, over the years, to be a very capable family beachcruiser

Sea Venture: designed to handle open water, and to run through a chop easily. Will almost entirely self-bail

Bad Points

Heron and Sea Venture 22 require 200–300 pounds ballast for daysailing. Centerboard "L" shape moderately disruptive to interior

Wilce's Heron, Navigator, and Sea Venture 22

Designer: Stephen Wilce in the early 1980s
Builder: Stephen Wilce Boats, Box 962, Winters, CA 95694
Cost: Heron: $6,240 with trailer; number built: 1. Navigator: $5,350 with trailer; number built: 9. Sea Venture 22: $7,276 complete, number built: 3. $3,959 for bare hull

Cruises/Articles/Books

Ken Ward ran a successful charter operation in Baja using a Sea Venture 25. The Sea Venture was designed specifically for him so that he could have a large boat that he could roll out of the water. Small Boat Journal #65, Oct./Nov. 1981, "The Evolution of a Thermoplastic Sharpie" by Stephen Wilce. Small Boat Journal #65, Feb./Mar. 1989, "Navigator: Light and Unsinkable Thanks to a Thermoplastic Sandwich Hull" by Mike O'Brien. Stephen Wilce Catalog: 20 pages of information and cruising accounts

Line drawing courtesy of Stephen Wilce Boats

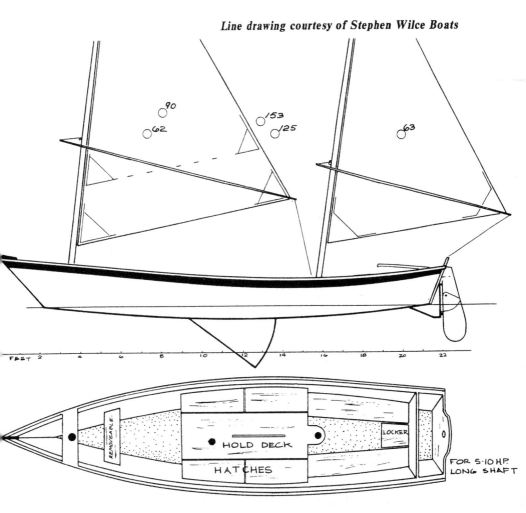

Sea Venture 22 **comes with optional tent system that would require a cat-yawl rig, stepping the after mast in the lazarette**

Sea Pearl

L.O.A. 21'

L.W.L. 19'

Beam: 5' 6"

Draft board up: 6"; board down: 2' 6"

Weight: 550 pounds with sail rig

Capacity: three adults plus about 500 pounds of gear/water (built-in tanks optional)

Sail Area main: 80 sq. ft.; mizzen: 56 sq. ft.

Sail Rig: loose-footed Marconi rig, cat ketch

Reefing System: roller furling around the mast

Hull Shape: whaleboat tradition, flat, narrow bottom with soft chines. Material: fiberglass with ½" balsa core on bottom for extra strength when beaching

Decks: the boat is three-quarters decked

Cockpit length: center cockpit: 6' 6". Footwell molded into stern deck. Footwell self-bailing

Flotation: foam. Self-rescuing if center cockpit closed

Masts length: about 18' in two sections. How stepped: through the deck. Material: aluminum

Sheeting Arrangement main: cam cleat aft of mizzen mast; mizzen: cam cleat on tiller

Rudder: kick-up. Mounted on gudgeons on stern

Centerboard/Leeboards material: fiberglass/cored lead shoe. Weight: 40 pounds. Lifting tackle: 1:1 rope pendant with cam cleat

Rowing Ability: oarlocks with 10' spruce oars optional; rows moderately well

Motor Provision: optional motor bracket on stern for 4.5 H.P. motor

Racing: light-hearted races organized at Sea Pearl get-togethers. Annual Sea Pearl Nationals in Panama City

Stowage: center cockpit and under decks

Covers: tonneau cover for center cockpit under way. Dodger/Pram hood for shade (useable under way). Camping tent with 3' 6" headroom (for use with leeboard model)

Good Points: trailer optional. 400-pound water ballast built in as option. Split rig makes balance helm. Mizzen reduces sailing around at anchor and allows boat to heave-to. Soft chimes give great ultimate stability and a more comfortable ride. Ron and Sammye Johnson of Marine Concepts very active in promoting the boat, events, and cruises

Bad Points: tender initially (though the water ballast helps). Narrow. Low freeboard and non-flaring bow gives wet ride in blustry weather

Modifications/Additions: waterproof tonneau cover

Designer: Marine Concepts. Expanded version of L.F. Herreshoff's 18' carpenter dory tender design of 1929

Builder: Marine Concepts, 159 Oakwood St. East, Tarpon Springs, FL 33589. 312 built since 1982

Warranty: 1 year unconditional warranty against defective parts or workmanship

Cost: $5,400

Associations and Newsletters: "From the Oyster Bed," a Marine Concepts Newsletter that includes updates on designs, cruising stories, announcements of get-togethers

Articles: Sailors Gazette, Feb. 1987, "Keeping Yourself Real Liquid" by Chris Harkness. This is an interview with Shane St. Clair who sailed a Sea Pearl from Tarpon Springs, FL up the east coast and across to the Great Lakes and down the Mississippi and across the Gulf coast back to Tarpon Springs—a trip of 5,000 miles in 6 months. Small Boat Journal #26, Aug./Sept. 1982, "A Pair of Open Cruisers from Florida" by Dan and Judy Segal. Small Boat Journal #45, Oct./Nov. 1985. Review of the Sea Pearl

Photo by Ron Johnson

Here's Shane St. Clair, who at the age of 21, took his *Sea Pearl Voyage through America* on a 6-month cruise of 5000 miles circumnavigating the eastern part of USA. These light boats (550 lbs.) have great carrying capacity. Some are rigged for sleeping aboard under the waterproof tonneau cover

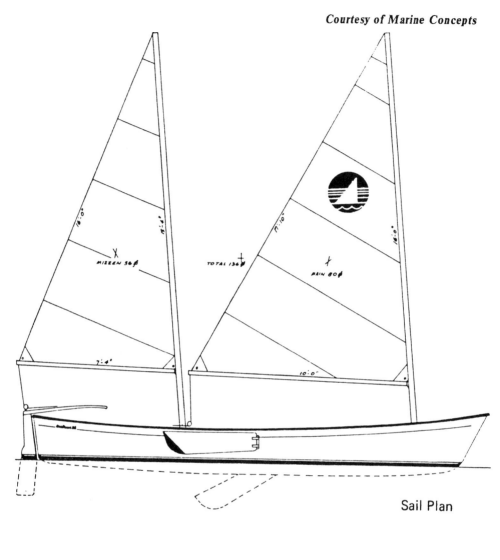

Sail Plan

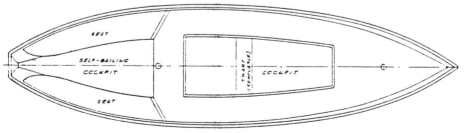

Deck Plan

Sail and deck plans for *Sea Pearl*

Leeboard version of *Sea Pearl* running wing and wing.

Board Boats Used For Cruising
Sunfish

'*The Sunfish Book* by Will White, from Sail Books 1983. One chapter titled "The Cruising Sunfish"

Small Boat Journal Feb./Mar. 1981, "Virgin Charter, Small Boat Style" by Lucien R. Greif

Small Boat Journal #46, Dec./Jan. 1986, "A Sunfish Custom Cruiser" by Thomas E. Lisco. Illustrated by Marya Butler

Sail Magazine, August 1987, "A Mighty Good Time" by Dom Degnon. Sunfish Connecticut River Classic—annual race and camping for 2 days from Hartford to Essex, CT

Builder: AMF Alcort Sailboats, South Leonard St., Waterbury, CT 06708. Over 230,000 sold in 25 years of production

Phantom

Small Boat Journal, Apr./May 1982, "3200 Miles Aboard a Board" by Jeremy Barnard. Describes cruise from New Orleans to Friendship, ME in 5 months, plus details of how he modified his Phantom for the trip

Builder: Howman Boats, Inc., Edison, NJ

Hobie Cat

Sailor's Gazette, Aug. 1985, "Sail Camping Coastal Waters: So What if all You Have is a Hobie Cat? Go Cruising!" by Bob Burgess

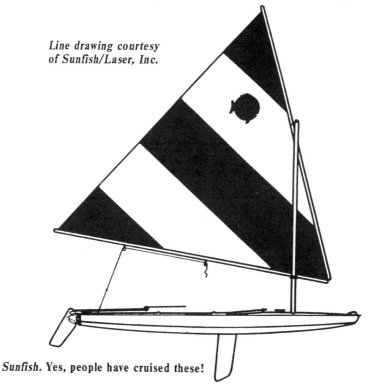

Line drawing courtesy of Sunfish/Laser, Inc.

Sunfish. Yes, people have cruised these!

172

Hobie 16. Your author cruised in a *Hobie 14* towing a canoe!

General Resources

Old Wharf Dory Co., Walter Baron, Box W, Wellfleet, MA 02667. Builder of beach boats and shallow-draft cruisers since 1977. Built over 60 hulls including sharpies and dory boats. Write for list of plans @ $10

Sailboat and Equipment Directory, Sail Publications, Charlestown Navy Yard, 100 First Ave., Charlestown, MA 02129-2097. Listing and description of boats and builders' addresses

Articles: Small Boat Journal, June 1980, "In Search of the Perfect Boat" by T.N.F. Shaw. About using the Sun Cat boat. Small Boat Journal #40, 41, 42, 1985, "Easy Down with Gypsy Girl" by John Garber. A rowing cruise of 150 miles from Sea Harbour to Beals Harbor, ME. Small Boat Journal #59, Feb./Mar. 1988, "Carolina Cruising: Down Pamlico Sound in a 17' Open Boat" by Tim Lemmond

Association Bulletins: Dinghy Cruising Association, Westfield, Western Road, Hailsham, E. Sussex BN27 3EN, England

SOURCES FOR ADDITIONAL INFORMATION

Books

Open Boat Cruising, by John Glasspool, 1973

Dinghy Cruising With Phillips: A Manual on Camping and Sailing in Small Open Boats, by Alan Phillips, available from Ken Elliott, 56 The Esplanade #403, Toronto, Ontario M5E 1A7, Canada. Includes a list of the Wayfarer log anthologies

Dinghies For All Waters, by Eric Coleman, Hollis & Carter, 9 Bow St., London, England WC2E 7AL

Open Boat Cruising: Coastal and Inland Waters, by Frank and Margaret Dye, 1982

The Dinghy Owner's Handbook, by Dave Jenkins, 1975

The Thousand Dollar Yacht, by Anthony Bailey, $6.95, 220 pages, reprinted 1988, International Marine, TAB Books, Inc., Blue Ridge Summit, PA 17294-0840. An account of fitting out and cruising a San Pierre dory; nice preface

Roving in Open Boats: The Guide to Low Cost and High Fun Boating, by Ian Nicolson, 1988, Ashford Press Publishers, RFD 1, Box 182-A, Willimantic, CT 06226

Associations

Atlantic Wooden Boat Association, John Wermescher, 953 Virginia Circle N.E., Atlanta, GA 30306

Traditional Small Craft Association, Box 350, Mystic, CT 06355

Dinghy Cruising Association, 4 Medlars Mead, Hatfield Broad Oak, nr Bishops Stortford Herts, England CM22 7JB. Newsletter filled with information and cruising stories and people seeking crews for small boat cruises. Librarian: Elizabeth Baker Westfield, Western Rd., Halisham East Sussex, England BN27 3EN

Catalogs and Directories

Sailboat and Equipment Directory, Sail Publications, Charlestown Navy Yard, 100 First Ave., Charlestown, MA 02129-2097. Listing and description of boats and builders' addresses

Equipment Catalog, West Marine, 2450 17th Ave., Santa Cruz, CA 95063, 800-538-0775

Builders

Check listings and ads in Small Boat Journal and WoodenBoat

Old Wharf Dory Co., Walter Baron, R.R. 1 Old Chequessett Neck Rd., Wellfleet, MA 02667. Builder of beach boats and shallow draft cruisers since 1977. Built over 60 hulls including sharpies and dories. Write for list of plans at $10 each

Boat Builders International Directory, Pirvateer Publishing Co., Benica, CA 94510. Source for plans and kits

Charters

Small Boat Cruising Center, Douglas Knapp, Box 881833, San Francisco, CA 94188-1833. Crewed, floating backpack adventures in open boats in Sea of Cortez (Baja)

Oceanic Society Expeditions, Fort Mason Center, Bldg. E, San Francisco, CA 94123

General Magazine Articles

"Open Boat Cruising," by Billy Ray Sims, WoodenBoat Magazine, May/June 1986

"Open Boat Cruisers Compared," commentary by Steve Redmond, WoodenBoat Magazine, May/June 1986

"Mississippi Odyssey: 75 Days in a Sneakbox," by Christopher Cunningham, Small Boat Journal #53, Feb./Mar. 1987. Author and 100 pounds of gear in a 13' 6" sneakbox cruise from Pennsylvania to Florida

"In Search of the Perfect Boat," by T.N.F. Shaw, Small Boat Journal, June 1980. About using the Sun Cat

"Easy Down With Gypsy Girl", by John Garber, Small Boat Journal #40, #41, #42. A rowing cruise of 150 miles along the Maine coast

"Carolina Cruising: Down Pamlico Sound in a 17' Open Boat," by Tim Lemmond, Small Boat Journal #59, Feb./Mar. 1988

CHAPTER 7

SOME CUDDY BOATS RECOMMENDED FOR BEACHCRUISING

We include a few boats that are not commercially available. However, you may purchase plans for *Dugong* from Philip Bolger and try your hand at building; or like Matt Layden, design and build your own *Swamp Thing*.

ADVANTAGES OF A CUDDY CABIN

There are some places where a cuddy cabin makes more sense than a tent shelter. Some shorelines have no camping places because of private property, or inhospitable geography. Other places are so wet or so cold that you cannot cruise happily without a cozy, hard shelter. It's all relative to your own threshold for hassles (putting up a boom tent) and discomfort. For most of us, if we're going to be cruising where we **know** we'll be sleeping aboard, and staying aboard quite a bit, we'll want a cuddy. When Michael and I decided to cruise the southern Florida coast, we moved out of our open canoe into a canoe with a cuddy. *Dugong* was designed for and used for cruising where we'd often be sleeping aboard.

Cuddy boats have more room and more dry stowage space than open boats.

We can close up a cuddy cabin against bugs a lot easier than closing up a tent against bugs. This is of great importance because we're cruising and overnighting within Bug Kingdom.

DISADVANTAGES OF A CUDDY CABIN

Once you have a cuddy cabin, it's there for good. Unlike an open boat with a boom tent, the cuddy doesn't just fold up and get tucked away when you **don't** want it. It will provide some shelter, but it'll also be in your view all the time.

When you'd like to get the boat out of the water overnight, the cuddy weighs it down so much you can not do it. That weight will require more horsepower to trailer, too.

If you've got a cuddy, you've got one more big part of a boat to maintain. It'll need painting or varnishing, leak-proofing and opening port inspections. It'll take up more room when you want to store the boat.

SOME CUDDY BOATS RECOMMENDED FOR BEACHCRUISING

Following this list are more detailed descriptions of each boat.

PAGE NO.	BOAT	L.O.A.	MATERIAL	COST
Production Boats:				
177	Peep Hen	14' 2"	Glass	$6,295
179	Bay Hen	21'	Glass	$10,900
182	Great Pelican	16'	Wood	$40 for plans
184	Dovekie	21' 5"	Glass	$9,950
186	Drascombe Coaster	21' 9"	Glass	$13,500
Non-Production Boats:				
188	Dugong	26'	Wood	$10,000
195	Swamp Thing	13' 2"	Plywood	$600

Peep Hen

L.O.A. 14' 2"

L.W.L. 13' 3"

Beam: 6' 4"

Draft board up: 9"; board down: 3'

Weight: 1,050 pounds rigged

Capacity: four adults

Sail Area main: 115 sq. ft.

Sail Rig: gaff, cat sloop rig

Reefing System: jiffy reefing from cockpit

Hull Shape: hard chine, flat bottom, 18" wide, 9" deep box keel (hollow). Material: fiberglass

Cockpit: about 6' long. Self-bailing

Flotation: PVC foam core hull and positive flotation. Self-righting

Mast length: about 16'. Weight: about 30 pounds. Material: aluminum. No stays. How stepped: hinged into a tabernacle

Sheeting Arrangement: cam cleat on tiller

Rudder: not kick-up; bottom of rudder level with bottom of hull. Mount: with gudgeons on stern

Centerboard material: aluminum. Weight: about 40 pounds. Lifting tackle: one block and cam cleat. Case closed

Rowing Ability: poor

Motor Provision: 2–4 H.P. short shaft outboard mounted on transom

Not built for racing

Stowage: galley counter big enough for a camp stove; 25-quart ice box, dry storage space for groceries and cooking utensils; forepeak room for duffles; space at foot of the bunks; forepeak well for anchor/chain; cut-out room under starboard seat for cooler and gas can

Covers: bimini. Summer cabin over cockpit

Cuddy headroom: 4'. Galley: sink, ice box, counter for stove. Berths: two 6'+ quarter berths (your legs go under the cockpit seats). Ventilation: companionway only. No opening ports

Good Features: higher than normal seat backs. Swim ladder on transom swings up. See-through window on the bottom. Good headroom under the boom—sail up or down. Boom gallows across stern. Mast way forward out of the way of the cabin. Designed for secure, relaxed, overnight, shallow water cruises. Keel provides resistance so boat can be sailed with board up

Bad Features: laborious to steer due to rudder design. Clunky looking. Mediocre performer under sail

Modifications/Additions: install opening ports. Install deeper, kick-up rudder

WATCH AS THE TEENAGERS TRY TO CAPSIZE THE PEEP HEN !!!

Drawings by Reuben Trane, Florida Bay Boat Co.

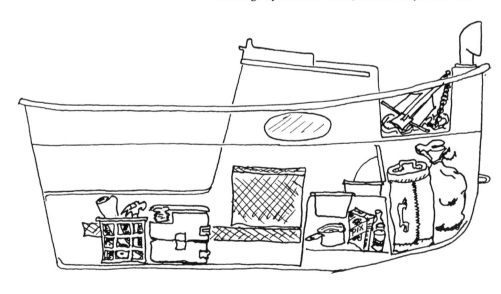

You can stow a lot of gear in this small boat. Then pull it out and enjoy a spacious camp ashore

Bay Hen

L.O.A. 21'
L.W.L. 18' 3"
Beam: 6' 3"
Draft board up: 9"; board down: 3' 6"
Weight: more than a thousand pounds
Capacity: six adults
Sail Area main: 175 sq. ft.
Sail Rig: gaff-rigged Cat sloop
Reefing System: jiffy reefing
Hull shape: hard chine, flat bottom, New Haven Sharpie. Material: fiberglass
No aft deck
Cockpit length: about 6' 9". Not self-bailing
Flotation: PVC foam core and positive foam flotation. Self-rescuing
Mast length: about 19'. Weight: 40 pounds. Material: aluminum. No stays. How stepped: hinged into tabernacle
Sheeting Arrangement: cam cleat on tiller
Rudder: does no kick-up; mounted with post through stern
Bilge Boards weight: about 50 pounds. Lifting tackle: Line through a block to cam cleat. Cases are closed
Rowing Ability: poor
Motor Provision: outboard well for 2–5 H.P. motor; room to tilt. Cut-out by motor well for fuel tank
Not designed for racing
Stowage: bins port and starboard in cuddy. Cockpit lockers under seats port and starboard
Covers: bimini which can be used under sail. Summer cabin tent encloses cockpit
Cuddy: completely open on the inside with space for personal gear, bedding, galley gear, and provisions. Porta-Potti stows under bridge deck, under slide-out counter that has a drop-in sink and room for a stove. Ventilation: four opening ports, companionway, and large foredeck hatch. 4' x 6½' sleeping area inside with bilge boards to the sides and out of the way
Good Features: very well thought-out camper cruising boat. Boom rides high enough to allow use of a bimini under way. Boom gallows to catch rig to ease mast lowering for bridges. Bow sprit for anchor roller. Mast and boards out of the way of the cabin
Bad Features: clunky looking. Noisy; and pounds in a chop. Mediocre performer under sail

Peep Hen and Bay Hen

Peep Hen

Designer: Robert Johnson, as a Lightfoot Sharpie with deck and cuddy added

Cost: $6,295

Bay Hen

Designer: Reuben Trane

Cost: $10,900

Builder: Mirage Fibreglass, P.O. Box 1489, Palatka, FL 32078-1489. Phone: 904-328-6052. Dave Kolodzik: Business Manager. Donnie and Keith are owners. Over 300 Hens of all models sold. The builder plans to keep the Peep Hen in continuous production. A Maxi-Peep (19-ft. version of the 14-ft. Peep) and the Bay Hen will be available from local dealers. The Sand Hen, a 24-ft. Cat ketch, will be available through custom orders only

Articles: Small Boat Journal #39, Oct./Nov. 1984. A comparison of the Bay Hen, Dovekie, Drascombe Coaster and five other boats at the Newport Small Boat Show. Small Boat Journal #67, July, 1989, "The Appealing Peep Hen" by Steve Henkel

Associations: Hen Owners Association, Tom Thatcher, Pres., 17 Tillman Pl., Willingboro, NJ 08046. About 220 newsletters to about 70 percent of all the Hen owners

Drawing by Reuben Trane, designer of Bay Hen

With a small, light beachable cruiser, you can travel like this to exotic places and cruise-camp different shores each vacation. Or trailer her to the beautiful lakes, rivers, and shores of the USA

FL0365EY

This 21' *Bay Hen* off Seahorse Key, FL has room for a double berth and a small galley in her cuddy cabin. She's a good choice for areas where you aren't allowed to camp on the beach

Great Pelican

L.O.A. 16'

Length on Bottom: 13' 2"

Beam: 8'

Draft board up: 4" (9" loaded); board down: 4'

Weight: 480 pounds

Capacity: six to eight adults

Sail Area main: 130 sq. ft.; jib: 60 sq. ft.

Sail Rig: standing lug with full length battens; sloop

Reefing System: reef points and cringle

Hull shape: banks fishing dory (widely flaring, straight lines). Pram, or sampan, bow. Material: plywood

Aft deck

Cockpit length: about 6'. Not self bailing

Flotation: asymmetrically stowed foam secured permanently in space under starboard side deck for self-righting

Mast length: about 16'. Material: wood. Stays: fore and side stays. Stepped into tabernacle on deck

Sheeting Arrangement main: runs forward under boom to center of cockpit. Jib: cleats amidships

Rudder: kick-up. Mounted with gudgeons on stern

Centerboard weight: 35 pounds of lead. Optional swing keel with 200 pounds of lead. Case is high-walled and swamp proof

Rowing Ability: no provision

Motor Provision: outboard bracket may be mounted on transom for up to 7 H.P. motor

Not designed for racing

Stowage: beneath cockpit seats. Lockers inside cuddy cabin

Covers: none available

Cuddy: two bunks. Ventilation: louvered doors, and screens in companionway. Two large opening ports forward and one each side

Good Features: all sail control lines lead aft to cockpit. Very stable

Bad Features: rudder does not kick up far enough to clear bottom

Modifications: self-bailing cockpit. Cockpit cover for storage. Fully lifting kick-up rudder. Winch to help raise the centerboard. Remove small bunks and use pad on floor. Samson post for anchoring. Boom crutch. Devise jiffy reefing

Designer: Capt. William Short

Design: Enlarged version of Short's San Francisco Pelican

Plans: Laurie M. Short, 9 Blue Heron Court, Sacramento, CA 95833, or Muriel S. Short, San Francisco Pelican Boats, 203 Hawthorne Ave., Larkspur, CA 94939. You need the standard 12' San Francisco Pelican plans (**$30** for plans and 48-page instruction book) and the "Great Pelican" conversion plans (**$10**)

Smith's Boat Shop, 764 Samish Island Rd., Bow, WA 98232. Offers plans, kit, or finished boat. Over 20,000 Pelicans have been built since 1959

Associations and Newsletters: International San Francisco Pelican Association, 481 Irvine Ct., Tiburon, CA 94920. Quarterly newsletter: The Pelican Post, ed. Howard Mackay, 2249 Tamalpais Ave., El Cerrito, CA 94530

Books/Articles: "How to Build 20 Boats," Fawcett Book #628. Rudder Magazine, Nov. 1967, detail of self-righting ability of the Pelican. Small Boat Journal, Sept. 1979, "Grateful for Small Favors." Small Boat Journal #36, Apr./May 1984, "The Great Pelican Bird of Play" by John D. Williamson. In 1973 Kim Tucker sailed a Great Pelican from San Diego, CA to Hilo, HI in 32 days

Photo courtesy of Laurie Short

Coming at you are a *Great Pelican* (l) and the smaller *San Francisco Pelican* (r). Both are popular on the west coast. The *Great Pelican* shown here doesn't have the cuddy cabin, which has two bunks

Dovekle

L.O.A. 21'

L.W.L. 19'

Beam: 6' 8"

Draft board up: 4"; board down: 2' 6"

Weight: 600 pounds empty; 750 pounds with sail rig

Capacity: two adults with gear for a week easily

Sail Area: 143 sq. ft.

Sail Rig: Bermuda spritsail sloop

Reefing system: modified jiffy

Hull shape: double-ended, flat bottom, canoe-like. Material: Airex foam core, fiberglass composite

Aft deck with lazarette under

Cockpit length: about 6'. Not self-bailing

Flotation: will float full of water. Self-rescuing

Mast length: under 20'. Material: aluminum. Stays: fore and side stays. Weight: about 30 pounds. How Stepped: pivoted onto stand on deck

Sheeting Arrangement: cam cleat on tiller

Rudder: kick-up. Mounted on gudgeons on stern

Leeboards weight: 60 pounds, with positive flotation. Lifting tackle: Stainless steel handles incorporating a cam to lock the board in any position; unlocks automatically if board strikes

Bow Centerboard: falls of own weight: kick-up; pendant for lifting

Rowing Ability: oar ports to accomodate 9' oars. Rowing possible for short distances. Sculling lock aft for sculling out of tight places

Motor Provision: outboard bracket on rudder for up to 2 H.P. or 25-pound motor. Optional 9.9 H.P. inboard in bin under helmsperson's seat. Drive produced by a high pressure jet of water that squirts from a nozzle just above the waterline next to the rudder (nothing extends below the bottom)

Not designed for racing; raced locally for fun

Stowage: anchor and rode forward in bow behind bulkhead. 5-foot long stowage bins along hull either side (canvas covered). Special recess on centerline for Porta-Potti

Covers: cockpit dodger. Coated fabric hatch covers. Back Porch (for use with bimini) for aft end of cockpit (no-see-um proof screens on three sides with canvas blinds on the outside). Bimini: stainless frame used to raise and support the standard supplied canopy as sun shade. Can be used underway

Cuddy: uncluttered and open with few bulkheads or furniture. Used mostly for stowage and cooking, though a small person could sleep in the aisle. Two hatches, wide-open companionway, and opening oar ports for ventilation. Cockpit used in conjunction with cuddy gives living area with 4' headroom and 7' long sleeping area for two

Good Features: will heave-to. Special trailer optional which makes launching, retrieving and motoring easy—a lot of thought and engineering has been put into this special trailer. Hawse pipe for anchor rode forward for tidy anchoring. Loose-footed sail won't bang your head, nor will sprit. Cockpit seats well designed for more comfortable seating than most small boats have. Hatches allow sail work from the security of inside the boat. Owners enjoy gathering and cruising together. Deucedly clever sail furling device for quick and easy furling

Bad Features: rudder blade occasionally "sticks" and must be shoved down. Fixed gallows over cockpit below head height (means having to duck). Centerboard forward needs raising when coming about—sometimes a hassle because you have to go forward to do it. Cuddy open to cockpit so not watertight.

Modifications: good suggestions in "Shallow Water Sailor." Devise easier reefing system. Devise method for dropping the anchor from the cockpit instead of having to go forward. Mount a regular outboard bracket on the side of the stern instead of on the rudder

Designer: Philip Bolger, N.A.

Builder: Edey and Duff, 128 Aucoot Rd., Mattapoisett, MA 02739, Phone 508-758-2743. Over 150 built

Cost: $9,950 ready to cruise—even includes anchor; $1,385 for trailer

Associations and Newsletters: "The Shallow Water Sailor," John Zohlen, 3 Wilelinor Dr., Edgewater, MD 21037. More than 80 members, most of whom are Dovekie and Shearwater (Dovekie's big sister) owners

Books/Articles/Cruises: 20-page booklet from Edey and Duff is well worth the $5 in information, entertainment, and philosophy. Small Boat Journal #39, Oct./Nov. 1989; Dovekie compared to the Bay Hen, Drascombe Coaster and five other boats. Cruising World Magazine, Oct. 1986, "Beautiful Skimmers" by Bill Rosen. Small fleets and individual Dovekies have cruised the Bahama Islands. *Editor's note: These boats are quite popular in southern New England. They move easily and are a pretty sight under sail.*

Photo by Chris Harkness

A group cruise of *Dovekies* anchored. *Dovekies* are beachable with a kick-up rudder, leeboards and centerboard

Drascombe Coaster (Longboat With Cuddy Cabin)

L.O.A. 21' 9"

L.W.L. 18'

Beam: 6' 7"

Draft board up: 1'; board down: 3' 10"

Weight: 1,060 pounds

Capacity: four people and gear

Sail Area main: 86 sq. ft; jib: 56 sq. ft.; mizzen (jigger): 22 sq. ft.

Sail Rig: loose-footed, sliding Gunter yawl

Reefing System main: reef points and cringles. Jib: roller

Hull shape: simulated lapstrake, hard, double chine. Material: fiberglass

No aft deck

Cockpit length: about 6'. Teak floor grating option. Not self-bailing but cabin is watertight

Flotation: Foam. Not self-rescuing

Mast: wood; stepped through the deck, about 20 pounds. Stays: fore and side stays

Sheeting Arrangement main: cleated on tiller; jib: cleats amidships, mizzen: cleated aft

Rudder: kick-up. Mounted through a rudder trunk

Centerboard: lifting tackle: rotary winch with line to cockpit. Case is closed. Weight: about 121 pounds

Rowing Ability: oarlocks and sculling lock provided for moving the boat short distances

Motor Provision: outboard well for 6-8 H.P. motor than can tilt

Racing: not designed for racing

Stowage: under cockpit seats (access from inside the cuddy). Under berths. Forward of berths. Lockers abaft cockpit footwell

Covers: folding pramhood over hatchway. Camping tent to enclose cockpit. Cockpit cover

Cuddy: two 6' berths 15" wide. Chemical toilet and galley unit with single burner stove stowed beneath bridge deck. Side cabinets next to bunks. Just barely high enough to sit upright. Ventilation through companionway only

Good Features: cuddy cabin nice and dry. Proven seaworthy and liveable for cruising

Bad Features: cuddy so tall you can't see over it when sailing. Sails poorly off the wind. Cuddy disrupted by mast and centerboard (very narrow sleeping space)

Modifications: step mast in tabernacle on deck. Increase sail area

Designer: builder. See Drascombe Boats in Chapter 6

Cost: $13,000 including oars, delivered to closest USA container port

Number Built: 225

Articles: Small Boat Journal #39, Oct./Nov. 1984. Comparison of Coaster with Dovekie, Bay Hen and five other boats. "Swamped," Dinghy

Cruising Association Bulletin #115. Summer 1987, "Eight Years Cruising in a Drascombe" Longboat, by Peter Knape. Great story of his living and cruising aboard a Drascombe Longboat (converted into a Coaster). Available from: Dinghy Cruising Association, Librarian and Deputy Editor, Westfield, Western Road, Hailsham, E. Sussex BN27 3EN, England

Photo by Chris Harkness

Lee Martin has equipped *Ibis*, his *Dovekie* with the optional full tent cover. Added to the cuddy cabin, this makes her a roomy camper. Leeboards are handled easily from inside

Dugong (Phil Bolger's "Canoe Cruiser")

L.O.A. 26'

L.W.L about 25'

Beam: 5' 4"

Draft board up: 8" @ 1,800 pounds displacement; boards down: 3'

Weight: 1,000 pounds

Capacity: about 800 pounds

Sail Area main: 165 sq. ft.; jib: 15 sq. ft.

Sail Rig: sprit rigged sloop (one or two sprits)

Hull shape: like a canoe; flat bottom, double-ended, no rocker. Material: cold molded with three layers of ⅛" red cedar veneers

Aft deck with watertight lazarette under

Cockpit length: 8'. Side decks: 5". Not self-bailing. Removable floorboards with bailing pump under

Flotation: wood. Watertight cabin, lazarette and forepeak. Foam inside mast and sprits

Mast length: 16' (as are sprits). Material: Sitka spruce with foam core; Weight: 20 pounds. No stays. How stepped: into a mast step box through the deck onto the cabin sole

Sheeting Arrangement main: through block to cam cleat on tiller. Jib: jam cleat on cabin top

Rudder: kick-up. Mounted on gudgeons on stern

Leeboards: weight: 20 pounds of lead imbedded in each board. Lifting tackle: Single lines to cam cleats on side decks

Rowing Ability: oar ports for 8' oars. Possible to row short distances with effort

Motor Provision: outboard bracket permanently mounted to rudder cheek for regular shaft 2 H.P. motor. Moves the boat along at about 5 knots in smooth water

Racing: not designed for racing, but like all shallow draft boats with lifting boards and rudders, where allowed, she can take advantage of shortcuts

Stowage: watertight lazarette (about 10 cu. ft. area). Cockpit: under seats and along sides. Cabin: watertight stowage for gear and supplies. Under bridge deck (companionway seat): shelves and drawers accessible from inside the cabin

Covers: bimini/awning with removable side curtains. Complete cockpit tent covering cockpit, half of cabin and half of the stern deck

Cuddy: a real cabin: waterproof and big enough for two large adults to lie down or sit up comfortably (double bed measures 6½' x 5'). Ventilation: one opening port on each side, forward hatch, and companionway

Designer: Philip C. Bolger. See "Different Boats" by Philip C. Bolger, International Marine, TAB Books, Order Dept., Blue Ridge Summit, PA 17214. (*Dugong* is the design called "Canoe Cruiser")

Builders: Michael Walsh and Ida Little in 1979-1980

Dugong was designed to go aground—flat bottom, pivoting leeboards, kick-up rudder, and knot log propeller. The awning proved too cumbersome for casual use.

Editor's note: In their list of good and bad features, Ida and Michael failed to note that *Dugong* was one of the prettiest small cuisers I've ever seen. This boat became a conversation piece any time it was near a gathering place. Admiration is good, but loss of privacy is bad.

Dugong's Good Features, Bad Features, And What We'd Do Differently Today

What prompted us to want a cuddy boat when open daysailers had worked so well for so long? It would be hard to name any specific thing. We always wanted extreme shoal draft, a flat bottom for beaching and a kick-up rudder and boards. But we wanted more comfortable seats, more protection from seas, a place to sleep aboard regularly, and greater cruising range across open waters.

The interesting result was that using a heavy cuddy boat limited us to certain cruising areas the same way our lightweight open boats had. Now, instead of searching for areas where we could be assured of camping ashore, we needed areas where we could either anchor securely very close to shore, or dry out on a flat. Although our open water crossings were more comfortable and safer, we rarely attempted conditions that a 17-ft. sailing canoe couldn't have handled. The big jump we thought we'd be able to do, crossing the Gulf Stream in winter, looked far too iffy once we actually launched *Dugong* and started learning to sail her.

As it happened, we went with the flow determined by the capabilities of the boat. Instead of cruising the Bahamas, we ended up cruising south Florida, the Florida Keys, Florida Bay, the Intracoastal and the Georgia islands. This had not been our intention. So we received our first lesson on the principle of "not planning" a set itinerary but rather preparing to adjust our itinerary to current conditions. We had to let the ultimate decision of where to cruise depend first on the boat, then the sea and the weather. We happened to have to flex quite drastically because our expectations had been so far removed from the reality of our craft and our courage (if we had been resolute in our plan to cruise the Bahamas, and had we had more coin at the time, we'd have had *Dugong* shipped across on a freighter).

Dugong was in her element in south Florida and coastal Georgia. Her 8-inch draft, ability to carry a heavy load of water and gear, a complete galley, roomy sleeping accommodations, her ability to be sailed, rowed or motored, her covered cockpit when anchored or beached, and dry cockpit under sail, made her an idea craft.

Our main trepidation with *Dugong* had to do with cruising in a boat that was too heavy to lift out of the water. We dreaded those dragging anchor blues. Sure, *Dugong* only drew 8 inches, but so what? Since we couldn't haul her out, it looked like we were back to square one where all the deep draft boats hang out—at anchor.

It took us about a month to overcome the mental block against running a boat aground intentionally. But once we did, we were home free. Thanks to *Dugong's* ability to be "beached" on the tide, we enjoyed secure beachorages almost everywhere we went. And as our allegiance to the taboo against closing with the shore and running aground weakened, the stronger grew our new credo that was all for those acts. We began running aground, drying out with the tide, tying up to trees, pushing the boat up creeks, scooting into unchartered by-ways—all casually with liberated abandon.

Regrettably, we had to pass up some ideal beach campsites because we couldn't haul *Dugong* out. But we knew a cuddy would be a compromise, and we opted for the opportunity of cruising more comfortably, for longer periods of time, in places where we couldn't always set up a shore camp.

The coast of Georgia with all its islands, rivers, and streams, entertained us for months. We sailed, rowed, motored, and pushed *Dugong* up creeks through miles of marsh to reach solid land. There we'd tie up to a tree, an overhanging limb, or anchor to the bank. In some places, we could have camped ashore, but many times the land was private or the bugs so bad we preferred *Dugong's* screened cabin.

We'd never before attempted a camping cruise of the Georgia coast. We'd never had a motorized canoe to help us buck the strong tidal currents. With *Dugong's* horsepower, we wound our way through creeks, tide or no tide, and so explored to our hearts' content; and thanks to her accommodations, we enjoyed shelter from the deluge rains, hot sun, and swarming insects.

Florida Bay and the lower Keys were made for a boat like *Dugong*. Between the minimal tide range and shoal waters, we found secure beachorages everywhere. Most of the time we anchored out, we were completely protected from any threatening weather. And now that we know how perfect the Bahamas are for beachorages, we would not hesitate to ship a boat like *Dugong* over there for a cruise of the islands.

So what **didn't** we like about *Dugong*? The sprit rig was number one. It took us weeks of going through the raising sail, furling sail, and reefing to get the procedure down. You have to have a low sail rig on a small, light, shoal-draft boat. But you don't have to have an unwieldy one. The 16-foot by 2-inch square sprits are a little too long and too fat to rearrange easily. In order to reef, one of us had to go forward, release the upper sprit's snotter and let the sprit fall. The other person would unclip the sprit from the sail and re-clip it lower down. Then the person at the snotter would haul it tight again. This was downright dangerous when we were using the lower sprit as well. We learned to move nimbly!

But not as nimbly as we'd have had to move if we had gone with the original design method of handling the sail from **inside** the cabin. As with Dovekie, the idea is to go forward through the cabin and pop up through the forward hatch. This way you can handle the sail without having to balance precariously on deck. In the long run, this contortionist routine was unthinkable to us. Particularly since our cabin is our castle, and no dirt, salt, or sand is allowed inside. So, it was up and across a heeled 5-foot deck with no lifelines or handholds or anything remotely resembling security. Whatever we needed to do forward, we had to do it fast. Sixteen-foot sprits are very cumbersome, and catching the luffing sail with its attached hardware is dangerous.

To make life easier, we did without the lower sprit except when running downwind in easy winds. We later planned to devise a balanced lug or Bermudan sprit rig with all the control lines leading to the cockpit.

Modifications
The Cuddy Cabin
The most important modification we made to *Dugong's* original plan was to make her cabin liveable and completely watertight. We much prefer to sleep in an already made, clean, dry, unsalty bed, so we made the cabin one big bed with a thick foam pad. Under way, we may store water jugs, stove and gear inside on a tarp, but at night we move all this stuff to the cockpit. When we establish a shore camp, we take our cooking and galley gear ashore.

We're pretty fussy when it comes to cleanliness and to keeping our sheets dry and salt-free. Our fastidiousness about keeping everything orderly borders on fanatical. Such fussy standards may not be as important if you're only out for a few days or for a week, but for any longer that that, most of us need basic comforts, like a clean dry bed. To keep going happily, we also need freedom from too many daily frustrations, like being able to find things easily.

Since the cabin is kept dry, we carry an AM/FM radio tape deck (ghetto blaster) with 12-volt battery lashed to the mast step box, and all our gear, food, and books without fear of water damage.

We installed two opening ports, one on each side, to add to the ventilation from the forward hatch and the companionway. On all openings, we installed velcro to hold mosquito screens.

For our companionway hatch, we used clear Lexan so that we could see up, and out, from the inside of the cabin.

Although we had a comfortable, sitting head room cabin, we spent most of our time in the roomy cockpit. After all, we're out here to be **out**. To make life in the cockpit easier, we installed floorboards to keep our feet out of the water. When it rains, or if any sea sloshes aboard, we bailed the cockpit with a bilge pump mounted on the sole, under the floorboards. A hose ran overboard through an oar port.

We built two wide seats, port and starboard aft, which folded down to allow us to lift the floor boards and to store things more easily when we trailered.
The Lazarette
We fitted the aft cabin with a large, screw-down, gasketed port so that we could stow gear there and keep it dry. We also devised a special brace to hold the Seagull outboard motor. Like plenty of other clever schemes, this one proved impractical in practice. When we carried the motor, we stowed it under one of the cockpit seats.
Leeboards
Instead of having the leeboards on a pivot fitting that allows them to swing away from the sides of the boat, we mounted them with a bolt that

allows only fore and aft motion. The addition of a leeboard brace outside the leeboard keeps the boards in a slot between the hull and brace and allowed us to leave both boards down. The brace also served as a step for climbing aboard.

We fashioned an **enormous** wooden wing nut to tighten down on the pivot bolt.

Kick-up Rudder

The oversize rudder sometimes sticks, both up and down, between the rudder cheeks. We kept the inside of the rudder cheek greased as best we could and this helped.

Outboard Mount

We attached a wooden outboard bracket permanently to the rudder cheek. Because small outboard motors have integral gas tanks, we had to crawl out on the stern deck every five hours or so to refuel. We planned to either install a new bracket on the side of the hull closer to the cockpit, or to run a fuel line back to the outboard from a tank in the cockpit. We'd raise the motor higher off the water in any case, and use a long shaft. When the motor is mounted low, waves and wash swamp it too easily.

Sails

Dugong was not designed to use a jib. We had a 15 sq. ft. jib made and it added a full knot of speed. When we had to reef the main, we could barely make headway without it, and it was our storm sail. When running with winds of more than 25 knots, we let the jib alone do the job. Since it

Photo by Michael Walsh

Ida Little at work helping Michael build *Dugong*. Building *Dugong* took one year. Costwise we would have done better to purchase a similar boat, the *Dovekie*, and modify her to our tastes.

is such a tiny handkerchief of a sail, it looked ridiculous, but it sure did the trick.

The Hull

We are historically prone to going aground. We recognized this characteristic of our boating style early on. Instead of resisting it, we count on it and plan for it.

In *Dugong's* case, we beefed up her bottom with 2-inch yellow cedar inside the ⅜-inch red cedar veneer hull. Outside, we epoxied a hard ⅛-inch thick ultra high molecular weight polyethelene sheet. The stuff is called Dura Surf and is sold by Crown Plastics, 115 May Dr., Harrison, OH 45030. The same material is used on skis and river dories.

Covers

The canvas tent we made seemed like a good idea. But after weeks of cruising, we'd only used it once. We came to the realization that a tent that's too much work to put up just won't get put up. Our tent required us to take down the mast, lay it and sprits on a crutch, haul out an enormous swath of heavy canvas, and fold it over the mast and sprits. We then had to tie the whole thing in place and roll up the sides. In the best conditions, it took a half-hour. In bad weather, when we could have used it most, neither of us felt like leaving the cosy cabin to struggle with it.

The tent was beautiful but too big and elaborate for casual use. So we had a full bimini made with a frame that folds down on the stern. We used this awning daily.

Splash Guard

We mounted a splash guard on deck to deflect spray overboard before it reached the hatch or cockpit.

Dugong aground at ebb tide. Though this bay faces the stormy northwest, the shallows protect her from any sea.

Swamp Thing

L.O.A. 13' 2"

Beam: 3' 8"

Draft: 7" (uses no board)

Weight/Capacity: 900 pounds fully loaded (one adult and cruising gear for a month)

Sail Area: 73 sq. ft.

Sail Rig: standing lug sloop

Hull shape: flat rockered bottom with chine runners. Material: plywood and fiberglass

Reefing System: the sail is rolled onto the boom for reefing

Furling System: sail is furled between boom and yard on deck

Cuddy: designed to sleep one but room for two on the cabin sole. Companionway and oar ports for ventilation. Space for galley and cooking. Serves as enclosed steering station

If you happened to boat past Matt Layden a couple of summers ago, you could have had *Swamp Thing* for nothing. As it is, somebody beat you to it! Matt had done all the cruising in *Swamp Thing* that he'd wanted to do, so when a kayaker came by with compliments, Matt gave him the boat! By then, Matt had started planning a bigger one.

We met Matt in February of 1986. We were beached on a wide sand flat in the Bahamas, painting *Beachcomber's* topsides, when we saw him sailing towards us. At first, we thought he was a big boat far away. Then we thought he was not quite so big a boat as all that, and fairly near. Then we stopped brushing paint as it dawned on us that he was a teeny boat close by. He sailed past us in 8 inches of water, rounded up, and anchored.

This 13-foot decked boat had carried him from the Connecticut River to Florida, then out to the Bahama Islands—Bimini, across to the Exumas, and up to the Abacos. In previous years, he'd cruised up to Maine as far as the Canadian border. Last summer, he took a short cruise (for him) from Connecticut up to Cape Cod.

At 27 years of age, he's on his third or fourth or maybe fifth self-designed and built beachcruisers. His latest boat is a 15-foot somewhat modified version of *Swamp Thing*, which I call "Son of Swamp Thing." This past winter, he sailed it down the east coast from Connecticut, out to Grand Bahama, and on around to our first beachorage meeting place. There he reported his pleasure with the boat, and pleasure with anticipation of using what he's learned, once again, to design yet another.

That's what strikes us about his boats. They are so well thought-out, and so simple and cheap. It's amazing. He designs 'em, puts them together in a few months with plywood, a little glass, and hand-fashioned hardware. His latest 15-footer cost less than $800 in materials.

Economy is not the only attraction of his boats. Their design for seaworthiness, sailing ability, ease of handling, versatility, and liveability are enviable. Look at his drawings and see all the simple and innovative design features.

Swamp Thing draws 7 inches and uses **no** board at all for lateral resistance. Instead, Matt incorporated chine runners (thick pieces of wood that jut out beyond the chine) to offer sideways resistance. No centerboard or leeboards to worry about.

The standing lug sail is reefed by merely pulling the boom aft to release the jaws from the mast, then rolling the sail around the boom until it's reduced appropriately. The pull of the sheet on the boom keeps the boom jaws locked onto the mast.

Matt's boats are steered with a knotted line that runs on blocks under and along the gunwales, with each end attached to a yoke on the rudder. Thus Matt steers from the shelter of his cuddy with his head just above the cuddy top. Inside he has a pad on the cabin sole (the bottom of the boat) and storage space for books, food and a gimbaled kerosene stove.

On his way back to the States from the Bahamas a few years ago, he suffered a knockdown. It was a dark night and he was about halfway between West End, Grand Bahama, and West Palm Beach, Florida, 30 miles or so into the Gulf Stream, a notoriously rough body of water. A freighter seemed to be bearing down on him. Without thinking, he jumped up to shine a lantern on his sails. A rogue wave hit the boat right then, and threw it over. Instead of rolling with it, Matt lunged for the upwind side. Clutching the side, he continued falling backwards, thereby pulling the boat over on top of him. He managed to roll the boat on over, climb back in, and sail on. Thanks to the small cockpit opening, the boat shipped very little water and he was able to bail her dry. He said he was mighty grateful to have had his life line securely fastened to the boat, and that it had been long enough to reach all the way around *Swamp Thing* when she rolled. Matt was none the worse for wear through the dunking.

"Son of Swamp Thing"

Many of the design features of *Swamp Thing* went into one of the following boats that I refer to as "Son of Swamp Thing." "S.O.S.T." is a couple feet longer and a foot wider than his predecessor. He carries a small centerboard which is far enough forward that it does not interfere with the luxurious cabin interior. In fact, when you peek inside this boat, you can hardly make out the centerboard case for all the gear and bicycle and bags up there. But what strikes you most is the spaciousness and uncluttered comfort of the "main salon." Matt could fit even a not-so-skinny person in there with him now. A wide pad covers the sole so that he almost has a full double bed.

The last time we met up with Matt, he blew into our beachorage before a 30-knot blow. The boats anchored in the bay had all they could do just to stay anchored. So here comes Matt screaming down towards us with spray flying, looking on the edge of control, when all of a sudden, sure enough, he loses steerage. The boat luffs up and it looks like the sails will flog themselves to death. Up pops Matt like some sort of marine cowboy and lashes the second reef into the sail. The boat turns and Matt continues our way. When he was settled in behind us on the flats, I asked him about the Moment of Truth out there, reefing the sail. He gave me a "what's the big deal?" look. There was nothing to it, he explained. He has the jiffy reefing lines inside so except for the few ties right on the boom, he has little to do that is at all precarious.

That's one of the reasons why he can enjoy months of delightful cruising using the most minimal of "cruisers." He's got a boat that is simple, safe, easy to run, and comfortable enough to provide him with basic comforts.

He'll be cruising "S.O.S.T." along the coasts of Maine and Nova Scotia this summer.

Matt Laydon in his own designed and built *Swamp Thing*. When we met in the Abacos, Matt was returning to the Connecticut River from the Exumas

SOURCES FOR ADDITIONAL INFORMATION

Books

Sailing on a Micro-Budget, by Larry Brown, $15.60, 163 pages, 1985, Seven Seas Press, TAB Books, Inc., Blue Ridge Summit, PA 17294-0840. Well written and clearly illustrated book about using a trailerable boat to go cruising more places more often than non-trailerable boats

The Riddle of the Sands, by Erskine Childers, $4.95, 352 pages, 1976 (originally published 1903), Dover Publications, New York. Cruising spy adventure

Magazine Articles

"Dugong: a 26' Cruising Canoe by Phil Bolger," by Ida Little, Small Boat Journal, Aug/Sept. 1981

"In Praise of the Beachable Boat," by Michael Walsh, Cruising World, August 1984

Equipment Catalogs

BOAT/U.S., 880 S. Pickett St., Alexandria, VA 22304

West Marine Products, Box 6030, Santa Cruz, CA 95063

Organization

Seven Seas Cruising Association, 521 S. Andrews Ave., Suite 10, Ft. Lauderdale, FL 33301. $18 a year for the monthly bulletin. Full members (Commodores) of this association are liveaboards, but anyone can be an associate member and receive the member-written monthly bulletin. Beachcruisers who expect to roam far and wide (by plane or train or car and then by sea) can learn all the current scoop on places from people who are there right now

Charterer

Key Largo Shoal Water Cruises, Box 1180, Key Largo, FL 33037. Bareboat charters of shoal draft sharpies on Florida Bay

Following is an article by Ida Little, describing "how it was" cruising in their cuddy boat Dugong, in Florida Bay.

Reprinted from SAIL Magazine, April 1984 with permission from Patience Wales, Editor. Their address is Charlestown Navy Yard, 100 First Avenue, Charlestown, MA 02129-2097.

CRUISING THROUGH A BIRDBATH
FLORIDA BAY BY SAILING CANOE

By Ida Little

This is how it goes in Florida Bay.

Dugong's leeboards keep fouling on the bottom of Eagle Key Pass as we try to sail around Eagle Key. We are making no headway, so Michael jumps overboard and takes our canoe cruiser in tow. Now he slogs through the murky water, sinking shin deep into sticky ooze. It looks as though we'll make it. Michael moves forward and sinks to his waist. The waters roil. Less than 5 feet away I see masses of fins circle and dive. Michael's torso disappears. He is up to his armpits. "Michael!"

"I don't know if I can make it, Ida. It's too damn deep."

He lets the towline go and pulls himself on board. The feeding fish are gone. Slowly we move along. We'll make it around the key after all.

Eagle Key, Snake Bight, The Boggies, Black Betsy Key, and Crocodile Dragover are places that lie in a triangular area bounded by the Florida Keys to the south and the Everglades and Cape Sable to the north. This 15- by 25-mile expanse is called Florida Bay, and it's just a big birdbath. A large part of it is only knee-deep, riddled with shoals and inlets, and alive with birds, and most of it is inside Everglades National Park. Florida Bay is perfect cruising territory if you crave isolation and privacy and wish to view the natural world close at hand. There is one drawback: You need a boat that draws virtually nothing, like our canoe cruiser.

After cruising awhile in a 17-foot sailing canoe, we commissioned naval architect Phil Bolger to design something larger for us—a 26-foot sailing canoe with the shallow-water capabilities of our old vessel but with greater capacity and seaworthiness. Our choice of such a shoal-draft boat necessarily meant the rig would have to be low aspect. Most effective would be a dipping lug, but we knew it would be too much of a chore for just the two of us to shift the sail to the lee side of the mast at each tack. A spritsail would work as well. After 18 months of building *Dugong* in New Hampshire, from lofting the plans to varnishing the fancy inlays, we trailered her south to a ramp in Biscayne National Monument, just south of Miami, to try out the boat and her rig before attempting any cruising. A short sail took us to our base at Elliot Key, which would be home while we learned how to handle the rig.

There are very few sprit rigs around, so our learning was trial and error. We struggled with the halyard, the sprit snotter, and the hardware. Setting and striking sail were traumatic even in the most planned and benign conditions. But gradually we evolved our own method of dealing with it. Instead of lowering the spritsail on a halyard, we kept it rolled to the mast. Getting under way was simply a matter of releasing the sail, catching the clew as it lashed across the cockpit, and clipping it to the sheet. Letting go the helm, I would race forward, lift the sprit, and clip it to the flapping peak. To raise the peak, Michael would haul tight on the snotter, and then he would secure it to the mast. With practice we gained some finesse in handling it.

Finally the day came when we felt secure enough with *Dugong* to leave Elliot Key. We sailed in company with Wayne and Amy Norwood, who enticed us to head for Florida Bay with tales of the natural world they had seen from their Bahamian smack, *Bohemian*. Even with a 20-knot breeze, the seas in Biscayne Bay remained easy, and we had an exhilarating 6-knot run down Card and Barnes sounds for our first passage. At Jewfish Creek, *Bohemian* towed us through the channel under the bridge, as we had no engine. From the bridge we cut across the banks for The Boggies, three winding, narrow mangrove channels that connect Blackwater Sound and Florida Bay. *Bohemian* kept to the main Intracoastal Waterway channel. Raising the leeboards, we rode zephyr and current down the only navigable Boggie to Florida Bay.

We pulled into North Nest Key, one of the few designated campground, get-out-and-walk-around keys in Florida Bay. For a breeze, we anchored off the point and then tied a line to a scrub bush so we could get ashore easily. In the morning, we went exploring—much easier to do on Nest Key than on most of the others, which are solely for the birds by combined design of nature and National Park Service. The majority of the keys in Florida Bay are barely above water and are composed entirely of mangroves. Roots descend from branches, spreading fingers across to form a tangled jungle gym. In comparison, Nest Key is high, dry, and clear—easy walking.

From a rise behind the beach we could see a large rust-colored puddle in the middle of the key. Sidestepping brush and skirting cactus, we approached its wide muddy shore. Flashy roseate spoonbills, unaware of our presence, marched forward in raggle-taggle rows. Swishing their bills from side to side, they strained food from the shallow pond. We mimicked the stalking cranes as we inched forward, hesitating between steps. With each step our feet sank deeper into the ooze.

Photo by Miachel Walsh

Dugong secured with lines ashore and a stake in the shallows. We're set up with beach chairs and a tent under the trees

200

Finally, neither of us could move. Through sweat-fogged sunglasses I saw Michael swatting mosquitoes.

"I can't get either foot loose," he whispered.

"Me neither," I whispered back. I began to laugh hysterically. The pink flashers jerked to attention, gave us frozen stares, and then resumed their feeding. We remained stuck and sinking. After experimenting cautiously, we found that by wiggling our feet back and forth, we could lift out one at a time with a resounding *tskuup!* We backed out to the beach very slowly.

After a hard night at Black Betsy Key, we awoke to find conditions far from favorable. A hard north wind whipped across the key as we debated the virtues of staying in a lee or using the wind to run the lee between Betsy and the Manatee Keys. Once we left, there would be no turning back. And if we missed Manatee Pass, assuming it really existed, we would careen into drying shoals. My mind hovered and backpeddled, tensed apprehensively on the brink.

After wrapping ourselves in mantles of foul-weather gear, we paused momentarily to brace ourselves and then sailed out. The world exploded. Crashing seas and howling wind reduced us to gestures and primitive fear. Eons passed before Michael yelled. "There's the pass. Full speed ahead!" Clinging to the tiller, he wove us between port and starboard stakes.

In a minute it was all over. The large bight in Manatee Key neatly encircled us with arms of shimmering green mangroves. Steel-blue herons, roseate spoonbills, and brown pelicans with splotches of white, like monks in variegated robes, regarded us from their perches as if to say, "Shhh! Sanctuary." And it was.

We were entranced for two days. Although there was no place to get ashore, we were comfortable on board. We prepared our meals on a Coleman two-burner stove fed by an aluminum propane tank lasted down in the cockpit. We baked bread in our folding oven, and between storage forward and in the stern we carried enough food and water to last us a month.

Dawn. Pink, flashing spoonbills fled across the sky. Michael pulled on his wool cap and put away the bread. A great white heron stalked *Dugong* for bread crumbs. I disconnected the stove from the tank and put it and the pressure cooker below. Michael replaced the coffee, milk, and sugar in the daybox and checked the lashing. With the cockpit cleared, he went forward to raise the sprit, and I turned *Dugong* away from Manatee.

We had a narrow channel to negotiate, and with the clear blue sky that came with the norther, it should have appeared distinctly as a slash of blue. We sailed beyond it before realizing that scattered stakes marked the way. A group of porpoises followed us as we worked our way back. They were comforting company, but one by one they chickened out and returned to deeper water.

Within 2 miles of the main Florida Keys that shield Florida Bay from the Straits of Florida, we joined the inside passage of the Intracoastal Waterway and followed it southward from buoy to buoy. At dusk, near Marathon, we slipped so closely behind Bamboo Key that the wading birds shrieked at us. Bamboo Key was our turning point; on the following day we headed north on the western fringes of Florida Bay aiming for Sandy Key, which the literature for the Everglades National Park listed as a campground.

That afternoon, 15 miles north of Bamboo Key, we searched for our destination. The water had lost its blue-green clarity and was looking more like a tossing pool of milk chocolate. Toothpick stakes marked the encroaching shoal some wit had named the First National Bank.

"Go forward and tell me you see Sandy Key, Michael."

Michael went to the bow and said, "I see Sandy Key."

"Really? You're not just saying that?" The wind was blowing 18 knots, and *Dugong* would fall off rapidly if I left the helm to take a look.

"Sure. It's directly ahead." Michael said, stepping back into the cockpit. I was nervous about my navigation; we'd sailed a 5-mile area that was not covered by our Waterway chart, and I had had to semi-imagine the course.

Shallow banks were close to starboard. We trusted blind luck and held our course, moving too fast to sound with an oar. In the medium high tide, leeboards dragging, we slid deftly over a hidden shoal to anchor in a 2-foot-deep pocket next to Sandy Key's shore. Within an hour, as the tide ebbed, we bellied the bottom.

Sandy Key and neighboring Carl Ross Key typify the best of the Florida Bay keys: long sand beaches and multitudes of all kinds of birds. They also demonstrate the worst aspect of the keys as far as sailors are concerned; shallow waters prevent landings or even close approach. At Sandy Key, while observing a bald eagle, we were warned off the island by a park ranger who said that they were protected. "You could be disturbing the birds. The spoonbills are nesting now."

The campsite is actually on Carl Ross, and at high tide we sailed around Sandy Key to find the channel between them. It was so well disguised that, discouraged by skepticism and the ebbing tide, we sailed on, heading for Flamingo—the only town in this part of the Everglades and headquarters for the national park. It was an easy broad reach along the shore of the mainland, and we made such good time that when we came to the East Cape Canal we ducked in for a look. To our regret the 3-knot current swept us in 600 yards before we knew it. There was nothing to do but anchor for the night, so we steered for the mangrove shore, dropped anchor, and instantly whirled around, bow in the current.

Inside *Dugong*, there's sitting headroom. Cloth pockets snap to stringers, and net bags forward hold food. The radio-tape deck runs off batteries strapped to the mast.

"Well, it's not such a bad place for the night," I said cheerfully.

Michael stared at me. "You look like that cartoon character who always had a swarm of bugs around his head." I felt them, tiny hypodermic no-see-ums, whirling like dervishes around my head. We rinsed off, prepared drinks, and dove below.

When the tide began to ebb on the following day, we escaped the canal, again sailing east toward Flamingo. A well-marked channel leads eastward between extensive shifting shoals to Buttonwood Canal, where the marina and boat basin are located. Thanks to the northwest wind we were able to negotiate this narrowing funnel of a channel until we were in a position to run across to the shores of the Flamingo campground, where we tied to an old dock piling.

Our next move was to sail up the canal to Whitewater Bay, a shallow inland lake north of Flamingo, sail through the lake along what the park map calls the Wilderness Waterway to the Little Shark River, then exit to the Gulf of Mexico and follow the beaches of Cape Sable south until we were back in Florida Bay—in effect, circumnavigating Cape Sable.

The abrupt change from the Florida Bay seas to enclosed Whitewater Bay provoked us to notice details. Jellyfish writhed on the bottom, turtles came up for air, porpoises raced for fish, and raccoons stalked the mangrove roots. At night, we could anchor securely almost anywhere.

At noon of the third day of lake voyaging, we entered Little Shark River. Puffs of wind accompanied the steady 2-knot current as we hurried out to the Gulf, where a northeast breeze quickened our pace. We turned south to sail along the mangrove shores of the cape, dodging sand shoals by eye. After three days of being confined on board we longed to stretch our legs, and the beach at East Cape beckoned 7 miles southward. Long before sunset we were there, the boat beached, a tent set up, and our propane stove and tank sturdy on a home-made shelf of gathered driftwood.

By the third day, after having seen but one other boat, a trimaran, sail by, plus a boatload of tourists from Flamingo power by, we decided to brave the shoals again. Rounding East Cape we headed now due east back to where we had started. Our route was by way of Tin Can Alley through at least a foot of water to the Dump Keys and then on to the noted Crocodile Dragover, the last blue channel on our trip.

Three stakes beckoned to the southeast. "Can you tell on which side we should pass...?" *Dugong* slid to a halt, Michael running forward as I released the sheet. *Dugong* lurched, floating again suddenly. The stakes didn't seem to mark anything. We decided to ignore them and steer directly for the Dragover.

We ran hard aground within sight of the channel. *Dugong* didn't budge. Resolutely we lowered the sail and glumly peered at the channel. So close. "We could try pushing with the oars," I suggested.

Each to a side, we pressed an oar into the soft muck and walked bow to stern, shoving *Dugong* forward. At twilight the faintest glow finally ushered us into Crocodile Dragover, our last long, wavy pass through Florida Bay. Gratefully, we anchored for the night. In *Dugong's* womblike cabin, we fell asleep to the familiar snapping sound of tiny shrimp accompanied by a mysterious muffled croaking. "Crocodiles," Michael muttered.

In the morning, Crocodile Dragover stretched before us, a blue-green channel running eastward around Eagle Key and toward the Boggies. With tanbark sails drawing, we ran with the wind at our backs toward home.

CHAPTER 8

GENERAL MODIFICATIONS
CANOE, OPEN AND CUDDY BOATS

MAKE IT STRONG AND SEAWORTHY

Parts of the boat which are essential to seaworthiness must be inspected and modified if necessary. This means checking the rudder mounts, stays, shrouds, lines, centerboard, leeboard mounts, etc. In common with most of the small boat cruisers I've read about and met, we routinely beef up all essential equipment and hardware. Our sailing canoe *Manatee* got a stronger leeboard bracket and stronger leeboards: our Hobie Cat *Kohoutek* got heavier stays, and an extra layer of fiberglass on the bottom of the hulls; *Dugong* got heavier pintles and gudgeons for her rudder and a tough plastic cover on her bottom. Most small boats are equipped to be only raced or daysailed. Cruising loads stress boats more than daysailing and modifications are needed to meet these stresses. Some general modifications to consider include:

Heavier stays

Heavier rudder, leeboard, centerboard mounting hardware

Build a kick-up rudder to replace one that doesn't

Beef up the bottom of the hull with high density polyethylene, fiberglass or wood

Epoxy any wood below the waterline to prevent the hull from drying out ashore, then leaking like a sieve when launched

Reinforce mast step at deck and base

Reinforce chain plates and other through hull fittings

Install a manual bilge pump under floorboards so that you can easily bail the boat

Carry break-down oars, obtainable from Carlisle Paddles, P.O. Box 488, Grayling, MI 49738

MAKE IT EASY TO SAIL

If any of the control lines, like sheets, halyards, and centerboard pendants, are difficult to reach, make them handy. Use hardware that makes line handling both handier **and** easier. Run as many controlling lines to the cockpit as you can. If you can drop the sail, pull in a reef, tend the main and jib sheets, and lift your board from the cockpit, you'll be safer and more secure than if you couldn't.

Take advantage of hardware to ease the strain on yourself. Install cam cleats and blocks to relieve your hands of service.

Twin fuel tanks fit snugly into closed compartments in the *Lowell Sailing Surf Dory*
Editor's note: Fuel storage should be as safe as possible. Tie-down straps should
be added. Small boats get kicked around in heavy seas—or even heavy wakes!

Put a downhaul on the jib and install a jiffy reefing system for your
main sail. Install lazy jacks where appropriate to help the sail fall neatly
into a pile and out of the way.

Consider installing a little sprit boom on the jib so that it will be self-
tending. If you do this, you are relieved of having to re-sheet the jib on
each tack.

Re-build short, wide, non-lifting rudders into thinner, lifting rudders.
This will make steering easier and make you worry less about damaging
the rudder.

Re-mount any rudder post that follows the angle of a reverse transom.
Alter the transom, or fittings, so that the rudder enters the water from a
vertical position. This will help steering, and prevent broaches on a
downwind run in a seaway.

MAKE IT EASY TO ANCHOR AND/OR BEACH

A lot can be learned from other peoples' experiences and modifications. But mostly you'll learn what you need to do from your own experiences. In general, though, the following suggestions are recommended on
all daysailer-size boats used for cruising.

Install appropriate mounts and fittings so that the anchor may be dropped and raised from the cockpit. Run the anchor rode through an eye at the bow then aft to the cockpit so that the anchor can be released from the cockpit, cleated temporarily, then cleated off the bow after the sails are dropped.

Provide for two anchors if you plan to anchor a lot. Two anchors set at a 45 degree angle or so will prevent your boat from sailing around at anchor. This is a common problem with most light, shoal-draft boats.

If you have a split rig, carry a tiny mizzen sail to keep up at anchor. This will keep the boat headed into the wind and so prevent it from sailing around the anchor.

Install handles or non-skid on the boat where you need to grab it to lift it or roll it ashore.

MAKE IT COMFORTABLE

The more comfortable you are, the more often, for longer periods of time, you'll actually go out cruising. Don't presume beachcruising is a masochistic sport. Some discomforts can be reduced with a little thought and effort. Various association newsletters and sailing, boating, and camping magazine articles are invaluable sources of ideas and plans. It's incredible just how many ingenious beachcruisers are out there. Some starter projects might include:

Consider widening the seats

Carry plywood or fabric hammocks to make wide bunks across seats and centerboard

Install opening ports in cuddy cabins

Remove unnecessary bunks, shelves, etc. to create more sleeping area on the floor of the cuddy

Make a bimini, sturdy awnings and a sleeping tent

Editor's note: *Many specific modifications are described in the boat descriptions in Chapters 5, 6, and 7, each for a specific design of boat.*

SOURCES FOR ADDITIONAL INFORMATION

Books

100 Small Boat Rigs, by Phillip C. Bolger, $18.60, 217 pages, 1984, International Marine, TAB Books, Inc., Blue Ridge Summit, PA 17294-0840

Understanding Rigs and Rigging, by Richard Henderson, $32.45, 272 pages, 1985, International Marine, TAB Books, Inc., Blue Ridge Summit, PA 17294-0840.

These books compare the advantages and disadvantages of different types of rigs; includes information about how to set up reefing systems, run halyards, etc.; illustrated

Magazine Articles

"Lug Rigs: The Ultimate in Low Aspect Sailing," by Chris Wentz, Rigs and Rigging Section, Small Boat Journal #38, Aug./Sept. 1984

"The Gaff Rig," by Chris Wentz, Rigs and Rigging Section, Small Boat Journal #39, Oct./Nov. 1984

"Tame Your Sail," by Dave Gerr, Small Boat Journal #43, #44. Describes rigging lazy jacks and topping lifts

"Sprit Rig Basics, by Ernie Cassidy, WoodenBoat #89, August 1989

Equipment

Balogh Sail Designs, Rt. 1, Box 462B, Newport, NC 28570. Mark Balogh's fully battened sails with reefing system; also offers leeboards, rudders, and masts for kayaks, canoes, prams, and rowboats

"Dura Surf," from Crown Plastics, 115 May Dr., Harrison, OH 45039. Heavy duty plastic sheeting for the bottom of your boat. We used this on *Dugong*

"Mini Reefer," from Cruising Design, Inc., Box 151, Peabody, MA 01960. Jib roller furling system for small boats

Photo by Ron Johnson

Sammye Johnson preparing breakfast on the *Sea Pearl*. The awning over the cabin keeps sleeping quarters snug and dry

CHAPTER 9

OUTFITTING THE BOAT

ANCHORS AND ANCHORING SYSTEMS

Loaded with camping gear, clothing, food and water, the boat is likely to be too heavy to lift, slide or roll onto even a gently inclined beach. Before beaching, we've always lightened the canoe or small boat of at least the heavy stuff—water, camping backpack, dive gear, food, and the galley box. We've carried these ashore before beaching the boat. If seas are calm, the boat can be unloaded while it floats gently against the sandy beach. If there's a surf, the boat will have to be held off, in deeper water, during the unloading.

We used an anchor to hold *Manatee* in place. An anchor serves in so many ways that it's an essential item even on a boat that's always beached. Get the best and the biggest anchor you can accommodate, and fit it with close to 10 feet of light chain, and 150 feet of ½-inch nylon rode. We've found Barnacle anchors effectively self-burying and easily stowed. Bruce anchors are effective, but less easily stowed. Danforth anchors are not easily stowed, and we often have to bury them by hand—not a problem in wading depths.

At other times, we've used an anchor to stay offshore during buggy nights or when we can't find a suitable landing; to stream astern to slow down and minimize broaching; to keep us in place while diving on a reef or casting for fish; to open coconuts and conch; and to make a pulley mooring in places where we didn't want to or couldn't keep the boat ashore.

To make a mooring that lets us retrieve the boat from shore, we tie a pulley to the anchor shank where the rode or chain is usually fastened to the anchor. The anchor rode is run through that block or pulley, the anchor dropped well beyond the low tide line, and we come ashore with both ends of the anchor rode, and knot the ends together. After unloading the boat, we tie a painter to that knot in the anchor rode. (A "painter" is a shorter line tied to the bow of a boat.) By pulling on one side of the looped anchor rode, the boat can be hauled back out into the deeper water where the anchor was dropped. The shore end of the mooring loop is tied to a tree or to a stake that's within dry reach at high tide.

Another anchoring-off tactic is more primitive and works as well, but use this method only as a temporary anchor, and never in any seas. We tie one end of a 50-foot plus line to the bow. We find a heavy rock (20 pounds plus) and tie it to that line about 10 feet from the bow, depending on the depth of water. The rock is usually contained in an old towel or canvas bag. When we're ready to leave the boat, we balance the rock on the edge of the bow deck and give the boat a gentle push-off. When the boat is a safe distance off, a jerk on the line tumbles the rock off the deck and anchors the boat. We tie the shore end of the bow line to a stake or under a rock. After lunch and an exploration of the shore, we pull the line in and the boat and rock come ashore.

Anchor

An anchor should be on board and as ready to use as you can possibly stow it. Our experience is that anything under 15 pounds is going to be hard to set. We tried the old anchor-weight-to-boat-length formula and found that when you get down to small boats, the formula fails. Sure, a 7-pound anchor will **hold** a 12-foot open boat, but you'll first have to set it by hand. It is too light to set itself. On *Dugong* we tried using a 10-pound Danforth for about four months. It took us about two months to figure out that it was just too light to set itself. The last two months we either set it by hand or shoved it into a soft bottom with the oar. This got to be tedious, even if we were only anchoring in 3 to 4 feet. Who feels like getting in the water when it's cold, or dark, or if the water's so murky you don't know **what's** down there? When we switched to a 15-pound Danforth, we didn't have any more trouble.

Five to 10 feet of chain between anchor and rode will increase the effective scope on the anchor and cushion the jerks in a strong blow. Chain won't chafe on the bottom as a line will. About 90 feet of line will suffice to anchor in depths to 15 feet. The rule of thumb is to pay out seven times as much anchor rode as depth in feet under the hull. If you're anchoring in 5 feet of water, you'll want at least 35 feet of rode including the chain.

Photo by Shane St. Clair

Sea Pearl 21 beached in the ICW, South Carolina. Note she carries a Bruce anchor on the bow and an outboard astern, both at the ready. The framework over the cockpit supports an awning. Shane St. Clair cruised this boat single handed more than 5000 miles. There's only a faint breeze but the sails should be furled

BEACHING YOUR BOAT
(See also Chapter 10, "Landing Your Boat")

On most beaches we're able to lay down some plastic sheeting, the stuff that comes in rolls that house painters and building contractors use. Wet it, and slide the boat up onto dry ground. On steeper beaches, we put inflatable fenders under the hulls, and roll the boat up the beach. Non-skid tape at the right spots helps us keep a firm grip on the hulls. With wide, nylon shoulder harnesses tying us to the boat, we lift, pull, and drag the boat ashore. At the end of a long fatiguing day, we've had to apply all these methods.

Even a 1500-pound boat can be beached using a four-part tackle or "come-along" tied to a tree or to a well-buried anchor, if the boat is rolled on long, fat, air rollers. These 10-inch by 4-foot sausages make comfortable seating aboard or around camp, and add a safe margin of flotation to any boat. They're available from Defender Industries, 255 Main Street, New Rochelle, NY 10801.

Anchoring and beaching gear are essential, but it would be rare to need sheets of plastic **and** rollers. Usually one will better serve the needs of a single cruise. Plastic sheet is cheaper, takes less room, weighs less, and has a lot of other uses around camp. Bumpers and rollers add to flotation and last for several cruises.

Bottom Paint

Because we cruise for extended periods, we paint the bottom of our boats with a toxic, anti-fouling paint. Any boat that's kept in the sea for longer than a month will develop a growth of marine things like weeds and barnacles. Unless you plan to scrub it off regularly (every three days), an anti-fouling paint is a good investment, and easily applied. We've tried several kinds and now use a paint that's hard enough to not get worn off during our daily groundings and beachings. It's named The Protector, Z-Spar, by Kopper Company. It's not cheap, but a small boat needs only a quart every other year.

Getting off the Beach

In the morning, rested, with the beach sloped in our favor, it's always easy launching. Ashore, we'd have relaxed over breakfast, explored the island, exercised our legs and washed up. Though we hope to go ashore for lunch, we prepare and pack a lunch of sandwiches or fritters or pancakes or cereal and dried fruits and cookies and nuts, within reach on the boat, in case we are unable to get ashore before lunch time. A bottle of drinking water and some snacks go next to the compass-binoculars and the chart. Even when we get up at sunrise, getting all the camp gear repacked and these daily needs organized, takes time. We're seldom afloat before ten.

SAFETY EQUIPMENT

Exactly how and what we prepare for each day depends on the cruising area, the boat we're on, the weather, how far we plan to sail, and our mood. How you outfit your boat will depend on this same set of criteria, and on your resources and personal needs and prejudices. Following are items you should consider.

Anchors and beaching gear have been described before.

Bailing the Boat

Another necessary item is some device or devices to bail water out of the boat. It's so obvious, we've sometimes overlooked it. It's a good idea to install a self-bailing device, but because it may fail to keep up with the

Photo by Chris Harkness

Author Ida and Michael Walsh loading gear aboard a Drascombe Dabber after shore camp is struck. If you beach the boat, launch it before stowing all that gear. They pack small like items in a single container

rain or waves, you should also have a manual backup. We usually use an empty plastic Clorox bottle with the bottom cut off, and a sponge. Plastic gets brittle with age, so flex-test Clorox bottles found on beaches.

At times we've been happy to have a self-bailer and have used a small hand pump. Most often we keep the sponge in use as it leaves the surface driest. Sponges are so useful for all sorts of chores that we carry a few sizes. To prevent them from floating away when they are most needed, we keep a bailer and a sponge tied to the boat with a strong line and a tight knot. Indeed, almost everything is tied to the boat. Even the assortment of lines used to tie things, is itself tied to the boat! A capsize is such a disorganized event that to have to go swimming around retrieving stuff that's floating free makes recovery dangerously delayed.

On *Dugong* we installed a small bilge pump so that we wouldn't have to lift the floor boards to bail. If we had to lift the floor boards every time we had to bail, we'd wait 'till the water rose above the boards. Something as routine as bailing should be made as easy as possible. When we suffered some real deluges in Key West, we were sure glad to be able to pump 15 gallons a minute without having to stoop, lift, toss, stoop, lift, toss. The inch and a half hose on the outlet side of the pump snakes overboard through the oar port, so we didn't even have to cut a hole anywhere for it. If the oar port weren't there, we'd just increase the length of hose and run it over the gunwale.

Photo by Michael Walsh

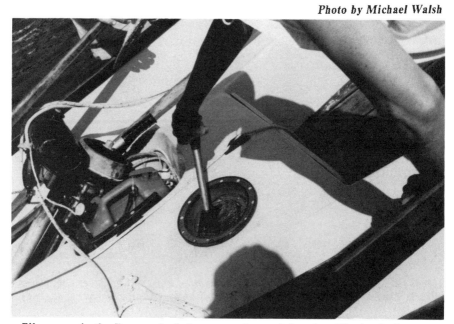

Bilge pump in the *Drascombe* is in an easy-to-reach location. The intake hose runs down beneath the floor boards. On small boats with no bilge, a large plastic scoop will do, but keep that bailer secured to the boat with a line!

Oars or Paddles

Your boat and layout will help you determine whether to carry paddles, oars, or a scull. Be sure to carry at least one of these choices and a spare. For most small boats, oars and oarlocks should be handy in case the wind dies, or you have to negotiate a narrow channel, or if the sail tears, or your outboard dies. Oars were impractical on our Hobie Cat and our sailing canoes, but we sure carried paddles at all times. Whenever possible, we install oars because they are a much more powerful way to propel the boat. Many a time they got us where we wanted to go when sailing couldn't.

An oar or scull serves as an emergency rudder as well as alternative propulsion. Of these, the scull is the most effective for propulsion. Well-placed oars are more effective than paddles. Sculling is a skill that must be learned with patience.

Editor's note: Our 17-foot day sailer Pow Wow had a terrible weather helm when we sailed her 100 miles home using an oar in place of our lost rudder. We could only last by spelling each other every hour. We never rigged an outboard bracket on Pow Wow. When we needed power, we lifted the big, heavy oak outboard rudder off the transom where it was attached with bronze pintles into bronze gudgeons. Then we'd mount the outboard motor. When sailing, we'd reverse this procedure. Coming north out of Sag Harbor, NY, under power to where we could catch the light westerly shielded by the North Haven peninsula, I took the outboard off and stowed it, and was in the process of fitting the heavy rudder onto the transom. At that moment, this three-story glitzy 50-foot power yacht came close by at flank speed, throwing a wake that rocked us violently. I would have gone overboard with the rudder, but I saved myself by letting the rudder go and grabbing the traveler for support. After all, the rudder is oak and that floats, right? I saw it shimmering away, confident that it would bob up, but it sank into murky depths to bury itself in mud. Evidently the bronze straps holding the pintles overcame what little buoyancy the oak had. We dove after it in 19 feet but couldn't see much down there and never recovered it.

A local yard back home made a replacement out of plywood, but it wasn't strong enough. I borrowed Earle Bragdon's Pow Wow rudder and bought oak, which a local lumber company machined for me, and I put together a fine new rudder that worked.

Life Jackets

The U.S. Coast Guard requires life jackets. They must be handy, effective, and there must be at least one for every person aboard. Some types also serve as a seat cushion, back pad, and/or pillow. Although we have put them on in rough seas, we are also tied to the boat by a line. Our boats have good flotation. Some sharks are attracted by the color of the orange-yellow life jackets! Yum-yum yellow!

Highest quality Type III life jackets are a must. Even in sheltered waters, a squall can capsize a boat and separate it from its occupants. Life jackets, immediately available and put into use, have saved many lives—and would have saved many more had they been used. We have met people whose lives were saved because they wore life jackets. It is important to get a jacket that is so comfortable that you almost prefer wearing it to leaving it off. I was glad to have mine on when I accidently flipped the Hobie Cat. The capsize took me completely by surprise, so when I fell off, I fell hard. My life jacket cushioned my fall against the stays. Once I was in the water struggling to right the boat, it buoyed me up. *Editor's note: Be sure you have yours on in rough seas. You may not find it if you swamp or capsize or have to abandon ship.*

Photo by Chris Harkness

Outward Bound of Florida takes people under sail to camping spots where they practice survival skills. Note that *everybody* is wearing life jackets

Fire Extinguishers

Editor's note: Except on canoes and other small open boats, the Coast Guard requires that you carry one or two of these, depending on the size of the boat. You certainly want a fire extinguisher handy if you're using a stove aboard your boat or ashore. A bucket of water is handy near a campfire. Water will put out an alcohol fire, but it may spread the fire. We use dry chemical extinguishers that will smother a fire. Be sure you get one that will extinguish fuel, electrical, and wood fires. Our authors prefer a Halon extinguisher. We have one extinguisher mounted on the bulkhead at the galley, and we keep a package of baking soda in the galley. It will put out grease fires.

A second dry chemical extinguisher is mounted on the bulkhead in the forepeak. Try to mount them so you can grab one from anyplace on the boat.

Beachcruisers will seldom, if ever, cook underway. If you ever have to, be very careful of stove-top frying. You can blow up the boat. Galley fires are the main cause of boat fires. The only time I ever feared fire aboard was off Cayos Cochinos in the Bay Islands of Honduras. We'd had bacon and eggs for breakfast and it was time to get underway, but the cook wanted to cook the rest of the bacon for future use. He persuaded me that he could manage while we sailed in light air. Famous last words! Some bacon fat spilled, and he had fire on the stove spreading to adjacent teak. I yelled to him to put the extinguisher on it but his priority was to save the bacon. Finally, they got the fire out and we emptied the flaming pan over the side!

Signaling Gun and Flares

If you plan to sail at night or very far off shore, carry a signaling gun and flare in some waterproof pouch. They don't take up much room, and provide a measure of security.

The Coast Guard also requires that a kit of light flares and smoke flares be on board. These may help others to find you if you become disabled. Small boats in large seas are difficult to find. These flares are cheap, small, and could be used as a defensive weapon. *Editor's note: Signaling guns are not considered firearms, but at close range, will repel boarders.*

Whistle

We wear a whistle on a string around our necks whenever we go out in the boat. If one of us were to fall overboard, the whistle will help us be found. When we're caught in bad weather, it warns other boaters of our presence. I never thought we'd need our whistles for fog but we sure did once. We were sailing *Kohoutek*, with *Manatee* in tow, south of Miami's Government Cut. It was November, very early in the morning. A thick fog descended, obliterating everything from sight except for us and our two little boats. Us on the I-95 of Miami's waterfront! Around us we could hear speed boats tear by, completely unseen. I can tell you we blew our whistles and hard. We've also made rare use of the whistles attached to the life jackets.

215

Fog Horn

We also have a small, cheap, but ear-splitting horn that is powered by a button release compressed air can. We've used these to attract the attention of other boats and bridge tenders.

We've not yet had to signal a large ship. We've seen them and been able to evade them. Beachcruisers don't spend much time in shipping lanes. When we do, we maintain a sharp lookout and always give them right of way.

Radar Detectors and Reflectors

In poor visibility conditions, a radar detector can warn us that a larger vessel is within radar range. These devices are like the speed trap radar detectors sold to warn speeders of radar traps ahead.

We use the passive equivalent to the radar detector—a radar reflector that makes us appear on a radar screen much larger than we are. Without a reflector, a little boat in fog, rain, darkness, or by the boredom of constant vigil, might be overlooked by the bridge of a big steamship. We carry a cheap one that we hang from the mast only while we're crossing a shipping lane. *Editor's note*: *Radar reflectors provide best reflection when hung from a spreader, with the bottom end tied down. You don't want it banging the sails or mast.*

A recently available device is a "personal" radar reflector. It is an inflatable balloon, coated to reflect radar frequency, which is tethered aloft on a long line. In a strong wind, I'm not sure how high it would loft. It would surely help a search party to find a small boat or floating person in distress.

Survival Kit

A last essential piece of safety equipment is a survival kit for each of us. It's small enough to be stuck into a pocket of our foul weather gear or tied to a life jacket. In it are some things we want if we are suddenly separated from the boat. Our experience (we and our boat have been suddenly parted!) recommends a few small silver coins, a few 10 and 20 dollar bills, some vitamins and chocolate bars, antibiotic ointment and pills, credit cards and identification documents, paper and pencil, a butane lighter, small flares, and that Swiss Army knife. Depending on where you are, a hand held VHF in a waterproof pouch and/or a personal E.P.I.R.B will help you be found. Some hooks and a fish line are in ours. Our compass and sandals are always at the ready.

TOOLS AND SPARES

On beachcruisers which have wire rigging, or wire pendants to control a centerboard, a replacement wire, fitted with end fittings, may allow you to continue a cruise that would otherwise be aborted. On our Hobie Cat, a very specialized wire halyard failed. Again, on a sharpie, we let the heavy iron centerboard push into the well as we ran over a shoal. We didn't take up the slack on the pendant. As we sailed off the edge of the shoal, into a deep channel, the centerboard fell hard enough to part the wire pendant and continue forward with enough momentum to crack the case and tear out the pin. Conceivably, it could have split the boat in two! Some cold diving recovered the board, and a tube of Sikaflex patched the case. However, as we didn't have a replacement pin or replacement wire, we continued sailing by using the board as a leeboard.

To keep even a small boat going will require a few tools to help replace and repair damages and failures. On our beachcruiser we keep the following:

Pliers and/or ViseGrips
Screwdrivers
Adjustable crescent wrench
Hatchet with hammer back
Hacksaw blades
Soft stainless wire
Stainless or bronze nails, bolts, nuts, and washers
Stainless self-tapping screws (sheet metal screws)
Sikaflex or 5200 marine sealant-adhesive
Marine-Tex: an epoxy that hardens under water and adheres to wet surfaces
Pliobond (contact cement) and black Autoseal
Fiberglass and epoxy resin and hardener
Duct tape, masking tape, air hose tape & gaffers (electrical) tape
A diamond sharpening stone (DMT)
An 8-inch stainless blade knife
For each person, a Swiss Army knife with everything
Needles and thread
A piece of inner tube rubber
A cutting board
Pieces of wood, thin plywood, and aluminum sheet

When we use an outboard we've added to the above:

Spare plugs and points, or power pack
Spark plug wrench
Shear and cotter pins, or hub
Spare prop
Fuel pump diaphram
Water pump impeller

Some of these get old (Sikaflex, tapes, epoxy) or rusted (pliers and hack saw blades) and have to be replaced periodically.

Some items deserve explanation. "Pliobond" is a very liquidy contact adhesive that comes in a three-ounce bottle. It's applied to both surfaces with a brush inside the cap. We use it to seal minor holes and cracks in anything; and to stick anything together—shoe soles, torn sail, one side of

217

Velcro to wood. Sikaflex and 5200 (3M) are much thicker, stronger, and messier adhesive-caulking compounds that come in large tubes. They are applied with a caulking gun. Sikaflex sets up fast—sometimes even before you open the tube! We use them to make major patches and permanent repairs. These polysulfides are so strong that once they set up, the materials can't be taken apart without destruction.

Our diamond sharpening stone is so much faster than any other, and we appreciate sharp knives so much that it is worth the higher cost. We fillet many fish, and this requires sharpness.

Gaffers tape is used by theater electricians and lighting technicians. It is super sticky. Air hose tape is used by divers and sticks well even when it's wet and applied to a wet surface. Both are specialty tapes that may not be easily found.

ITEMS REQUIRED FOR COMFORT

Protection Against Sun

Among personal spares we carry:
>   prescription eyeglasses
>   a hat (sunstroke can lead to death)
>   sunscreen
>   clip-on polarized sunglasses

We can't see clearly beyond inches without our glasses. Without a hat covering our heads and shielding our faces and eyes, we could sail in the tropics, comfortably, only at night. The polarized sunglasses are essential for navigation as well as to protect our vision. These eliminate surface reflections on the water so we can see the bottom. They also stop 95% of the ultraviolet radiation that contributes to glaucoma. To see the bottom is entertaining as well as cautionary.

Editor's note: In the tropics, we've seen people from northern climes suffer severe sunburn in short times. They do not realize the difference between the strong tropical sun and the sun back home. You must cover up, and apply a powerful sun screen (SPF 15 to 30) to your face and any other exposed parts. We wear loose fitting long-sleeved shirts and long pants, and always a broad brimmed hat. Some prefer pajamas. Bring an extra hat in case one blows away. A chin strap or a string tied to your belt will prevent loss.

Protection Against Cold and Rain or Spray

Kohoutek, the 14-foot Hobie Cat with which we cruised the Bahamas, was a very wet boat. Sometimes we were cold. We tried using our wet suits in which we dive. They helped, but they are bulky and restricting. For such wet sailing today, we would wear "dry suits" that have been developed for divers and cold-weather board sailors.

We guessed wrong when we first started cruising the Florida Keys. Though it was late November and we'd be cruising throughout the winter, we thought that south Florida weather was like the Exumas. There, in the central Bahamas, we'd cruised many winters and the temperature never dropped below 60 degrees. Sure, we had cold fronts, but nothing a light flannel shirt couldn't handle. Lilo, an old friend who'd moved to Florida from the Exumas a year before we came down, tried to warn us. She told us it got **cold** in the winter in Florida. We didn't listen, didn't bring a heavy blanket, and froze at night. We didn't start to enjoy ourselves until the wool hats, gloves and blanket arrived by post in Key West.

Foul Weather Gear

Summer is the wet season in the tropics, but it sometimes rains in winter too, sometimes heavily in storms. It's important to know how often and how much it might rain so that you know your chances of getting

Photo by Chris Harkness

Author Ida starting the Seagull outboard lowered through the well of a *Drascombe Dabber*. Note her broad-brimmed hat, good protection against skin cancer, used with sunblock. An outboard is a safety factor for a small boat. When the wind dies, an adverse current might take you into danger

caught in it. If prepared, you'll have **comfortable rain gear** and a way to catch the rain for your fresh water supply. If caught unprepared, you can suffer wet cold even in 80-degree temperatures. We managed to get caught unprepared one summer in the Exumas. We stopped on a small island made up of rough coral and a large sand spit. We set up camp on the only flat space, the wide open spit of sand. Thunderclouds threatened in the distance. By the time we quit fooling around and had camp set up, the storm was upon us. We thought it would pass quickly, so didn't secure our gear carefully. The torrential downpour drove rain into our canoe through an unsnapped part of the cover, collapsed the tent, soaked our bedding and left us like limp wet rags shivering in the aftermath. It was 80 degrees and we were **cold!**

Even if you're planning to cruise in a place where it hardly ever rains, you'll want good foul weather gear. Spray wets your clothes and makes you cold. Foul weather gear keeps you clothes dry and your body warm. When we started cruising, we afforded ourselves the cheapest of foul weather pants and jackets. They were such a joke. they passed water right through and tore to shreds within weeks. They weren't worth the little they'd cost. Over the years, we've bought better and better foul weather gear. Not 'till three years ago did we really appreciate the difference **superior** foul weather gear makes. We now use Rukka gear which comes from Finland. The bib pants and jacket with hood sell for about $170. They are so comfortable that we wear them casually for warmth as much as we wear them for spray and rain. They never leak; the hood is secure and visor clear; the wrists and ankles tight against dribble; the material soft and not suffocating. I'm sorry we didn't put good foul weather gear high on our list of priorities a long time ago.

Water Makers

Although many islands in the Caribbean are singularly arid, we've always been able to find fresh water. At times it took some searching and digging and experience to find it. If we didn't want to look for it, or if we cruised a region with even less rainfall, like Baja, we might carry one or two hand-held and hand-powered reverse osmosis water distillation units to use for making sea water drinkable. These are not cost effective if the water contains any sediment like fine sand or clay, or if there is any low tech alternative. ***Editor's note***: *If you're camping for longer than overnight, set up a catchment for rain water. Even while you're underway, a bucket will catch rain water coming off the sails or boom. You may have to funnel it to the bucket.*

Boom Tents and Awnings

Whether we sleep aboard or ashore depends on where we choose to cruise. In some places, particularly populated areas and shorelines that make landing dangerous, we try to sleep aboard. Also, if our intention is to continue sailing each day, then it's expedient to set up the boat for camping aboard instead of ashore. We've found a boom tent a necessity. A medium weight, highest quality cotton or cotton/synthetic is our choice of fabrics. Light weight and stiff synthetic fabrics make a lot of noise in even a gentle breeze, and the interior condensation of non-wicking fabrics will drip all night sufficiently to make the bedding wet.

All these fabrics are quite flammable. If you're cooking aboard under a tent or an awning, keep a good fire extinguisher handy. If you get one that's charged with Halon, you'll be more likely to use it. Halon is effective on all types of fire, and it makes the least mess.

Make a mock-up with old bed sheets. Raise the aft end of the boom with the halyard for added headroom aft while minimizing wind resistance forward. Avoid zippers as they require close tailoring and are apt to get jammed with salt. Favor loop and toggle fastenings backed by Velcro for additional weatherproofing. Include openings fore and aft for visibility, attending chores like the anchor warp, and for venting in fair weather. Even though they do drip condensation, we appreciate the sewn-in plastic windows on each side.

With hooks and elastic lacing, our boom tent can be made quite tight to minimize flapping in a breeze. In a small cockpit the same can be accomplished by threading the oars through laces along the outboard edges. To minimize sagging and flapping, we've added glass battens sprung across the boom inside the tent.

We keep the fabric and seams waterproof by brushing on a seam sealant. It is also coated with a fire retardant and with a mildewcide. Still, unless it is completely dry when folded, it will rot. Choose your color carefully. Blue is visually cool and dark. White looks old quickly. Red, orange and yellow are conspicuous but cheerful. A pale green or tan is an easy compromise.

In the tropics, an awning that shades us while underway is a necessity. If you can't think of a way to install such a well-framed contrivance under the low boom of a small boat, then equip yourself with a sun umbrella that you can mount over your steering station. The best of these are made for farm tractors and are available from farm machinery dealers. On gentle days, when you most need the shade, a cheaper model would serve. Cruising in Buzzards Bay, MA, I didn't think we'd need shade while underway. But even at that high latitude, wearing a cap, I suffered too much sun.

NAVIGATION EQUIPMENT

We use our senses as we would a sextant or a compass. We navigate by watching the coast, the color of the water; by paying attention to where we've been, looking back often, and to what's ahead. Our eyes and ears tell us about bad currents, rocks, weird swells, surf, rip tides and breaking seas. Since it often doesn't matter if we know **exactly** where we are on the chart, we stay tuned in to respond to the changing condition of our surroundings.

Editor's note: You can avoid many problems if you learn to keep track of your position at all times. If visibility socks in, or the wind becomes a bit much, you want to know exactly where you are. Keep track!

The main tools we use for navigation are: a mounted compass for steering and a hand-held compass for bearings; waterproof binoculars; polarized sunglasses; a parallel rule for plotting courses; charts; tide tables; tidal current tables; and guide books.

Photo by Michael Walsh

While author Ida (under that hat!) is at the tiller following the box compass at her feet, Chris Harkness plots a course. Following a course will enable them to do dead reckoning to have an approximate position even when they can't see land

Compass

Actually, we didn't even have a reliable compass, mounted or otherwise, the first three months of cruising in the Bahamas with *Manatee* and *Kohoutek*. Shore was always right there. Well, almost always. When we crossed 10 open ocean miles to Little San Salvador and another 10 to Long Island, all we used was a Boy Scout compass. It made us a little nervous. Therefore, when we needed to cross **30** open miles, some of which would be out of sight of land, we did mount a good steering compass on *Kohoutek's* trampoline where it was easy to see. After it was mounted, we checked it against our own little Boy Scout compass, which we had checked previously for deviation. This way we could be assured that when we steered 90 degrees by the compass, we were either doing 90 degrees magnetic or knew by exactly how much we were **not** doing 90 degrees. Steering with an error of just one degree means a difference of a half-mile 30 miles later. We're always very careful not to put any ferrous metal near the compass that will disturb its readings.

We now carry a lighted compass mounted to the boat, and a hand-held, hockey-puck, Mini Morin compass. It helps us feel more confident to check them against each other. Whatever iron is aboard, and where it is placed in relation to any compass, will affect the readings. Sometimes the effect is drastic. Once we've got all the iron stowed, we take an early opportunity to check a few corrected compass bearings against some conspicuous landmarks that appear on the chart. Thus we have a note of the deviation of the mounted (fixed) compass. Deviation should be noted at 45-degree intervals (8 points), for the mounted boat's compass. We use a compass deviation card. Compass deviation is not the same as magnetic variation. As long as we stow our iron stuff in the same places, the compass deviation doesn't change. Our portable compasses provide a check only if we remember to keep them away from iron. Our stainless steel Swiss Army knives, in our pockets, and flashlights, have thrown off the compass enough to fool us. But usually, when we've not believed the compass, it's been right and our sense of place has been wrong.

You always hear about people out hiking or boating who get all turned around and think they're headed one way, when the compass tells them they're headed another. We were cruising in the Canadian lakes when we had this classic situation happen to us. A fine mist enveloped us as we groped through a maze of islets, deep bays, and long inlets. Finally we got so confused about where we were headed that we stopped, got out of the canoe, and took some compass readings. The compass pointed north, to our right as we stood on the shore looking out at the lake. We both agreed that by no means could north be that way! We even walked down the shore a ways to be sure there wasn't some iron ore or something affecting it. But we knew the compass was accurate. Finally we just had to believe it, and it was right!

That little hand-held Mini Morin hockey puck compass is our survival compass. We carry it with us ashore. If we are separated from the boat, it's the one we'll take with us.

Binoculars

Many navigational tools are fun to use as well as necessary. Our binoculars are Fujinon. These are powerful (x8), bright (50 mm), and include a built-in, lighted compass which we use to take bearings of distant objects. Don't get any stronger because binoculars magnify your movements (and the boat's) and distant objects will appear to not be still; and stronger magnification implies more weight. The lighter, the better. *Editor's note: We find 7 x 35 easier to use on cruising sailboats.*

Waterproof, floating binoculars have always been an essential part of our gear. They help us see landmarks, channel stakes, and other boats in time to plan ahead. They are especially handy in Florida Bay where some channel stakes are very hard to make out until you're on them. We were cruising *Dugong* there one winter when it seemed we were running downwind before a northwest blow every other day. During one particularly hard blow, we were running for a channel between two dry shoals. If our course took us a little too far to port, we'd have to gybe to make the channel, if we could make the channel at all by then. With the help of binoculars, we were able to make out the two thin white stakes ahead. This gave us time to alter course and skid right through the channel. I'd feel a little lost without my binoculars.

We're out here beachcruising for fun. Binoculars expand our view of the world around us. We use our binocs as much for watching birds, other boats, houses, people, the moon, as we do for watching for practicality's sake.

Editor's note: I'll never forget coming into the Puerto Cortez Naval Base on the west shore of Baja California, at night during our cruise from Acapulco to San Diego in 1964. We were on the Isla Mangrove range looking for the Marcy Channel range 4.5 NM to the SSE, me on the tiller, Earle Bragdon looking out from the bow. I saw one light, but I knew there should be two. The land configurations looked strange, and I thought the light must be part of Puerto Cortez. We quickly ran out of fathoms, lined up the Isla Mangrove range and hightailed it back where we came from, before we ran aground. When we got back to the light we'd seen, I put the binoculars on it, and sure enough it was two lights, the Marcy Channel range we'd been looking for!

Never mind whether it looks right or you're not sure. I learned to put the binoculars on it!

Polarized Sunglasses

Polarized sunglasses or clip-on shades eliminate glare and they allow us to see color and depth where we otherwise would see only reflected light. They are a pleasure and ultraviolet light protection to the eye, and a real aid to navigation. We use clip-on polarized shades for our prescription eyeglasses. You can buy prescription polarized sunglasses. The day on *Dugong* when we were running for the downwind channel, polarized shades helped us discern the exact edges of the shoals. Stakes and privately kept markers mark approximate edges at best. Polarized shades allow us to see exactly where deep blue meets shallow brown, and they let us see the individual shoals.

Polarized shades also let us see the reefs where we can dive for fun and for fish. They even make it possible for us to see individual fish swimming around in the shallows. In Florida's Marquesas, our greatest entertainment is fishing on the flats for barracuda. We wade out 100 yards or so until we see a school of barracuda. Polarized shades allow us to see so clearly that we can cast for **the** barracuda we want. *Editor's note*: *Polarized sunglasses are also helpful fishing for bonefish or tarpon.*

Photo courtesy Viscom

Viscom Mini 2000 hand bearing compass has an internal tritium gas light (no batteries needed). When you can see anything, these are great for taking bearings to confirm your postion

Tennis Ball on a String

From time to time, it's handy to know just how fast we're moving through the water. A handy little trick is to take a tennis ball and tie it to a 34-foot length of string. Toss the ball overboard and count the seconds until the ball runs out all the string. Divide the number of seconds into 20. This formula gives your speed in knots. Just keep in mind that this is speed through the water and not necessarily speed over the bottom. If there's a current running for or against you, this will affect your true speed over the bottom.

Communications and Electronics

For more effective communication of distress, we carry a hand-held VHF transceiver which is equipped with Channel 16, and we carry a **Class C Emergency Position Indicating Radio Beacon (E.P.I.R.B.).** These are more effective than flares, and much more costly. They require maintenance.

Editor's note: Originally, 121.5/243 MHz EPIRB frequencies were monitored for aircraft, ships at sea, and monitoring stations ashore. Many foreign countries do not monitor nor recognize this frequency. In addition, EPIRB. transmissions on 121.5/243 develop incoherent emission problems that result in up to 25% of the signals being lost by the satellites that they're beamed to. To make matters worse, the emissions on 121.5/243 are too broad or unstable for an accurate position to be calculated.

Because of these problems, the U.S., Canada, the United Kingdom, France, Norway, Sweden, Denmark, Brazil, Bulgaria and the Soviet Union have established a primary emergency rescue frequency on 406 MHz. This new frequency will also reduce false alarms received by satellites. All present 121.5/243 EPIRBs will be phased out over the next few years. If you buy an E.P.I.R.B., be careful to get one of the new 406 MHz ones. Both Soviet Union and U.S. satellites are in place to receive 406 MHz. An additional U.S. satellite was launched in 1989. Availability of the 406-EPIRBs in the U.S. was delayed by FCC approval of test facilities. By the time you read this, they'll be available, but they won't be inexpensive, likely $1000+. 406 EPIRB's will not only tell rescuers where you are, but who you are! Wonders will never cease.

The VHF is a very useful two-way communication device in non-emergency conditions. We use it daily, to talk to other boaters and to listen to what's going on around us. For cruising in company with other boats, each boat should be equipped with a VHF transceiver.

For emergency signaling and other more common uses, we also carry an unbreakable plastic mirror, a strobe light, glow sticks, and several flashlights, some of which are waterproof. We've practiced signaling with the mirror. We monthly check the strobe lights on the life jackets. We keep fresh batteries in the flashlights. We feel we are abundantly and redundantly equipped with safety, security and emergency devices. But we've beachcruised year 'round, for years. If we cruised only occasionally, and in secure waters, we'd carry only the strobes, an E.P.I.R.B., the flashlights, the mirror, and the hand-held VHF. In some areas, a hand-held CB unit might be more useful than a VHF.

VHF radio has limited range, practically line of sight. A small radio with AM/FM, Short Wave and Single Sideband is both entertaining and essential. **LORAN** radio receiver-screens are very accurate and immediate in giving position and speed and other navigation data. Recently, portable models have become available. Pencils and paper are certainly our most useful tools.

Conventional **AM radio** transmissions give local weather with reliable regularity, but their point-of-view is more likely to serve the landsman than a mariner. For the Atlantic and Gulf Coast weather conditions, we listen to U.S. Coast Guard transmissions from Portsmouth, VA, Station NMN. Reception is good but requires a SSB short wave receiver. The broadcast schedule is listed below:

TIME (EST)	FREQUENCIES (kHz)			
0500	4428.2	6506.4	8765.4	
1100		6506.4	8765.4	13113.2
1700		6506.4	8765.4	13113.2
2300	4428.2	6506.4	8765.4	

Commercial High Seas Radio communications services such as AT&T, WOM and WLO rebroadcast the Coast Guard weather reports regularly or on demand. You can write them for a timely schedule, or call (305)587-0910.

We mounted a good compass on our *Hobie Cat*'s trampoline, strapped water stills to the mast, and tucked a paddle under the hiking straps. Here we are approaching one of our Bahama base camps. No matter how small your beachcruiser, a good compensated compass (or with in accurate deviation table) is your most essential navigation tool

Editor's note: For many of the beachcruising areas suggested by Ida in Chapter 3, you won't need any supplementary position-locating devices other than your compass, your charts (with course and positions plotted), and a hand bearing compass. We've become good at dead reckoning and we never stay in port because of poor visibility. In most recommended areas, you are seldom out of sight of land, and there's never any fog. Beachcruisers can make imprecise landfalls that deep draft boats would never dare. Your shallow draft is a safety factor and an aid to navigation.

If you want to beachcruise some of the world's best areas like Maine or southern New England, you may want to equip your beachcruiser with Loran-C or GPS (Global Positioning System). You're loaded down with so much gear already that this must be considered optional, but it's a blessing when unexpected poor visibility socks in, or you can't stay in port for fog because you have to get back to work.

You can locate yourself within a small triangle if you are adept at using a Radio Direction Finder. I cruise New England waters extensively and this is all I carry. Portable RDF's are battery operated and I get good results with mine.

I'm seriously looking at GPS. If you needed any evidence, Desert Storm was a convincer. Our side had it and Saddaam Hussein's men didn't. Our tanks, vehicles, and men knew exactly where they were night or day, smoke or no, all the time.

The GPS system was developed by the U.S. Department of Defense, but the consumer market for it is soaring. One of the many civilian uses is for navigation on boats, both commercial and pleasure boats. When completed in 1993, there will be 21 satellites and three spares. At this writing, there are 17 Navstar satellites in place. They will orbit 10,900 miles above the earth in six orbital planes. Each satellite has four atomic clocks that give the time in seconds to nine decimal points! The satellites are designed to last 7½ years. At least four satellites will be receivable at any time from any position on earth. GPS receivers measure the time of arrival of three or more Navstar satellite signals and then compute the one place in the world where these signals could have arrived at these precise times. GPS also provides very precise velocity measurements. Changes in velocity are measured to 1/10 meter per second. Accuracy will vary from about 25 meters to 100 meters, depending on whether the U.S. Defense Dept. continues their degradation of the satellite signals for security reasons. Loran-C is generally accurate to within ¼ mile or less. Loran-C repeatability is about 20 meters.

GPS degradation takes place by the Dept. of Defense altering signal accuracy. They do this by changing the satellites' orbit parameters, and creating errors in satellite clock signals. While the war was on, degradation was turned off, but this policy was reinstated last July. The Global Positioning System Association of Sunnyvale, CA is lobbying for this "Selective Availability" to be turned off except in national crisis.

To get around the degradation problem, manufacturers have built "differential" GPS receivers. This requires locating a receiver at a known position, to be a reference point. This receiver will monitor the GPS signals, calculate out the error from its known position, and transmit the error correction to all the GPS receivers in the area that are equipped to receive it. This will defeat the degradation that our military puts into the system. Differential GPS is currently in use by ferries between Stockholm and Helsinki. Accuracy is claimed to be less than one meter! Other tests elsewhere have indicated accuracy to four meters. I won't quibble.

Which to buy, Loran-C or GPS? As we've noted, GPS is much more accurate, but it's also much more costly. Loran-C receivers have come down in price to as low as $300. Present GPS prices range from $2000 up, though several manufacturers have announced plans to introduce 1992 sets for less than $1000. They need the increased volume that Loran-C achieved in order to lower the price. If you have a Loran-C set that's interfaced with a plotter and/or an automatic pilot, GPS can be linked to them so you won't lose this linkage. GPS sets can also be linked to other bells and whistles without Loran-C. Besides greater accuracy, GPS is worldwide. Loran-C reception is poor in some parts of the Bahamas, and you lose it as you go south in the Gulf of Mexico and the western Caribbean. It's non-existent in the eastern Caribbean. You need GPS if you're going to make long passages. It's far superior to Omega, Omni, or SAT-NAV. It is planned to continue Loran-C coverage into the next century, but coverage in Hawaii will be dropped by the end of 1992. Overseas Loran stations are being transferred to the host countries. There will be no further expansion of Loran. The U.S. Dept. of Defense will cease using Loran and Omega in late 1994. GPS will be their designated satellite system.

Cruising Guides

Cruising guides give important and interesting information about a cruising area: weather, aspects of the coast, effects of land masses on winds, and what the locals are like. Knowing what to expect helps plan a safe cruise and a safe landing. Keep in mind that some guides are more complete and more appropriate for a beachcruiser's needs. Look for guides that cover coastal geography over ones than focus on marinas and offshore courses.

Government Charts (See also Chapter 3, "Charts")

We've used charts published by National Ocean Survey (N.O.S.—N.O.A.A.) for coastal waters and inland waters. Offshore and foreign water charts are published by the U.S. Defense Mapping Agency and by foreign governments. These, as well as the appropriate cruising guides, are essential, and available at your chart agency. Or you can order them directly from the publishers listed at the end of this chapter. In some cruising areas, good road maps are useful.

Consulting the chart for shoals, bays, peninsulas, points, rivers, streams and settlements helps us plan our route. Any break in the shore may serve as a refuge, so it's good to know where they can be expected. It's also important to know where potential hazards lie. This may seem uptight, considering that we're rarely more than 100 yards offshore. However, we can be caught by a sudden squall, and must know the safe way to shore. Reading the Wayfarer logs of cruising in Lake Superior has made me even more aware of how important it is to study the chart ahead of time. Even on nice days you can find yourself in trouble for not having paid attention to the chart before you get there.

We've been caught in breaking seas on a flat calm day. All it takes is a freak shoal in an otherwise deep sea to cause a wave to lift. It's the same phenomenon as we've all observed at the beach. The waves roll in, lift, and fall over as they approach shore, creating surf. The same thing happens when a wave rolls over a shallow area farther offshore as at Whale Cay Passage in the Abacos, or a shallow hump in deep water inshore. We were sailing our canoe *Crapaud* close to the south coast of Martinique. It was a pretty day, little wind, and we weren't really paying attention. Ignorant of both chart and visual clues, we sailed over a 10-foot deep shoal just as an ocean swell lifted, and started to break. Paddling furiously, we managed to escape, but it notched another scar into our hearts.

We did a little better on another occasion. We were sailing *Kohoutek*, with *Manatee* in tow, from Little San Salvador to Cat Island in the Bahamas. The passage was only about 10 miles, about three hours for us. Winds were southwest at 10 knots. Though we hadn't received a weather report on our little radio, we knew that southwest winds precede a cold front. A wind shift to the northwest, with cooler air and stronger breezes, could be expected any time. But we estimated that we had time to zip across to Cat Island. This time we did our homework. We studied the chart of Cat Island carefully. Predicting a landfall on the coast south of Bennett's Harbour, we searched that area for suitable landings. If the front hit before we reached Cat Island, we'd be caught sailing towards a rough, windward shore. Beaches, even gently sloping beaches, can be rough in a storm if there's no reef or bar breaking the seas ahead of them. We made a mental note of two small rivers that would make good landings, and set off.

About a mile from Cat Island, the storm came toward us from astern. The winds clocked, increased to 20 knots, and soon we were struggling to keep *Kohoutek's* pontoons from nose diving and *Manatee* from crawling up on the tramp. A half mile from shore, the front hit with cold wind and driving rain. If we hadn't studied the chart earlier, we'd have been driven down on an unfamiliar shore, completely at the mercy of the storm. All of our attention and effort went to keeping the boats upright and scanning the shore for our river. The wind drove us down towards jagged coral where the river should have been. Then suddenly, the entrance opened up, and we careened into the sheltered stream.

Road and Topo Maps

These maps are often helpful as a supplement to nautical charts. They describe where roads run, where people live and where people aren't likely to be living, and where beaches, swamps, cliffs, hills, and inland lakes lie. Many times these maps will show landmarks for navigation that a chart wouldn't have.

A Word to the Wise about Guides, Charts and Maps

Use your own head and always pay attention to your own senses. No printed information is infallible. We're fortunate as beachcruisers that we can usually laugh off errors, but every once in a while they do matter. We have set our beach chairs at a special place near Key West just to watch cruisers routinely run aground where Government charts indicate 4 feet more depth than there is. Again and again, the skipper and crew disregarded their own observations and piled up on the mucky grass. We've been chagrined ourselves, though, when we've run 6-inch draft *Dugong* aground in places where we could see that it was too shallow despite what the charts promised. We too fall prey to the "it can't be **that** shallow" syndrome.

STOWAGE

Stowing a selection of essential equipment on board a small boat takes some thought and practice. We have fitted the interior surfaces with large, accordion-pleated fabric compartments. These pockets or saddlebags are kept in place with snaps and can be removed for use on shore. Most of the small items that we want to keep handy are kept in these "boat pockets." Our boom tent has some sewn into the walls.

Larger items are grouped according to use, and stowed according to anticipated need. All the dive gear fits into a net nylon duffel bag that is pulled into a remote corner with a line that goes around a block. Our typewriter, papers, and books go into a sealed cooler that protects them from mechanical damage, keeps them dry, and serves as well when carried ashore to be used as a desk. Our bedding and clothing are in waterproof canoe packs that have shoulder straps. Foods are in a framed back pack that will hang on a tree or stand up on the ground by the galley box. What won't fit into easily accessible stowage, gets sealed into waterproof bags of heavy plastic or rolled into taped and labeled plastic lawn and leaf bags.

Additional information at the end of this chapter lists, illustrates, and describes some of the equipment recommended. Some suppliers names and addresses are included.

SOURCES FOR ADDITIONAL INFORMATION

Local Marine Chandleries are the best places to learn what is available and where to purchase your urgent needs. Look in the yellow pages. Some chandleries have knowledgeable people who can demonstrate and explain uses of equipment.

Discount Mail Order Marine Chandlers Catalogs

These are the best places to learn of a wider selection and to make purchases at lower cost. We've used those listed below.

Defender Industries, P.O. Box 820, 255 Main St., New Rochelle, NY 10802-0820. Catalog $3 Offers the widest selection at least cost and least service

BOAT/U.S., 880 S. Pickett St., Alexandria, VA 22304. Annual membership fee is $17 that includes the privilege of purchasing almost as wide a selection at almost as low a cost with considerable service and courtesy that includes an 800 number and national lobby on behalf of boating interests

West Marine Products, 500 West Ridge Dr., Watsonville, CA 95076-4100. Offers a wide range of marine hardware and supplies in an attractive catalog at prices comparable to BOAT/U.S., has an 800 number, and considerate service

Sling-Light, 1539 Monrovia #23, Newport Beach, CA 92663. Offers a light weight, comfy, folding sling chair available nowhere else. It sets inches above the ground or boat sole

Wildwater Designs, 230 Penllyn Pike, Penllyn, PA 19422. Specializes in equipment for kayaking and canoeing. Some have application on any small boat

Ecomarine Ocean Kayak Center, 1668 Duranleau St., Vancouver, B.C. V6H 3S4 Canada. Has a shipping center for U.S. customers in Ferndale, WA. They specialize in equipment and supplies for ocean kayaking and canoeing. They carry such unusual products as grizzly bear repellent, a pocket E.P.I.R.B., and a hand-powered desalinator. They also lead trips to such exotic places as the Maldives, Bahamas and Patagonia

Epoxy Repair Kits

Gougeon Brothers, Box X908, Bay City, Michigan 48707
System Three, Box 70436, Seattle, WA 98107

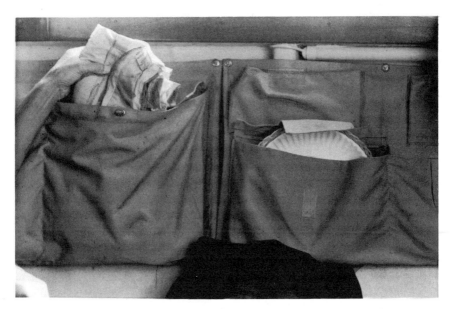

Cloth pockets provide organized storage for any boat. These are mounted with snaps onto stringers

Following is an article by Ida Little describing ways that they keep comfortable while beachcruising.

Reprinted from SAIL Magazine, April 1985 with their kind permission. Their address is Charlestown Navy Yard, 100 First Avenue, Charlestown, MA 02129-2097.

Gunkholing in Comfort

by Ida Little

"You look comfortable," a woman's voice said enviously. Michael and I, reading in chairs set on the island beach, hadn't noticed the couple approach. We replied that we were indeed comfortable, and the conversation drifted to cruising—to their new-found delight in weekending and to our over 10 years of extended, and sometimes liveaboard, sailing. "Which boat is yours?" the woman asked, looking about the bay.

"The little red one. Twenty-six feet . . . the one drawn up on the beach."

The couple exchanged a quick glance. "But how" she asked, "can you be comfortable on a boat that size for such long periods of time?"

Her companion quickly answered for us, "Comfortable chairs, for one!"

He was right. Our two folding sling chairs are one item we number among our cruising comforts. We lash them on *Dugong's* deck, and although they are big, they are important enough to us to warrant the space.

For us it makes sense to equip with as much of what we really need and want as we possibly can. There are things you can do without for a few days of cruising, but if they are important to you, you won't be happy without them for long. The

At high tide we shoved *Dugong* over the shallow grass flats to enter the narrow creek that wound through miles of island maze. No other boats in there!

point when you're long-term cruising is that life on board is the Real World. You equip for it just as you would for your life in *any* situation.

Since eating is a big part of any life-style, it follows that cooking is a big part of cruising. To keep it easy, clean, and economical, we use propane aboard. We carry 20 pounds in an aluminum tank, about 90 hours' worth, or enough to serve us for three months. The aluminum tank costs triple a steel tank, but it won't corrode and at 13 pounds is half the weight. It's light enough, in fact, to carry ashore for refilling. Our tank is lashed in the cockpit for ventilation and convenience. As propane is heavier than air, many people rightly worry that if there's a leak the gas will settle in the bilge. For this good reason, the tank should be kept on deck or in an airtight compartment that is vented to the outside.

Why bother? Propane, besides being efficient, is hassle-free compared to liquid fuels. It requires no priming and no pumping. On an early morning, what a pleasure it is to simply turn a knob and light the propane to heat the water for coffee. Using a "gun" to shoot a piezoelectric spark makes the ritual just that much easier. Our two-ounce, yellow-barreled "gun" (whose trigger causes a hammer to hit a crystal that "shoots" a spark at the end of the 8-inch barrel) has had six years' daily use and shows no sign of wear or tear. It doesn't need refueling and has a longer life expectancy than we do.

We cook on a two-burner folding Coleman stove. While we're under way it's folded and put away. It's light, even with a separate small fuel cylinder, and easy to carry ashore for cooking out. Its portability allows us to move it inside the cabin, too. After a year's daily use it looks like rusty flotsam found in the nick of time. We might have done better getting a stainless steel model, but at less than $40 ours can be economically replaced. Coleman also makes a nifty folding oven. Of sheet metal, it encloses a 10-inch cube that fits on top of one burner. One or two grills fit inside for baking cookies or bread. A built-in thermostat on the door gives fairly accurate readings. It rusts the same way the stove does, so it's kept well oiled. We also carry a stainless folding toaster that fits on top of a burner; it is well worth the small space it consumes. A pressure cooker is our most-used cooking pot. It saves time, gas, and water. It'll cook a chicken in one-third the normal time and rice in half the time with half the water.

We don't use refrigeration or ice. The foods we use daily are kept in a wooden "day box," 2 feet by 4 feet by 1 foot, which is kept in the cockpit, where we spend most of our time aboard. In the morning, we take out of the box coffee, sugar, and powdered milk, some bread and cereal, silverware and bowls; at lunch, cheese, cabbage (a lettuce substitute), mayonnaise, salt and pepper, and some guava paste and crackers for dessert. We carry mustard, jam, margarine, ketchup, and mayonnaise sold in the toothpastelike tubes designed for backpackers. They are easier to handle and keep the mayonnaise from being contaminated by dirty utensils. If it is stored in shade, opened, unmixed-with-food mayonnaise keeps at least two weeks. Bulk food such as soups, brown rice, flour, nuts, dried beans, and noodles, as well as extra stocks, are stashed in labeled waterproof plastic canoe packs. Cabbage and onions keep for two weeks when slung in nets, which we have strung all through the boat. Cheese and eggs will keep a couple of weeks unrefrigerated, and unopened margarine even longer. For variety in greens we carry hijiki, a dried seaweed available at most health-food stores. A few ounces of water rehydrates it in 15 minutes to a consistency and taste of tiny green beans. We've tried growing sprouts, but they require rinsing three times a day for three days, after which they quickly spoil—so on day three you'd better feel like eating sprouts. Tahini, a sesame seed paste available at health food stores and at many supermarkets, can be used as a salad dressing and as a sauce for fish and vegetables.

The heaviest precious item any cruiser carries is water. In a week, the two of us go through a minimum of 9 gallons. We generally carry 20 to 25 gallons in collapsible, 5-gallon plastic containers. They're easy to clean and fold flat when empty. A cloth cover keeps the sunlight out and green slime at bay. It also protects the bag from puncture. An on-off faucet makes it as handy as plumbing, without the maintenance. Auto-Seal, a black sealing rubber in a tube, repairs small leaks quickly. These containers can be purchased at department stores for about $6 or collected gratis from a hospital lab. We have also used internal tanks, but they are hard to clean and take up space even when empty.

We indulge ourselves with a pint each of fresh water for our evening bath. The indulgence serves two purposes. It keeps the bedsheets from getting salty and absorbing moisture, and makes us feel good. We approach the evening bath as an important daily ritual. It freshens and invigorates, washing away the grime, the salt, and the mental grungies. First, we rough-sponge with a sudsy mix of seawater and Joy or Prell (two detergent soaps that really do suds in salt water). Then we rinse with more seawater. Then comes the final rinse: a pint of fresh water. This water is kept in a black-coated, heavy plastic bag with hose and spray nozzle attached. The black coating on the "under" side absorbs heat from the sun during the day. With the bag hoisted on a halyard, we can have a real shower. Commercial models are available, but we've made our own plastic shower bag by using heavy plastic and a triggered spray nozzle.

As with the shower bag, we've made other gear that may be available commercially but is easily home-built. Custom-made cloth pockets are designed to keep all our gear organized and accessible. Using a sun-resistant, medium-weight fabric, we made rectangular backings onto which various-sized pockets were sewn. Each piece is then snapped to fittings on the hull stringers. In the cabin these hold clothing, sheets, and towels. In the cockpit they hold foul-weather gear and whatever. A few small pockets are handy for holding bandages, combs, glasses—small items that get lost easily. We keep charts in one big, flat pocket. Bigger, pleated pockets hold bulkier items.

In the pocket closest to the hatch we keep the mosquito coils and screens. Velcro sewn to the edge of the custom-cut screen fastens to Velcro super-glued to the inside rim of *Dugong's* hatch, so the screen is easy to install quickly. Speed here means a lot when you are suddenly besieged by voracious mosquitoes or no-see-ums. Our screening is kept coated with Screen Proof. We've been caught up many a Georgia creek at sunset with nothing but a thin screen between us and torture. Experience has taught us that no-see-ums can penetrate any screen—even fine mesh—that isn't coated effectively.

To run our multiband radio, stereo tapedeck, fluorescent reading lantern, and two waterproof flashlights we need about 1.25 ampere-hours a day at 12 volts. For two years we've used a 6-volt solar panel to charge rechargeable D-cell batteries that in turn power all but the tapedeck. The portable fluorescent lantern is the wrench in the works. It uses too many amps too fast to be powered by D-cells. And the model we use overheats, thus draining the batteries even more. But we have become accustomed to the handiness of moving it where it's needed and to its brightness for reading. Our plans now call for a six-pack of 2-volt rechargeable batteries for the fluorescent lamp and tapedeck and the D-cells for flashlights and radio. A 12-volt solar panel will fit under the forward hatch so that the sun will replace the energy we use nightly. We use the multiband radio and stereo tapedeck enough to justify their energy appetite. Shortwave radio brings us National Public Radio. Likewise, we appreciate time signals and weather reports. With the tapedeck we can listen to the music we like. We don't use a transmitting radio. If we run into trouble, we have a strobe light, an EPIRB, and a VERY pistol.

We've tried to avoid using a dinghy ever since we lost our first one in a heavy sea. It was a nice wooden dinghy, but it was heavy. Every time the seas got rough, we felt compelled to haul it on deck, a laborious process. The one time we didn't labor, we lost it. Although *Dugong* draws only 8 inches, less then a dinghy, we still prefer to use a dinghy in a busy port or to go diving on reefs, so we carry an inflatable. It's a dinghy but not "another whole boat." It's light, folds out of the way, and needs almost no maintenance. We've used the same inflatable for two years and have patched four holes. If we don't repair a puncture in time, it sags and our fannies get wet. It's easy to puncture and easy to repair, and it will have to be replaced in a couple of years. For the convenience of stowing it on deck, we trade time in inflating and deflating, plus the occasional fanny wetting. Folded in a 2-foot-by-3-foot packet, the inflatable fits snugly on deck between the legs of our folding chairs.

Every boat, every cruiser, has unique shape and personality. Outfitting—especially a small boat—is a matter of fitting gear snugly to each curve and idiosyncrasy. We outfit with as much of what we need and want as we can, rather than trying to get by with as little as possible. Phil Bolger, *Dugong's* designer, put it this way: "The attitude indicated by their equipment listing delights me. We will be austere and independent, and they are. But by all the gods we'll have this, that, and the tapedeck, and they do. But they don't seem to have *anything* they don't really want and use frequently. That is something worth aiming for."

CHAPTER 10

SAFETY AND SECURITY UNDER WAY
(See also Chapter 9, particularly Sections on
Anchoring, Safety Equipment and Navigation)

SKILLS

Two skills you must know before going beachcruising are how to sail and how to swim. Take lessons, practice, and become skilled **before** attempting to cruise. As long as you lack confidence handling the boat you'll be too anxious to enjoy beachcruising. If you can't swim, or dogpaddle without fear of drowning, you won't be able to think of much else the whole time you're out. Both skills are fun to learn and fun to practice. They will not only keep you alive, but make **being** alive more fun.

A third skill to practice is camping. Go out for hikes and overnight cruises. Learn how to select sites, get water, and set up your tent. Learn from your own needs what special things to look for in a good campsite, and what gear you'll want to carry. Learn to know two basic traits about yourself—the kind of geography and climate that turns you on; and the equipment **you** need to make **you** comfortable enough to enjoy it. This will give you the criteria you need to choose where to cruise and what boat to go in.

WHERE TO CRUISE (See also Chapter 3)

Whether you choose to cruise in your own home waters or in some foreign sea, do as much research as you can before you start. Check guide books, encyclopedias, magazine articles, local sailing newsletters, books, maps, charts, and weather reports. Talk to people who've been where you want to go. When we were planning a cruise of Dominica in the West Indies, we wrote to the librarian in the capital city of Roseau for timely information. We also went out of our way to talk with some travel writers in town who'd just returned from the island. The writers told us that there were some troubles with groups of Dominican youths terrorizing people, and that living conditions were harsh. The librarian's letter gave us the name of the postmaster so that we could be assured of receiving our mail there, and invited us to visit her home when we arrived. This sort of current, personal information is worth going out of your way for.

Editor's note: The worst of these gangs was known as "the Dreads." They preyed on white people and were responsible for several murders and some beatings, never attacking groups, only single people. They are long gone. Prime Minister Eugenia Charles has improved Dominica for tourists. She's one of the best in the Caribbean, though economically,

Dominica is a basket case, having been flattened by a hurricane a few years ago.

In your research you'll want to learn specific features about the cruising area to decide if it will be a good place to cruise, and to know how to plan for it.

WEATHER PATTERNS
(See also Chapter 9, "Items Required for Comfort")

Every place has its own predictable pattern of weather. The pattern of prevailing winds, average temperatures and amount of rain varies with the time of the year. Knowing what the pattern is, and what forces affect it, will help you prepare for dealing with it. For example: in south Florida, summers are hot and buggy, but the winds are reliably east to southeast, generally 10 to 15 knots. Winters are frequently cold, night temperatures in the 40s and few bugs, sometimes with blustery winds out of the north.

Photo by Dave Buckma

Here's a *Lightning* coming into North Haven, Maine. Some skippers have converted these popular daysailers into cabin cruisers. This is a good conversion example

Winds

We failed to do our homework before cruising the Bahamas the first time. When a winter cold front came through, we hadn't a clue which way to jump. Had we read the chapter on weather in the "Yachtsman's Guide to the Bahamas" or the "Cruising Guide to the Abacos and Northern Bahamas," we'd have learned how to predict wind direction based on present conditions. So, although our radio wasn't picking up a weather broadcast, we'd have known that the winds "clock" in the wintertime. That is, since the current winds were southwest, they would soon clock northwest and north. In our ignorance we chose to find shelter from the hard southwest winds by anchoring in the lee of the northwest shore. When the cold front blew down on us from the northwest, we were caught. This little mistake on our part nearly cost us our lives, and did cost us our boat.

Storms

Many small, beachable, boats have made ocean crossings. During 1988, Ed Gillet crossed 2200 miles from Monterey to Maui in 63 days in a 21-foot kayak! Few small boats have been lost at sea, and these were lost in extraordinary storms that caused many large vessels to founder. Many experienced ocean voyagers on large and little boats recommend a sea anchor. This is a heavily constructed water parachute or drogue that is put in tow on a long heavy line when seas are so big and winds are so hard that the boat cannot be controlled. Presumably the sea anchor slows the boat and keeps it advantageously oriented to the wind and seas while you go below and keep warm with a hot toddy. *Editor's note: Others recommend trailing long warps if you're running downwind in heavy seas. These are long heavy lines that will slow you down and help prevent broaching and ease the motion of your boat.*

Barometer

In some regions a barometer can be used to predict weather change or violent weather. In areas where there are no reliable radio forecasts, such as Baja California, a barometer becomes essential. With practice at reading and recording, and some practice at cloud watching, our barometer has enabled us to stay out of the worst weather and helped us recognize fair weather. Ours is a small, hand-held altimeter used by mountain climbers.

Lightning

Lightning came with a summer downpour in the Exumas. When the storm hit, I was standing knee-deep in the sea, hunched over *Kohoutek's* trampoline filleting fish. Lightning struck close by and caused my muscles to spasm so hard that the fillet knife went flying. I got **out** of the sea, joining Michael where he was standing oddly still, looking up at *Kohoutek's* mast. A peculiar menacing hum seemed to emanate from the aluminum. Both of us looked upward to the top of the mast. There, to our horror, was a small, power-packed glow, St. Elmo's Fire. In unison we began to back away. We got 20 yards when there was a sharp crack and a spark leaped from the masthead. The humming ceased. From that time on, we have been very careful to put to shore as soon as we detect thunderclouds headed our way so that we have time to find a protected landing. When we land, we prepare for strong winds and rain without dilly dallying around. When the thunderstorm is on us, we stay out of the sea, under the cover of a tarp set back among some low trees.

It is not always possible to get out of the way of lightning. We have been struck. Equipping our mast and wire rigging with short, heavy, grounding jumper cables has minimized the trauma. We clamp #4 insulated, high voltage brass cables to the mast and stays. *Editor's note: Copper is an even better conductor than brass.* When lightning threatens, we drop the other end into the sea—or better yet, to the ground ashore. Short lengths of chain would work almost as well. At sea, we tie ourselves to the boat. Thus, if struck unconscious and overboard, we won't get totally separated from the boat. Ashore, we seek low ground and keep away from high, solitary objects. Note that an AM radio receiver will receive the crackle of lightning long before your ears can hear the thunder. If you hear lightning on your radio, and a storm hasn't passed recently, it's probably on its way toward you.

SEA PATTERNS

As in weather, there are consistent, predictable patterns in the sea. These patterns include tides, currents, and water temperatures. Just like the weather, these patterns affect our and our boat's safety and security. Like weather patterns, they are known, described, and available for study. One of the sources I enjoy reading for information about sea patterns are the sea kayaking books. The kayaking books that we list in the Additional Information section at the end of this chapter, give information based on personal experience. You have the opportunity of learning through another boater's actual experience.

Tides

Tides rise and fall regularly. In some places there will be one high and one low tide a day. In other places there are two high and two low tides each 24-hour day. Tide tables indicate times and heights of high and low water. In some places, like along the coast of Georgia, the tides have an 8-foot range. In other places, like the Florida Keys, the range is only a couple of feet.

Where there are two tides a day, one of the high tides will be higher than the other, and one low tide lower than the other. This matters if you are dried out or want to sail over a shoal. You may be afloat on the morning high tide, go for a walk inland, have a picnic, and in the evening, find you are stuck there for the night. The tidal range also fluctuates on a monthly basis. If you were able to get into that cove last week, you may not be able to today.

For years we cruised without tide tables because our boats were light enough to carry to the sea if the tide didn't come to us. When we started cruising *Dugong* and could no longer lift the boat, we neglected to think of tide tables. A day came when we were high and dry with a falling tide. We were ready to go but couldn't. The sunny, gentle weather passed and by the time we got off four days later, thanks to storm-driven seas, we had a hard sail.

I used to think that tide tables were only for big boats. Now I realize it doesn't matter if you're concerned about 6 feet or 2 inches. In either case a difference in the depth of the water and what your boat draws will determine where you can go. With tide tables you can plan a safe time to cross a strong tidal current area, or a time of high tide so you can sail close to shore if the winds or seas are bad, or where you can take short cuts, or when to arrive at a cove so that you can cross over that shallow bar and snug up way inside.

Tidal Currents

The rise and fall of tide generates a current. As a general rule, the greater the range between high and low tides, the stronger the current. Shallows and geographic constrictions can also cause strong currents, even where tidal range is minor. When we read that British Columbia has a tidal range of 10 feet or more, with currents approaching 6 knots, we gave up our dream of beachcruising there. We might have rejected the Georgia coast on these grounds. The tides there can run 8 feet, and the currents are very strong, but the water is warm. If we capsized, or had to wade with the boat in tow, we wouldn't freeze. As it turned out, sometimes we just had to sit tight and wait for the current to flow in the direction we wanted to go. In the Bahamas and Florida, the range is only 2 to 4 feet, so the currents, while swift in places, are easier to deal with.

The narrower the slot through which the tide has to flow, the stronger the current. Though we know to expect this, we are still taken by surprise in places. When we first landed in the Exumas we were shocked to find out just **how** strong the currents **do** run between the islands. We'd sailed *Kohoutek,* with *Manatee* in tow, from Eleuthera to the northern Exumas, a distance of some 30 miles. As we approached the narrow slot between Ship Channel Cay and Bird Cay, we prepared to meet some tidal current. The cut is only about 20 yards across and the tide was in mid flood, the time of strongest current. We never expected to be sucked right through the cut without being able to make shore. The lesson stuck.

Ocean Currents

There are currents in the sea independent of tidal currents. The Gulf Stream is an example. It flows northward along the Atlantic coast of Florida at a velocity between 3 and 6 knots. The El Niño current on the Pacific coast, also flows northward. The equitorial current sets westward through the Caribbean. Unlike tidal currents, these currents are not easily observed, so it's important to find out what the ocean currents are where you plan to cruise. These currents will affect the speed and direction of your course. They also affect the condition of the surface of the sea. Whenever the wind opposes a current, steep seas develop. I met a sailor who sailed to the Bahamas from a port on the coast of Florida that is north of the Bahamas. This meant he had to sail southward against the Gulf Stream. He thought that would be okay, since he had a following wind. The northwest wind he was counting on for help created enormous, standing waves in the Stream. I overheard him say to someone that he'd been warned about crossing that way, and with that wind, but he just hadn't believed it could be so bad.

Anomalies

It's misleading to have you believe that tides and currents are fixed factors in this constantly flowing universe. They aren't. Neither are the tables, guides, and statistics. Factors that you could never predict might affect conditions in a way that paperwork theories can't account for. Whale Cay Passage in the Abacos, the northern Bahamas, is a treacherous passage to the ocean. Here ocean swells roll in, meet an abrupt shallow shoal, lift, and sometimes break clear across the passage. A couple winters ago I overheard a sailor speaking with a freighter captain over the VHF radio. Both were planning to use Whale Cay Passage that day since the winds had been calm for a couple of days. The freighter captain entered the Passage and radioed to the sailor that there was a terrible sea— "a rage"—despite the calm winds and slack current. When the sailor expressed disbelief, the captain invited him to give it a try but said that he "might could meet with disappointment." Whenever I see people trust what ought to be over what is, I remember the captain's words.

Let me give you some examples of the forces, like wind and storm and planets, that affect the condition of the sea, tides, and currents. Sometimes when the wind blows hard and constant for a few days, it blows the water right out of parts of Florida Bay. It didn't matter that the Tide Tables predicted a 3-foot high tide at noon when we were sailing through Crocodile Crossover. We got stuck in mud. Winds can cause greater or lesser tides, and sometimes, no tide at all. Storms hundreds of miles away will send surges of water that easily increase tide height a foot. Barometric pressure does the same. Last year the planets lined up at high tide during a heavy northerly blow and the sea flooded parts of New Plymouth settlement in the Abacos.

Appreciating that anomalies exist is the first step toward dealing with them. Note personal observations in a log and look for recurring patterns. Talk with the locals, and use your own senses. Remain flexible, refer to your guides and charts and tables, but forget absolutes.

Editor's note: Strong winds will not only make for higher or lower tides than are predicted, but they can delay the times of high or low tides.

Sharks

Shark attacks upon boats are very rare, but they do happen. Small boats have been totally destroyed and lost to sharks. If you're taking a small boat, like a canoe or kayak, on seas that nurture aggressive sharks, like the Great White of Australia, . . . no problem. Carry a shark deterrent, a "bang stick" that on contact inflates the shark with a jet of compressed air. (Maybe make that two or three.)

Photo by Chris Harkness

Author Ida at Atsena Otie Key off the west coast of Florida surveying some of the paraphernalia of a *Drascombe Dabber* beachcruiser—life jacket, Teva sandals, canvas duffle bags, ice chest, and a plywood board that serves as a navigation table

TIMES TO BE ESPECIALLY CAREFUL

Our experience has been that we're more likely to have problems if we're tired, if we're hungry or thirsty, if it's dark, or if we're changing activities.

Fatigue

Cruising in an open boat, exposed to the elements, is tiring. We stop frequently to stretch, lie down in the shade, and generally change position. Setting up camp also takes a lot of energy, so we don't wait until late to do it. If we do go too long and stop late in the day, we find that we are not having a whole lot of fun, and that we pinch fingers, stub toes, trip on rocks, bruise thighs, burn fingers in the cook fire, and generally abuse our tired bodies. As beachcruisers, we're not out to set speed or distance records. We choose to beachcruise because it is a slow and intimate way to cruise and get to know a coast or shore. We are fortunate to have the **choice** of stopping frequently and walking around.

Nourishment

Hunger and thirst are demons if not regularly satisfied. We always carry food and water readily available. We carried snacks and a quart of water on *Kohoutek's* trampoline, and refilled the supply every time we stopped. By the time we feel thirsty, it's already past time to drink. Drink regularly, a couple of quarts a day, whether you feel like it or not. Food keeps us fueled and agreeable. Keep snacks and water handy and you'll have a more good-tempered and happy cruise. So many references and articles on provisioning address minimum requirements. When it comes to water, and to good food, we always carry double or more of what we need.

Night Sailing

Once in a while, we've sailed at night. Many places, a hard wind will die down at night. When we were trying to get 'round the south tip of Martinique past Diamond Rock into the everlasting strong easterly, we'd never have made it in the daytime. Having inquired of the local fishermen about the winds, we learned that we'd do better sailing after sunset or before dawn. We tried it and it worked. We try not to do this unless we have to because it's too easy to make mistakes in the dark. Stop **long** before dark and leave plenty of time to scope out a camp site, explore, make dinner, and relax.

Landing Your Boat (See also Chapter 9, "Beaching Your Boat")

Beachcruising is such a slow and gentle activity that you almost have to go out of your way to hurt yourself. Landing provides one of the few great opportunities to do so.

Prepare to be more alert than usual when you make a landing. Most accidents happen during a change in activity. You move around more and begin doing things you haven't yet gotten used to, even though you may have done them hundreds of times in the past. When starting to change activities, move slowly.

When landing, some dangers to look out for are: intermittent breaking seas, undertows, currents, steep drop-offs, and quicksand or deep muck. Many times the chart or coastline itself will warn you off such a landing. Test the bottom in a marshy area before throwing your weight overboard. Michael sank to his waist once. He leaped overboard to slow our landing and not only found himself stuck but surrounded by a dozen or so small sharks. Charts show where the coast is cliff. Steep cliffs often indicate steep drop-offs. Had we been more alert to the chart's warning when we landed at Anse Dufour, Martinique, we'd have avoided the shock of finding ourselves unable to gain our footing less than 10 feet from shore. We hadn't planned on having to swim our canoe *Crapaud* to shore and then haul her up such a steep beach. It was a real struggle.

Underwater creatures and debris are hazards as well. Sharks, rays, sea urchins, conch, glass, tree stumps, and broken shells are just a few. Avoid putting your feet down where you can't see what they'll land on, and even then, with caution. Sharks bite, stingray barbs jab and tear, urchin spines stick and break inside your flesh, and conch shells cut. They all infect, and hurt like crazy. Wear shoes or sandal-style flip-flops for every landing and you'll avoid some nasty wounds. Regular style flip-flops won't do, really. They leave too much of your foot exposed; they tend to slide from underfoot; and they fall apart quickly. Tevas and Hey! Sailors have been our best bets. ***Editor's note:*** *I use an old pair of boat shoes kept specifically for dingy landings, reef walking, and beachcombing. They have hard rubber bottoms and leather uppers, not easily pierced.*

No problem beaching these beachcruisers on a sandy isle off Cedar Key, Florida

Surf

It's sporty fun to land through a gentle surf. It's downright dangerous to land through a heavy surf. We've been forced to make some frightening landings through breaking waves, and in each case were tossed around like so much trash. You just can't control a sailboat in breaking surf. All we could do was time our approach with the least fearsome set of waves, and have bow and stern lines ready to grab.

Editor's note: On that same Mexican cruise, I was rowing a Sabot dinghy to the beach at Zihuatanejo, having great fun timing the breaking waves to deposit me gently on shore. After a couple of successful landings with passengers, I went in by myself. I timed a wave pretty good and took off like a shot. It was a great sensation, but I did something wrong. All of a sudden I was tumbling head over teakettle in a wave, the dink with me. It came down on top of me when I finally came to rest, seated and sputtering. The gunwale just missed my thick head, hitting my shoulder, no damage, only a bruise. Before that trip was over, I worked out with the heavier canoas that Mexican boatmen land in surf and learned how they do it with nary a mishap. I was a volunteer "canoa boy" at Puerto Vallarta! They keep these double-enders lined up to the waves, and let the big waves do the work. Once the boat touches, they're out on the beach on both sides, and help the next wave lift the boat higher on the beach without broaching or getting pooped. Don't try it in a square-sterned dinghy!

Getting **out** through surf is a lot easier than coming in because you can observe the waves from a better perspective ashore. When you're sitting on the back of the waves, feeling them roll in under you and go tumbling toward shore, you feel like every wave is a monster. Ashore, it's easier to judge their height and rhythm and be able to time your launch accordingly. Also, when you are ashore and the waves look impassable, you can just wait. If you're sitting out there in your boat waiting to come in for the night, you're compelled to run the surf. After making a compelled landing through the hard surf at Anse Dufour, we were very cautious about our leave-taking two weeks later. In fact, we were so cautious that we delayed our departure long enough to run out of food. A fresh water stream provided us with all the water we needed. We ended up hiking four hours inland for more French bread and brie, to a village marked on our topo map rather than attempt a risky launching.

CAPSIZING

Boat Buoyancy

The Dinghy Cruising Association of England recommends using a boat with sufficient positive buoyancy to support itself together with stores and partially immersed crew, plus a reserve of not less than 112 pounds. This buoyancy should be arranged so that it is possible for the crew to put the boat back in sailing condition after capsizing or swamping. They also point out that sails, mast, rigging, and fittings must be strong enough to withstand capsizing forces.

The only real way to know if your boat can handle a capsize is to test it. The best time to test it is when **you** choose to test it. Before taking our Hobie Cat, *Kohoutek* and sailing canoe, *Manatee* to the Bahamas, we practiced capsizing both. We knew what to expect if it ever happened by accident, which it did, of course. What we learned was very interesting. The canoe, when swamped with only Michael aboard and no gear, was impossible to bail if there was any sea at all. We ended up dragging the swamped canoe ashore. Thereafter we were especially careful not to risk a capsize. When I took *Manatee* for a week's cruise by myself, I ran into some heavy weather. I remember spending a whole day jumping onto the windward gunnel then sitting back down in the canoe and back up again and releasing the sheet and throwing myself to windward. I knew that if I went over, I'd have a terrible time swimming my loaded, swamped canoe ashore.

Now the Hobie Cat, *Kohoutek*, was different. We could right it. However, Michael's 175 pounds had a lot easier time of it than my 125 pounds.

Photo by Stephen Wilce

Lee Wilce standing by their *Wilce Navigator* in Baja California. They've cruised this clipper yawl all over the Pacific coast

What we learned helped later when we each capsized alone. Knowing that it could be done, and how, was an enormous help. We had all the righting lines rigged and ready and knew instantly where they were. We also knew what problems would make righting more difficult. The mast gets shoved under and spears the bottom when the water is shallow enough. Therefore, we learned to swim for the end of the mast and quickly pull it around to windward before it had a chance to dig in. The first time I went over by accident, I felt panic even though I'd been through a capsize before. I kept thinking how scary it would be if I had never done it before and was having to deal with an unfamiliar process as well as fright.

You won't want to swamp the bigger, cuddy boats like *Dugong*, Dovekie, or the Hens. You'll just have to check for built-in buoyancy. The descriptive literature should explain how the boat will respond to a swamping.

Capsizing isn't fun. Better to do all you can to avoid it in the first place. Try to select a boat that is stable enough for the crew to sit on the gunwale without dipping it under or capsizing it. The DCA recommends that the beam not be less than the cube root of the waterline square. If your boat has 16 feet on the waterline, squared, that's 256 feet, the cube of which is a little over 6 feet. So your boat should be a little over 6-foot beam for stability. By this formula, our sailing canoes *Manatee* and *Crapaud* had only half the beam they needed for stability, and it showed! We had to be veeery careful.

Reefing

A quick, efficient reefing system will be your best insurance against a capsize. Even though you may start out with what seems to be a mere handkerchief of a sail, you'll want less when the wind comes up, and you will want to have less **Right Now.** Ingenious systems have been devised and advertised for lateen, lug, sprit and Bermudian rigs. If your boat's rig doesn't come with a reefing system, or that system is awkward and slow, consider devising or adapting your own. An easy and quick reefing system is so important that it should influence your choice of rig to cruise with. You may think you won't get caught out in a blow but it's more likely that you will. I've been caught out playing around on a windsurfer and had to reef just to get back to shore!

If You Capsize

We have had boats capsize and roll under us. When we landed *Crapaud* through the surf in Martinique, we did our best to keep from broaching or getting pooped and capsizing. Michael straddled the stern and I straddled the bow, both of us perched on top of the spray cover which we had closed completely. Despite our desperate attempt to paddle fast enough to keep ahead of the waves, we broached and rolled over.

We'd read enough to know to hang onto the boat and scramble to hang on we did. Michael was able to grab the line we'd tied to the stern in time to slow her down just as I latched onto the bow line. Had we not had those lines, *Crapaud* would have continued rapidly and uncontrollably for the sheer rock cliff. We were only 10 feet from shore but we couldn't touch bottom. About 5 feet from the pebbly shore abutting the cliff, when we **could** get our footing, the steep slope and rolling rocks nearly kept us from getting any farther. At least we had the boat to hang onto and a boat to eventually get back out with, and a boat full of supplies to support us in our wild jungle camp. If you capsize in open water, always hang onto the boat. If you capsize in surf, hang onto the boat only if you are sure the boat won't come crashing down on you. Lines from the stern and bow allow you to hang on more safely in these conditions.

PEOPLE THREATS

Beachcruisers tend to be left alone. We don't have enough fancy equipment to attract thieves, nor are we likely to cruise in populated places.

However, there are places on this earth where the local people are just **bad.** Often, it's poverty that compels them. Sometimes boredom compels them? Sometimes it's hard to say **what** really compels them. Cruising in areas where the people are known to be "unfriendly" is just asking for trouble. Guide books, word-of-mouth, and timely magazine articles describe areas to stay away from. The Seven Seas Cruising Association Newsletter publishes timely, personal information about places all over the world. We pay close attention when we're warned away from a place, because we didn't pay attention several years ago and got the shock of our lives. We were still in our innocence regarding the basic nature of all Mankind and were rudely awakened by banditos holding a gun to our heads. Mind you, this was the roughest part of Columbia—the Guajira— and we were in a big, no doubt loot-laden yate, but still, we'd just come from a wild part of Venezuela and those very poor natives were the gentlest, most considerate people we'd ever met. So it pays to listen up when you're warned away from a place.

Diplomacy and soft talk have been our best ways of dealing with threats from people. If worst comes to worst, the best aggressive defense we have is tear gas. Ever since reading "Sitting Ducks" by Betsy Hitz-Holman, we've carried it. Who knows, mad dog or crazed human, it'd come in handy. We were sure glad to have it once when some drugged-out thugs from Key West straggled into our camp. Turned out a dose of water and food served better.

Guns (See also Chapter 9, "Signaling Guns")

A lot of times we're asked if we carry a gun. No, we don't. Even though we cruise in remote areas, we choose those areas carefully and do not expect to have to defend our lives against villains. There have been times when we were caught in a place where some sneaky nighttime activities are being carried out. We just stay still and keep a low profile. So far, so good.

Unless you are already an expert, we don't recommend carrying firearms aboard a small boat. If you must cruise along hostile shores like brown bear country, make yourself an expert with a HEAVY arm **before** you go. If you carry firearms, use at least a 12-gauge shotgun loaded alternately with double O shot and slugs. An expertly handled .44 Magnum is another minimal choice. A large animal can do lethal damage even after it has been separated from its head!

Editor's note: Most foreign countries do not allow you to bring guns into their jurisdiction. Some will let you carry firearms if they are sealed in a locked compartment. Others will take away any guns you declare at customs and hold them for you until you leave the country. To recover your guns, this requires you to return to the same port where you entered. If you fail to declare firearms, and they find a gun on your boat at an inspection, or later when you use the gun, your gun will be confiscated, your boat may be confiscated, and you may wind up in jail. No other country in the world has gun laws as permissive as the USA. Check the gun laws of each country that you plan to visit with the nearest U.S. consulate of those countries.

While you are in their country you are subject to their laws. *Woe unto you if you use a gun on one of their citizens! American consuls or ambassadors can't help you. All they'll do is visit you in jail and make sure you have a good English-speaking lawyer.*

For 50 years I've cruised in many parts of the world and never encountered a situation where I felt need of a gun. Courtesy of Uncle Sam and more recent employment at Winchester, I'm familiar with firearms and I'm a crack shot. I leave my guns at home!

We have mistakenly cruised a hostile and hungry shore. When we were confronted with guns, because we were unarmed, we were compelled to negotiate. Although we were apprehensive, the exchange with bandits was remarkably peaceful and friendly. At one point, one of them almost shared his purse with us! Had we been armed and violently responsive, a few minor losses would certainly have instead been major trauma. Other cruisers have had this experience.

A friend cruising nearby fired her pistol toward pirates as they approached her sailboat. Her intention was to warn them off and to defend her crew and property. The pirates did withdraw, but their return fire killed our friend. If you consider applying firepower, before you use it, be certain you shoot first with totally overwhelming force and destruction.

Negotiation is not always possible and the results are uncertain. Unless you have the advantage, and use it first, then armed confrontation is even less certain than negotiation. As most of us are unpracticed and shy with guns, the aggressive and practiced attackers are likely to have the advantage.

If you expect to defend your beach cruise against armed attacks, then only long range weapons will serve. In salt water environments all weapons require devoted maintenance. Mossberg offers a variety of semi-automatic 12-gauge configurations in marinized coatings that are as effective as stainless steel. Other manufacturers make stainless steel guns.

We recommend choosing friendly or benign coasts.

Editor's note: Amen! Why cruise where they don't want you, or where they're hostile? Our State Department puts out bulletins that tell you which countries are currently not safe for Americans to travel in.

Mace and other Cannister Deterrents

For those rare, surprise hostilities, we carry "MACE" or tear gas, and pepper gas in handy compressed cylinders. These are lightweight and come small enough to pocket. Larger cylinders fit on a belt holster. They have an incapacitating effect upon mad dogs, humans, polar bears and lions.

They have an effective, no wind, or downwind range of 20 feet. Bears and wild animals often come from downwind. These chemicals are very painful to the target and cause severe, but healable, tissue damage. Eye damage is usually severe. These chemicals are not to be used casually. Their damage is so much less traumatic and permanent than bullets, that we would not hesitate to use them at the first sign of hostile intent. They are useless at long range.

Safety In Numbers

Cruising in company with others provides some of the best security around. The time off Key West when we watched thugs chase down cormorants and kill them by smashing their heads against mangrove roots, we really did fear for our own vulnerable necks. Luckily, another couple sailed into our remote bay and we enlisted their support. Two boats, one with a VHF radio now, and four people joining in a concerted effort (not to mention calling the Coast Guard), provided immeasurable psychological and actual physical strength.

Float Plan

Whether we're in company with another boat or cruising alone, we file a "float plan" with a friend, or a dockmaster or dependable acquaintance, that describes where we are going, the route we plan to take, and how long we'll be gone. Then we **stick to** the plan.

SOURCES FOR ADDITIONAL INFORMATION

Sailing Books

The Craft of Sail: A Primer of Sailing, by Jan Adkins, $4.95, 64 pages, 1984, Walker & Co., 720 Fifth Ave., New York, NY 10019. Fun sketches and lessons in the theory and practice of sail

Sailing School, by Douglas Schryver, $19.95, 192 pages, 1987, Barrons, Box 8040, 250 Wireless Blvd., Hauppauge, NY 11788

Handling the Racing Dinghy, by Uwe Mares and Kurt Schubert, 1974

Small Boat Sailing: The Basic Guide, by Bob Bond and Steve Sleight, $15.45, 157 pages, 1983, Alfred A. Knopf, New York

Navigation Books

Coastal Navigation for the Small Boat Sailor, by Jeff Markell, $15.50, 256 pages, 1984, TAB Books, Inc., Blue Ridge Summit, PA 17294-0840

The Practical Pilot: Coastal Navigation by Eye, Intuition, Common Sense and Cunning, by Leonard Eyges, $19.95, 192 pages, 1989, International Marine, TAB Books, Inc., Blue Ridge Summit, PA 17294-0840

Books About Weather

Wind and Strategy, by Stuart Walker, $20, 416 pages, 1973, W.W. Norton, New York

Instant Weather Forecasting, by Alan Watts, $9.95, 96 pages, 1988, Putnam Publishing Group, New York

Instant Wind Forecasting, by Alan Watts, $14.95, 128 pages, 1988, Sheridan House Inc., 145 Palisade St., Dobbs Ferry, NY 10522

Books About Waves

Waves and Beaches: The Dynamics of the Ocean Surface, by Willard Bascom, $8.95, 366 pages, 1980, Doubleday, New York

Waves, Tides and Currents, by Elizabeth Clemons, 1967, Alfred A. Knopf, New York

Magazine Articles

"Staying Alive at Force 5 (and Beyond)!" by David Buckman, Messing About in Boats Magazine Vol. 4, No. 16, Jan. 1, 1987, 21 Burley St., Wenham, MA 01984. This is a well-written article about how to secure yourself and your boat for harsh weather conditions by a man with experience

"The Ins and Outs of the Surf Zone," by Wayne Haack and Eric Soares, Sea Kayaker Quarterly, spring 1987. All about landing and launching through surf by a couple of very experienced people

Gear

Viscom Mini-Handbearing Compass. Available through marine/camping catalogs

Self-sticking, clear vinyl contact paper. Easily applied to charts to make them waterproof and durable. Available from stores like Eckerds, K-Mart, etc. It will be in housewares or kitchen equipment departments, as its main use is for lining shelves

Sailing Programs

National Outdoor Leadership School, NOLS Mexico, P.O. Box AA, Lander, WY 82520. The NOLS program for sailing is currently (through spring 1990) offered as part of a semester program which caters mostly to college folks. Plans are in the works to add a regular sailing program to the format soon

Photo by David Buckman

A *Lightning*, converted to a cabin beachcruiser, is tied to shore and anchored in Willsboro Bay, Lake Champlain. Note the extra line to pull the boat ashore. See page 208 for a detailed description of how to do this

CHAPTER 11

BEACHCRUISING FASHION

This chapter is short because beachcruising requires only one item of special professional clothing. Just take the most comfortable and holey wear in your closet. Ours come from the Goodwill, and we take little of that, even on our six-month cruises. Favor what dries quickly, is cooling when it's hot, and is warming when it's cool, wet, and windy.

Our choice of beachcruising climate favors nudity, but sometimes the weather is too cool and breezy, like wind chill to 30 degrees while we're wet. When the sun does shine, we know it's destroying our skin just as it destroys the tent fabric. Sometimes it's so hot that wearing clothing helps us cool, especially if we wet it. So most of the time we have something on, even when modesty doesn't require it.

Editor's note: Don't fool around with tropical sun. I've seen many sun worshipers become badly burned in a short time, ruining their vacations. Few of us northerners have any idea what that strong Caribbean sun can do to you. Like Ida and Mike, I wear my old clothes when I go cruising, carrying along a decent pair of gray flannels, a jacket and tie. In resort areas, you won't need the jacket or the tie, but some fancy restaurants and clubs want you dressed up. In the tropics, I wear loose-fitting, light-colored long pants and old white long sleeved shirts. Many long term Caribbean sailors wear pajamas. Polarized sunglasses, a light-colored wide brimmed hat, socks, and boat shoes complete my wardrobe. I bring two bathing suits because I'm in the water a lot. When I'm snorkeling, I wear a white long-sleeved shirt to avoid a sunburned back, and I wear a tank cap to protect my bald head.

The ladies that sail with us in the tropics also cover up. They bring one or two dressy outfits for evening shoreside jaunts, but otherwise, they wear loose-fitting, light colored cover up clothes. White clothes reflect heat better than anything else. Ladies also need wide-brimmed hats and protective sunglasses. Bring an extra hat in case one blows off.

We continue to try any promising fabric that comes along. Most of the time we find ourselves wearing "natural" fabric—cotton or wool. A notable exception is our one professional costume, our foul weather gear. Because small boats don't have the elaborate shelter of big boats, our need for particularly effective foul weather gear is critical to our comfort and health.

Even though we're fortunate enough to be ashore during the foulest weather, we're as dependent on the foul weather gear ashore as we are in our cockpit. Get the best you can afford. Consider that it can serve you during your non-cruising life if you choose one that doesn't have that exclusively nautical, stormy look. Ours look nice. With the hood up, they keep us dry even while standing in front of the garden hose. On cold nights, the full lining prevents condensation from wetting the insides.

They are not heavy or hot. They are soft, supple, fully lined and comfortable. We choose a dark blue color for warmth. Ours are made by Rukka of Finland. *Editor's note: I'm on my 16th year with a set of Helly-Hansen storm gear purchased for me in Norway. They're available in the USA now. Mine has had heavy use and still keeps me warm and dry. Mine has no fly which requires me to take it all off when nature calls.*

Because they aren't heavy, we wear our Rukka's over cotton pajamas in mild foul weather. In colder weather, we use a hooded cotton sweat suit under the foul weather gear. In the Caribbean, we've rarely had to add a wool sweater to our outfit.

With the exception of our nylon windbreakers, the rest of our wardrobe is of cotton and wool. Light colors for hot, sunny days. Darker colors for cool days and evenings. We choose bright colors because they're more cheerful than white, grays, or black.

Camping in colder climates we've had to apply the principle of vapor barrier wear for lightweight warmth. Over our underwear, and next to our skin on the rest of our body—hands, feet, legs, arms, neck and head, we wear a thin layer of material which will not pass moisture. Yes, it's clammy, but it's warm, and our body moisture doesn't dampen our overclothes. Our overclothes stay dry and effectively warmer. On our hands we put plastic gloves **under** our wool gloves or mittens. On our feet we wear plastic booties **under** our cotton liners. On our legs and arms we

Photo by Michael Walsh

Ida hiking a coral shore in the Bahamas (this is locally called "ironshore." It's dead coral.). We've learned to protect ourselves from skin cancer by covering up. We rarely go barefoot, but use comfortable sandals like Teva or Hey! Sailor

use a plastic-coated rip-stop nylon fabric jacket **under** the woolen underwear. To stay warm, we avoid wicking and evaporation from our bodies. To stay cool, we induce moisture to evaporate from our bodies.

The head and neck are the most sensitive parts of our anatomy. We always carry a hat to help regulate our temperature and to shield our head, face, ears, and neck from the sun and wind. Our sun caps have a visor and a personally sewn-in neck drape (like the French Foreign Legion caps). They are light-colored and can be dipped in seawater when additional cooling is desirable. To be fashionable, we sometimes use a straw hat with a brim. To all of them we've added ties to keep them from going with the wind. When it's cold, we wear a wool scarf and a wool cap that has a nylon shield across the forehead.

During sunny, clear days on the water, enough U.V. radiation is reflected off the water or beach surface to sneak under the brim or visor and burn our faces. A bandana of light, open weave cotton draped over the nose and mouth works well. The fishing guides in Key West wear these "bandit" outfits. We also use Bullfrog sunscreen amphibious lotion. It doesn't wash or sweat off. It may irritate sensitive skin, so try it before you count on it. If you don't mind looking like a clown, zinc oxide or your nose and lips works very well. Theatrical supply houses have it in various colors. As I wear glasses, I sometimes choose a leaf that covers my nose. The bridge keeps the leaf in place. Others use a nose guard that lightly straps around the head, or one that clips to your sunglasses. Lips are very sensitive to U.V. To avoid cancerous lips, use one of the suggestions mentioned above.

In Chapter 9 we've remarked on the effectiveness of polarized sunglasses in shielding eyes from U.V. radiation. Some opticians can test your lenses for U.V. filtration. The phototropic lenses that darken according to the brightness, are very poor U.V. filters—worse than none because they cause your cornea to open and admit **more** U.V. radiation!

Infra-red radiation is not quite as damaging to the eyes, but it's tiring. Cruising glasses should filter out most of the infra-red as well as all the ultraviolet. Such darkened glasses will cause your cornea to remain more open, and enough radiation may come in through the sides to cause damage. On strong-sun days, we wear glasses that are fitted with side-shields. This style, pioneered by glacier climbers, are called "Glacier glasses."

Because of the activity involved in sailing and camping, ordinary glasses slip down and easily fall off. We wear glasses with ear pieces that wrap around the ears. Bollé makes a good, tough, nylon frame that includes all our needs. Before we found these, we tied down our glasses to our heads with elastic bands. *Your editor favors Croakers, that fit snugly on the ear pieces and behind your head.*

Colorful cotton t-shirts, a windbreaker, and underpants is what we wear most. On hot, sunny days, we cover more flesh with light pajamas that tie around the waist. On cooler days, we cover with colorful, soft, cotton sweat pants and a hooded top. We went out of our way to get pajamas and sweat suits of colorful cotton with a tie waist and pockets. Elastic waists give up quickly.

We carry a long-sleeved shirt of cotton, an oiled wool sweater, and wool socks. These are likely to be worn in the evening, over a different set of pajamas, evening pajamas. And because our life is almost exclusively lived beachcruising, we do carry a carefully kept dress-up costume for those rare formal invitations.

We wear socks with our shoes because they are easier to wash than the shoes. Because they are comfortable, protective of the feet, and light, if we could carry only one pair of shoes, it would be our pricey jogging sneakers. However, where we walk, these are usually hot, and they take too long to dry between wadings. Since we have the room and the choice, during the days, walking and wading, we almost always wear sandals. We use TEVA sandals, high quality and expensive flip-flops with an ankle strap that keeps it snug to the foot. These were originally developed for river rafting guides. We also wear Hey! Sailor sandals. Both are secure, well made, comfortable and cool foot protection. The Hey! Sailors are marginally better looking and more comfortable.

In colder climates, we've substituted knee-high wading boots, with room for bulky wool socks, in place of the sandals. In the Pacific Northwest, shores are deeper and seas are always cold, making full-length waders an appropriate substitute for the sandals we use in the tropics. Wetsuit "booties," or the more heavily soled "river booties" are useful footwear in some conditions where you're frequently getting in and out of a small boat and having to wade short distances in cold water. These are popular among canoeists and kayakers.

In the intense sun of tropic summers, we've covered our hands with cheap cotton gloves. Where it's cold, we use medium weight deer skin gloves because they stay soft even after many salty wettings. A thin plastic or rubber underglove (vapor barrier) under the wet deerskin keeps our hands dry and warmer. These liners are available from epoxy and paint dealers or from surgical supply houses. Good deerskin work gloves are available from Smith and Hawken, the garden tool suppliers. Davis Instruments also makes good cold weather boating gloves.

Our only cold climate cruising has been on Lake Superior and in Northern Canada. There we did find polypropylene underwear an adequate but smelly substitute for soft wool. Over that, we wore a skiing outfit on the water. On shore, after an evening bath, we changed to wool slacks and a down parka. Watch out for sparks on any synthetic, especially the thin nylon shell on an expensive down parka. The synthetic bunting clothing from Patagonia is almost as warm as wool or down, and it is much easier to maintain. In the North Country cold, we've found mittens warm the hands better than gloves. The ones we use are tightly knitted of boiled wool, called Dachstein mittens.

Oily wool is slightly water repellent and makes for a good sailing sweater. A modern substitute for wool is synthetic pile. The nicest aspect of pile is that you can shake it almost dry. It's light, colorful, and easy to wash. Good qualities are expensive. Poor qualities pill and open. If we did our boating in a cold climate, we would use more of it.

Before we got good waterproof stowage bags, our clothing would get wetter and dirtier in carriage than in wearing. Now we have tough, dry bags and sealed canoe portage-packs that keep all our fashions dry even in a capsize. These bags, and the waterproof gear box provide sufficient flotation to keep my small boat afloat. They're available in a variety of qualities, sizes, and prices from the canoe, kayak and camping mail-order outfitters.

SOURCES FOR ADDITIONAL INFORMATION

All of the **marine mail order chandlers** listed at the end of Chapter 9, **Outfitting the Boat,** also sell nautical clothing. Clothing devised for canoeists and kayakers is particularly appropriate for beachcruising and camping

The **camping outfitters** listed under catalogs at the end of Chapter 12, **Making a Shore Camp,** devote many pages to outdoor camping fashions.

We also like some of the clothing sold by **Patagonia, P.O.** Box 150, Ventura, CA 93002. Excellent quality, fairly attractive and comfortable, and correspondingly pricey

Wildwater Designs, 230 Penllyn Pike, Penllyn, PA 19422, also catalogs an excellent selection of clothing for small boaters

Recreational Equipment Company, P.O. Box 88125, Seattle, WA 98138-0125, is a leading mail order outfitter of outdoor equipment that includes clothing

Bermudes, 51 Milina Dr., Easthampton, NY 11937, manufactures "dry suits" for wetsporting in cold weather

Masterpeace Footwear, Rte. 1, Box 39E, Bloomington, IL 61704; (309)662-9011, for Hey! Sailor sandals

Foul Weather Apparel

Rukka, 201 N. Washington Hwy., Ashland VA 23005

Henri-Lloyd MRC, Box 1039, Manhasset, NY 11030

Douglas Gill, 6087 Holiday Rd., Buford, GA 30518

Look for these and other brands in most **marine supply stores,** and in **marine supply catalogs.** Talk to users before you buy

CHAPTER 12

MAKING A SHORE CAMP

SELECTING A SITE

We'd been cruising the Bahamas for five months before we found what I still consider the Ideal Beachcruiser's Campsite. At first blush, the tiny, uninhabited islet resembled many of the better sites we'd camped at throughout the island. We could see it'd be easy landing the boats on the gently sloping beach on either side of Lansing Cay, that casuarina pines would provide shade, and that onshore breezes would help keep the bugs down. It wasn't until we started walking around that we began to recognize it as Paradise.

The ground cover of pine needles cushioned a wide, level space for the tent, high and dry above the high tide line. No coconut trees threatened the space with their heavy bombs. Although we'll walk beneath coconut trees by day, we try **not** to at night. Cooler evening temperatures cause the stems to snap then. And we **never** pitch camp under one.

In among some scrub brush was a wind sheltered setting for a kitchen fire and food tables. Exploring further, we found a location just as suitable on the opposite side of the island, including a gently sloping beach and place with trees to which we could secure the boats. If there were a storm with wind, we could always move camp the 20 yards across to the leeward side of the island.

We weren't really worried about storms. This being spring, we had no fear of fierce storms or freak storm tides. The contrary. Our greatest fear as summer approached was lack of wind and consequent onslaught of no-see-ums, stinging gnats.

Although by day the islet appeared ideal for bug-relieving breezes, we'd been fooled before. Right at sunset the winds usually ease and often don't resume until mid-morning. All along we'd tried everything to stay in what little breeze remained. We'd built a tree house. That didn't work. We'd tried camping atop a lighthouse knoll that towered above all the land around it. But no, when the breeze died, it died up there too and the no-see-ums ate us alive.

In the Bahamas and other tropical lands and isles, the consistent, inescapable problem was the no-see-ums. We rarely had any trouble suiting the basic requirements of a good campsite: a gently sloping shore on which to beach the boat; a dry, level clearing with shade for the tent; some wood for a fire; and protection from storm winds. We were almost always able to avoid swampy sites and completely windless shores in an attempt to minimize bugs. Even if we did get bugs, we could retreat from the bigger ones like mosquitos, biting house flies, deerflies and horseflies. But the tiny no-see-ums could get at us through the screening. Sometimes it was windy enough or cold enough or the insects hadn't had a recent hatching, and we were left blissfully alone, but usually they found their way to us.

For several days after we set up camp on this ideal little islet, we were blessed with a steady breeze. Then came the Real Test. The breeze eased, the temperature climbed, and by mid-day there was no wind at all. It became so still and quiet that we could hear the hermit crabs crawling over the pine needles. Dusk came—the worst part of the day for bugs. There was nary a bug. At night, we prepared to go through our suffocating and ineffective routine of wrapping ourselves like mummys in our sheets. We waited for the painful sting of the no-see-ums, but nothing happened. Having suffered months of defenseless bloodletting, we declared this Paradise.

We are better prepared for dealing with no-see-ums now. We carry Screen-Pruf, and insecticide that you can paint on your screens (after checking to be sure the chemical won't melt your tent); mosquito coils that when lit give off an insecticidal smoke; and Skin So Soft, a hand lotion whose smell repulses insects (repulses me too). For the short term, these repellents are fine. For the long term, day after day, we hate to keep putting this poisonous oil on our skin and smearing it on our clothes, and breathing poisonous smoke in our lungs. Had we had Screen Pruf back in the '70s, we'd have used that. But all we had then were the insecticidal skin oils.

So—what else was so ideal about our little islet? Rainwater filled the coral potholes we'd cleared out and provided us with enough sweet water for drinking and bathing. Fresh fish and spiny lobster thrived in the nearby reef and suppplied us with fresh seafood (and entertainment) daily. Food staples, mail, and the society of people were all accessible in the small Bahamian village just an hour's sail away. We made this islet our base camp for four years.

Priorities in Selecting a Campsite

Priorities in selecting a good campsite vary with the cruising grounds. Along the leeward western coast of Martinique, our top priority was finding a landing site that wasn't already occupied. Our second priority was finding a safe place to land the boat. Unlike the Bahama Islands which have sand bars, shoals and islets protecting their western, or leeward, shores, Martinique has nothing. The ocean swell rolls in from the Atlantic, swings 'round the north and south ends of the island and breaks in waves along the western shore. We always had to look carefully to find a gently sloping beach without much surf. Once ashore, our top priority was finding a clear area for camp. This was especially important here, where we didn't want to disturb the deadly fer de lance snake. In one place, rather than sleep among the tall, thick grasses, we went so far as to pitch the tent on a dirt car track. We nearly got run over in the morning.

Oddly enough, we weren't ever bothered by stinging bugs along the northwestern coast of Martinique. Therefore, we never worried about finding a campsite with a good breeze. Only once were insects of any sort a pest. We'd climbed up a river to pitch camp in the jungle. That night, as we began to eat some hot soup, swarms of gnats surrounded us. It was impossible to eat soup without eating gnats. The next day we smartened up and ate earlier, in the tent.

We moved into the tent earlier not just for the gnats, but for the rain. On the jungle mountainside of Mt. Pelee, where we were camped, it rained every day in the DRY season. Many days it stopped raining only for three or four half-hour intervals. We got to where we just ignored it. It was warm enough, 85 degrees to 90 degrees anyway. But after a week we were desperate to hike down to the sea where we could dry our mouldy skin and allow our scratches and punctures to heal.

When we tried to return to our mountain camp in the afternoon, we learned why it's not a good idea to pitch camp too near a mountain river. A particularly heavy rain running down the mountain had flooded the river. Where we had to cross it to reach camp, there were 6-foot diameter boulders rolling down with the torrent. We waited 2 hours, watching the sun go down behind the steep mountainside. In the dimming light, we fidgeted and imagined fer de lances behind every bush. We waited another hour and the boulders stopped crashing by and whole trees, ripped up by the roots, finally ran aground. We crossed with rushing water shoving against us up to our waists.

Camp had survived. The worst of it was only that our tent apparently straddled a slight depression in the ground, which had filled with the hard rain. So we had a floating bed for the night. It could have been much worse if we'd pitched camp any closer to the river. We made this mistake

Photo by Michael Walsh

This beachcruiser is equipped for comfort—chairs, a drftwood table, and a palatial tent

in Mexico. Luckily, a Mexican found us in time to warn us about the likely posibility of the river rising suddenly and actually sweeping us away.

In Florida Bay, where mangroves predominate, our top priority is finding some dry land for our camp. There isn't much dry land. We're also on the look-out for a breezy site as well since the bugs are pretty ferocious.

In Canada, where bugs and bears and falling trees are a threat, we camp on small, detached, rock islets where we're less likely to get attacked or crushed. This often precludes other priorities like having better shelter or a flatter space for the tent.

In every case, we select a site by judging it for privacy, easy landing, room to set the boat above the high tide line, height above sea level (or flood level of rivers), clearings for tent and cook area, availability of firewood, protection from hard winds but access to some breeze, shade and distance from reputed dangers like snakes, bears, people, etc. If we plan to stay long, we seek places that offer a source of fresh water and some food gathering. In Martinique, we camped by a safe, clean river from which we hunted crayfish with gigs (a small metal trident mounted on a short stick). In the Bahamas, we camp near reefs that have a lot of sea life. Not all do. In the Florida Keys, we camp near wide, flat shoals where we can cast for barracuda. If it is at all possible, we try to locate our camp near a village for the services and pleasures of mail, food supplies, and companionship.

WHEN YOU DON'T HAUL THE BOAT OUT

Drying out

In some places you can't haul your boat out. There may be no dry land, as in the mangroves of Florida's Everglades, or the land may be too rough or too steep. Or, you may be cruising in a boat that is too heavy to wrestle ashore. In either case, the best compromise between hauling out and anchoring out, is drying out. By this I mean running your boat into a shallow area and letting the tide run out from under it.

When we started cruising *Dugong* we knew we wouldn't be able to haul her out. Yet we wanted to enjoy being in some places for days, weeks, or even months at a time without worrying about the boat. And we wanted to make a day camp ashore. Drying out became the perfect answer.

It took us a while to recognize potential beachorages. Coming from a background of either anchoring out or hauling ashore, the thought of going aground on purpose seemed heretical. But when we got sick and tired of having to anchor out with *Dugong*, the 6-inch draft cruising canoe we'd had designed specifically to go into shallow, supposedly protected, waters, we were driven to consider the alternatives.

We couldn't haul her out. She weighed a ton. We could anchor her in a mere 6 inches, but there were 6-inch spots that scared the wits out of us when the wind came up from the wrong direction. At Christmas Tree Island, Duck Key and Cumberland Island, to name just a few, we jerked and dragged at anchor despite the shallow depth. Finally, one day in the atoll-like Marquesas Islands west of Key West, we sailed into a beach on a falling tide and got stuck for the night. I immediately went into a panic. "We've **got** to get out of here," I kept thinking. "We're wide open—absolutely nothing out there to protect us from wind and sea." But gosh, we were fine. There were about 50 yards of inches-deep shoal between us and deep water. So even if the wind did come up from our unprotected quarter, no sea could get to us. What a great night! We slept serenely and soundly for the first time since the commencement of our cruise—no anchor watch, no anxiety, no scary drama.

The next time we dried out we were more selective with our site. We chose a small cove on the northwest side of an island where we'd have access to a long beach. Now choosing this site was truly boating heresy. It faced the direction from which the cold fronts blast down. And nothing, again, between us and the weather. I still felt panicky about being so exposed, but less so. Again, we were fine. The little scoop of a bay we were in not only had 100 yards of shoal around it, but a tiny spit of sand curving protectively around us. For the first time in our cruise we actually **enjoyed** a storm. We watched the black wall approach from our cozy shore shelter. We'd located camp so as to keep an eye on the boat, which we could see to be high and dry and perfectly safe. Preparing for this storm meant putting up extra tarps to catch the rain rather than more anchors to hold

Photo by Michael Walsh

Tall grasses sometimes indicate fresh water. Four inches down here, we struck sweet water on this Bahamas deserted island

the boat. It was wonderful! It was liberating! It was exciting and dramatic and **fun.** The 40-knot northwest blast whistled loudly around us when we crawled into *Dugong* that night. We fell asleep listening, without fear, to the howl. About midnight I awoke as we began to float, and lay there enjoying the gentle rocking and lap lap lap of wavelets against the hull. By morning we were aground again, steady as a rock. This was bliss.

In our favorite beachorages we even go so far as to build a little walkway from the boat to shore so we won't have to wet our feet at high tide. Although we spend most of the time ashore where we have a sheltered camp for cooking and eating and reading and generally hanging out, we return to the boat each night to sleep. We like to keep our feet dry and warm when we return.

Requirements: The Boat

Boats with flat bottoms or twin keels dry out upright. Ones with shallow, thin skegs tip a few degrees to one side. Ones with deeper skegs or keels may fall over far enough to risk endangering the boat. We met a spunky Canadian couple in the Marquesas Keys who ran their 19-ft., full keel sailboat aground on a falling tide. During the night, the boat flopped over. When the tide started to rise, the waves lapped over the side into the cockpit, through the ports into the cabin, and threatened to swamp them before she'd float.

If your boat doesn't dry out level but has a wide or sturdy keel, you can help it do so by using supports. Some boaters, especially in Europe, carry wooden legs along the sheer and when they've found a place to anchor that will leave the boat high and dry, they just swing the legs down for support. Boats with very shallow keels can use blocks or bumpers. Care should be taken in all cases in seeing that the rudder or any other part of the boat won't be harmed when the boat does rest on the bottom. If your boat doesn't come with a lifting rudder, make one that will lift.

Requirements: The Bottom

Any firm, level bottom will do as long as it is beyond the reach of waves **or** wakes that could pound the hull. By firm, I mean sand, hard mud, grass, and even rock if it's level and surrounded by plenty of shoal water. The bottom must be firm for twin keel boats and leg-supported boats especially. Our friend Doug grounded his twin-keeled Westerly in soft mud and actually saw the keels being forced apart as she sank into the mud. Leg supports are very susceptible to sinking and could cause the boat to topple. Even for cruisers in flat hulls, a firm bottom is desirable since you'll want to be able to walk ashore.

If the bottom is a little sloped, say, one to five degrees, no problem. But if the slope is over five degrees and you dry out parallel to it, you'll feel it. Cooking, eating, and sleeping aboard will become pretty uncomfortable. As a rule, you should try to ground out perpendicular to the slope. Generally, shoals and shallows have a gradual slope downward towards deeper water. Waves that might lift and pound your boat will come from the deeper water. For this reason, the boat should not only lie perpendicular to the slope, but bow towards the deeper end.

Before grounding out we check carefully for obstructions that the boat might come down on. Tree stumps, conch shells, rocks or other hard objects might damage the hull. Once we've got an area checked out, we then position the boat with anchors and stakes so that she dries out **exactly** where she should.

Tides

You must watch the tides. They allow you to get into a shoal area, and they allow you to get out again, sometimes. It depends on whether the high tide that brought you in is higher or lower than the one you try to use to get out. In places where there are two tides a day, as in Florida, one high tide is higher than the other, and one low tide lower. Over a period of a month, the daily tides gradually increase and then decrease as moon and sun exert their influences. So if you dry out in a place with little water to spare on the high tide, you better check the tide tables to be sure you'll be able to leave when you want to. Conversely, if you plan to sail into a shoal area to dry out at your favorite beachorage, check to see if the tide will let you in. Remember to leave yourself a little extra margin of tide in case the elements conspire to increase or decrease the expected tide

Photo by Chris Harkness

This gently sloping beach makes a perfect camp landing. That's Heather Caron and *Beer Budget*

height. As I write today, aground at Allans Pensacola in the Abacos, the barometer reads a whopping 30.05. This abnormally high pressure has actually decreased the high tide half a foot from what it should be. The 55-ft. ketch that ran aground during last night's storm doesn't have a prayer of getting off now, despite what the tide tables say.

ANCHORING OUT

When the boat, or the place, or the time, or all three aren't suitable for hauling out or drying out, then you'll have to anchor out.

I offer anchoring out as the last and least favored alternative. One of the greatest features of beachcruising in small boats is having the ability to secure the boat so that you don't have to fret over it. You are completely free to enjoy shore explorations. After living and cruising aboard a 6-ft. draft boat for a year, we turned to beachcruising to get **away** from anchor watches and continual attention to the boat. We've had some great evenings anchored out, and we still do anchor offshore when we have to, but it's not first choice. Maybe it's just us, but my feeling is that the people who prefer to anchor out either don't appreciate the alternatives, or they entertain romantic visions of clear, calm, starry evenings, followed by an easy row to a nearby beach for a walk. It's possible to get that, sometimes.

Editor's note: When we beachcruised in our sail canoe, we always hauled it up on shore. Our 17-ft. flat-bottomed, lapstrake Amesbury Pow Wow was heavy to drag or even roll, so we nosed her into the beach, unloaded our camping gear, and anchored her offshore. We had oversized ground tackle and she never dragged.

Requirements: The Place

You want an anchorage that is as secure as possible. If the wind comes up or shifts to a new direction, you don't want to spend your time shuffling the boat around. As we all know, these anchor drills happen at midnight with no moonlight! Lagoons, narrow rivers, and shallow-mouth bays, all offer complete protection. In these places you can anchor with a line to shore, making the boat and gear accessible to land. Then you can safely set up a shore camp to be enjoyed for several days or more.

This was the method we used among the Georgia islands. We'd leave the main river channel that winds between the islands and mainland, and follow a smaller river through the marsh towards high land. Sometimes it took two or three tries to find a river or creek that reached dry land as most just snake back and forth through marsh. At Cumberland Island we found a creek that wound inland to a place where we could tie bow and stern lines to a couple of trees. We even had a low-lying bough that we used for getting back and forth from boat to shore. This is a pretty important feature in many rivers where you don't want to have to wade through muck. In another creek along this same island coast, we again tied to a tree but had to use an anchor off the stern. When we returned to the boat after a long walk over to the ocean beach, we found out that our little creek dried out at low tide. The 6-ft. drop in water left *Dugong* hanging like an outlaw from a noose. We slept at attention until the tide rose and lifted her from the steep incline of the creek bank.

Small islets, narrow peninsulas, and points are second best choices as anchorages. These places offer a variety of protected anchorages, all close-by, for various wind directions. If conditions are right, you'll be able to anchor off and, with a line to shore, enjoy some temporary shore life. But, unless the weather is very settled, you won't want to set up a camp ashore. In an anchorage where you may have to move suddenly, you can't count on being there tomorrow to collect the gear you took ashore.

We were sure glad to have picked a small islet for our anchorage one night in Florida Bay. About midnight, the winds shifted, and we found ourselves on a windward shore. We just raised the jib, sailed the anchor out, and ran around to the other side of the island. It **felt** dramatic since there was **no** moon and it was pitch dark. We found our way by sailing close enough to the island to feel the mangrove branches slap against the hull. I believe we tied to a mangrove root for the rest of the night. Next day the sea was a mess where we **had** been, so we couldn't have returned for any gear left ashore there.

The third, and least attractive choice for an anchorage, is a place where the boat is plenty secure but where there's nowhere to go ashore. The Shark River and Whitewater Bay areas of south Florida's Everglades National Park offer very few landings. It's mostly mangrove. It's the same

Photo by Ron Johnson

Beachcruiser moored with a bow anchor and a stern line ashore. This keeps the bow into any waves

along the back side of Great Exuma, in the Bahamas. In both places we've had secure anchorages among the mangroves but we've been confined to the boat day and night.

CAMP EQUIPMENT

Tents

I need to be sheltered and protected from insects and crawling things to sleep well, and I have to sleep well to have a good time. This goes hundredfold over a long period, but even if I'm out just overnight, I want a good tent. By that I mean a tent that's easy to erect, has a sewn-in floor, big screened windows on every side, a sturdy frame and leakproof seams. At the end of a day's cruise, I don't ever feel like hassling with a complicated procedure. The simpler the process of erecting the tent, the better. With a tent floor and zippered entry, I don't have to worry about creepy crawlers like snakes, cockroaches, scorpions, mice, or hermit crabs, sharing my bed. Screened windows let in breezes, moonlight, and light by which to read if it's a rainy day. Leakproof (sealed) seams keep me dry and in better temper in a downpour; and a sturdy frame keeps it from collapsing in a blow.

Photo by Fred Jacobs

Beachcampers on one of Douglas Knapp's Baja beachcruises. *Drascombe Longboats* are anchored off this cove in the Sea of Cortez

This frame should be self-supporting. Too many times there are no trees or shrubs to tie to. It should also be made of some non-corroding, lightweight material. Our Stephenson tent uses aluminum tubing that requires occasional waxing to prevent surface pitting. Fiberglass and carbon make good frame material too.

When we started beachcruising, we used a two-person tunnel-shaped tent that weighed about three pounds. It was fine for under a month, but for longer cruises we prefer a little extra room. In the tropics, even at night, small tents get stuffy and hot. A four-person tent that covers a 10-ft. by 6-ft. area suits us well. The extra space and larger windows keep us cooler than a smaller tent would. We no longer have to draw straws to see who has to get out of the tent and go to sleep in the hammock! The spacious accomodations give us a dry, cozy, bright place to hang out if the weather's bad. With all that extra room, we can keep personal gear at hand—books, writing material, radio/tape deck, kerosene lamp, jug of water, spare clothes, etc. The tent sports double walls to prevent condensation but weighs only six pounds. It's a cinch to set up. We just slide two sets of curved poles through sleeves sewn into the front and into the back of the tent, stretch out the tent so that the poles arch upward, and stake the two ends down.

Packing up is when we really appreciate having a tent that rolls into a light, compact package. This big tent of ours folds into a 6 by 20 inch roll. The roll fits into a backpack along with the bedding. In taking down and setting up, things that belong together can be kept together.

The tent is so very light because it's made of the same stuff they use for making parachutes: lightweight rip-stop nylon. Although it's light, it's tough. The only tendernesses we take with it, are laying a tarp under the floor to prevent it's being torn by something sharp, and laying some material over it to shade it from destructive ultraviolet rays. The only maintenance we give it is an annual coat of Trewax and a coat of seam sealer on the seams.

Most canvas is too heavy, too bulky, and holds too much moisture to be used for a shore tent. If canvas is packed damp for as short as an hour, it begins to rot. Nylon deteriorates too, but not from wet. Sunlight destroys nylon. Our two-person nylon tent that was still youthful after four years of use in Minnesota, lasted only five months in the tropics. We had no idea that it would deteriorate so rapidly in the tropical sun. When a fierce windstorm came through and the tent exploded into a thousand thin shreds, we were shocked. There was no spare tent to take its place.

Our larger nylon tent is going on eleven years now. We've used it for four years in the Bahamas, one summer in Canada, one summer in the Sierras, two years in the Florida Keys. The magic to such longevity? Shade. We treat it like we treat our own skin. We rarely leave it exposed to the sun. In the Bahamas and Martinique, we either cover it with palm fronds or a tarp, or collapse it under a sheet during the day. In Canada and the Keys, we've been using an aluminized cover that slips over the tent like a rain fly.

A tent designed to stand up to weather and screen out insects is essential to comfortable camping. We choose rounded shapes that fare better in a blow; sturdy but flexible frames that flex without breaking; and sewn-in double walls that shed rain and condensation. Zippered panels that drop from the inside, and matching panels that lift on the outside, cover the large screened side windows in our tent. This way if it's cold, we have two layers helping keep us warm. If it's hot, the panels allow cross-breezes to cool us off. A sewn-in floor, together with securely zippered panels and doors, keep out insects and snakes. Sewn-in pockets on the inside walls keep small items visibly handy.

Cockpit Tents

For those who prefer to sleep aboard, a cockpit tent is necessary. Because it's sturdy, won't flap and make noises in the breeze, and won't drip condensation even though it's only single-walled, canvas is the best material for a boat tent. Lightweight, treated canvas is available for fabricating cockpit covers. You must be particularly careful to dry canvas thoroughly before folding it away, and when it's in use, to avoid touching it and causing water to be wicked through the fabric to the inside.

As with shoreside tents, cockpit tents should be designed so that they're easy to erect. Otherwise you just won't use it as often as you'd really like to. We went to a lot of trouble designing and sewing a cockpit tent for *Dugong*. We thought it clever as anything. Using the mast and two sprits for frames, we could cover the boat from cockpit to forward of the companionway hatch. The only extraneous piece of gear we needed was a small cross-arm to support the sprits and mast fore and aft. Simplicity was **not** the catchword. On a good, calm, good-tempered day, we needed about half an hour to put it all together. Lifting the mast out of the step seemed to be our biggest mental hurdle, although it wasn't hard to do unless the boat was rocking around. In practice, the tent was just too much hassle to bother with. Once we came to terms with our own laziness, and the fact that if it takes half an hour to set up an awning, it's just not worth bothering with for anything less than several hours' use, we set to designing a much simpler tent. This one is really an awning that folds up, frame and all, onto the stern deck. We unfold it and snap it over the cockpit in about three minutes. If we feel like it, we can zipper curtains to the sides. This awning we use.

There are many different designs and shapes to consider today. The Florida Hens, Dovekie, the Wayfarers, Sea Pearls—all these have wonderful tents. Look around at other designs. Often you have to design your own, and seeing others' ideas is a real help. An awning or tent maker will also help with design, as ours did with *Dugong's* awning.

Bedding

We choose our bedding for comfort and versatility. Foam sleeping pads, sheets, a thin and a thick blanket, a coated nylon tarp (vapor barrier), and pillows have traveled with us on all our cruises.

A combination of egg crate patterned, open cell foam with air-trapping capability feels soft and warm and dry. An air mattress is fine when it's warm out, but feels cold if laid on cool ground. And ever since I went camping as a child with my family and awoke every third night with all the air out of my mattress, I have mistrusted them. Many dinghy cruisers who sleep aboard, like Frank and Margaret Dye, use them. I think they may be less susceptible to punctures when kept aboard. Closed cell foam is the firmest alternative. It's not as soft, as cool, or as easy to roll into a small packet as open cell foam, but it doesn't absorb water, and it provides better cushioning than open cell foam.

Editor's note: We used air mattresses and sleeping bags in our two-man nylon mountain tent when we camped on beaches. Later we double-decked one bunk on our 22-ft. sloop, to sleep three in the cabin instead of two. We hung plywood from the deck frames using hooks and nylon webbing. An air mattress was used on the plywood. You can get many years' use out of a good air mattress. We used sheets and blankets aboard the 22-ft. sloop and on our Pearson 30.

For the energetic, long-term beachcruiser, we recommend a waterbed. We used one when we made a base camp on that Perfect Beachcruiser's Islet in the Bahamas. We dug a 6 by 6 by ¾-foot deep hole in the sand (checking to be sure our hole didn't go below sea level), stretched out the waterbed in the hole, and filled it bucket by bucket from the sea. When the bed was filled to comfortable firmness, we put up the tent over it. Our

Photo by Chris Harkness

The *Dovekie* has a comfortable roomy cockpit tent, right on the beach. Lee Hardin's "Ibis" at Atsena Otie Key

big tent covers the water bed with room to spare all around. This firm edge gives us place to set personal items safely beyond bed waves.

A cotton sheet, a thin flannel blanket, a thick wool blanket, and coated nylon tarp have given us all the versatility we've needed to suit varying degrees of temperatures and humidity in southern waters. These are easier to wash, quicker to dry, and more variable than a sleeping bag. When it's hot, the sheet's enough. Below 75 degrees we'll pull up the flannel blanket. If that's not quite enough we'll pull the tarp over the blanket. Although we're really using it for a little more warmth without adding weight, it also serves to reduce evaporation of our perspiration. So we feel warmer and less thirsty. When temperatures plunge into the 60s, we haul out the wool blanket. So far, this has served down to 40 degrees. If it gets that cold, we'll pull on caps. Since we always have acrylic caps aboard for chilly sails (anything under 70 degrees), we'll use these at night if we don't have our soft polyporpylene caps aboard. In Canada, where we're talking frost and hail storms in **summer,** we do carry a down comforter as well as the wool blanket. It may seem redundant to have both, but when it's warmer than 40 degrees, the down cover feels suffocatingly hot.

FURNITURE

Chairs

It took about three months of cruising without chairs before it dawned on us how uncomfortable life is without something comfortable to sit in. Not **on. In.** We had our life vests and seat cushions, but no back rest and no height off the ground. The comfort factor rose dramatically when we added a couple of lightweight backpacker chairs. The more room we have, the bigger the chairs we carry. On *Dugong* we lash two full-size, wooden, folding sling-chairs on deck.

A hammock was part of our gear during the five years cruising *Manatee* and *Kohoutek* in the Bahamas. It gave us a place to lie back in the breeze and read or nap. In summer, it gave one of us an alternative sleeping place when the little tent got too hot. It also served as a platform for food stocks and personal gear when we were forced to overnight in a marshy area.

Storage Shelves and Tables

Parts of our boat contribute to the furniture ashore. *Manatee's* leeboards become shelves; *Dugong's* sprits become table supports. In Martinique, our canoe *Crapaud* became one huge table/storage area. By lashing bamboo into a pair of tripods, we made a cradle on which to rest the canoe at waist height, so creating a convenient table and storage chest. At night or during rains, we snapped on the rubberized cover and kept everything dry. With whatever materials you can carry or scrounge, it's worth building a table. As with a chair, once you've got table, you realize how uncomfortable you were without one. Camping catalogs have cleverly designed tables that roll into conveniently small packages.

The best organized shore storage we've used are backpacks. They're easy to stow in the boat, and easy to suspend from a limb ashore. Separate pockets keep gear organized and easy to find. The main body of our pack holds all our bedding and tent, which makes moving all that stuff from boat to tent site and back again a lot easier. However, backpacks aren't waterproof. You need to pack your gear in a tough (3 mil) plastic bag **before** stuffing it into the backpack. Ashore, when it's hanging or leaning upright, we cover the outside of the backpack with a garbage bag or waterproof canoe bag.

Michael washing laundry on a makeshift table at a deserted island in the Bahamas. A spring-fed well provided all the fresh water we needed

273

LIGHTING

Candles

The simplest, lightest, easiest, and dimmest lighting is a candle. During the first six months cruising the Bahamas, that's all we used: a dripless candle and a flashlight for brief scurries. This meant pitching camp, preparing food, washing up and bedding down before dark. Many nights we lay in the tent reading by candlelight, barely able to stay awake, and looking to find it was just six o'clock. If we'd had one of those fancy camper's brass candle lanterns, or then known the Outward Bounders' trick of using a plastic milk container to keep the candle flame from blowing out in a breeze, we might have stayed out longer. But we hadn't made these technological breakthroughs. In retrospect, I realize that it wasn't just exhaustion that made us sleepy by six. It was somewhat the effort of squinting at a very dim book page.

Lanterns

We might have continued using the unsatisfactory light of a candle several more years if the incident with Corene hadn't happened. We'd been out diving all day and had had incredible luck spearfishing. In fact, we'd speared ten crawfish, two heavy groupers, a porgy and a margate. This was too much for us to eat or preserve, so we decided to sail on down to Little Farmers and give the extra to Corene and Stafford. They were glad to get the seafood and we were glad to have something to offer them for all their kindness to us. We stayed and visited and enjoyed the novelty of being there on a day when the mailboat wasn't in. But the time passed quickly and we realized we'd get back to camp just at dark. Corene realized this before we did and disappeared inside the storage shed. When she came out, she had an old train conductor-style kerosene lantern. She dusted it off, shook it to see if it had fuel, and offered it to us. She knew we'd only used candles up to then. We bought them at her store. She said we could have the lantern. They didn't use it, and we might want it when we got back to camp that evening.

Well! It was as if we'd received the gift of fire, or the notion of the wheel. The lantern made **that** much of an improvement in our life. When we got back to camp, we had enough light to secure the boat, fillet our fish, bathe, cook dinner, eat, and read in bed without straining our eyes. It was really hard to imagine how we'd managed without the lantern.

The problem with the kerosene lantern is fuel. It'll spill if the lantern's knocked over. Mrs. O'Leary's cow burned down Chicago by knocking over her lantern! To prevent spilling, we empty it before packing it into the boat. Also, you've got to carry enough kerosene to keep it running for however long you're away from stores.

Pressurized kerosene lanterns are much brighter than the non-pressurized types. But they are impractical for most beachcruisers because they guzzle fuel; eight times as much as the non-pressurized types; their ash mantles are extremely fragile; they require pumping; and they're too noisy.

If I'm going for brightness, despite inconveniences of fuel and fragility of parts, I'll go with a propane lantern. They too use a fragile ash mantle but they don't require pumping, they're quiet, and they don't reek noxious fumes. Small propane lanterns screw onto one pound, non-refillable propane cylinders which cost about $3. They can be fitted to larger refillable tanks which can be refilled for about 30 **cents** a pound. Rigging a system for attaching the lantern to a refillable tank is particularly worthwhile if you are using propane for cooking as well. A pound of propane will run a two-burner lantern for about 10 hours; a stove for 20 hours.

For convenience, durability, hardiness, brightness, availability, and cleanliness of fuel, the portable fluorescent lantern tops the list. These lanterns, made by Coleman and Eveready among others, are half the size of a loaf of bread and weight a couple of pounds with batteries included. They require no messy fuels or fragile mantles. Our lantern uses eight "D" cell batteries every 4 hours or so. I estimate that it's costing us about 70 cents an hour.

In order to cut costs and the quantity of replacement batteries we had to carry, we tried using rechargeable batteries. A small six-volt solar panel did recharge the batteries, but when we went to use them it seemed there was always one whose polarity was reversed, or one that was weaker than the rest. Rechargeable batteries are more hassle than they're worth for these reasons, and because they don't store as much energy as non-rechargeable batteries. Now we use two six-volt batteries which are kept outside of the lantern case and wired to the lantern with a plug that fits into a 12-volt socket. Using these bigger batteries, we get twice the lasting power of the "D" cells. The cost comes out about the same, but we don't have to carry so many spares. We keep a couple of extra fluorescent tubes on hand.

Flashlights

Imagine **not** having a reliable, waterproof flashlight. You get up at night to check out the stars and on your way back to the tent you trip and drop your flashlight in the water. It's not waterproof so suddenly everything goes black. You can't see a thing. A hermit crab walks by and mashes your little toe in its claw. You manage to shake it loose, but in doing so, you kick a sharp stick sticking out of the sand. Stumbling forward blindly, distracted by pain, you lose your way. You call out to your mate. No answer. You remember the hole in the coral that was close to camp, the one that looked like the very jaws of . . . You feel yourself fall—the old Worst Case Scenario! Not so funny in real life.

Two, and preferably three, reliable, waterproof flashlights, a couple of spare bulbs and spare batteries, deserve a permanent place in your gear. A good flashlight costs as little as $5. Choose one that uses the larger "D" cells. The more expensive alkaline batteries will stay **bright** longer than the cheaper batteries which dim sooner and continue dimming over a longer period of time. I'm not convinced that the krypton bulbs are worth the additional expense though they are supposedly brighter than the regular bulbs.

We've taken to carrying disposable one and a half-inch squeeze-switch pocket flashlights. The size of a disposable lighter, they are small enough to carry in your pocket, and to hold in your mouth when you need to use both hands.

PORTABLE ENTERTAINMENTS

In keeping with our philosophy of beachcruising for fun and pleasure, we bring along a selection of entertainments: books, games, a miniature cassette tape player, and a transistor radio. One of the joys of being "away from it all" is having the undistracted time to be frivolous and indulge our passions. Some of these include reading the books and magazines that we never had time to read before, playing a day-long game of "GO," listening to John LeCarre read his "Little Drummer Girl," listening to A Prairie Home Companion, and All Things Considered on public radio.

We choose our books and magazines with as much care as we choose our food stocks. This past year we subscribed to The New Yorker so that we'd have a bunch of those magazines to peruse at our leisure on some deserted beach. We give these away when we meet other readers. We trade books when we can. Most people favor murder mysteries, Gothic romance, westerns and spy stories. We favor non-fiction travel adventure, nature, and classics, so we don't count on being able to replenish our supply casually.

For Big Thrills, we turn to recorded books. A tiny player, like the Walkman, plays these dramatically read stories very well. It's like going to the movies in your own mind. Besides recorded books, we carry our favorite music: a little Vivaldi, J.J. Cale, Laurie Anderson, and Julian Bream.

When we're cruising the coast, we can use our portable AM/FM radio not only for weather reports, but for entertaining programs like Reading Aloud, and for music. Since we especially enjoy the thoughtful news reporting on national public radio stations, we eagerly tune our dial to those stations morning and evening. It is a real pleasure to relax over coffee, no rush, and listen to varied and probing reports while the Great Blue Herons feed nearby. It puts a different perspective on things. The phone's not going to ring, nor the doorbell to chime, nor traffic to frustrate.

Board Games, Cards, and Play Toys

Even if you've never enjoyed a board game or cards or frivolous sport, beachcruising can give you the leisure to learn this lighthearted way of human play.

Our board games include backgammon, chess and GO. Because backgammon is a fast moving, light-spirited, relaxing game, we play it the most, usually at the end of the day. Chess demands more attention so we play it when we have more time and energy. The GO board comes out of the box only when we're hunkered in for a few days. This game requires the most concentration and the most time. In our case, it takes days. We were originally attracted to the game through a revue of it in The Whole Earth Review Magazine. The reviewer remarked on a story going around about a GO master in Japan who was for several years teaching a student the game of GO by never playing it. Then one day the Master announced that the time had come for the two of them to play. After three or four moves, the Master suddenly smiled, placed his hands together, bowed formally to the student, and resigned.

For size, portability, and entertainment value, a deck of cards is hard to beat. We play a form of two-handed bridge nearly every evening. When other cruisers are around we play "Spades." Some of our beachcruising friends became so addicted to the daily 5 o'clock game that they'd schedule their whole day around it; that is, do their beachcombing, fishing, shelling, varnishing, reading, and writing early so as to be ready for another hilarious game at 5.

Frisbees, Aerobies, and kites take little space and weigh next to nothing. These come with us, too. A guitar used to come along, but the wet environment didn't agree with it. We bring the play toys we know we enjoy, and new ones to try. Doug introduced us to the controllable kite, and Nadine to the frisbee-like ring called the Aerobie. We're playing with both new toys this year, and thinking in terms of going pro!

•

Regarding our outfitting *Dugong*, her designer Phil Bolger made this observation in Small Boat Journal: "The attitude indicated by their equipment listing delights me. We will be austere and independent, and they are. By all the gods we'll have this, that and the tape deck, and they do. The weight ... suggests to me that they don't have **anything** they don't really want and use frequently. That is something worth aiming for."

ADDITIONAL SOURCES FOR INFORMATION

Catalogs

Don Gleason's Campers Supply, Inc., Box 87, 9 Pearl St., Northampton, MA 01061-0087. Camping and backpacking equipment

Recreational Equipment, Box 88125, Seattle, WA 98138-0125, 800-426-4840. The catalog is full of information that helps you choose the right equipment for your purpose

Coghlan's, Ltd., 235 Garry St., Winnipeg, Manitoba, R3C 1H2 Canada. Piezoelectric lighters, folding toasters, waterproof matches, etc

L.L. Bean, Freeport, ME 04033, 800-221-4221. General and specialty catalogs for quality gear

Magazines

Backpacker
Canoe
Outside

Portable Games and Entertainments

"Go" board, and how-to books from Ishi Press International, 1101 San Antonio Rd., Suite 302, Mountain View, CA 94043

"The Stars," by H.A. Rey. Guide to identifying planets, stars, and more

Books

Roughing it Easy: A Unique Idea Book for Camping and Cooking, by Dian Thomas, $3.95, 248 pages, 1976, Warner Books, New York

Magazine Articles

"Fitting Out for Camp Cruising," by John Burleson, Small Boat Journal #13, August 1980

"Hanging Duffles," by Steve Callahan, Small Boat Journal #32, Aug./Sept. 1983

Equipment

Screen-"Pruf", Protexall Products, Inc., Box 216, Maitland, FL 32751. Insecticide to put on your screens to keep no-see-ums out. Also available through some grocery and hardware stores

Sling-Light, 1539 Monrovia #23, Newport Beach, CA 92663. 16 oz. folding aluminum chair with headrest

Stephenson Tents, Gilford, NH 03246. Quality lightweight camping equipment. We use their tents and ponchos

Moss Tents, Camden, ME 04843. Uniquely designed tents and tarps

Voyageurs, Ltd., Box 409, Gardner, KS 66030. Waterproof gear bags. We've used their bags for over 10 years

CHAPTER 13

THE GALLEY

Beachcruisers have an advantage over beach hikers and backpackers; we have a boat to carry our load. Unlike blue water cruisers with their cramped quarters, we have lots of space ashore. When we land, we just pull out our gear, spread it around, and make as spacious a living area as we like. In the Bahamas, in Canada, in the Massachusett's Elizabeth Islands, in Martinique, and in the Florida Keys, we set up elaborate living rooms and galleys ashore. They were comfortable and entertaining places to hang out, and had easy space in which to prepare food. We had big driftwood tables, driftwood chairs, shelves, stools, waist-high counters for our stove and oven, stone benches, and palm-frond or tarpaulin roofs.

The Site

The shore galley site itself should be level; free of insect nests; clear of brush, stickers, poisonous plants, and coconut trees; shaded if possible; and protected from strong breezes. The site should be as close as possible to a source of water, be that lake, well, or sea, for cooking and cleaning.

Tables and Shelves

There are two good reasons to keep your gear off the ground. First, it discourages ants, crabs, roaches, scorpions, rats, mice and snakes from making themselves at home in that dark, damp space between your gear and the ground. Second, just as important, it makes using the gear easier on your back and your disposition.

Tables rate as high as chairs on our Desirability Scale. Tables can transform a caveman condition into Yuppie camper comfort. Look around for natural tables and shelves. On Little San Salvador in the Bahamas, we found shelves carved into an old coral wall. You can use your boat gear for tables and shelves. We've used sprits for table supports, leeboards and canoe seats for table tops, paddles and oars for shelves, galley box for a table, and cloth pockets and backpacks as hanging shelves. In Martinique, we used the whole canoe as one big table/pantry/shelf. We set it in the crotch of two bamboo tripods, so that it rested upright at waist level. A canoe seat supported the Optimus stove, while the rest of the space held all our supplies. At night, and during rain or sun, we used the rubberized cover to keep things dry and shaded.

Roofs

John Burleson makes a strong case for carrying a good tarpaulin fly in his article, "Fitting Out for Camp-Cruising," in the August 1980 issue of Small Boat Journal. We agree with him. Having a cover to protect you, gear and cooking area from rain and sun, makes life in the outdoors enjoy-able rather than marginally endure-able. John's "Seagull Fly" of seven-ounce poplin has worked so well that it's worth copying. He's reinforced edges with webbing, sewn leather into stress points, and used only six extendable poles, one at each corner and two opposite one another at the ridge seam. He says it's worked great for 12 years, and that you can buy one from Moss Tents if you don't want to make it yourself. We have generally used ordinary rip-stop nylon rectangular tarps, but these are flappy in a breeze. We've also used heavy Sunbrella acrylic fabric. We secured this to one of *Dugong's* sprits, which we tied between two trees about 7 feet up. When we needed shade or cover, we unrolled the fabric from the sprit to tie the two outer corners to posts which we'd driven into the ground at the appropriate distance. This made a good roof and a good rain catcher. Rain poured off the fly, down a line to which a stone was tied, and into a beachcombed plastic bucket. We sometimes collected as much as 25 gallons in one downpour, without ever getting wet ourselves.

Galley of our camp in the Exumas. Driftwood tables, rat-proof containers, nesting billypots. Crawfish tails are cooling in a pot lid. Dinner will soon be ready

EQUIPPING YOUR GALLEY

There's a little bad news and a little good news, about equipping the galley of a small boat. The bad news is that everything has to be small, light, portable and compact. The good news is that technology has been working to give us what we need. Today, we have available portable stoves, ovens, cookware, and utensils that fit, fold, and roll into tiny spaces. Backpacker/camping catalogs and stores offer the best and cheapest choices of equipment for us. Camping and hiking equipment is not made as corrosion or rust-free as marine equipment, but if cared for, will last long enough to pay for itself many times over.

Stoves

To help you choose, here are a few questions to ask yourself:
1. How big, and how heavy, a stove can my boat carry?
2. Will I be cooking aboard?
3. How long will I be away?
4. How much cooking would I like to do? Or, put another way, how much do I enjoy eating?
5. How many people will the stove be cooking for?
6. How handy will fuel supply stores be?
7. How handy am I with tools and repairs?
8. How high/low is my frustration level?
9. How klutzy am I? (Be honest, ask someone else)

Once you've answered these questions and feel a little more familiar with your situation, you can consider the characteristics of stoves in general. You'll have an idea of what matters most to **you.**

1. **Effectiveness:** I've rated stove fuels by how long each takes to boil a quart of water. If you're lucky, you'll find two stoves in one catalog rated this way. I spent several hours converting pints of fuel burned per hour, quarts of water boiled per half-hour, number of BTUs per burner to one comparable standard. The following is a rating of the four basic fuels, from **most** effective to **least** effective.

White Gas (or Coleman fuel): 5 minutes

Liquid Propane Gas (LPG. propane and butane): 8 minutes

Kerosene/Mineral Spirits: about 11 minutes

Wood (hard, dry wood): about the same as kerosene

Alcohol: 19 minutes, or about twice as long as LPG

2. **Efficiency:** How much fuel will you have to carry or buy to keep the stove running? All the stoves seem to consume about 1 pint of fuel per hour. The less time it takes to heat, the less fuel will be consumed. So the rating for efficiency is the same as for effectiveness except in the case of wood.

A wood fire, for which the fuel is collected at each site, can be the rule breaker here and turn out to be the most efficient of all the stoves. It only takes a dozen 10-inch by 1-inch diameter dry, dense sticks to boil a quart of water.

3. **Ease of operation:** You ask anybody who cooks much what fuel they like best and I bet you ten to one they'll say propane. It is far and above the easiest to start and easiest to run, requiring only the turn of a knob and the flick of a lighter. The open can and jellied alcohol Sterno stoves are easy too. Just open the can and light, but they're slow cookers. Because white gas and kerosene/mineral spirits stoves need pre-heating and pumping to start up, they are more hassle. Pressurized liquid alcohol stoves have the disadvantages of the kerosene/white gas stoves, with the added disadvantage of being slow as Christmas. Enough people are wising up to the myths surrounding alcohol stoves that conversion kits are now available for turning alcohol stoves into kerosene/mineral spirits stoves. In some cases all it takes is changing the burners. From easiest to most hassle, the rating goes:

LPG (propane/butane)
Jellied alcohol
White gas
Mineral spirits (cleaner than kerosene)
Kerosene
Liquid alcohol

Wood Fires

It takes some time to become familiar with the heat producing qualities of different woods. Wood fires are not easy to operate at first, and are never fully controllable. However, the most un-handy person can usually gather some twigs and light a match. On that score, wood "stoves" have all the other stoves beat. We switched to wood fires after five months of using a tiny Svea white gas stove. Klutz here knocked over the stove one day and set her toe on fire, spilled the tea, and soaked the clothing pile. That was the final blow to the frustrating daily hassle of fueling the tank, pre-heating the carburetor, then heating one small pot of food at the end of a tiring day. I screamed I'd never cook on that thing again, and I didn't. Much to my surprise, a wood fire was easier, quicker, and could be used to heat two or three or four pots of food and drink at the same time. We do now carry an Optimus kerosene stove for times when we can't build a fire, but it's second choice to wood.

Having used simple wood fires for cooking for several years, we've learned a few simple and very helpful procedures. First and foremost! You don't need a bonfire to cook food. If you want a bonfire for fun, fine, but make a separate, smaller fire for cooking. When we want a fire to heat water in a pot, we'll use several **small**, hard, dry sticks of wood, just enough to fill the area directly under the pot. Set ablaze, this small stick-fire will boil a quart of water in about 10–11 minutes. When we want a fire to cook a grill of fish, we'll first burn 15 to 20 1-inch thick sticks and 4 or 5 3-inch thick sticks in a foot square area. After these have burned down to

This small wood fire will cook two fish grills of fillets—three eight-pound fish

Basket grills make turning a no-mess affair. Ida places onion rings between the grill
and the fillets, so that the fish tends less to stick to the grill

Grilling fish over a slow smoky fire gives a nice flavor and helps preserve the fish for future use. Here Ida checks it out with a fork. The grill is balanced over the fire and held by a rock or driftwood. Start your wood fire on the beach where it won't spread to a forest fire, stand by your grilling fish, and keep a bucket of sea water handy

coals, we'll add the same amount again, letting this burn to coals also. By now, we'll have a good 2 inches of very hot coals that will cook the fish quickly and dry the flesh without burning. We try not to let the fire flame when grilling.

Today, we grilled three grill-loads of grouper, hogfish, and mutton snapper, and I was reminded of a few more things we've learned through time and experience. We choose our wood carefully. Today, for example, we shunned the dead tree nearest our fire pit, although it was convenient, and dry, but not rotten. Not knowing if it were poison wood or not, we left it alone. Woods with poisonous resin give off a poisonous smoke. When you breathe this smoke, it causes a systemic reaction whose **least** trouble-some symptoms are external blisters, like the ones you get from touching poison ivy, poison wood, etc. If you're lucky, as we have been, the poison is expelled through your sweat, raising blisters that itch like craa-zee. If you breathe too much poison wood smoke, you can fatally injure your lungs, so it's to be avoided.

We weren't having any trouble finding plenty of safe, good wood to burn today. We'd selected a grilling site on a beach fronting rows of casuarina (Australian pine trees). We know the wood is hard, burns very hot, and is safe. All we had to do was walk through the grove and break off branches that were dead, but not rotten, as the ones on the ground might be. Near the casuarina grove lies a semi-marshy area with loads of soft mangrove and dead scrub that rots standing upright. We've used these woods before and been dismayed at how long their flame takes to cook anything. It's like using alcohol compared to propane.

During the 3-hour process of grilling three grill-loads of fish, the wind shifted and started blowing harder. Our beach got quite breezy and the fire started flaming. To keep the fire hot but not aflame, we sprinkled sea water over it. We built a short wall of sand around the coals to keep keep the draft down.

4. **Availability of fuel:** If you will have to restock your fuel supply while cruising, then you'd better use a stove whose fuel is easy to find. From most to least available:

Wood

White gas

Kerosene

Propane

Alcohol

Keep in mind that availability will vary from place to place. You might want to check before you head out.

Nowadays, multi-fuel stoves make it easier to re-stock your supply. If you're uncertain of available fuels, these type stoves would serve you best. Fuels that come in special tanks, canisters, and cans will always be harder to find.

Editor's note: We used a Sterno stove when beachcruising. It folded flat, and the fuel took little space and was readily available. On our 22-foot cabin sloop, we had a two burner Swedish Optimus kerosene stove with an alcohol prime. One filling of the two integral tanks would last for months, and that stove was trouble free for 20 years, and much faster than the Kenyon alcohol stove on our Pearson 30. Our alchol stove needs frequent fuel replenishment and needs care in use. Keep a container of baking soda nearby to throw on flames, and always have a dry chemical fire extinguisher hung in the galley.

We've cruised in faraway places in many parts of the world and have found kerosene readily available nearly everywhere. Stove alcohol is scarce outside the USA. Propane and CNG are increasingly available most places. Propane is the fuel on most charter boats.

5. **Size and weight:** "The bigger and heavier the stove the better" may sound strange, but it's true. If I have room, I'll take a two-burner 12-inch by 20-inch Coleman propane stove that weighs 11 pounds, rather than a Svea 3½-inch by 5-inch stove that weights one pound. I like having two burners to cook on, a support for a large pot, and the stability of a broad base. If I don't have room for a two-burner stove, I'll choose a one burner that is stable under a wide pot. Check to see that the stove has the legs or base to support such a pot without falling over easily. When reading stove dimensions, note whether these include the fuel tank or not. If you plan to cook aboard, you might want to consider a gimbaled stove, even if it means carrying a little more weight. Small, marine, one-burner gimbaled stoves weigh about eight pounds.

6. **Design:** Look for quality of materials. Non-corroding stainless or brass are preferable, but aluminum and steel will serve if you can keep the salt off. Look for simplicity of design. In most cases, the fewer the removable parts, the better. The main exception to this is the propane stove with its removable tank. In this case, removability is good because this makes storage so much easier. Butane tanks cannot be removed from the stove once the tank's seal has been broken. This makes storage awkward. Look for built-in windshields, sparking devices and reflectors.

7. **Maintenance: wood "stoves":** Portable grills won't "break down" but they and your pots and pans get sooty. It's best to take an attitude of likeing the soot and adapt to it, rather than to try and clean it off. We've tried the trick of slathering the pots with soap or detergent before cooking for "easier" cleaning later, but it wasn't easier enough. Instead, we carry the grill, pots, and pans, soot and all, in a protective plastic bag.

Jellied alcohol stoves: These stoves have only a wind shield to be kept free of corrosion. This is the simplest of chores and shouldn't intimidate the least handy person.

Non-pressurized liquid alcohol stoves: Stoves like the Origo operate like the jellied alchohol stoves, in that they don't use pressure. The only moving part to maintain is the flame adjusting shield, if it happens to pop a rivet. Lloyd aboard *Lloyds of Michigan* says his is virtually maintenance free.

Propane: Camper stoves like the Coleman that use non-stainless burners require new burners every couple of years as the old ones rust. We used ours for five years, and the only thing we replaced were the burners, and those only once. Otherwise, all we did was keep it oiled to slow the rusting. Lately we've come across marine stainless propane stoves that use asbestos gaskets between burner and stove top. We had to replace one this year and discovered how hard it is to buy asbestos gasketing material in the U.S. Be sure to get some spares **before** you need them.

White gas: Although it is a fairly clean fuel, it will sometimes clog the orifice through which it is vaporized. These stoves will need some special tools, spare parts and know-how.

Kerosene: Kerosene is dirtier by nature than white gas. Stoves using this fuel, then, take more than the routine maintenance. The orifice on our Optimus needed cleaning so often that we kept a wire orifice reamer handy. Nowadays these wire reamers, called prickers, are built into many kerosene stoves. This makes them a lot handier and less likely to get lost. On the other hand, they sometimes get fouled up and either don't ream or don't close down tightly so that the fuel control won't close down tightly either. Enough clever people have gotten sick and tired of the dirty orifice hassle to either strain all their kerosene, or better yet, switch to the ever so much cleaner mineral spirits. Bob and Connie on *Cookie Monster* swear by mineral spirits. A gallon lasts them a month even though they're baking bread with it. They say mineral spirits are cheap if purchased at paint stores, 50 cents more per gallon than kerosene. In the U.S., mineral spirits are easier to find than kerosene. Outside the U.S., kerosene is easier to find.

Pressurized alcohol stoves: These stoves can both strangulate at the orifice or spew fuel if not preheated sufficiently. They require as much maintenance and replacement parts as the pressurized kerosene stoves.

From least to most maintenance:

Wood

Jellied alcohol/liquid alcohol

Propane

White gas

Mineral spirits/kerosene

Pressurized alcohol

8. **Safety: propane:** You may have surmised that propane stoves are **our** first choice. Here's the catch—they **can** be the most dangerous. If the tank leaks, propane will spill out and fall to the bottom of the boat. If you've got a cuddy or a tent over the boat, it is possible to trap the propane inside. Then, any spark will blow you up. Or, anyone breathing it will slowly asphixiate without noticing a thing. Since we are talking about open-style boats and generally cooking ashore, propane leaks should rarely be a problem. We usually get **too much** ventilation.

Ida and Michael enjoying coffee. We could eat and sleep aboard *Dugong*, or go ashore to make full camp or galley only. Our stove, propane tank, and galley gear are all easily portable

White gas: This fuel rates a close second to propane on the danger score. A spark will cause its fumes to explode. Since gas floats on water, you can't use water to extinguish it. You have to smother it.

Kerosene: Kerosene won't explode but its flame is as difficult to put out as a gas flame. Again, you have to smother it. Look for stoves that are designed so that if upset they will not burst into flame.

Alcohol: Alcohol has always been considered the safest of all fuels because it doesn't explode (it will flare up if you're not careful), and the flames can be extinguished with water. However, you can spread the flame of alcohol with water as easily as you can with gas. You should smother it like all the others. The myth of alcohol is rapidly losing believers.

Wood: A wood fire, generally the safest fuel flame around, can also be the most dangerous of all. In a fire hazard area when the ground is very dry and easy to ignite, wood fires are **not** safe. There have been summers in Canada it's so dry that the Ministry of Natural Resources flies around making sure nobody lights a fire. Even in the safest areas you must clear a space for your fire, build some sort of low wall to contain it, and keep water handy to control any rebellious flames. Care must also be taken to avoid getting sparks on your clothing.

From safest to least safe:

Alcohol/wood

White gas/kerosene

Propane/butane

All of the fuels could be considered intrinsically "safe" **or** "unsafe" depending on how careful you are, how good a job you do filling and starting your stove, and how carefully you maintain all the parts.

Fire Extinguishers (See also Chapter 9, "Fire Extinguishers")

A wet towel is about the easiest and should be about the handiest for the size stoves we're taking about. If you are cooking aboard, you ought to carry a small Halon fire extinguisher. Halon is a gas that smothers fire. We carry one called FLAM-X that weighs less than a pound and fits in the palm of your hand. We ordered it through one of the marine catalogs. *Editor's note: Keep your extinguisher near the stove.*

A SELECTION OF STOVES IN EACH FUEL CATEGORY

Now that you've answered the personality quiz and know some good things and some bad things about each fuel supply, here are some stoves to consider:

White Gas

Hottest flame, doesn't need pumping.

1. **Svea 123 "Backpacker"** (about $43)
   Size: 3¾ inches x 5 inches
   Weight: 18 ounces
   Material: Solid brass
   Good things: Requires no special fuel tank; compact and easy to pack; won't corrode or rust
   Bad things: Bursts into flame if upset; unstable, supports only a small pot

2. **MSR Whisperlite Stove** (about $41)
   Size: 4½ inches x 6 inches
   Weight: 12 ounces
   Material: Stainless steel and brass
   Good things: Small and compact (legs fold); built-in heat reflector; quiet; very light; won't rust or corrode
   Bad things: Requires a special fuel tank

3. **Peak 1** (about $33)
   Size: 4⅝ inches x 6 ½ inches
   Weight: 32 ounces
   Material: Steel
   Good things: Small and compact (no removable parts); built-in pump and orifice reamer; won't burst into flame if upset
   Bad things: Corrodible

Some galley equipment that we consider essential. Gimbaled propane stove with oven, bread board, pressure cooker, folding toaster, piezoelectric lighter, insulated plastic cup, vitamin dispenser, waterproof matches

4. **Coleman Sportster®** (about $33)
Size: 4⅝ inches x 6-1/16 inches
Weight: 34 ounces
Material: Steel
Good things: Small and compact; built-in windshield; won't burst into flame if upset; comes with a hard plastic carrying case
Bad things: A little heavy; corrodible

Propane
Easy to use, hot flame
1. **Primus two-burner Gour-Mate** (about $67)
Size: 12 inches x 4 inches x 21 inches
Weight: 10 pounds
Material: Steel
Good things: Two burners; broad base for stability; large suface for large pot; little maintenance; uses **refillable** propane tank; spill tray under burners
Bad things: Large and heavy, corrodible, requires special fuel tank
2. **Coleman two burner camping stove** (about $50)
Two-burner like the Primus above. A little easier to find but of a little poorer quality
3. **Balmar Seacook** (about $129)
Size: 14 inches x 15 inches including the propane tank under the burner
Weight: 8¾ pounds
Material: Cast aluminum and stainless steel
Good things: Gimbaled (for cooking aboard); regulator heat valve rather than needle valve for more precise heat adjustment
Bad things: Must use unrefillable 16.4-ounce propane tank; expensive, big and bulky

LPG—Butane

Easy to use but fuel tank not detachable; harder to find than propane
1. **MiniGalley II** (about $93)
Size: 7½ inches x 12 inches with tank (located under stove)
Weight: 32 ounces
Material: Stainless steel
Good things: Gimbaled basket; has custom-sized pots and pans
Bad things: Uses a special 6.75-ounce cartridge
2. **Mini Mark III** (about $25)
Size: Folds flat and pocketable without tank
Material: Steel
Good things: Tiny and easy to carry; built-in windshield; cheap
Bad things: Unstable; supports only small pots; corrodible; needs a special 14-ounce butane tank

Kerosene
Non Explosive
1. **Optimus 00** (about $60)
   Size: 7½ inches x 5 inches
   Weight: 32 ounces
   Material: Brass
   Good things: Small and compact; needs no special fuel tank; built-in windshield on burner; comes apart for easy storage
   Bad things: Needs priming and pumping

Alcohol
Safe and easy
1. **Origo Heat-Pal 5000** (about $87)
   Size: 10½ inches diameter by 11¼ inches high
   Weight: 5 pounds
   Material: Stainless steel and aluminum
   Good things: Simple and easy to operate; no maintenance (no jets, valves, pumps), doubles as heater
   Bad things: Bulky, dirties pots with soot
2. **Sterno** (jellied alcohol)
   Size: about the size of a 1½-pint can
   Weight: Under a pound
   Material: Steel
   Good things: Simple and easy; won't spill fuel
   Bad things: Supports small pots only

Multifuel
1. **Peak 1 Multifuel** (about $56)
   Size: 5-inch diameter x 5½ inches high
   Weight: 18 ounces
   Material: Steel
   Good things: Will run on kerosene or white gas; built-in sparker, built-in windscreen
   Bad things: Corrodible
2. **MSR X-GK** (about $80)
   Size: 3⅜ inches x 3½ inches
   Weight: 16 ounces
   Material: Steel
   Good things: Runs on nine fuels including: kerosene, white gas, leaded gas and diesel; built-in sparker; stability built in with widespread flat legs; all in one piece yet compact
   Bad things: Complexity may call for more maintenance; need for more tools, know-how, and spare parts

OVENS

You should consider taking along an oven if you are going to be away from stores for longer than two weeks, or if you really enjoy baking breads and other foods.

When we started cruising in the Bahamas, we had no oven. We were forced to fry a sort of pancake bread if we wanted bread at all. The time and effort required to make ten "cakes" every few days got to be so much a pain in the neck that we started improvising ovens. Being able to bake real loaves of bread raised our standard of living significantly. As a result of our efforts with ovens, we were able to bake fish, cookies and other treats that we hadn't been able to enjoy before.

1. **Underground ovens.** For baking fish, meats, potatoes, etc. These are the easiest to build and the hardest to control. You simply dig a hole in the sand and build a big enough wood fire in the hole. When the pile of wood has burned enough to make a heap of charcoal, it's ready to use. Place damp seawood, moss, whatever, on the coals to provide a little buffer for the food. Then lay the food, wrapped in heavy aluminum, on this bed. Cover the whole thing with a layer of damp seawood followed by sand, leaving one small hole for air. Smoke should rise through the sand as air is sucked in through the hole. The bigger the hole, the more air gets sucked in, and the hotter the fire. Now comes the tricky part—guessing when the food is done. We'd wait 45 minutes to an hour for a 10-pound fish or a 5-pound chicken. Only once was a fish underdone, and that because we didn't check the oven enough to make sure enough air was getting in. From time to time, the oven needs to be checked and air holes poked into the sand, if no smoke can be seen coming up through the sand. I don't think we've ever baked anything for too long a time. We're always much too hungry. All the fish we've baked this way has been very tasty, and given us both a change from our usual ways of preparing fish, and a means of cooking things like chicken.

2. **Barrel ovens.** For baking anything, including bread. We've lucked out with our beachcombing and come across junk with oven potential. In the Bahamas, we used a 50-gallon fuel barrel turned on end for both stove and oven. First we'd cut out the end of the barrel. This took hours to days, depending on our patience and the strength of our machete-cum-barrel-opener. After filling the barrel three-quarters full of sand, we cut a gap in the upper edge for receiving wood sticks, and poked holes along the upper edge for receiving supports for a grill. This gave us a place to cook at a comfortable waist level. To convert the stove into an oven, all we did was place the top of the barrel over the top edge. This held in enough heat to bake bread or anything else. We had no thermometer, but it was easy to check for doneness by lifting the lid and just looking.

3. **Pressure cooker.** The most practical way to bake while beachcruising is with a pressure cooker. You can bake anything from a roast to a bread

292

in it. The cookers are necessarily heavy (the four-quart size weighs five pounds) but are worth carrying for both baking and preparing foods that require a lot of cooking. Keep in mind that an alcohol flame burns so cool that it has a hard time bringing a pressure cooker up to pressure.

4. **Reflecting ovens.** Reflecting shields of tin or aluminum foil placed before a fire work to bake small things like cookies, biscuits, and thin fillets of fish. Canoeists use this method frequently.

5. **Folding ovens.** When we have the room, we prefer to carry the Coleman folding oven. It measures 12 inches x 12 inches x 2 inches folded flat, and 12 inches x 12 inches x 11 inches opened out. It does require a 12-inch base of support so we only use it with a two-burner propane stove. The worst thing about the oven is that it's made of corrodible steel so it needs care around salt water. Even with the best care, it'll rust away in two or three years. I've tried spray painting the oven with high temperature paints, and found I could prolong the oven's life by a year or two. The round Optimus stainless oven is preferable as far as materials go, but the ring mold design is peculiar. It will not take two regular bread loaf pans nor a large cookie sheet. As with the pressure cooker, keep in mind that alcohol stoves just don't burn hot enough to run an oven.

LIGHTERS

1. **Piezoelectric lighter.** a $5 item, indispensible for lighting LPG stoves. The lighters work by using a trigger to pressure a crystal which causes a spark. The crystal never wears out but the trigger does. Our lighter from Coghlans is 10 years old and still going strong. However, the one we bought in Martinique developed a bad trigger after only two years' use.

2. **Disposable lighters.** These cheap lighters come in mighty handy when it's too damp out to light a match.

3. **Windproof/waterproof matches.** Windproof matches burn a little like a sparkler and blaze away impervious to the strongest wind. Waterproof matches will light even when wet. We get both kinds from Coghlans and always carry them along.

Editor's note: I have a **refillable butane lighter** *that has lasted two seasons. It has a "window" that lets you see how much butane is left.*

POTS, PANS, AND OTHER GALLEY EQUIPMENT

If your budget can handle the higher cost, go for stainless.

1. **Pressure cooker.** A pressure cooker has these advantages: It can be used as an oven; it cooks food twice as fast as a regular pot; and it will hold leftover food in a sterile environment. Use the size appropriate for the amount of food you plan to cook so that you don't waste fuel on heating up the pot.

2. **Frying pan and lid.** Look for a pan with a double thickness bottom for more even cooking.

3. **Double-sided grill.** We carry the heaviest gauge stainless grill available. We use it for toasting bread and for grilling fish and meat over a wood fire. The basket design allows you to flip the whole grill rather than just each piece of food. Once the food is cooked, you can leave it in the grill for storage. We hang the grill, covered with a paper bag in the shade of a tree so that it hangs in a cool breeze. This way, we can keep grilled fish for two days in the tropics.

4. **Folding toaster.** The round, four-slice, open design toasters work best. They are very light and fold completely flat. We take ours beachcruising, canoeing and backpacking. Having toast somehow makes you feel less like you are "roughing it."

5. **Nesting billies.** These half to four quart pots fit inside one another and make a neat package. The big pot top doubles as a frying pan. The rest of the pots have tops too so can be used for steaming foods. Because they nest inside one another, they don't have handles. These handle grips come separately and a couple spares should be carried along.

6. **Storage bowls.** Some stainless bowls are designed to nest like the nesting billie pots. These bowls can be used for cooking, then used for storing the leftovers when the lid is clamped down tight. These are the most effective food containers for keeping creatures out.

7. **Plastic bags that zip lock.** Ziplock brand heavy duty freezer bags are tough enough to withstand abrasion and gentle pokes without tearing or splitting. We re-use the bags two or three times. Other brands give out before the first use is finished. We use the bags for storing rice, coffee, powdered milk, and leftovers. The only problem is you must keep the bags inside a hard container in order to keep the creatures out.

8. **Heavy duty aluminum foil.** Don't even bother with regular foil. The heavy duty material won't tear so easily and can be used as a pan, food wrapper, heat reflector and pot cover.

9. **Basins.** Plastic Rubbermaid basins will serve well for years as dish pans, clothes and body washing basin, bread dough bowl, etc. It's one of these items that keeps primitiveness at bay.

10. **Detergent.** Joy detergent wins hands down as the best detergent to use in salt water. We even use it as shampoo and body soap when we bathe in the sea.

UTENSILS

Stainless or wood handled cutlery looks, feels and lasts better than other materials. Plastic may be easier and lighter, but it's one of those things that can make beachcruising feel a little tacky.

You'll want a **spatula,** a **can opener** (there's one on the Swiss Army knife), a **small-bladed bowl-cleaning spatula,** and possibly a **grater** for coconuts, citrus peel, etc.

A **stainless steel fillet knife**, thin and long, will double as a kitchen knife. For a smaller blade, the Swiss Army knife will do.

Disposable paper plates serve well and look nice when placed in straw plate holders. These holders support the flimsiest of paper plates but juices can soak through. As with so many items, don't bother with the light weight stuff. Buy the heaviest grade paper plate you can find. *Editor's note: Plastic coated paper plates resist soaking through.* The tops of your nesting billies serve as both plates and bowls.

The only esoteric galley item we always carry is a **conch pounder.** Conch flesh has to be pounded before it's used in chowder and fritters. A regular meat pounder will do. *Editor's note: We've seen natives use Coke bottles to pound conch in the Abacos, and to pound abalone in Mexico. They lay it on a flat rock. The bottoms of Coke bottles are very strong.*

A **cutting board** has many uses besides those of providing a surface for

Photo by Chris Harkness

Ida with *Cold Bag* at impromptu beach galley set up adjacent to the boat, everything handy in the shade of an awning. The ice cream is long gone but the early a.m. purchase of orange juice is still cold by mid-day

filleting, chopping, spreading, etc. Ours serves as chart table, seat, wind break for the cooking fire, and on and on.

STORAGE CONTAINERS/ORGANIZERS

The ideal traveling galley is carried and stored so that it stays dry, safe from creatures, and organized in one portable container.

1. **Galley box.** some sort of box that holds the essentials of your galley so that you've got it all in one place, and all in one container to ferry ashore.

"Campers Kitchen": an aluminum box with piano hinges that allow the top, front and sides to fall away revealing either plain shelves or a complete kitchen. Available from Gleason's Campers Supply.

Beer Cooler: 24-quart, plastic hinged-lid coolers are tough, waterproof, light and easy to carry. Their plastic material and rounded corners are easier on a boat than metal is. We carried two coolers when we were cruising in *Manatee* and *Kohoutek.* One cooler had stationery supplies and the other galley equipment. We fitted both with extra snap-down catches to make sure the lids would stay locked down.

Home-made boxes: we made a large wooden box with a simple latch for carrying all our galley gear aboard *Dugong.* It served both as table and storage container. It was tough enough to keep raccoons and rats out. A design error caused a leak through the lid when it rained, so we eventually had to add some gasketing.

Editor's note: I built a stout wood sea chest for 17-foot Pow Wow, *permanently mounted aft of the centerboard trunk. It carried our food, radio, binoculars, matches, some clothing, tools, spares, extra outboard fuel, sterno stove, and served as a table aboard the boat. The tent, life preservers, anchor, and other bulky items stowed under the foredeck.*

In the Bitts and Pieces section of the April/May 1984 issue of Small Boat Journal, Jim Beauchamp describes a very simple home-made plastic galley storage box of Rubbermaid nesting dishpans.

One of the niftiest home-made galley boxes I've seen is Thomas Fulk's plastic galley box for his Drascombe Lugger. He described and photographed it for the Bitts and Pieces section of the August/September 1982 issue of Small Boat Journal.

2. **Waterproof plastic/fabric storage containers.** These tough bags are available from camping, canoeing, and kayaking stores. They're a lot tougher than plastic garbage bags and well worth the investment. We're still using the set of Voyageur packs we got in 1973 and they're still keeping our gear dry without fail, through many a swamping. If you are determined to stick with plastic garbage bags, buy the thickest mil you can find. Then pack your gear inside the plastic bag and place **that** bag inside a canvas duffel bag. This way you're actually making your own tough, waterproof bag.

3. **Cloth pockets.** Cloth pockets are particularly handy for carrying and organizing gear both aboard and ashore. You can sew your own to fit the contours of your boat, equip them with snaps and grommets, and attach them to the hull or swing them from a tree. Steve Callahan describes how to put together what he calls "hanging duffels" in the Bitts and Pieces section of the August/September 1983 issue of Small Boat Journal.

Backpacks come with pockets of all sizes, including a main compartment divided into a couple of big pouches. They're strong, flexible (without the frame) and made for carrying. When we carried a large backpack in our canoe *Manatee,* we decided to leave the aluminum frame attached to the bag. This frame kept the pack just a little above the floor of the canoe so that small amounts of water couldn't get at the gear inside. We also used a heavy plastic garbage bag inside the large compartment to make sure our bedding stayed dry. The smaller backpack was no problem. For traveling, we just threw it into a waterproof Voyageur pack.

SOURCES FOR ADDITIONAL INFORMATION

Magazine Articles
"Gunkholing in Comfort," by Ida Little, Sail Magazine, April 1985. Reprinted at the end of Chapter 9

"Galley in a Box," by Thomas Fulk, Bitts and Pieces, Small Boat Journal #26

"Multi-Purpose Dishpan Locker," by Jim Beauchamp, Bitts and Pieces, Small Boat Journal #36

Equipment
Worthington Cylinders, Box 391, Columbus, OH 43085. Aluminum propane tanks

Basket-style fish grill. Kitchen supply stores

Cold blanket. Lightweight insulating blanket that you can use to keep you warm or to keep the food in your ice chest cold

Cold bags. Insulating bags for keeping food cool or hot. Available economically from Baskin Robbins

Nalgene plastic containers. Found in camping supply stores

Folding toaster and piezoelectric lighter from Coghlan's

Coleman folding oven. Metal foot-square oven that folds to about 2 inches deep. We've used one over our propane camping stove for about 10 years. The problem is that they rust something terrible

Collapsible 5-gallon water jugs. Sometimes available free from hospital labs

Swiss Army Knife from Victorinox

"Dry Box," P.O. Box 525, Germantown, WI 53022. Plastic waterproof storage box about 30″ x 25″ x 17″ deep

"Dri-Pac," Skydyne, 21 River Rd., Port Jervis, NY 12771. 800-428-CASE. ABS storage box about 33″ x 27″ x 18″ deep. Other sizes available

Though we slept on the boat in Florida, we built a day camp ashore for our galley and our shower. Use driftwood from the beach. Barrel on the left holds rainwater

CHAPTER 14

FOODS
THE BEACHCRUISER'S WEIGHT LOSS BODYBUILDING PROGRAM

The subtitle to this chapter is used only partly in jest. Everybody seems so conscious about weight and exercise. Beachcruising does seem to be a very natural, certainly more fun, weight loss and bodybuilding program. The daily exercise of climbing in and out of the boat; loading and unloading gear; raising and handling sails; shuttling back and forth from port to starboard; landing; pulling the boat out; walking through bush and up and down slopes; setting up camp; adjusting to heat, then chill; to parching dryness then soaking wet; now bracing into a breeze then abruptly perspiring from lack of a breeze, builds muscles and reduces fat faster than any Jazzercise, Aerobic or Doctor Whoever diet I know of. Not only that, but with this "diet" you can eat more and tastier food than you usually eat at home and come away looking and feeling sleeker and healthier than ever. You swim every day, hike a lot, and you're never in a car. You'll stay slim and trim. *Editor's Note: Both Ida and Michael have stayed slim and trim ever since I met them years ago, and they're both strong.*

EVALUATING WHICH FOODS TO TAKE

Some considerations in choosing which foods to take:
1. **Desirability**: What foods and drinks do I enjoy daily at home? Or what will I miss if I don't take it along?
2. **Necessity**: Do I need to carry this item, or can I catch, hunt, gather or buy it along the way?
3. **Nutrition**: Will this food sustain a healthy energy level?
4. **Calories**: Will some foods provide quick energy when I need it?
5. **Flavor**: Will I actually want to eat it?
6. **Texture**: Will I get enough soft, enough chewy, enough brittle textures in the food?
7. **Spoilage**: Does the food require refrigeration to keep from spoiling or hatching out in weevils?
8. **Volume and weight**: Is the watermelon **really** necessary, or would dried fruit serve?
9. **Ease of preparation**: Am I actually going to bother preparing it?
10. **Cost**: What foods can I afford?

Here are some thoughts about these considerations.

Desirability

Some foods and drinks play such an important part in our daily routine that they give us physical and spirtual comfort by the very familiarity of their repetitiveness. They serve, in many ways, to make us feel at home even when we are in remote, strange places and in unfamiliar circumstances.

Our daily meal rituals need a selection of these foods and drinks:

Breakfast: coffee, milk; toast or bran muffins with butter and jam; fruit, or fruit juice from the Ocean Spray boxed concentrates.

Lunch: hot days: sandwiches of fish, cheese, canned liver paté, canned chicken, etc. With alfalfa sprouts or cabbage, thinly sliced onion, pickles, olives or green peppercorns; cookies; fruit juice, beer or Coke.

Cool days: hot soup with barley; fried peanut butter sandwich; or grilled cheese sandwich.

Tea time: mid-afternoon, cool days only: Market Spice Tea, or Lapsang Souchong Tea, with digestive biscuits and guava jam.

Cocktail hour: lobster dip, sliced cheese, fresh fish liver paté, fish roe, or canned smoked oysters on crackers; or peanuts. Cold beer or a drink made with rum or bourbon.

Dinner: fish, beans, canned turkey, etc. with brown rice, pasta, or potato; canned peas, asparagus, or green beans; homemade suet pudding, some chocolate, or cookies, for dessert.

Of all these items which we regularly take aboard, the ones we'd miss most are the powdered coffee and milk, tea, bread, crackers, soup, and the bottle of rum. Without them we couldn't enjoy the daily eating and drinking rituals that give our day structure and familiarity, and that give us the opportunity to regularly commune with each other.

Necessity

Since we usually cruise waters abundant with fish, and carry equipment for catching it, we don't carry much canned protein. We carry just enough for times like today, when the wind is howling and neither or us feels like going out for a dive.

Though we have managed to gather some vegetables and fruit in Martinique, the Bahamas, and Canada, there has never been enough to count on. We'd thought perhaps that in The Jungle we'd discover trees dripping with wild avocados (we did once, because we stumbled on the ruins of an old plantation), oranges, breadfruit, coconuts, palm sprouts and wild beans but we were sorely mistaken. The Romantic Idea doesn't match the realities of a jungle thick with wild trees that bear next to nothing, or very little, and **that** beyond reach. And besides, do you dare experiment with eating unknown pods or fruits in a remote wilderness?

Nutrition

If you asked us what exactly are our daily requirements for a healthy diet, neither of us could tell you. But the facts are certainly available in most good cookbooks and health references. We follow the old fashioned basics of eating a good mix of protein, starch, carbohydrate, green leafy vegetables, fruit and bran. And we carry the following vitamin supplements to cover times of want or heavy demand:

Vitamin A (10,000 I.U. capsules): one a day if we expect to be, and then when we are, in the sun a lot

Vitamin B Complex (50 mg. pills): for stress and general good energy

Vitamin C (500 mg. tablets): if we feel we aren't getting a regular dose of it naturally every day

Vitamin E: as a burn ointment

Calories

It's rare to have a good excuse for eating junk food. But quick energy foods like sugar and chocolate are a beachcruiser's powdermilk biscuits. They give us the energy to do what needs to be done **right now**. Believe me, you work it off. So don't scrimp. Your regular, well balanced meals, will provide slow-burning calories to sustain good energy over the long haul.

Flavor

Since your boat is small and your stores necessarily limited in variety, size, and weight, you need even **more** flavor additives than you use at home. With the liberal use of spices, herbs, and condiments, you can make the most bland foods taste delicious. We both like flavors that, as Michael puts it, throw you up against the wall! So we seek out spices and condiments with the strongest possible **natural** aromas and flavors. We

never use monosodium glutumate (MSG). On the short term it causes headaches, and on the long term?

Spices and Herbs

We carry the following spices, herbs, seeds and condiments in small plastic containers or bags:

Janes Crazy Salt: a spicy **partial** substitute for salt

Coarse ground black pepper: more flavorful than the fine grind

Dill: for fish, dips, salad dressing

Basil, margoram, sage, ground anise, parsley: for fish and chowders

Laurel and bay leaves: for soups, chowders, and spaghetti

Oregano: for spaghetti and tomato dishes

Thyme: for almost everything

Curry: for sauces; to sprinkle on egg or crawfish sandwiches

Garlic: for fried fish and pastas

Paprika: for potatoes

Cinnamon: for buttered toast and for spice tea

Vanilla beans: for flavoring the sugar in the sugar container

Genuine vanilla: for cocoa and muffins

Hershey's cocoa: for drinking and baking

Dried mint leaves: for mint tea and mint coffee

Seeds

Caraway: for breads and cabbage

Sesame: for breads and rolls

Poppy: for cakes and cookies

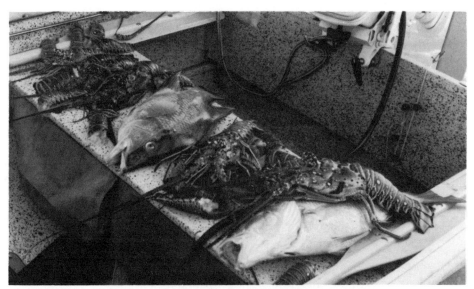

An average catch from a day's spearfishing on Bahamas reefs. Catching our food is fun, and you can't beat fresh-caught flavor

Teas
Wagners Spice Tea
Market Spice Tea from Market Spice, Inc.
> P.O. Box 2935
> Redmond, WA 98073-2935

Celestial Seasonings' Morning Thunder
Twinings' Lapsang Souchong

Condiments
Heinz Ketchup: a hearty tomato flavor for cocktail sauce, barbeque sauce; on hamburgers or soyburgers
Mayonnaise
Canned butter
Coleman's Hot English Mustard: good on sandwiches and on fried fish. Plochman's Natural Stone Ground mustard has a nicer texture but it's not hot enough for our taste.
Tabasco, Worcestershire Sauce, Pickapeppa Sauce
Lime juice
Malt vinegar: for fried fish
Red wine vinegar: for salad dressings
Extra virgin olive oil: strong olive flavor for sauteeing and for salad dressing
Chutney
Capers
Green peppercorns in brine: to mix with canned liver paté
Imitation (soy) bacon bits
Honey
Molasses
Parmesan Cheese
*Anchovy sauce: essence of anchovy
*Toasted sesame oil: packs a roasted sesame flavor wallop
*Tamari: a type of soy sauce
*Wasabi: a green horseradish powder that you mix with water to make a very pungent sauce for fish; served with raw fish in "sushi"
*Tahini: a paste of ground sesame seeds mixed with crushed chick peas, garlic, lemon juice and onion to make a mix called Hummus

Texture

Michael's mom warns us that our teeth are going to fall out if we don't find something firm to chew on. To this end we pack and create as much variety of textures and firm "chew" as we can.

Quaker 100% Natural Cereal: crunch, delicious, **expensive** granola
Whole wheat flour and whole grain breads
Peanuts, pecans, and sunflower seeds
Dried fruits and fruit leathers

*Sprouts: fresh packed and sealed alfalfa and wheat seeds from Arrowhead Mills, Box 2059, Hereford, TX 79045 or from your local health food store if they carry the specially sealed-to-last packets.

*Dried seaweed: There are several varieties available through health food stores. The variety called Hijiki looks, tastes, and feels like French-style green beans when hydrated.

Cabbage: a crunchier, long-lasting substitute for lettuce

Brown rice: a chewier texture than white rice

Wild rice: firm, nutty grain

Bulgur: wheat grain; good in salads; or as a side dish like rice; or by itself when mixed with spices and olive oil to make Taboule

Barley: a cereal plant grain that gives a hearty "chew" to soups

Smoked/grilled fish: cooking fish this way makes the flesh firmer

Canned turkey and canned beef chunks: we use canned meats from Brinkman Turkey Farms Inc., 16314 S.R. 68, Findlay, Ohio 45840. The Brinkman family raise their own turkeys which they put up in cans, along with high quality beef, without additives or salt. The texture of their meat is firm and the flavor is good.

*Items available through health food stores

Left to right: crawfish, grouper, chub (in Michael's right hand), Nassau Grouper (in left hand), and conch

Spoilage

None of the foods listed in the previous sections require refrigeration. However, some of these foods **will** spoil if kept in a warm environment for too long. The "too long" is a time difficult to define. You don't know where to begin counting, really, unless the food is marked with an expiration date. And even then you don't know what conditions its shelf life has endured.

Some common foods to keep an eye on are:

Grains: rice, etc.

Flour

Oatmeal

Almonds

Unsulphured dried fruit

Bran

Corn meal

To minimize loss, store these items in small, separate, packets so that if **one** packet goes bad you won't have lost the whole lot. To control bugs put a few bay leaves inside the packets of grains, bran, rice and flour. We've carried brown rice aboard for as long as eight months in the Bahamas and never seen a weevil. However, we have gotten bugs in the corn meal, flour, oatmeal and bran after only a few weeks. So it's best to play if safe. We did encounter maggots in our dried apricots this year, so we won't plan on keeping the unsulphured type for longer than a couple of weeks.

Some vegetables keep surprisingly long unrefrigerated. Cabbage, potatoes, onions, acorn and butternut squash, and waxed rutabaga keep two weeks anyway. All we do is store them in paper bags in a dark place.

The best commercially available bread we've found in terms of both flavor and staying fresh the longest, is Honey Wheat Bran. The package says it doesn't contain preservatives so it's surprising that it outlasts (it'll go two to three weeks) many of the other whole wheat breads. The plain white fluffy breads packed full of preservatives will keep a month or more.

Fruit cake is a natural for keeping a long time. It's certainly seen us through many a lean day. We arrived in Martinique with ten pounds of it in our canoe. This lasted four months and assured us of a daily "meal."

Leftovers

Many foods last longer when they're cooked than when they're raw. Foods like fish last even longer if they're cooked slowly over a smoky fire to dry out the flesh. We learned this the hard way. When we started out cruising in the Bahamas we merely boiled our crawfish and fish, then used the leftovers in sandwiches the following day. Because the flesh was so damp, it lost all texture and even spoiled in less than a day. So we experimented with grilling the seafood over a hot coal fire. This **did** work to preserve the flesh for up to three days. The grilling also gave the food better flavor and texture.

For the most part we reheat leftover food to kill any bacteria that might cause stomach problems. This too we learned the hard way. We kept a fish chowder one day too long then served it cold. We really suffered cramps and diarrhea for that mistake. Without anti-diarrhea medicine like Parapectolin we'd have been in real trouble, since we were days away from help.

Though we have endured maggots in some of our meals, and some iffy leftovers, we do try our best to minimize such incidents. If food doesn't taste "right" or tastes bland when it should taste good, we throw it away.

There was only one occasion over a period of fifteen years, when either of us might have been seriously poisoned by bad food. That was when Michael licked the top of a mayonnaise jar which he'd just emptied. Next day he was doubled up with stomach pain and cramps. This was the only lesson we needed to be extremely careful with foods like mayonnaise. Now we keep our unrefrigerated mayonnaise in the shade and dispense it with clean utensils only. And if we're only out for a week or so, we'll go to the trouble of putting the mayonnaise in a campers' plastic squeeze tube so that it can be dispensed without utensils.

Photo by Michael Walsh

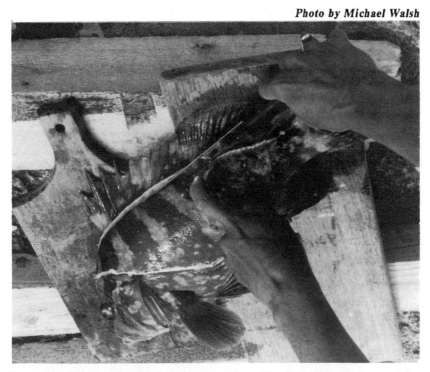

First step in filleting most fish is to cut an outline of the fillet. From the top, cut down and across the belly, taking care to avoid slicing into the gut. Editor note: We prefer to cut off the head and tail first and de-gut and wash out the organ cavity, then start the fillet procedure

2nd step in filleting fish. Gently strip the fillet away from the spine and rib bones, being careful not to disturb any internal organs. *Editor's note: Internal organs should all be gone*

Volume and Weight

One of the main considerations in choosing food is how much water you can expect to collect during your cruise, or whether you will be carrying it all with you. If portable water will be scarce, you should not stock up on dehydrated foods, as these require water that you might just as well

Once the fillet is cut from around the belly area, the knife can be run straight back along the spine, as shown

Here is the top fillet, cut free from the grouper

bring along in the food. For example, canned tomatoes might be just as practical and tastier than dried tomatoes; a can of turkey as practical and tastier than freeze-dried fare; or boxed full cream milk instead of powdered skim milk, especially if you're a milk freak and are accustomed to

Place the fillet skin side down on a flat surface. Starting from the tail, the knife is held nearly flat to the hard surface, and slices from the tail towards the head

drinking real milk. Volume will play a part in your choice but remember that water jugs take room too.

The only esoteric backpacker-type food we carry is powdered egg for baking. Some friends go to the trouble of drying meats to take along, since they don't fish or dive. They also dry their own vegetables to carry along, but then they plan to stop for water pretty frequently. Companies devoted to backpackers' needs sell dried and freeze dried foods. It's expensive and, to us, not very tasty.

Grocery stores sell relatively inexpensive and flavorful dried fruit, juices, potatoes, nuts, and milk. We use skimmed milk because it's easier to mix than most full cream powdered milk. Some stores even offer the delicious concentrated boxed juices from Ocean Spray. You'll also find boxed burrito meals, tortellini, and pastas in the grocery store. They're all light weight, low volume, inexpensive, and tasty items that don't have to be refrigerated.

Considering the limitations of space and weight, what about liquor? After all, for a non-essential, it's pretty heavy and takes up a lot of room. But we really enjoy a drink at sunset. We consider liquor a "desirable" though not an "essential." To minimize weight, we have carried liquor in Nalgene plastic bottles, but we've found that the liquor loses some flavor and alcohol through the plastic. Lately we've been using Old Crow bourbon that comes in plastic bottles and that's been fine. Sometimes we'll carry 151 proof rums so that each drink requires less liquor by volume. If we have room, we'll carry a little wine. The boxed wines carry well and are easy to dispense and store after opening. We've carried opened wine for weeks this way without it spoiling.

Ease of Preparation

You can pre-mix a lot of things at home before getting under way. It's a sure way to encourage better eating. Some items, like Bisquick, rice dishes, etc., come pre-mixed right from the grocery store. We usually carry Bisquick; pancake mix with eggs and milk included; tortellini with various fillings; boxed burritos with sauce included; muffin mix; boxed rice with various sauces included; and taboule in the box (bulgar with spices). All of these foods taste good, and don't take much time or brain power to prepare. This makes them perfect for beachcruisers.

Cost

The bigger your budget, the more you will end up spending on food. My experience is that the more expensive items cost more because they taste better. Not always, but eighty percent of the time. That's why we recommend certain brands in this book, even though they're more expensive than other brands. But if you can't or won't afford Quaker Oats Granola, then your own less expensive, but more time consuming, mix will do.

Here's the good news. Most of the food that's appropriate for beachcruising is inexpensive, especially if you plan ahead by shopping at markets where grains, etc., are available in bulk. Flour, rice, bran, barley, pastas, and bulgar cost only a few cents per pound. Sometimes it costs only a few cents more to go first class—like buying LeSeur peas; or Coleman Hot English mustard; instead of the store or generic brands; and buying fresh, aromatic spices from a natural foods store, rather than from the volume stocked shelves of a grocery store; and ordering canned meats by mail rather than taking whatever the local store has to offer.

●

When you've got your stock of foods all ready to go, reconsider one more time what your daily eating and drinking habits are. If you eat like a horse, carry enough food to satisfy your appetite. If you don't eat like a horse, take along more than you think you'll want. Beachcruising tends to build an appetite, and you don't want to risk hunger. If you drink coffee like a fiend, better bring along a lot of coffee. You'll suffer headaches and nausea and grouchiness if you don't. If you need salty potato chips once a day, pack some bags along. The point is to have enough of what you like to make the trip a pleasure.

SOURCES FOR ADDITIONAL INFORMATION

Books
Good Food Afloat: Every Sailor's Guide to Eating Right, by Joan Betterly, $14.95, 188 pages, 1986, International Marine, TAB Books, Inc., Blue Ridge Summit, PA 17294-0840. Good suggestions about nutrition, foods, equipping a galley and how to keep foods from spoiling

Foods and Sources
Canned meats (turkey and beef), Brinkman Turkey Farms, Inc., 16314 State Route 68, Findlay, OH 45840. Tasty meats without all the hormones, preservatives and salt that most canned meats have

Sprout seeds (alfalfa, mung, wheat, radish), Natural Food Stores. Arrowhead Mills packages sprout seeds in nitrogen to preserve the seeds; we buy these to use a couple months later

Dried seaweed (hijiki), Natural Food Stores. We soak hijiki for a half-hour or so until it looks and feels like thin string beans and then we throw them into a salad

Concentrated fruit juices (cranberry, cranapple, apple, grapefruit, etc.). Ocean Spray products available at most grocery stores. The concentrate comes in small boxes; tastier than canned juice and more portable than bottled juices. Sweetened, unfortunately, but better than no fruit juice at all

Whole grain rye bread in a stay-fresh box; grocery stores

CHAPTER 15

FORAGING, FISHING AND DIVING

Explorers, travelers, and students may rely on the generosity of those met along their route. Because we're beachcruising for fun, we should be self reliant. If we err badly, we too many have to beg. And indeed, human generosity to those in need is part of the communal contract in which even beachcruisers are certain to participate. But good planning, good health, comfort and survival will favor those who can give over those who must receive.

Unless you're practiced and equipped to gather and hunt **before** you begin your cruise, take along more than enough food stores to feed yourself. Consider anything you catch or gather en route to be an unlikely bonus. If you're cruising along a shore that's sparsely populated, it's probable that the shores can't support many lives. The few who do wrest a living from such shores are probably well-equipped experts who don't want to spare much of their catch. To obtain any food along your cruise in sparsely populated areas, you'll have to become at least partially practiced and equipped.

Until you're familiar with the lake or sea shores along which you're cruising, you won't even know what game you're going to play. You won't know what equipment to take or what skills to practice. Reading local guide books, talking with and watching local hunters and fishermen, and making an observant first cruise will give you some idea of what edibles can be found and how to get them. You may learn you need a whaling ship instead of a beachcruiser!

We hunt and gather as a sport as much as to supply ourselves and our friends with fresh and tasty protein. Initially frustrating, it's become more entertaining as our skills improved. Expect initial failure and frustration. Plan for failure. We have been fishing, hunting and gathering in tropical and arctic waters for 15 years. Though we are well equipped, we are frequently frustrated even though we are entertained by our blundering. We are well fed in spite of our failures.

When inexperienced friends have visited us, some for as long as a month, even with the benefits of zeal, select equipment and patient instruction, all have left without bringing home any bacon. Though coconuts don't run away, most guests were never able to even down a coconut, much less open one! Our own first eight months at diving and angling cost more energy than we gained by the little we brought home. But our efforts did entertain us and our occasional teachers.

The tropical, clear, warm seas of the Caribbean and southwest North Atlantic are clear because they are barren. These seas don't support many fish, compared to murky, cooler shores. As a beachcruiser, the only fish you are likely to get are those that shelter between the shore and an off-shore reef—along the shore and in the reefs. Most live in or around the reef.

Shellfish

The only fish that are easily caught are the ones that can't move fast, the shell fish. If you can see shellfish, you can usually get them. Often you can't see them, but you can dig them out anyway. Along the coasts of North America we've found **mussels** and **oysters** growing in patches. More often we've dug out hard shelled clams, **quohaugs**, from soft sand and hard mud in any comfortable depth of tidal water. In bare feet we feel under the mud with the toes and heels, then dig them out with our fingers. (Watch out for broken glass and sharp shells!)

Lobster

We saw our first spiny lobster under a coral head in the archipelago Los Rocques, about 100 miles off the coast of Venezuela. We chanced to look under a single rock in 8 feet of water. More than 30 lobsters were crowded into its shadow. We had no spears. I put on a pair of heavy work-

Photo by Michael Walsh

Ida's regular dive outfit: wet suit, snorkel, prescription mask, gloves, Hawaiian sling, spring steel spear, and flippers

311

ing gloves. But even gloved, I was too timid to grasp firmly enough. Ida sharpened a broom stick. But the point wouldn't nick the shell. All we did was push them around until they got so irritated that they walked off across the sand. A few days later some experienced divers anchored nearby. That night we shared our first Great Dinner. They gave us our first spear and showed us how to use it.

We particularly like spiny lobster. These taste like their North Country cousins—good, firm, fresh, nutritious protein. They're so lean that they're improved with melted butter. If you find one, and can see it, it will give you at least one good shot before it crawls deeper into its crevice. Once on the spear, it can't fight back much. Instead of claws, it has very sharp spines, Dont't touch it without gloves.

Queen Conch

In coral seas we find Queen Conch. One of these 8 to 12-inch conical giants of tasty white muscle will make a meal for two. They are well camouflaged and difficult to distinguish as they graze on the bottom in 3 to 30 feet of water. On a grassy bottom they grow green weeds on their shell. On a white coral sand floor, they color their shell with white. It takes a practiced eye to recognize the shape and size from the background on which they crawl. If you see a rock moving, it's probably a conch. Pronounced "konk." The ones that live in calm, shallow bays are clean-shelled and easiest to recognize. Few of these are left. We usually dive for them in 15 feet of water. Non-divers use a "look-bucket" and fish them up with a "grains." A look bucket is a pail with a glass bottom through which you can see clearly through the surface of the water. A grains is a very long pole with two metal tines, bent over to 90 degrees at one end. It's handy for pulling coconuts down as well as pulling conch up.

Michael brings up a crawfish (called spiny lobster in the Bahamas). We usually dive 10-12 feet for them

Snails and Chitons

Between the tides on the shoreline coral rock we sometimes gather **West Indian Tops**. These spiraled, black and white shelled snails are mistakenly called whelks. They graze on algae that grows on the rock, and are active at night (as active as snails get). During the day they hide in small cavities and cracks in the shoreline rock. In some places, as in Martinique, you'll find them only at night.

The **chiton**, another common edible shellfish, live alongside the Tops, and are less easily pried from their hold. They're more plentiful. You must use a knife or sharpened spoon to pull these off. The chitons are less fleshy and tasty. Some people like them a lot. Birds also like them. I consider them a survival food.

Preparing Shellfish

As a survival food, any of these small or large shellfish may be eaten raw, out of the shell. Some are best this way. But to make any of these into the tasty fresh protein of a balanced meal is an artful, time consuming, labor intensive chore that takes some study, tools, imagination, practice, spices, vegetables, and sauces. The easier a thing is to find and catch, the more work it takes to prepare it.

Oysters must be individually washed and scrubbed. Any bivalve should be well scrubbed. If you prefer them raw, learn to pry them open with an oyster knife. And learn to sneak up on them, with the knife, when they're relaxed. We prefer our oysters roasted for 5 minutes over a hot bed of coals. While creating a hot bed of coals is no easy matter, roasting brings out the flavor and makes them easily opened. Gloves are a necessity in this process and are helpful for any fire cookery.

Mussels are common along many fertile shores. Like **clams** and **quohaugs**, they should be individually washed and scrubbed clean. The shells open after about 5 minutes of steaming. Use only a minimum of water. We've dipped them in a tasty sauce. We've chopped them into a spaghetti sauce. We've made them into a chowder of veggies and herbs. Decant the juice, or don't drink what's on the bottom of the pot. It's always a little sandy. Especially so if you didn't let them set in a bucket of salt water overnight. All these shellfish toughen as they become cooked. Don't cook them any more than necessary to get them out of the shell. If you learn to open them, the tenderer, smaller specimens may be eaten raw.

Chitons are easily scraped off the rocks with a sharpened strong spoon. The same tool is used the scrape the guts off the flesh then the flesh out of the shell. There's not much meat on chiton, so plan to pick a lot of them. They can be eaten raw, improved with a sauce dip, chopped into a newburg or a chowder, or used as bait.

It is easy to clean **lobster** and just as easy to cook. We clean them in the water, as we spear them. To clean a spiny lobster we grip its head firmly with one hand and grip its tail very firmly with the other. The spear and sling are held in your armpit. By twisting the head and tail in opposite directions, the tail is torn off. Big ones may need a little severing with a knife. And watch out for those flailing, sharp feelers. Professionals wear a forearm guard—the sleeve is torn off a discarded wetsuit. Before the head is dropped, snap off the last 5 inches of one antenna-feeler and keep it handy. Looking at the underside of the end of the tail, you'll notice the vent. Push the piece of the feeler, large end first, into the vent about 2 inches; jiggle it; and withdraw it. The inverted spines on that antenna should have snagged the lower intestine, and that tube will come out with the antenna. Discard the intestine and antenna. Keep the tails in a bucket of cool sea water, in the shade, with occasional changes of water, until you can drop them in boiling water for about 8 minutes. The rinse will wash away the blood of the lobsters' tails. Unrinsed tails may become slightly discolored.

After boiling, the hard shell can be easily removed. Place the tail on your gloved hand with its backside facing your palm. By squeezing each section of the shell, the back will crack and can be peeled off the meat. Sometimes the next shell is developing under the outer one. This layer of tough skin doesn't crack. But it can be easily cut and peeled off. One medium-sized tail, about a pound, makes a meal for two.

We like the freshly cooked lobster cut into bite-sized chunks and dipped in a mild garlic-lemon butter. The second day we cut a slice of cheese over each half and roast them, covered, on a grill over slow coals. If we've been lucky, we'll have enough for a third day. By cutting the meat into fritters on the second day, we've found they'll keep a couple more days. Certainly we eat fritters as they come off the pan, but we make a sufficient amount to have fritters as a fine meal underway the next day, and reheated on the grill two evenings later.

Photo by Michael Walsh

What's wrong with this photo? Ida has no gloves! She's separating the tail from the head of this crawfish. The spines can wound you

Photo by Michael Walsh

Ida using a piece of feeler to extract the intestines from this crawfish tail. This removes the bits of shell and sand that the crawfish has ingested. Now the tail is ready to be boiled for 10 minutes. *Editor's note: We throw some seaweed and/or a small onion into the boiling water and melt some butter on the side*

The **Queen Conch** is so big and so varied that it deserves a book to itself. (Available and in print.) For a novice, even opening them is a herculean task. For many years we didn't know them to be edible. Then, for several more years we had no idea how to extract them and clean them. But, once we learned, we were able to earn a little extra cash whenever we found a big herd of them. Now we make them a regular treat in our own diet.

The shell must be punctured with a hatchet at the second turn from the apex. Through that hole we slip a narrow knife blade along the central shell core, to separate and cut the muscle from its hold on that shell. Once the muscle is parted from its grip on the core, the whole conch snail will pull easily out of the shell by tugging on its nail. Once out of the shell, the snail can be gutted and skinned. Cut away all the loose mantle. Inspect the mantle for a pearl before you throw it away. Cut off the nail, eyes, phallus, mouth, and guts and discard them. Slice open the throat from the mouth down and scrape and wash out this passage. Notice that the remaining muscle has a covering, a layer of dark skin. You've got to get that all off so that you keep only a piece of firm, creamy meat. We've peeled this skin off in narrow, 1/8-inch strips. And we've peeled it off as a whole piece by working our thumb between the skin and firm muscle. Neither way it easy. It's more difficult at the end of the day when you're tired, the wind has calmed, and the insects are biting.

The white meat may be diced into 1/8-inch cubes, lightly marinated in salt, seasoned lime juice and enjoyed raw in a salad. Until it's cooked, the meat is fairly tender. To prepare it for cooking, it must be pounded with a serrated hammer of wood or aluminum, into the consistency of butter. Then this buttery paste must be cut or chopped. We enjoy it best in conch fritters. A meat grinder works well too. A rock against a board works too.

Michael bringing up conch from 15-20 feet. They're difficult to see because they become covered with sand and grass

The **"tops"** we pick in the rocks need to be individually scrubbed then allowed to cleanse themselves in a bucket of seawater. Keep them in the shade. After 5 minutes in boiled water, they are easily picked out of the shell. Dipped in garlic butter and eaten with French bread is the best way to enjoy these. They taste like a strongly flavored clam. A short boiling in

Photo by Michael Walsh

First step in cleaning conch. Ida chops a 1″ hole between the 2nd and 3rd spirals, counting from the top

316

Once you have the hole, run a thin, sharp knife inside, down the surface of the spiral, to cut the muscle from the shell

Once the muscle is cut, the conch slides easily out of the shell. *Editor's note: Please don't throw the empty shells back in the water. You'll see piles of empty shells everywhere on shore in the Bahamas. Shoreside disposal prevents some poor diver from bringing up a shell from the briny deep only to find a hole in it!*

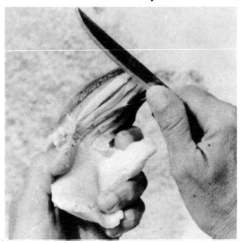

The conch organs have been cut free from the firm white flesh. Now Ida is stripping the dark skin from the firm flesh. *Editor's note: Then you're ready to make cracked conch (pounded and fried), conch chowder, or conch fritters. This rubbery stuff is the national dish of the Bahamas, along with peas'n rice*

a change of water can be used to mellow them. A few, chopped into a white chowder add much flavor.

Red Tide

Consider that bivalve shellfish may at times become poisonous. Saxitaxin is caused in them by a "bloom" of dinoflagellates. A heavy infestation of these causes a "red tide." Saxitoxin has been fatal and is certain to cause severe intestinal distress. There is no cure. Drinking a lot water helps wash out or expel the toxins. Be sensitive to local conditions; i.e., the Pacific N.W. bivalves are likely to be toxic during the summer months.

FISHING

At any time these shellfish make effective bait. The hermit crabs caught on land also make good bait, and make tasty human nourishment too. We use a small, baited hook to catch small pan fish on a simple hand line. We prefer to catch big fish because they are more exciting to land, and make a more abundant, easily prepared, series of meals.

Barracuda

To catch and land big fish requires fairly costly equipment and maintenance and practice in using it. To make it easier for ourselves, we've elected to specialize in casting for barracuda. Where we live, barracuda are abundant. When we've used the same equipment and technique to cast for permit or troll for dolphin, we've spooked them or lost them or bored them. Learn what fish are available to you in the area you're going to cruise, then choose the fish that will best entertain and feed you. Mangrove snapper bore us. But while we are stalking barracuda, our cruising friends caught all the snapper they could eat with a baited hand line. If the kind of fish you choose to go after requires specific equipment, then get the best equipment you can afford.

We particularly enjoy barracuda, grilled on a wood fire on the beach, or, in colder weather, as a major ingredient of a milk-based fish chowder. That barracuda are good sport to tease, hook and land, has made many days playfully competitive and introduced us to the specialized world of fishing the flats.

Late one evening, sitting on the beach, watching the sun set across the acres of shoal, we were surprised to see as many as six, 10 to 15-pound, 3-foot long barracuda lazily patrolling the foot-deep water only a few feet from the shore. As soon as I stood up for a better look, they moved off. The next time, I got up slowly and threw my baited and weighted hook ahead of them. They stopped. They studied my offering, and they moved on. The next trip we returned with a 6-foot casting pole and a bait-casting reel. When the 'cuda came by, I cast a 3-inch silver spoon ahead of them. As I reeled it in with long, fast jerks, one of them hit the lure. I never saw which one. It happened so fast, I was so unprepared, that the reel whined, jammed, and I tried to reel in, the 'cuda ran out, snapped the line, and kept on going. I'd lost that lure, and most of that line. I went through many more lures and much more line. These fish could break the lures. They broke hooks. They bit through the leader. After I learned to use steel lures, and steel leaders, and steel roller swivels, and steel hooks, the fish stayed on, but only long enough to foul my reel. By this time I was using 20-pound test line and the pole snapped.

Now we use a very good, strong, expensive, 6-foot casting pole. We use alternately a closed-faced and an open-faced spinning reel. We use a premium 15-pound test monofilament line. We use 30 inches of doubled, stainless steel leader with a swivel at each end. The lure is 14 inches of green surgical tubing that has two or three gangs of #10 treble hooks wired to the leader through the tubing. One set of hooks ends the tubing and the other two are evenly strung along it. A slip sinker of 1 ounce of lead is on the leader to aid the cast. This sinker weight must be varied to balance with your pole and casting style. We check the line knots and the drag set every other cast. Open-faced reels are easier to check. We sharpen and reshape the hooks after every strike.

No longer do we sit on the beach waiting for the 'cuda to come by. One of the most entertaining aspects of fishing in clear water is that we can see the individual fish for which we're casting, and we get to see its response to the presentation of our lure. In sandals we wade out until we see the fish we want, not so big as to risk damaging our tackle. We walk around to present our lure at an inviting angle. A poor presentation, too close, will cause it to spook. One too far will be ignored. If the lure is retrieved toward the target fish, it'll spook. Retrieved away will tease it so it might make a strike. Retrieved at 45 degrees away from the fish, or across it's line of vision, is most likely to provoke a strike. The retrieve must be fast and steady, not jerky, and begun before the lure strikes the water. Barracuda strike fast and hard. We've seen them strike a lure trolled at 20 m.p.h. We've watched them cut a 4-pound snapper in two at one pass. We've seen them miss their target and strike the bottom so hard they knock themselves out.

When barracuda strike a lure, they are not hooked. They simply have the lure in their mouth. With the lure they will make a fast run during which you must set a hook into their hard jaw, before they leap into the air with a shake intended to throw the lure. They frequently throw the lure even after you've set a hook. Sometimes their first run is toward you! Once hooked, they continue a series of runs between which we've had to walk toward them to recover enough line for their next run. As they tire, we ease the drag to relieve the strain on the tackle. Once exhausted they rarely recover while we gently, slowly, lead them to the beach for the coup de grace. The other one of us is on the beach with a club, ready to help— to hold the fish in place while the other delivers blows to the head, to collect firewood and start a fire, mix the marinade, slice onions, and admire the fish and the fisher.

Photo by Micahel Walsh

Ida showing off our catch after three hours diving. Fish on board at left, conch in center, grouper and crawfish tail at right

320

Graceful and experienced flats wading can often let us get within a few feet of barracuda. But because these big fish have such a menacing reputation (undeserved), and because they aren't particularly shy, it does take some faith and experience to get into the water dominated by schools of them. We have seen schools of well over a hundred.

During one of her visits, daughter Nadine tried for weeks to land a dinner. It does take practice to even learn to see them. Day after day she'd waded for hours on the flats and along the beach to return emptyhanded, sometimes without a lure, sometimes with a rats-nest of line. However, she was encouraged, excited, and provoked by getting strikes and runs. She never learned to set the hook. Maybe she was too excited. Eventually, she came back to camp triumphant, with a big one. She had tired it out as she worked it toward the beach, but, because the hook wasn't set, it fell off the lure. Nadine threw the pole shoreward, leaped on the barracuda, grabbed it, and threw the fish up the beach. We were proud of her.

Editor's Note: I caught my first barracuda while trolling south of Bimini. He flashed after the spoon like a silver streak, taking the bait as fast as any fish I've ever seen. I set the hook as he made off with it, then I let him take line. They're fun to catch on light line. 'Cuda are reef feeders. Never eat them without asking local people about ciguatera poisoning.

Barracuda are curious fish. When I've been swimming, they come close to hover off aways. If I move my hand fast towards them, they'll back off away but still watch my every move. They have teeth that could damage you, but will not attack humans unless they mistake the glitter of a ring for something else. Never wear jewelry while snorkeling or swimming.

Once, I swam over to a catamaran anchored near us in Marigot Harbour in St. Lucia. I made conversation with the pretty lady in the cockpit, hoping to be invited aboard. She pointed out a large barracuda near me. I said, "Oh they don't bother me. I just point my finger at them and they scoot." She answered, "Yeah, but you can only do that 10 times!" I laughed so hard I nearly drowned, and I didn't get invited aboard anyhow!

Once I hiked along a lonely beach in the Bay Islands of Honduras, and saw barracudas in the shallows, following me. When I stopped, they stopped. They stayed with me until I got back to my dinghy. Honduras people eat barracuda. My Bay Islander friend Charles Osgood says they're safe from ciguatera poisoning if you clean them meticulously immediately on catching them, then ice them down and have them for dinner that night. We caught some daily trolling off the reefy north shore of Roatan.

Spearfishing

We usually dive and shoot other kinds of fish with a barbed spear. This spear is made of spring stainless rod, about 3/8 to 1/4-inch diameter by 4 to 6 feet long, and is projected or shot with an elastic rubber that works like a sling shot. The sling is called a "Hawaiian Sling."

To find, see, stalk and kill underwater prey, we also need a prescription dive mask, a snorkel, a pair of gloves, and swimming fins. In colder water, under 70 degrees F, or for long immersions, a wet suit or partial wet suit, and matching weight belt is necessary. All this dive gear stows in a "gear bag" made of tough net fabric that keep it organized and lets it dry.

To stow all this gear requires quite a lot of space, so consider your priorities. All this gear is also quite costly and will pay its way only in entertaining or productive dive waters. We're nearsighted. Corrective face masks cost over $100. But squeezing an old pair of glasses inside our initial cheapo masks requires continuous adjustment that distracted from the fun. The breathing tube, snorkel, fits to the mask strap, and needs only to be comfortable to hold in your mouth. Before you buy it, try it. And test the mask for a snug, comfortable, water-tight fit, **under**water, as in the bath tub. If you're not smoothly shaven, expect it to leak.

Even if you never have an opportunity to hang onto a thrashing fish or spiny lobster, the gloves are necessary. As we dive under, we use our hands to hang onto rocks and live coral as we peer between and under; for it is in the crevices and caves that the fish hide. Our left hand glove wears out after about 40 hours.

The foot fins are used to add power to our swimming kick. Without them we can't descend gracefully, quietly or far. Get a pair that fit comfortably and snugly. A loose fit causes blistering and abrasion. A tight fit causes cramping. And when you start out, don't get those long or wide jobs that the macho use. They cause cramping. We use the kind that cover the whole foot sole because they help protect our feet better than the kind that slip over just the toes. If your interest in diving persists, you'll have opportunity to improve upon your initial choices. None of this equipment lasts long. Rubber rots, even if you rarely use it. Sweat, blood, tears and the sun seem to make the rubber rot faster.

Learning to Dive

Unless you use scuba gear, diving underwater requires holding your breath. The longer you learn to hold your breath, the deeper you will be able to dive. Diving deeper is desirable, even necessary, if you want to see larger fish and a variety of fish. Skilled champions decend to more than 100 feet and bring up more than 200 pounds of fish in one hour. Ordinary divers, like us, do well to decend to 30 feet and bring up just enough for ourselves and our friends to share a meal. We're limited not so much by lack of oxygen as by a painful inability to balance the pressure inside our head cavities to the pressure of the weight of water.

Unless you learn to "pop your ears" to equalize the pressure inside your eardrums and sinus to that of the water, you suffer a painful ear ache ... and eventually a fractured eardrum, infection, and hearing loss. Indeed, any cavities in the body may pain during a dive—sinuses and teeth do often. Practice and instruction make successive dives longer, deeper, and less risky.

Begin diving in calm, clear water only 6 feet deep. Pools and beaches are good. Learn to pop your ears by blowing against your pinched nose in the first few feet. As we decend it is necessary to continue equalizing the ears. But it's in the first few feet that popping them is most urgent and essential. If you can't equalize them during the first 6 feet, don't go deeper. Instead, see a nose and ear specialist. She may suggest an antihistamine.

Deep dives are necessary to spearing fish. But diving abilities are only a small part of the skills needed. We've sometimes found lobster in knee-deep water and missed every one! Stretching the sling, and holding the spear on target, while surf, swells, and tides alternatively pull us away then bash us into fire coral, is a chancy way to put food on the table. It's fun, as long as we have an alterative. Beans and rice may not be as tasty or exciting, but they are more certain than grouper.

Grouper

Large grouper, a kind of tropical sea bass, are elusive and difficult to spear. Unlike crawfish, (spiny lobster), grouper can, and do, move away. Fast. At times I've been surprised at how fast a lobster swims. Yet grouper are the easiest and most likely large fish to be speared. By "large" I mean over 10 pounds. That's a big enough fish to swim off with your spear. Unless you're assured of a paralyzing shot into the pea-sized brain, don't even try to spear a fish that's longer than your forearm. They are very strong and can swim faster than we can, even with a spear in them! The biggest fish we've ever speared weighed 45 pounds. It took the two of us to bring it up and get it into the boat.

It's rare to find a grouper out in open water. When we dive, we're usually swimming from hole to hole to small cave to a crack in the reef, peering in, looking for the tell-tale long feelers of the spiney lobster. Instead, we sometimes find ourselves staring close-up at a big grouper. If neither of us spooks, we might get a shot at it. More often we've got to resurface for air, then go down ready to shoot. By then, the smart fish have retreated or made themselves invisible. They really do. We only get to kill the retarded ones. Other times, we see the fish from the surface. Then we stalk it until it disappears, or we corner it in a hole in the coral rock below.

Another difficult aspect of diving is seeing, recognizing, descriminating the figure of strange creatures from the background in which they float. If they don't move fast, they are certain to be well camouflaged. Grouper even change colors to match the background. Lobster look exactly like the coral in which they shelter. Barracuda appear transparent and move like lightning. Their shadow gives them away. Chub are easily seen, but chub move in large schools of erratic, fast confusion.

Preparing Fish
A Fritter Recipe
You can put just about anything into a fritter batter. The batter itself is

made of flour, sugar, baking powder and baking soda, an egg, vegetable oil, salt, soured powdered milk or buttermilk powder, water, and spices and herbs (black pepper, garlic, dill, hot sauce or red pepper). This batter has to be made thicker than pancake batter. The final portions must be **pushed** off the spoon into the frying pan. To this basic batter we always add a mix of chopped vegetables, onions, cabbage, carrots, green pepper and celery, no lettuce. The protein varies. Ràrely do we have that much lobster. Usually it's ground conch. Err on the lean side with shellfish. One large conch per cup of flour is an easy average. Sometimes we put our fish, barracuda or grouper, cut into small bites, into the fritters. We cook these in hot oil or lard until well browned. Peanut oil works very well. While they're cooling, before you close them into put-away packs, do keep the flies off them. Indeed, unless you're going to eat it right away, keep flies and crawling insects off everything you want to eat. We cover cooling food with a piece of screening.

Cooking Fish

To prepare fish for cooking, we usually cut the sides (fillets) off the fish with a **very sharp** knife, then strip the skin off the fillets, again, using a **very sharp** knife. We've found this method to be the least work for the most meat. Practice and watching a skilled fish butcher, and a very sharp knife, has eased this chore and maximized the amount of boneless, uncontaminated by organ juices, meat we fillet off the fish. Filleting them on a flat, smooth, board, raised above the ground to a comfortable height, is so helpful that we now keep a scrap of plywood in the boat and on the beach.

Our favorite way to prepare large fish is to grill them. For this we carry a double-sided grill with a long attached handle. We cut the fish fillets into pieces that fill the grill. We place sliced onion rings between the grill and the fish. We baste the onions, the fish, and the grill with a mix of spiced oil. These flavor the fish and ease the separation of the fish from the grill. The critical ingredient is a long, slow, cooking over a fire that will not quite char the fish. If it is to keep, and have a meaty chew, the fish must dry during the grilling. A bed of hot coals works well. Of course, if you like moist, tender flakes, then cook it fast or boil it to keep it from drying out. But moist fish won't keep in the tropics even overnight.

On cool evenings we want a hot meal. Our favorite is a white fish chowder. As with fritters, you can put just about anything into a chowder. We start by frying diced salt pork in the big pot. Once browned we set these "little fried fat things" aside, and fry some sliced onions in the salty lard. Then a couple of carrots, potatoes, and celery are cut in and covered with water to cook. While these cook, I add herbs and spices—garlic, celery salt, ground star anise, sage, thyme and sometimes a little dill. When the veggies are about done, in goes the fresh protein chunks—grouper, grilled barracuda, any shellfish, lobster, or mix thereof. As these come to be cooked, add a can of milk and a can of creamed corn; or any creamed soup and canned corn. Don't let it boil after the milk has been added. It could curdle. And more water and spices depending on the number, the appetites and the taste of those you want to serve. In bowls, sprinkled with those little fried fat things and some broken crackers, it'll keep everybody friendly and warm through a cool night.

Hazards of Eating Fish and Diving

Are there risks in fishing and diving? There is less risk in the catching than in the eating. Tropical predator fish, including barracuda and grouper, carry a toxin named "ciguatera." It makes the victim who eats affected fish helpless and many have had to be hospitalized. To avoid ciguatera poisoned fish, we ask the locals what fish they don't eat, and we clean our catch carefully. Don't cut into the organs until you've removed the fillets. Then, after the autopsy, wash the knife and your hands well. Never eat a suspect fish. Big fish have a higher concentration of ciguatera than do small fish. See Chapter 16 for more information on ciguatera and puffer fish symptoms and treatment.

Puffer fish, that expand themselves like a ballon, are edible only at a very high risk. Their toxin, unidentified, is a hallosonigenic. Though they are prepared by expert Fugu chefs, licensed only in Japan, for entertainment of gourmets at special "bars," a few "puffer eaters" die there annually. Be sure you don't eat puffers during their reproductive season, and be certain to eat no skin or even touch the gonads, intestines, or the liver. See also Chapter 16.

A risk of diving is touching corals that sting. Some raise a welt or cause a blister. If you touch any, they will let you know. Immediately. Thus you'll quickly learn to identify them and become a more graceful diver. These correspond to the danger of catching a fish hook into yourself.

In fact, the sting of coral is caused by a barbed hook that is poisoned. It is injected or shot through the skin by a one celled creature named nematocyst. These are the same that cause excruciating, sometimes fatal, pain when the tentacles of a man-o-war and some other jellyfish touch our skin. Some nemtocysts are free floating. Our daughter Nadine once stuck a pretty sea fan into the leg of her wetsuit. It left her hands free. Within a minute she felt that her back was on fire and couldn't tear the wetsuit off fast enough. The stinging continued for a few hours but never raised any blisters. Don't stick things into your bathing suit.

Normal barracuda are not dangerous. They are likely to hang around a diver in hopes of a little action. We have never seen a barracuda over 6 feet long. But even these aren't likely to attack a normal size human. It may want your catch. If a big barracuda came after my catch, I would give it to him. I have. I have sometimes lured a barracuda with a wounded fish, and I have sometimes speared and landed the barracuda. These were under 4 feet. And sometimes they have swum away with my spear.

Some divers carry their catch along on a string or in a net bag. This is a

Michael with mutton snapper and a crawfish speared on the reef. *Beachcomber* **rests on a sand shoal in the background**

most likely way to attract sharks. Even though we take our catch directly to the boat or ashore, holding it out of the water, sharks have been attracted to our activity. We are watchful of them. And if a big one hangs around, we move to a different site. It is rare for a shark to make a sudden attack on a healthy, adult-sized human. They are cautious. If they do attack, they can be warded off with your spear, sling, or gloved hand while you swim to safety. The ones we've met while diving have usually continued on their way. One has taken my catch. One watched me. One chased me. I'm sure I didn't see all the sharks that came by. The aggressive ones are usually found where a strong current is running. Be especially careful when you dive in a strong current. Whenever you see them, watch them. They might be entertaining and exciting.

Don't go sticking your hand or head into dark, tight, underwater nooks and crannies. You might irritate a big mouth with sharp teeth—like a moray eel or an octopus.

Other Ways to Catch Fish

Thinking of sharks reminds me of our experience in setting a gill net to catch fish. In a tiny, shallow bay, we anchored a 4-foot x 30-foot x 4-inch gill net one evening. In the morning there was no trace of our net. We presume a shark, attracted by the sounds of all those snagged fish, had carried it off. Maybe a porpoise did it. I suppose that's the reason we seldom see nets set along seashores. In fresh water lakes gill nets are more successful. A set gill net kills so many more fish than can be eaten, that they are illegal except to commercial license.

We've also tried throwing nets to trap fish. Cast nets of 8, 10, and 12 feet in diameter are used in shallow, fresh and salt water to trap small fish, like shrimp, mullet and perch, and to catch bait fish like minnows and ballyhoo. Like all the other ways of getting fish, throwing these nets takes practiced skill and some developed strength. If you're in an appropriate area of expansive shallow water, and see others casting nets and catching fish, watch and ask for instruction.

We tried catching fish with a bow and arrow. We've tried kite fishing. We've even caught fish by hitting them with rocks and sticks as they swam by. Just about anything will work. Try to find a way that's fun for you, and works.

Editor's Note: I'm not comfortable at depths over 10 feet, so I don't dive deep, only shallow dives while snorkeling. We've caught snapper and grouper all over the Bahamas and in parts of the Caribbean, bottom fishing from boats. They're very good eating fish, and are now appearing on northern USA restaurant menus. We've trolled lines on interisland passages in the Exumas, the Leeward Islands, and the Windward Islands. We've rarely failed to pick up fish on the longer passages, mostly spanish mackerel and tuna. I've caught many thousands of fish in my northern USA home waters, all from boats, with rod and reel or hand lines. It takes less skill than the methods described by Ida, but many people enjoy diving and spearing fish. Make sure you have fishing licenses (mandatory in the Bahamas and Mexico) and know what fishing laws are applicable in foreign countries.

Following is a descriptive listing of books and magazines that cover the foraging, fishing, and diving scene. We've also included a descriptive list of equipment we use along with a choice of manufacturers' addresses.

SOURCES FOR ADDITIONAL INFORMATION

Local apprenticing to and instruction by an experienced diver or fisherman may be the only way to learn fishing and diving. By doing some **reading, studying videos,** and **visiting a local equipment shop,** you'll be better able to recognize and store the information you need to know to get started.

Books

Diver's Almanac Guide to the Bahamas and Caribbean, by Stephen Fl. Gutterman, $24.95, 208 pages, 1987, HDL Publishing Co., 1325 Antigua Way, Newport Beach, CA 92660. If you're a serious scuba diver, this full-color guide contains everything you need to know about diving the Bahamas and Caribbean—dive site information, dive services and re-sorts, dive lodgings and topside attractions, liveaboard dive boat informa-tion, and shipwreck mapping. It includes a section on safety and equipment

The Sport Diving Catalog: A Comprehensive Guide and Access Book, by Herb Taylor, $13.95, 320 pages, 1982, St. Martin's Press, New York. A good introduction

Sport Diving, by Carole S. Briggs, $9.95, 1982, Lerner Publishing Co., 241 First Ave., Minneapolis, MN 55401. Another of the useful beginners books

Skin Diving Made Easy, by Skin Diver Magazine, 1967. Was published before scuba became popular, hence includes good info and pictures on sim-ple snorkeling

Dinghy Fishing at Sea, by Phil Williams and Brian Douglas, 1985, Bee Kay Pub. Ltd., distributed in USA by State Mutual Book & Periodical Service, 521 Fifth Ave., 17th floor, New York, NY 10175. Better read **before** you share a small cockpit with a big fish

Spinning and Plug Fishing: An Illustrated Textbook, by Barrie Rickards and Ken Whitehead, $27, Longwood Publishing Group, Box 2669, Wolfeboro, NH 03894-2069. Out of print, but may be found in libraries

Angling: Fundamental Principles, by Barry Rickards, $26, 318 pages, 1986, Longwood Publishing Group, Box 2669, Wolfeboro, NH 03894-2069. A timely introduction to current technique and equipment. Out of print, but may be found in libraries

Long Range Casting and Fishing Techniques, by Paul Kerry, $40, 1985, Bee Kay Pub. Ltd., distributed in USA by State Mutual Book & Periodical Service, 521 Fifth Ave., New York, NY 10175. If you're planning to fish from the shore, this will help you get your lure out without a kite

Complete Book of Baits, Rigs & Tackle, 6th edition, by Vic Dunaway, $6.95, 224 pages, 1984, Wickstrom Publications, Inc., 5901 SW 74th St., Suite 310, Miami, FL 33143. The handiest, economical guide to get you started in fresh or salt water

Stalking the Blue Eyed Oyster and other foraging books by Euell Gib-bon are likely to be available at your local library. Good instructions and entertainment

Magazines

Text and ads in any of the below listed monthlies will introduce you to how seriously this subject can be taken. Look for them at a newstand or library: **Gulf Coast Fisherman, Salt Water Fishing, Gray's Sporting Jour-nal, Salt Water Sportsman, Scuba Times, Skin Diver Magazine.** Of those, Gray's is the most tasteful and sophisticated, and includes hunting as a major interest

CHAPTER 16

HEALTH AND HYGIENE

If you plan only a one week cruise, and if you suffer no major catastrophe or lengthy delay, then you can get away with ignoring even common sense rules of health and hygiene. And if your body does break down within a week, you can't have gotten too far away from the aid of others. This is certainly the plan to which Outward Bound and Frank and Margaret Dye subscribe. In the interest of traveling light and carefree they endure short-term deprivation. After surviving, overcoming, perhaps enjoying a week of hardship, they return to routine, self-indulgent, life support systems with heroic tales and strength of character. On more extended cruises, or in the interest of self-reliance and comfort, we devote attention to our health.

Don't set off on a cruise unless you're initially healthy and fit. Include health and fitness among your preparations for a beach cruise. Thus, once you set sail, all you need do is to sustain the conditions that led to your good health. And the demands of beachcruising will add to your fitness.

While food quality can be compromised for as long as two weeks without much effect on good health, it is so essential to our happiness that we've devoted a chapter to it. That's not much considering that whole books are dedicated to cooking aboard and cooking outdoors. It is **water**, quality and quantity, that is the most critical essential to our good health. We don't believe it is possible to drink too much good, fresh water.

WATER SUPPLY

Rationing water may be a survival necessity. Drinking as much or more than enough to quench our thirst, is healthy. While sailing and camping in the tropics, we've noticed that on many days we forget to drink enough water. Coffee, tea, fruit juices, sodas, even beer are better than not drinking. But unadulterated fresh water is best. We consciously try to drink at least one quart daily in addition to at least twice that much of other liquids. One conspicuous effect of this water discipline has been elimination of kidney, bladder, and urinary infections. It's difficult to know whether or not it's improved our dispositions. However, health scientists agree that insufficient water intake does lead to depression. So we drink three quarts of liquids daily. We gain still another quart or so in the foods we eat—fruits, vegetables, soups, cheese, etc. Aboard we carry at least one gallon per person per day for drinking and bathing.

When it rains we catch water off our tarpaulins. When we land, explore, and camp, we look for signs of underground water. Digging only a foot deep we've found abundant fresh water on sandy islets as small as 5 acres which stood only 4 feet above high tide. At ebb tide the sweet water level will be a little deeper than at flood tide because this lens of fresh water floats on the underlying salt water. This lens is thin near the edges of the shore, and becomes thicker further inland. On that 5-acre islet it was 2 feet thick only 100 feet inland—we dug through it and hit salt water under the fresh lens.

A certain sign of underground water is high grasses. But on that islet, there was only sparse, low bushes. We frequently find abandoned cisterns. On one small, long-abandoned, Caribbean island we found a cistern of over ten thousand gallons! These finds are opportunities to do laundry, bathe with abandon, and refill our cisterns. It's usually better than the chlorinated water we've brought with us.

Water Filters

We do filter some of the water we drink through a silver and charcoal filter. These small, portable, drinking water filters are inexpensive. We buy them from the manufacturer. But I've seen them available from camping equipment mail order catalogs. R.E.I. has one that is used like a soda straw, and is not much bigger. The one we use can filter about 100 gallons—the dirtier the water, the less volume the filter will strain.

We carry chlorine powder and iodine crystals along. If a well smells swampy and has larvae in it, we dump in a thimble full of chlorine the day before we plan to use it. We also dump a thimble full of vegetable oil on it to suffocate any surviving larvae. When we bathe or do laundry, we keep some yards from the well so we minimize contaminating it with our used water. If the water is used for drinking, then we drop in some iodine crystals, filter it, or boil it. Unlike chlorine, iodine crystals have an infinite shelf life.

Cautions

Be particularly cautious about your drinking water. Just because you see locals drinking it does not mean its safe to drink. The sickest intestines I've ever suffered were caused by drinking the water from a village well in Puerto Escondido, Oaxaca, Pacific Mexico. The villagers were all drinking it. I guess the ones who couldn't survive it had died as infants! On the other hand, far away from human settlement, I've drunk water straight out of standing puddles and suffered not even a burp. Not that "wild" water is necessarily clean. Maybe the wild bugs aren't quite as debilitating, concentrated, or fast. Before drinking wild water, be sure not too many animals live upstream or contaminate the surroundings. If in doubt, boil it for 20 minutes or treat it with iodine for 20 minutes before you drink it.

Michael taking water from an old well. We treat it with iodine drops before using it

Even bathing in water that has human settlement or domestic mammals nearby can be lethal. Three fifths of the world's rivers and lakes are contaminated by one of the oldest diseases known. Schistosomiasis, liver flukes, are found in the freshwater streams of several Caribbean islands. It is a slowly progressing parasite. Fifteen to twenty years after bathing in an infected stream, you die. This schistosome is a free swimmer that penetrates the skin even while you wash your face or clothes. Take heart, it can be diagnosed and there is a treatment. Better yet, be informed and guarded when using water from nearby an ignorant, impoverished, or dirty settlement, particularly if animals may graze upstream. Just because the locals bathe in a river or lake does not mean it is safe. We've met indigents who knew the water was contaminated, believed it to be deadly, but who also recognized they had no choice.

Use of Salt Water

All this caution seems to recommend salt water. It is usually less contaminated; and there's so much more of it. There is available a hand-held, hand-pumped, reverse osmosis unit that turns sea-water into fresh water. We prefer to carry fresh water, and we've always collected and found more than enough. Admittedly, on rare occasions we've bathed in sea water. But even then, we've had enough to rinse off with a quart of fresh water. We're out beachcruising for several months and we don't want to get our evening clothes and our bedding salty. Salty fabric becomes damp. We prefer dry bedding.

If we didn't like to bath; if we didn't enjoy this evening ritual; and if we were cruising for only a week at a time, then we might skip that evening bath. For a week at a time, bathing in the sea, followed quickly with a towel drying, would leave little enough salt on the skin. In two weeks the clothes and linen would get a little damp. If we took salt water baths, we'd save having to lug 5 gallons each (80 pounds each!) of fresh water. For only a week's cruise on a small boat that compelled a choice, I'd do without bathing in fresh water. On a two week cruise I'd take enough for three or four fresh baths. As it is, we bathe nightly with at least a gallon of fresh water each. We have the room to carry it. We enjoy finding it and catching it when it falls from the sky.

We keep enough fresh water to wash our clothing, linen and utensils as needed. For if these are washed in the sea, then a residue of salt will keep them damp and clammy. The use of a deodorant does minimize the clothes we must wash, and makes us more welcome at chance encounters.

Ashore, at a long term camp, cooking over a wood fire, we do wash the pots and the grill in the sea. When we pack them aboard, we keep them in a heavy plastic bag.

On a small islet, intended only as an overnight camp, stormy weather trapped us for ten days. We found no fresh water. In the interest of economy, we cooked a spaghetti dinner in sea water. It was tasty, but we had cramps and diarrea for two days. If you are forced to cook with seawater, dilute it with at least 50% fresh water. Seawater seems to have a laxative chemistry.

CLOTHING AND BEDDING

Clothing

On hot days in the sun, in the wind, much of the water we drink passes through us as perspiration which cools us by evaporation. We've found that we stay cooler, perspire less, and drink less water by keeping our shirt and hat doused with water—sea water or fresh water. In the tropics, wearing a long-sleeved shirt, and a hat that shades the neck is necessary even on cloudy days. While diving we keep a shirt on to shield our back from the U.V. rays. It seems like if we don't need clothing to regulate our temperature, we cover to keep from getting skin cancer. Bullfrog sunscreen on the face does a good job even after repeated wettings. But it's too costly to wear as a bodysuit. Cottom pajamas work well; and wetted, they are cooler than going about naked.

In the late afternoons, shaded by casuarina trees, on a gentle days, we enjoy wearing nothing. Even in the tropics such ideal conditions are rare. Gentle evenings in winter often compel a wool sweater over our pajamas.

If there is a cool breeze, we put on a wool cap to prevent sinus infection. In summer these wouldn't be necessary. But by then we're camping on Cuttyhunk, MA or the Apostle Islands of Lake Superior and we need even warmer clothing than during winters in the tropics.

Bedding

Coming from the Northeast we though all nights in the tropics are balmy. Often they are. But even as far south as tropical as Martinique, we've found many winter nights call for a wool blanket. Because wool is so bulky we've been tempted to take our down quilt instead. Down packs into half the space wool requires. But down becomes useless if even slightly damp. Wool serves even wet, and can be easily washed after a capsize. At Anse Dufour, on the northern coast of Martinique, we were grateful to have wool. Other warm beddings, of synthetics, are as bulky as wool, no more effective, but more costly.

When we've been caught without enough blankets, the "vapor barrier" principle has gotten us through the night. We use a tarp of thin rip-stop nylon between the cotton sheet and the blanket. Thin as this additional layer is, it keeps our moisture from evaporating and raises our temperatures significantly. An aluminized plastic "space blanket," or a sheet of plain plastic, though not as comfortable as our nylon tarp, would be equally warming. Don't put the vapor barrier layer outside the blanket, as there the vapor will condense inside the colder surface and wet the bedding. This same effect of a vapor barrier works in clothing, but must be carefully regulated as soon as you begin to exercise in response to increases in body temperature.

The point of having comfortable bedding is to get at least the rest and sleep you want. Living close to the elements requires more constant response and alertness. Nature is more fatiguing than our controlled home environment. We usually sleep about 10 hours and rest and read, in bed, an additional hour.

Boaters are easily subject to not making sufficient use of their legs. If we have trouble sleeping, it's usually because we didn't do enough ashore. We include time each day to play and walk—tossing the Aerobie, beachcombing, exploring tidepools . . .

Sleeping on the ground or the bottom of the boat does call for some padding under us. Not only is sand and wet wood surprisingly hard, but it seems to sap the warmth right our of the bones. An air mattress softens the surface. But unless it is filled with down or foam, the air, circulating within the mattress (convection) will transfer our bodies' warmth right into the earth. Feathers or foam in an air mattress prevent that convection loss. In Chapter 12 choices of mattresses are detailed.

We usually know when we're too hot more easily than when our body temperature drops. Be aware of the cooling effect of being wet in a breeze. As soon as you feel even a little cool, plan to do something immediate to get warmer. Once you begin to shiver your health is at risk, and your ability to think becomes impaired. Alcohol does not help restore warmth. Hot food, shelter, fire, another warm body, and warm, dry clothing will keep you from becoming seriously ill. I usually suffer a bladder infection when I get cold. The creatures that lie in wait to attack our body will find a weak organ as soon as our body temperature drops. Away from home, regulating our comfort is just as important as taking care of our garbage.

SANITATION

We observe civilized standards of sanitation and have usually avoided primitive illnesses. Our toilet and garbage are buried well away from the camp; away from bathing and dish washing and drinking water. We use a detergent to wash our dishes clean, and rinse them with clean, fresh water or clean lake or sea water, collected away from the shore. We don't lick serving utensils. We wash our hands before handling foods. If any food looks or smells spoiled or fermented, we bury it away with the garbage.

CAUTIONS

We use salt and sugar sparingly. We don't smoke tobacco or abuse substances. We take vitamin supplements almost regularly; especially vitamin A when we endure prolonged exposure to the sun; and B complex on exhausting days. We move gently and we become familiar with the plants and animals in our neighborhoods.

Insects
Of these, the insects are the most distracting and most common. Sufficient insect stings or bites cause debilitating reactions, particularly bees, wasps, and some spiders. Mosquitoess and no-see-ums can also put us out of commission. Screening keeps most of these at bay. An insecticide, painted on the screens, keeps more of them out. When we can't stay behind a screen we use a smoking repellent coil that mildly pollutes the air with an insecticide. As a last resort we carry an insecticide-repellant to coat our skin. We wash this off before we go to bed. Sometimes we've just had to pack up the camp and sail away from these pests.

Poisonous Plants and Trees
Other harmful animals or plants are less numerous, less aggressive, and usually more severe. Become locally informed. On tropical islands "poison wood" (Metopium toxiferum) and manchineel (Hippomane mancinella) are the equivalents to the poison ivy and poison oak of the higher latitudes. Touching them, camping near them, or burning the wood will at least cause severe itching and blistering in most of us. Don't

crash through the bush with naked abandon. Wear socks, long pants, a long sleeved shirt and a hat. After a bush walk, wash exposed skin with a detergent and put exposed clothing in a laundry bag. Severe reaction to these resins (urushiol) requires hospitalization. Do not sit on the fallen leaves of these because the toxin is undiminished by time and insoluble in water.

Along many tropical sandy shores grows a grass that packages its seeds in a small sphere, 1/8-inch in diameter, covered with tiny barbs. The plant is called sandbur (Cenchrus spp.). Masses of these await bare feet. They hurt exceedingly, are difficult to extract, and provoke infection. Sandals work very well to protect bare feet against them.

Watch Where You Walk

Without sandals, be careful walking on even the apparently clean beach. One of the worst cuts I ever suffered was when I jumped across the sand to land on a big, sharp, shell shard buried just under the surface. It might have been a broken bottle or a light bulb. My foot became infected and took a long time to heal. Even with sandals, be cautious. Nails in a board will easily penetrate the sole of a sandal with enough left over to impale the flesh. I've done that too.

We maintain our tetanus vaccination. Because at times we live so remotely, one of us has had a voluntary appendectomy.

Photo by Michael Walsh

The aerobie flies into the "poison wood" once again! We have learned to identify and avoid this plant like the plague. *Editor's note: I'd be tempted to leave the aerobie there, but maybe they were far from civilization and couldn't get a replacement*

Rabies

There are locally poisonous plants and venomous creatures in every area that's good for beachcruising. Learning of them and the prophylactics and treatments are part of preparing for a cruise. While exotic local threats must be considered, our experience has been that such common threats as bacterial infection and rabies are more likely to interrupt a cruise. We try to avoid animals that behave threateningly. If they persist we spray them with a deterrent—MACE, aerosol tear gas or pepper spray. If bitten, we are prepared to kill the animal so it may be analysed. If the biting animal can't be analyzed for rabies, then, on the assumption that the animal is rabid, an innoculation series must be started immediately. Rabies innoculation is costly ($800), lengthy (weeks) and painful. On the other hand, treatment begun after symptoms have developed is totally ineffective. Ony two humans are known to have survived rabies, and one of these suffers permanent, residual brain damage. Only Hawaii is free of rabies. Rodents are not known to carry rabies, although rats are a vector of bubonic plague in many parts of the world, including Colorado, even today. Skunks, foxes, raccoons, and bats are quite certain to carry rabies.

One cold morning in remote northwest Canada, as I pulled on my slacks, I was surprised to feel a sting on my thigh. I thought it was a bee or a spider. Slapping at my flank to kill it, I was surprised when a small bat rolled out the bottom next to my foot. We radioed a plane to land on the lake and by late that day the bat was en route to a lab. Two days later, I flew out to begin my shots. The public health doctor who had received the bat joined me at the hospital because in handling the bat, he had nicked a finger on one of the fangs. A costly lesson to shake out my clothes before putting them on.

Photo by Michael Walsh

Ida stepped barefoot on a conch once. A month later she removed the last bit of shell from her infected foot. Wear shoes or sandals

336

We always wear sandals when exploring inland. Sand spurs like this can hurt and will cause infection. *Editor's note: Boat shoes, socks, and long pants are better protection for inland exploration*

CAUTIONS AND TREATMENT FOR VENOMOUS BITES

Snakes, spiders, ticks, and scorpions are more likely than bats to nestle into the folds of clothing and then to inject their venom when you upset their rest. The only treatment for snake venom is incision and suction, combined with administration of specific antivenin. Spider and scorpion stings, although painful, are rarely fatal to healthy adults. Female black widow spiders are timid and prefer to run away than to attack. However, their venom is likely to cause shock, and death is a not unknown result. Specific antivenin for black widow bites is available in the United States from Merck, Sharp and Dohme, Inc. It must not be given to people allergic to horse serum. Snake antivenin kits are available from Wyeth Laboratories. It is effective to some extent against all North and South American snakes. It too is made from horse serum, and on allergic individuals, will cause more damage than the snake venom.

The best course is to move with caution and to shake out your clothes, including your shoes, just before you put them on. If you must cruise in an area that is known to have a high incidence of rabid or venomous creatures, like the Florida Everglades, then take special precautions. If exposure is likely, plan ahead for treatment. Vaccinations are available to high risk explorers.

When we arrived in Martinique and were attracted to jungle camping, we were warned that there were a lot of fer-de-lance pit vipers inhabiting the jungles and banana groves. We learned what they look like, and where the antivenin is administered. While climbing up the rock ledges, we looked ahead to where we were about to place each hand and foot.

Along grassy steppes we carried a long stick with which we beat the tall grasses ahead of our step. We never saw one.

Ticks are usually benign and painless bloodsucking insects that latch onto human flesh. If they're not too well dug in, they are easily brushed off. Others require a more deliberate excision, like removing a splinter. Leaving a tick head in the flesh may cause infection. Some ticks carry severe debilitating diseases. If a tick bite shows any abnormal signs, make a written note of it and report to a physician at an early convenience. In the northeast U.S., Lyme disease is carried by deer ticks. It is weakening and prolonged and requires professional treatment.

Anyone with a personal health condition (like angina or high blood pressure or a sensitivity to bee and wasp stings) must be responsible for carrying their personal medication on their person, and for instructing their companions in the administration thereof.

If exposure to excessive bee or wasp stings is possible, then epinephrine (synthetic adrenalin) should be ready—500 mg in a syringe. Don't use it on anyone with any heart disease, high blood pressure, thyroid disease, or diabetes. Don't count on an adrenalin inhaler to get this job done because loss of breathing is a likely reaction to bee venom.

VENOMOUS SEA CREATURES

In the sea, the venomous creatures corresponding to the bee are the hydra, some sea fans, corals, jellyfish and sea anemones. All these inject nematocysts into the flesh immediately upon contact. Pain is immediate. Death is rare. Death is immediate and certain if stung by the common Pacific Sea Wasp jellyfish. Sea Wasp antivenin is available from the Dept. of Health, Serum Labs, Melbourne, Victoria, Australia. Do not wash these stings with fresh water. Use cool sea water. Wear gloves if necessary. Use ammonia, baking soda, vinegar, gasoline, turpentine, and in severe cases shave the area. Apply a cortisone and take an antihistamine. Adolph's meat tenderizer or papaya juice will neutralize nematocysts. Pain usually eases after two hours.

Sea Urchins

Sea creatures with spines cause a more traumatic looking wound. The one we usually suffer is sea urchin punctures while wading without sandals. These little crinoids are hard to see because many are the color of sand, and because they camouflage themselves with weeds and shell fragments. Their spines impale flesh, then break off. They are like brittle sandy splinters as they break up in the flesh while we try to dig them out. Left in the flesh, even a grain will cause infection. We apply an antibiotic salve to the wounds we've created, while extracting them. *Editor's note: If you cannot extract sea urchin spines, then dissolve them by applying half a hot lime. It works faster if the lime is very hot, but be careful not to burn your skin.*

338

Other Venomous Fish

Stingrays, stonefish, scorpion fish, weaver fish, toad fish and surgeon fish don't attack, but you might accidentally step on one in some cruising areas. All inject a venom which is fatal in sufficient quantity and potency (i.e. Scorpion fish). The toxin is neutralized by heat. Very hot water should be applied to the wound. Antihistamines and cortisone are appropriate to reduce swelling and an antibiotic salve will reduce secondary infection. Antivenin is available from the Serum Labs in Australia.

Sea Serpents

The Lab also supplies sea serpent antivenin. Anyone beachcruising or shore camping and swimming the waters of the western Pacific or the Indian Ocean, including the Coral Sea, the Philippine Sea, and the South China Sea, would be well served to carry sea serpent antivenin. Sea serpents are not aggressive, but they do bite if handled or stepped upon. The bite is painless and frequently no venom is injected. If poison is passed, treatment is urgent and should be supported by an experienced hospital facility. Serum is also available from the Venin Research Laboratories, Penang, Malaya. If sea snake antivenin is unavailable, a polyvalent antivenin that includes a krait fraction is recommended. Corticosteroids are also helpful.

Photo by Michael Walsh

These sea urchins live in shallow grassy areas in warm seas. They become camouflaged with bits of grass and grains of sand. If stepped on, their spines penetrate and break off, and slowly infect the foot. *Editor's note: These are white sea urchins, whose orange-colored roe is prized by the Caribbean natives. Most sea urchins are black with longer black spines than these. Watch where you step in shallow water. Black sea urchin spines can penetrate snorkeling fins*

Ciguatera Poisoning

Ciguatera is an illness caused by eating fish whose flesh is contaminated with an accumulation of toxins made by a variety of microorganisms called dinoflagellates. The toxin is not unlike that injected by the nematocysts when you chance to touch fire coral or Man 'O War jellyfish. Many fish eat these dinoflagellates and the weeds on which they live. Then other fish eat those fish, and the fish at the top of the food chain accumulate a lot of these toxins in their flesh.

More than 400 species of fish have been involved with this serious and sometimes fatal poisoning. A person who eats a lot of fish so in-toxicated will accumulate the poison in her flesh until an intolerable threshold is reached and she breaks down with symptoms called ciguatera poisoning. Some call it fish poisoning. The symptoms are nausea within 12 hours after eating fish. Next comes diarrhea, numbness, tingling, dizziness, weakness leading to exhaustion, and occasionally, hallucinations. Dehydration may lead to death unless hospital support intervenes. Most people so poisoned survive it but then itch for months and must not eat any seafood for at least a year. Only recently has an antidote been found. Most physicians and hospitals can't be expected to know of it as a treatement for ciguatera poisoning. It is called Mannitol. It is a sugar commonly used in treating heart disease. It is applied intravenously and recovery is immediate and complete.

Ciguatera toxin is found in large specimens of reef inhabitant fish such as jack, barracuda, and grouper. Moray eels are notoriously toxic.

Puffer Fish

A different and far more deadly toxin contaminates the flesh of blow fish or puffer fish that inhabit warm seas. It is called tetrodotoxin, and becomes particularly concentrated in the skin, gonads, liver, and intestine during the reproductive season. It produces an euphoria, and for this reason, is served in "fogu" bars in Japan. An excess leads to paralysis, extreme pain, and death. A tingling sensation around the mouth, fingers and toes develops within an hour after eating. With hospitalization, there is a 50% survival rate. There is no known antitoxin.

CUTS, BRUISES, SPLINTERS

Most threats to good health are not likely to be so dramatic. More likely threats are cuts, bruises, splinters. These are minor annoyances that in one or two weeks of neglect aren't going to become life threatening. Because we're out for extended cruises, we give even these some nursing. On cuts, we don't use alcohol or iodine, because these damage the tissue even more than the bacteria would. We remove all foreign matter, encourage bleeding, wash the wound with soap and clean water, apply pressure to stop the bleeding, then salve the area with an antibiotic ointment. We cover, but avoid closing, puncture wounds. We hold together, but not close, slice cuts using butterfly closures or steri-strips. Then we cover the area loosely with a sterile bandage and immobilize the limb until the wound knits together. Inspect the wound twice daily while you wash the area and change dressing.

Photo by Chris Harkness

Ida enjoying shade provided by the *Drascombe Dabber* tarp. The lowered mast anchors one side, and oars support outer corners. Avoiding too much sun will help prevent dehydration, heat exhaustion, sunstroke, and skin cancer

MEDICAL KIT

After bad-mouthing fish so much, we've got to admit we eat fish at least once a day and frequently twice. We like it. Most fish are good for us. Not only are they nourishing and tasty, but the slime that covers them contains proteins that help to heal and restore human flesh! Nonetheless, we carry with us an elaborate medical kit based upon our special needs (Gantrisin for bladder infection and neosporin opthalmic drops for eye and ear infection) and upon the special aspects of the environment in which we beachcruise.

Our kit includes a copy of "Being Your Own Wilderness Doctor," by Kodet & Angier, published by Simon & Schuster; "Medicine for Mountaineers," by James A. Wilkerson and The Mountaineers; and a fairly recent copy of "Current Medical Diagnosis and Treatment." On short cruises, we carry only the first. We recommend the first two be read in advance by anyone who is planning to be more than 12 hours distant from professional medical aid.

Dark glasses are an essential health maintenance cover to our eyes. Ours are prescription, filter out the ultraviolet and infra-red light, and can be closed with snap-on "gracier" side curtains. These will help our eyes be healthy, while other sailors are recovering from eye surgery.

Another prophylactic we carry on us is a small cylinder of tear gas and/or pepper spray. The pepper spray is a solution of Capsicum, an ingredient of cayenne peppers. It has an effective range of 20 feet and is documented to have deterred several attacks by both grizzly and polar bears. We consider it a desirable, effective alternative to heavy firearms in that we use it with less reserve, and hence would be more likely to make the first move. It has yet to be field tested against snakes and rabid animals, but we'd not hesitate to try it.

If you can't take with you a fully equipped and staffed field hospital, then we suggest you consider taking some of the medical supplies listed below.

MEDICAL SUPPLIES

Equipment
Surgical forceps and tweezers
Scissors
Scalpel with blades
Needles
Thermometer
Hot water bottle
Snake bit kit with antivenin
Propane cigarette lighter
Pencil and paper
First aid manual

Supplies

Dimes and quarters in local currency
Sterile gauze
Band aids
Triangular bandages
Adhesive tape
Elastic bandages
Moleskins
Eye pads
Steri-strips and/or "Butterfly" bandages
Telfa pads
Dental tape and/or floss
Soap

Medications

Vaseline (so the gauze won't stick to the wound)
Zovirax (fever blister treatment)
Urushiol detergent (available from Technu, Albany, Oregon, 97321—
for washing poison ivy, oak, sumac, and wood off flesh)
Zinc oxide (to block U.V. and prevent sun poisoning. Comes in fashionable, decorator colors to match wardrobe)
Eugenol (mixed with zinc oxide makes a temporary tooth filling)
Cyclizine, Marezine (better than Dramamine to control nausea). Tends to cause drowsiness
Benadryl (another antihistamine to relieve allergic reactions. Tends to cause drowsiness

Photo by Michael Walsh

We avoided eating beach plums until a Bahamian man showed us that they were tasty and safe to eat

343

Tylenol with codeine (reduces pain)

Vitamin E capsules (to spread on burns)

Sun screen paste that isn't water soluble—Bullfrog

Adolph's meat tenderizer (a topical antihistamine-neutralizer. Good for jellyfish stings)

Cortizone lotion (reduces swelling and itching)

Aspirin (nobody knows why)

Dibucaine ointment (Nupercainal, a topical anesthetic)

Iodine crystals (to sterilize water)

Syrup of Ipecac (an emetic)

Parapectolin (a paregoric)

Neosporin ointment (an antibiotic topical salve)

Neosporin Opthalmic drops (an antibiotic for the eyes)

Coly-Mycin S (an antibiotic for the ears)

Sulfisoxazole (an antibiotic for the intestine and urinary tracts, effective if used with a lot of clean drinking water)

Benzalkonium Chloride (Zephiran is the only antibacterial effective in deep wounds that doesn't damage tissue)

Penicillin (study which you'll need. We use Duricef because it is broadly effective. Ampicillin is more effective on the anaerobic bacteria that infect wounds, gums, bones, the abdominal cavity, and the intestines.

No Alcohol

Abstinance from drinking alcohol will help any person recover from and avoid infection. The effectiveness of antibiotics is drastically reduced and compromised if the patient is allowed to drink alcohol. Injured and/or sick people must not drink alcohol.

Stainless steel pots with lock-down lids are the safest for food storage. Mayonnaise goes into squeeze tubes so that it can be dispensed without using utensils that might cause contamination

SOURCES FOR ADDITIONAL INFORMATION

A Sympathetic Physician or Physician's Assistant, practicing locally in the area you plan to cruise, can give you advice on avoiding local threats to good health. Your own physician or P.A. will probably provide you with advice and medication specific to your health needs. You can help them and yourself by becoming medically informed. We have found the following resources helpful.

Books

Emergency Survival Handbook, by American Outdoor Safety League State, $3.50, 48 pages, The Mountaineers, 306 Second Ave. W., Seattle, WA 98119

Boater's Safety Handbook, edited by Robert Brown, by American Outdoor Safety League State, $3.50, 52 pages, 1982, The Mountaineers, 306 Second Ave. W., Seattle, WA 98119

Medicine for Mountaineering, 3rd edition, edited by James A. Wilkerson, M.D., $12.95, 376 pages, 1985, The Mountaineers, 306 Second Ave., W., Seattle, WA 98119. In common with boaters, mountaineers are not likely to be within convenient reach of a trauma center. This tome details treatment well beyond first aid

Survive Safely Anywhere, the S.A.S. Survival Handbook, by John Wiseman, a retired instructor of Britain's Special Air Service, $29.95, 228 pages, 1986, Collins-Harvil. Published in paperback, $16.95, by Crown,

Photo by David Buckman

Here's a *Lightning* landed on the rock-bound coast of New Hampshire's Isle of Shoals. Beachcruisers can snug up to any shore

New York. This is a very pro book on tactics for surviving in a variety of nasty circumstances

How to Survive on Land and Sea, 4th edition, by Frank C. Craighead, $14.95, 488 pages, 1984, U.S. Naval Institute Press, U.S. Naval Institute, Annapolis, MD 21402. A comprehensive classic that includes tropical hazards

Dangerous Marine Animals That Bite, Sting, Shock, Are Non-Edible, by Bruce W. Halstead, M.D., $15, 220 pages, 1980, Cornell Maritime Press, Inc., Box 456, Centreville, MD 21617. May frighten you from engaging in any marine activity, but if you do, at least you'll know what gotcha'

People of the Deer, by Farley Mowat describes many of the insect larvae that infest residents of northern Canada as well as the dietary constraints that will doom that population to extinction. A caveat to not necessarily follow the example of the indigent

Other Sources

Survival Technologies Group, 101 16th Ave., S., St. Petersburg, FL 33701, 800-525-2747. Catalogs and mail, sells an exhaustive array of sea-safety equipment and supplies including dental supplies

Ecomarine Ocean Kayak Center, 1668 Duranleau St., Vancouver, B.C., V6H 3S4 Canada. Includes bear repellent among their cruising gear. It works on tigers, dogs, and people too

We camped in a T.V.A. campground at Land Between the Lakes, and enjoyed sailing Kentucky Lake in our sail canoe. Some boats had to watch out for stumps and shoals, but not our beachcruiser!

PLACE AND BOAT TYPE INDEX

Michael Walsh (center) with Hertha and Warren Bailey, beachcruising pioneers of the Florida Keys, and never without at least one canine crew

348

Photo by Chris Harkness

Outboard bracket mounted on transom of this Sea Pearl. Some boats
mount the bracket on the rudder itself. Handiest of all is an outboard well,
as in the Drascombe designs

Photo by Chris Harkness

Chris Harkness has his boat rigged and ready to go in a matter of minutes. He has peace and quiet, free from the nagging details of a complicated world

Photo by Michael Walsh

Ida Little (under the hat!) spreading a vinegar-soy sauce over fish fillets before grilling over a campsite fire. She says the sauce adds flavor and moisture. They carry a large selection of spices, herbs and condiments to add flavor to the basic foods they're limited to because of no refrigeration and small storage space or weight

Photo by Michael Walsh

Micro chases *Drascombe Dabber* in the bight at Cedar Key, FL